NX-OS and Cisco Nexus Switching

Next-Generation Data Center Architectures

D0506432

Kevin Corbin, CCIE No. 11577

Ron Fuller, CCIE No. 5851

David Jansen, CCIE No. 5952

Cisco Press

800 East 96th Street

Indianapolis, IN 46240

NX-OS and Cisco Nexus Switching
Next-Generation Data Center Architectures

Kevin Corbin, Ron Fuller, David Jansen

Copyright © 2010 Cisco Systems, Inc.

Published by:

Cisco Press

800 East 96th Street

Indianapolis, IN 46240 USA

Printed in the United States of America

Fourth Printing: January 2012

Library of Congress Cataloging-in-Publication data is on file.

ISBN-13: 978-1-58705-892-9

ISBN-10: 1-58705-892-8

Warning and Disclaimer

This book is designed to provide information about the Nexus Operating system and Nexus family of products. Every effort has been made to make this book as complete and as accurate as possible, but no warranty or fitness is implied.

The information is provided on an "as is" basis. The authors, Cisco Press, and Cisco Systems, Inc. shall have neither liability nor responsibility to any person or entity with respect to any loss or damages arising from the information contained in this book or from the use of the discs or programs that may accompany it.

The opinions expressed in this book belong to the author and are not necessarily those of Cisco Systems, Inc.

Trademark Acknowledgments

All terms mentioned in this book that are known to be trademarks or service marks have been appropriately capitalized. Cisco Press or Cisco Systems, Inc., cannot attest to the accuracy of this information. Use of a term in this book should not be regarded as affecting the validity of any trademark or service mark.

Corporate and Government Sales

The publisher offers excellent discounts on this book when ordered in quantity for bulk purchases or special sales, which may include electronic versions and/or custom covers and content particular to your business, training goals, marketing focus, and branding interests. For more information, please contact: **U.S. Corporate and Government Sales** 1-800-382-3419 corpsales@pearsontechgroup.com

For sales outside the United States please contact: **International Sales** international@pearsoned.com

Feedback Information

At Cisco Press, our goal is to create in-depth technical books of the highest quality and value. Each book is crafted with care and precision, undergoing rigorous development that involves the unique expertise of members from the professional technical community.

Readers' feedback is a natural continuation of this process. If you have any comments regarding how we could improve the quality of this book, or otherwise alter it to better suit your needs, you can contact us through email at feedback@ciscopress.com. Please make sure to include the book title and ISBN in your message.

We greatly appreciate your assistance.

Publisher Paul Boger

Associate Publisher Dave Dusthimer

Executive Editor Brett Bartow

Managing Editor Sandra Schroeder

Project Editor Seth Kerney

Editorial Assistant Vanessa Evans

Interior and Cover Designer Louisa Adair

Composition Mark Shirar

Manager, Global Certification Erik Ullanderson

Business Operation Manager, Cisco Press Anand Sundaram

Senior Development Editor Christopher Cleveland

Copy Editor Apostrophe Editing Services

Technical Editors Phil Davis, Eric Murray

Indexer WordWise Publishing Services

Proofreader Water Crest Publishing

CISCO.

Americas Headquarters
Cisco Systems, Inc.
San Jose, CA

Asia Pacific Headquarters
Cisco Systems (USA) Pte. Ltd.
Singapore

Europe Headquarters
Cisco Systems International BV
Amsterdam, The Netherlands

Cisco has more than 200 offices worldwide. Addresses, phone numbers, and fax numbers are listed on the Cisco Website at www.cisco.com/go/offices.

CCDE, CCENT, Cisco Eos, Cisco HealthPresence, the Cisco logo, Cisco Lumin, Cisco Nexus, Cisco StadiumVision, Cisco TelePresence, Cisco WebEx, DCE, and Welcome to the Human Network are trademarks; Changing the Way We Work, Live, Play, and Learn and Cisco Store are service marks; and Access Registrar, Aironet, AsyncOS, Bringing the Meeting To You, Catalyst, CCDA, CCDP, CCIE, CCIP, CCNA, CCNP, CCSP, CCVP, Cisco, the Cisco Certified Internetwork Expert logo, Cisco IOS, Cisco Press, Cisco Systems, Cisco Systems Capital, the Cisco Systems logo, Cisco Unity, Collaboration Without Limitation, EtherFast, EtherSwitch, Event Center, Fast Step, Follow Me Browsing, FormShare, GigaDrive, HomeLink, Internet Quotient, IOS, iPhone, iQuick Study, IronPort, the IronPort logo, LightStream, Linksys, MediaTone, MeetingPlace, MeetingPlace Chime Sound, MGX, Networkers, Networking Academy, Network Registrar, PCNow, PIX, PowerPanels, ProConnect, ScriptShare, SenderBase, SMARTnet, Spectrum Expert, StackWise, The Fastest Way to Increase Your Internet Quotient, TransPath, WebEx, and the WebEx logo are registered trademarks of Cisco Systems, Inc. and/or its affiliates in the United States and certain other countries.

All other trademarks mentioned in this document or website are the property of their respective owners. The use of the word partner does not imply a partnership relationship between Cisco and any other company. (0812R)

Dedications

Kevin Corbin: I would like to dedicate this book to my parents. You have loved and supported me through all my endeavors. Mom, you instilled in me a work ethic that has been at the root of everything I have done. Dad, you taught me perseverance, and that the only time something is impossible is when you think it is. Nothing that I will ever accomplish would have been possible without both of you, I love you.

Ron Fuller: This book is dedicated to my loving wife Julie and my awesome children: Max, Sydney, Veronica, and Lil Bubba. Thank you for showing me the world through your perspective and helping me appreciate the things I would have otherwise taken for granted. I can't thank you enough for believing in me when I told you I was going to write another book. Your support and encouragement has and always will be the key to any success I enjoy. Thank you for your love and support.

David Jansen: This book is dedicated to my loving wife Jenise and my three children: Kaitlyn, Joshua, and Jacob. You are the inspiration that gave me the dedication and determination to complete this project. Kaitlyn, Joshua, Jacob, you are three amazing kids, you are learning the skills to be the best at what you do and accomplish anything; keep up the great work. Thank you for all your love and support; I could not have completed this without your help, support, and understanding. I'm so grateful to God, who gives endurance, encouragement, and motivation to complete such a large project like this.

About the Authors

Kevin Corbin, CCIE No. 11577, is a technology solutions architect with Cisco. In this role for three years, Kevin works with Enterprise customers to help them develop their next-generation data center architectures. Kevin has more than 14 years of server and networking experiencing including routing, switching, security, and content networking. Kevin has also held multiple certifications from Microsoft, Citrix, HP, Novell, and VMWare. Prior to joining Cisco, Kevin worked for many large enterprises and most recently in a consulting capacity for large enterprise customers.

Ron Fuller, CCIE No. 5851 (Routing and Switching/Storage Networking), is a technical solutions architect for Cisco specializing in data center architectures. He has 19 years of experience in the industry and has held certifications from Novell, HP, Microsoft, ISC2, SNIA, and Cisco. His focus is working with Enterprise customers to address their challenges with comprehensive end-to-end data center architectures. He lives in Ohio with his wife and three wonderful children and enjoys travel and auto racing.

David Jansen, CCIE No. 5952, is a technical solutions architect for Data Center for Central Area. David has more than 20 years experience in the information technology industry. He has held multiple certifications from Microsoft, Novell, Checkpoint, and Cisco. His focus is to work with Enterprise customers to address end-to-end data center Enterprise architectures. David has been with Cisco for 12 years and working as a Technical Solutions Architect for 4 years and has provided unique experiences helping customers build architectures for Enterprise data centers. David has also been instrumental in developing data center interconnect solutions to address L2 requirements between multiple data centers to meet application clusters and virtualization requirements. David has been presenting data center interconnect at Cisco Live for 3 years. David holds a B.S.E. degree in computer science from the University of Michigan (Go Blue!) and an M.A. degree in adult education from Central Michigan University.

About the Technical Reviewers

Phil Davis, CCIE No. 2021, is a technical solutions architect with Cisco, specializing in routing and switching and data center technologies. Phil has been with Cisco for more than 10 years and has more than 17 years of experience in the industry. Phil currently uses his expertise with Enterprise customers designing their data center and multiprotocol network architectures. Phil holds multiple certifications, including VMware's VCP, and is often presenting on many of today's top technologies. Phil lives near Cincinnati, Ohio, with his wife and two children.

Eric Murray is a network engineer for a large healthcare company. He has more than 15 years experience with designing, implementing, and maintaining Cisco Enterprise networks in the fast-paced healthcare and manufacturing industries. Eric has implemented several Nexus data center network designs and migrations and is a subject matter expert in utilizing Nexus 7000, 5000, and 2000 series switches. Eric is currently involved with designing, testing, implementing, and providing technical support for a Cisco Unified Communications solution. Eric also has extensive experience in multiprotocol WAN and data center LAN environments utilizing Cisco switching and routing platforms.

Acknowledgments

Kevin Corbin: I would like to first thank my co-authors Ron Fuller and David Jansen. I truly enjoy working with you on a day-to-day basis, and I am truly honored to have the opportunity to collaborate with you, and to even be considered in the same league as you guys. You are both rock stars. I would also like to recognize Steve McQuerry for his role in getting me involved in this project and providing coaching throughout this process.

I would like to thank the Cisco Press team, specifically Brett Bartow and Chris Cleveland. Thank you for being patient with me as a I got ramped up for the project and keeping me motivated to make this project a reality. To Phil Davis and Eric Murray, thank you for keeping us honest throughout your review process.

The development of this content would not have been possible without a significant amount of access to equipment, and I'd like to thank Hongjun Ma and Jon Blunt for their commitment to ensure that gear was available and accessible to me.

Working at Cisco has opened up a world of opportunity for me and challenged me on almost a daily basis to accomplish things that I never could have imagined that I was capable of. For this I would be remiss if I didn't give my most sincere thanks to Joel Ekis for opening the door; Gary McNiel for taking a chance on me; and Scott Sprinkle and Jason Heiling for their support throughout my time at Cisco.

Ron Fuller: First I'd like to thank my co-authors Dave Jansen and Kevin Corbin. Dave, thank you for being such a good friend, a trusted co-worker, and a leader in our organization. You set the bar the rest of us try to reach. It has been great sharing a brain with you, and I look forward to more challenges and fun. Keep the goat rodeos coming! Kevin, thank you for stepping in to help complete this project. You are awesome to work with and your technical acumen is top-notch. People like you and Dave are the reason I love my job.

I'd like to thank Brett Bartow for his (almost) infinite patience with this project. It is a huge undertaking and his persistence and understanding and encouragement were greatly appreciated.

Chris Cleveland, it has been a pleasure working with you. Your guidance on the formatting and consistency makes the book something we all can be proud of. Thank you for making three propeller heads from Cisco look good.

To our technical editors, Phil Davis and Eric Murray—wow, you guys are picky! Thank you for the detail-oriented work and assistance making the book accurate and concise.

To Jeff Raymond, Marty Ma, and Charlie Lewis—thank you for allowing us access to the hardware. This book wouldn't have been possible without your help.

I'd like to thank my manager, Bill Taylor, for his support throughout this project and understanding. You are a great manager and I truly enjoy working for you. Thanks for the opportunity and the support you've provided over the last five years. (Time flies when you are having fun!)

To my family, thank you for the many times you wanted me to do something and hearing about a book on things you don't get to see. Your understanding and support through the weekends and late nights are truly appreciated.

For the extended teams at Cisco—thank you for responding to my many emails and calls no matter how inane you thought they were. There was a method to the madness—I think. Working with a world-class organization like this makes coming to work a pleasure.

Finally, I want to thank God for the gifts he has given me and the opportunity to do what I love to do with people I enjoy to support my family. I couldn't ask for more.

David Jansen: This is my second book, and it has been a tremendous honor to work with the great people at Cisco Press. There are so many people to thank, I'm not sure where to begin. I'll start with Brett Bartow: Thank you for getting me started in the writing industry; this is something I enjoy doing. I appreciate your patience and tolerance on this project. I really appreciate you keeping me on track to complete the project in a timely manner, as we have missed several completion dates.

First, I would like to thank my friend and co-authors Ron Fuller and Kevin Corbin. I can't think of two better people to work with to complete such a project. Cisco is one of the most amazing places I've ever worked, and it's people like you, who are wicked smart and a lot of fun to work with, that make it such a great place. I look forward to working on other projects in the future. I am truly blessed by having both of you as a co-worker and friend. I look forward to continue to work with you and grow the friendship into the future.

Chris Cleveland, again it was a pleasure to work with you. Your expertise, professionalism, and follow-up as a development editor is unsurpassed; thank you for your hard work and quick turn-around; this helped to meet the deadlines set forth.

To our technical editors—Phil Davis and Eric Murray—thank you for the time, sharp eyes, and excellent comments/feedback. It was a pleasure having you as part of the team.

Thank you to Jeff Raymond, Marty Ma, Lincoln Dale, and Ben Basler from Data Center Business Unit (DCBU) to provide access to hardware to complete this book. Also, thank you Charlie Lewis in RTP CPOC for scheduling hardware to complete this book as well.

Thanks to my manager at Cisco, Bill Taylor—I appreciate your guidance and your trust in my ability to juggle the many work tasks along with extra projects like working on a book.

I would like to thank the heavy metal music world out there—it allowed me to stay focused when burning the midnight oil; I would not have been able to complete this without loud rock 'n roll music. Thank you.

I want to thank my family for their support and understanding while I was working on this project late at night and being patient with me when my lack of rest may have made me a little less than pleasant to be around.

Most important, I would like to thank God for giving me the ability to complete such a task with dedication and determination and for providing me the skills, knowledge, and health needed to be successful in such a demanding profession.

Contents

Icons Used in This Book

Nexus
7000

Nexus
5000

Nexus 2000
Fabric Extender

Nexus 1000

Nexus 1KV VSM

Route/Switch
Processor

QFP

ASR 1000
Series

Router

Network
Management
Appliance

Web
Server

Laptop

Server

PC

Network Cloud

Ethernet
Connection

Serial Line
Connection

Command Syntax Conventions

The conventions used to present command syntax in this book are the same conventions used in the IOS Command Reference. The Command Reference describes these conventions as follows:

- **Boldface** indicates commands and keywords that are entered literally as shown. In actual configuration examples and output (not general command syntax), boldface indicates commands that are manually input by the user (such as a **show** command).

- *Italic* indicates arguments for which you supply actual values.

- Vertical bars (|) separate alternative, mutually exclusive elements.

- Square brackets ([ ]) indicate an optional element.

- Braces ({ }) indicate a required choice.

- Braces within brackets ([{}]) indicate a required choice within an optional element.

Foreword

More than five years ago, Cisco had the vision of unifying the fabrics in the data center to enable consolidation, virtualization, and automation. Cisco gathered input from customers and partners, and feedback from TAC and the sales team, to begin the design of the Nexus series of switches. With the launch of the Nexus 7000 in 2008, the years of planning, discussion, and hard work paid off as this new platform was released to our customers. The Nexus 5000, Nexus 2000, and Nexus 1000V quickly followed, providing a comprehensive end-to-end data center architecture designed to solve the emerging challenges faced in the ever-changing space that is the data center.

Supporting key innovations that make the 24×7×365 highly available data center a reality, while aligning with the increased demands of virtualization, the Nexus portfolio is truly game-changing. These innovations span the breadth of the product line and encompass both hardware and software changes. A subset includes capabilities such as In-Service Software Upgrade (ISSU), virtual device contexts (vDC), virtual Port Channels (vPC), VN-Link, and Unified Fabric for Fibre Channel over Ethernet (FCoE). This breadth of new capabilities brings increased efficiencies to how data center networks are designed, engineered, and operated.

To that end, a book like the one you are reading will hopefully become a convenient reference for best practices deployment of these new technologies. It is written by three of our Enterprise data center technology solutions architects, who work with our customers on a daily basis and help them develop next-generation data center architectures. Their breadth of experience makes them perfect candidates to drive a project such as this.

We hope that as you read this book and learn more about the Nexus series of switches, and NX-OS specifically, you'll see the years of effort that made this product the Cisco flagship data center operating system now and in the years to come. Enjoy!

Umesh Mahajan, VP/GM
Ram Velaga, VP Product Management
Data Center Switching Technology Group
Cisco, San Jose

Introduction

The modern data center is rapidly changing and evolving to support the current and future demands of technology. At the center of this change is the network—the single entity that connects everything and touches all components of the data center. With that in mind, Cisco has launched a new series of switches, Nexus, based on a revolutionary new operating system, NX-OS, to meet these changes and provide a platform with the scalability, reliability, and comprehensive feature set required in the next generation data center.

The purpose of this book is to provide a guide for the network administrator who might not be familiar with Nexus and NX-OS. It is intended to be used as a "go-to" resource for concise information on the most commonly used aspects of NX-OS across the Nexus 7000, 5000, and 1000V platforms.

Goals and Methods

The goal of this book is to provide best practice configurations to common internetworking scenarios involving Nexus products. Having been network administrators ourselves, we are conscious of the pressures and challenges with finding accurate and relevant information, especially on new technology. We intend this book to be a resource the network administrator reaches for first.

Although there might be more than one way to accomplish a networking requirement, we focused on the best way that minimizes operational complexity and maximizes supportability. We realize and respect that there might be corner-case scenarios that call for configurations not described in this book but sincerely hope we address the vast majority of common configurations.

Who Should Read This Book?

This book is targeted for the network administrator, consultant, or student looking for assistance with NX-OS configuration. It covers the three major Cisco Nexus products and highlights key features of them in a way that makes it easy for the reader to digest and implement.

How This Book Is Organized

This book has been organized following the OSI system model for the initial chapters starting with Layer 2 and then moving to Layer 3. We then add in network-based services such as IP multicast, security, and high availability. Next the embedded serviceability features of NX-OS are explored before moving to emerging data center architecture, Unified Fabrics. Last, and certainly not least, we focus on Nexus 1000V and its capability to provide insight, consistent network policy, and simplified administration to virtualized environments.

Chapters 1 through 9 cover the following topics:

- **Chapter 1, "Introduction to Cisco NX-OS":** Provides the reader with the foundation for building NX-OS configurations including command-line interface (CLI) differences, virtualization capabilities, and basic file system management.

- **Chapter 2, "Layer 2 Support and Configurations":** Focuses on the comprehensive suite of Layer 2 technologies supported by NX-OS including vPC and Spanning Tree Protocol.

- **Chapter 3, "Layer 3 Support and Configurations":** Delves into the three most common network Layer 3 protocols including EIGRP, OSPF, and BGP. Additionally HSRP, GLBP, and VRRP are discussed.

- **Chapter 4, "IP Multicast Configuration":** Provides the reader the information needed to configure IP Multicast protocols such as PIM, Auto-RP, and MSDP.

- **Chapter 5, "Security":** Focuses on the rich set of security protocols available in NX-OS including CTS, ACLs, CoPP, DAI, and more.

- **Chapter 6, "High Availability":** Delves into the high-availability features built into NX-OS including ISSU, stateful process restart, stateful switchover, and non-stop forwarding.

- **Chapter 7, "Embedded Serviceability Features":** Provides the reader with the ability to leverage the embedded serviceability components in NX-OS including SPAN, configuration checkpoints and rollback, packet analysis, and Smart Call Home.

- **Chapter 8, "Unified Fabric":** Explores the industry leading capability for Nexus switches to unify storage and Ethernet fabrics with a focus on FCoE, NPV, and NPIV.

- **Chapter 9, "Nexus 1000V":** Enables the reader to implement Nexus 1000V in a virtualized environment to maximum effect leveraging the VSM, VEM, and port profiles.

Chapter 1

Introduction to Cisco NX-OS

This chapter provides an introduction and overview of NX-OS and a comparison between traditional IOS and NX-OS configurations and terminology. The following sections will be covered in this chapter:

- NX-OS Overview
- NX-OS User Modes
- Management Interfaces
- Managing System Files

NX-OS Overview

Cisco built the next-generation data center-class operating system designed for maximum scalability and application availability. The NX-OS data center-class operating system was built with modularity, resiliency, and serviceability at its foundation. NX-OS is based on the industry-proven Cisco Storage Area Network Operating System (SAN-OS) Software and helps ensure continuous availability to set the standard for mission-critical data center environments. The self-healing and highly modular design of Cisco NX-OS enables for operational excellence increasing the service levels and enabling exceptional operational flexibility. Several advantages of Cisco NX-OS include the following:

- Unified data center operating system
- Robust and rich feature set with a variety of Cisco innovations
- Flexibility and scalability
- Modularity
- Virtualization
- Resiliency

- IPv4 and IPv6 IP routing and multicast features

- Comprehensive security, availability, serviceability, and management features

Key features and benefits of NX-OS include

- **Virtual device contexts (VDC):** Cisco Nexus 7000 Series switches can be segmented into virtual devices based on customer requirements. VDCs offer several benefits such as fault isolation, administration plane, separation of data traffic, and enhanced security.

- **Virtual Port Channels (vPC):** Enables a server or switch to use an EtherChannel across two upstream switches without an STP-blocked port to enable use of all available uplink bandwidth.

- **Continuous system operation:** Maintenance, upgrades, and software certification can be performed without service interruptions due to the modular nature of NX-OS and features such as In-Service Software Upgrade (ISSU) and the capability for processes to restart dynamically.

- **Security:** Cisco NX-OS provides outstanding data confidentiality and integrity, supporting standard IEEE 802.1AE link-layer cryptography with 128-bit Advanced Encryption Standard (AES) cryptography. In addition to CTS, there are many additional security features such as access control lists (ACL) and port-security, for example.

- **Base services:** The default license that ships with NX-OS covers Layer 2 protocols including such features such as Spanning Tree, virtual LANs (VLAN), Private VLANS, and Unidirectional Link Detection (UDLD).

- **Enterprise Services Package:** Provides Layer 3 protocols such as Open Shortest Path First (OSPF), Border Gateway Protocol (BGP), Intermediate System-to-Intermediate System (ISIS), Enhanced Interior Gateway Routing Protocol (EIGRP), Policy-Based Routing (PBR), Protocol Independent Multicast (PIM), and Generic Routing Encapsulation (GRE).

- **Advanced Services Package:** Provides Virtual Device Contexts (VDC), Cisco Trustsec (CTS), and Overlay Transport Virtualization (OTV).

- **Transport Services License:** Provides Overlay Transport Virtualization (OTV) and Multiprotocol Label Switching (MPLS) (when available).

Example 1-1 shows the simplicity of installing the NX-OS license file.

Example 1-1   *Displaying and Installing the NX-OS License File*

```
! Once a license file is obtained from Cisco.com and copied to flash, it can be in-
stalled for the chassis.
! Displaying the host-id for License File Creation on Cisco.com:
```

```
congo# show license host-id
License hostid: VDH=TBM14404807
! Installing a License File:
congo# install license bootflash:license_file.lic
Installing license ..done
congo#
```

Note   NX-OS offers feature testing for a 120-day grace period. Here is how to enable a 120-day grace period:

```
congo(config)# license grace-period
```

The feature is disabled after the 120-day grace period begins. The license grace period is enabled only for the default admin VDC, VDC1.

Using the grace period enables customers to test, configure, and fully operate a feature without the need for a license to be purchased. This is particularly helpful for testing a feature prior to purchasing a license.

NX-OS Supported Platforms

NX-OS data center-class operating system, designed for maximum scalability and application availability, has a wide variety of platform support, including the following:

- Nexus 7000
- Nexus 5000
- Nexus 2000
- Nexus 1000V
- Cisco MDS 9000
- Cisco Unified Computing System (UCS)
- Nexus 4000

Cisco NX-OS and Cisco IOS Comparison

If you are familiar with traditional Cisco IOS command-line interface (CLI), the CLI for NX-OS is similar to Cisco IOS. There are key differences that should be understood prior to working with NX-OS, however:

- When you first log into NX-OS, you go directly into EXEC mode.
- NX-OS has a setup utility that enables a user to specify the system defaults, perform basic configuration, and apply a predefined Control Plane Policing (CoPP) security policy.

- NX-OS uses a feature-based license model. An Enterprise or Advanced Services license is required depending on the features required.

- A 120-day license grace period is supported for testing, but features are automatically removed from the configuration after the expiration date is reached.

- NX-OS has the capability to enable and disable features such as OSPF, BGP, and so on via the **feature** configuration command. Configuration and verification commands are not available until you enable the specific feature.

- Interfaces are labeled in the configuration as Ethernet. There aren't any speed designations in the interface name. Interface speed is dynamically learned and reflected in the appropriate **show** commands and interface metrics.

- NX-OS supports Virtual Device Contexts (VDC), which enable a physical device to be partitioned into logical devices. When you log in for the first time, you are in the default VDC.

- The Cisco NX-OS has two preconfigured instances of VPN Routing Forwarding (VRF) by default (management, default). By default, all Layer 3 interfaces and routing protocols exist in the default VRF. The mgmt0 interface exists in the management VRF and is accessible from any VDC. If VDCs are configured, each VDC has a unique IP address for the mgmt0 interface.

- Secure Shell version 2 (SSHv2) is enabled by default. (Telnet is disabled by default.)

- Default login administrator user is predefined as admin; a password has to be specified when the system is first powered up. With NX-OS, you must enter a username and password; you cannot disable the username and password login. In contrast, in IOS you can simply type a password; you can optionally set the login to require the use of a username.

- NX-OS uses a kickstart image and a system image. Both images are identified in the configuration file as the kickstart and system boot variables; this is the same as the Cisco Multilayer Director Switch (MDS) Fibre Channel switches running SAN-OS.

- NX-OS removed the **write memory** command; use the **copy running-config startup-config**; there is also the alias command syntax.

- The default Spanning Tree mode in NX-OS is Rapid-PVST+.

Caution   In NX-OS, you have to enable features such as OSPF, BGP, and CTS; if you remove a feature via the **no** feature command, all relevant commands related to that feature are removed from the running configuration.

For example, when configuring vty timeouts and session limits, consider Example 1-2, which illustrates the difference between IOS and NX-OS syntax.

Example 1-2 *vty Configurations and Session Limits, Comparing the Differences Between Traditional IOS and NX-OS*

```
! IOS:
congo#
congo(config)# line vty 0 9
congo(config)# exec-timeout 15 0
congo(config)# login
congo# copy running-config startup-config
------------------------------------------------------------------
! NX-OS:
congo(config)# line vty
congo(config)# session-limit 10
congo(config)# exec-timeout 15

congo# copy running-config startup-config
```

NX-OS User Modes

Cisco NX-OS CLI is divided into command modes, which define the actions available to the user. Command modes are "nested" and must be accessed in sequence. As you navigate from one command mode to another, an increasingly larger set of commands become available. All commands in a higher command mode are accessible from lower command modes. For example, the **show** commands are available from any configuration command mode. Figure 1-1 shows how command access builds from EXEC mode to global configuration mode.

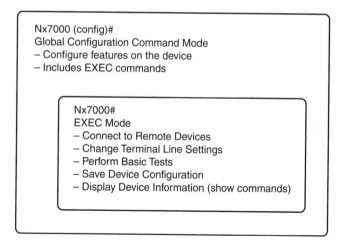

Figure 1-1 *NX-OS Command Access from EXEC Mode to Global Configuration Mode*

EXEC Command Mode

When you first log in, Cisco NX-OS Software places you in EXEC mode. As demonstrated in Example 1-3, the commands available in EXEC mode include the **show** commands that display device status and configuration information, the **clear** commands, and other commands that perform actions that you do not save in the device configuration.

Example 1-3   *Cisco NX-OS EXEC Mode*

```
Congo# show interface ethernet 1/15
Ethernet1/15 is down (SFP not inserted)
  Hardware: 10000 Ethernet, address: 001b.54c2.bbc1 (bia 001b.54c1.e4da)
  MTU 1500 bytes, BW 10000000 Kbit, DLY 10 usec,
      reliability 255/255, txload 1/255, rxload 1/255
  Encapsulation ARPA
  auto-duplex, auto-speed
  Beacon is turned off
  Auto-Negotiation is turned off
  Input flow-control is off, output flow-control is off
  Switchport monitor is off
  Last link flapped never
  Last clearing of "show interface" counters never
  30 seconds input rate 0 bits/sec, 0 packets/sec
  30 seconds output rate 0 bits/sec, 0 packets/sec
  Load-Interval #2: 5 minute (300 seconds)
    input rate 0 bps, 0 pps; output rate 0 bps, 0 pps
  L3 in Switched:
    ucast: 0 pkts, 0 bytes - mcast: 0 pkts, 0 bytes
  L3 out Switched:
    ucast: 0 pkts, 0 bytes - mcast: 0 pkts, 0 bytes
! Output omitted for brevity

Congo#
```

Global Configuration Command Mode

Global configuration mode provides access to the broadest range of commands. The term *global* indicates characteristics or features that affect the device as a whole. You can enter commands in global configuration mode to configure your device globally or enter more specific configuration modes to configure specific elements such as interfaces or protocols as demonstrated here:

```
Nx7000# conf t
Nx7000(config)# interface ethernet 1/15
```

Interface Configuration Command Mode

One example of a specific configuration mode that you enter from global configuration mode is interface configuration mode. To configure interfaces on your device, you must specify the interface and enter interface configuration mode.

You must enable many features on a per-interface basis. Interface configuration commands modify the operation of the interfaces on the device, such as Ethernet interfaces or management interfaces (mgmt 0).

Example 1-4 demonstrates moving between the different command modes in NX-OS.

Example 1-4   *Interface Ethernet1/5 Is a 10Gigabit Ethernet Interface—Show How the Interface Is Designated at Ethernet and Not Interface Ten1/15.*

```
congo# conf t
congo(config)# interface ethernet 1/15
congo(config-if)# exit
Congo# show interface ethernet 1/15
Ethernet1/15 is down (SFP not inserted)
  Hardware: 10000 Ethernet, address: 001b.54c2.bbc1 (bia 001b.54c1.e4da)
  MTU 1500 bytes, BW 10000000 Kbit, DLY 10 usec,
     reliability 255/255, txload 1/255, rxload 1/255
  Encapsulation ARPA
  auto-duplex, auto-speed
  Beacon is turned off
  Auto-Negotiation is turned off
  Input flow-control is off, output flow-control is off
  Switchport monitor is off
  Last link flapped never
  Last clearing of "show interface" counters never
  30 seconds input rate 0 bits/sec, 0 packets/sec
  30 seconds output rate 0 bits/sec, 0 packets/sec
  Load-Interval #2: 5 minute (300 seconds)
    input rate 0 bps, 0 pps; output rate 0 bps, 0 pps
  L3 in Switched:
    ucast: 0 pkts, 0 bytes - mcast: 0 pkts, 0 bytes
  L3 out Switched:
    ucast: 0 pkts, 0 bytes - mcast: 0 pkts, 0 bytes

Congo#
```

NX-OS supports different Ethernet interface types such as Gigabit Ethernet and 10-Gigabit Ethernet interfaces. All interfaces are referred to *Ethernet*; NX-OS does not designate Gigabit or 10-Gigabit Ethernet interfaces. In Example 1-4, interface 1/15 is a 10-Gigabit Ethernet interface.

Management Interfaces

NX-OS has many different type of management interfaces, all of which the following section covers:

- **Controller Processor (CP)/Supervisor:** Has both the management plane and control plane and is critical to the operation of the network.

- **Connectivity Management Processor (CMP):** Provides a second network interface to the device for use even when the CP is not reachable. The CMP interface is used for out-of-band management and monitoring; the CMP interface is independent from the primary operating system.

- **MGMT0:** Provides true out-of-band management through a dedicated interface and VRF to ensure 100 percent isolation from either control plane or data plane. MGMT0 enables you to manage the devices by the IPv4 or IPv6 address on the MGMT0 interface; the mgmt0 interface is a 10/100/1000 Ethernet interface. When implementing Virtual port-channel (vPC), a best practice is to use the MGMT0 interface for the VPC keepalive link.

- **Telnet:** Provides an unsecure management connection to the NX-OS device.

- **SSH:** Provides a secure management connection to the NX-OS device.

- **Extended Markup Language (XML) management interfaces:** Use the XML-based Network Configuration Protocol (NETCONF) that enables management, monitoring, and communication over the interface with an XML management tool or program.

- **Simple Network Management Protocol (SNMP):** Used by management systems to monitor and configure devices via a set of standards for communication over the TCP/IP protocol.

Controller Processor (Supervisor Module)

The Cisco Nexus 7000 series supervisor module is designed to deliver scalable control plane and management functions for the Cisco Nexus 7000 Series chassis. The Nexus 7000 supervisor module is based on an Intel dual-core processor that enables a scalable control plane. The supervisor modules controls the Layer 2 and Layer 3 services, redundancy capabilities, configuration management, status monitoring, power, and environmental management. The supervisor module also provides centralized arbitration to the system fabric for all line cards. The fully distributed forwarding architecture enables the supervisor to support transparent upgrades to higher forwarding capacity-capable I/O and fabric modules. Two supervisors are required for a fully redundant system, with one supervisor module running as the active device and the other in hot standby mode, providing exceptional high-availability features in data center-class products. Additional features and benefits of the Nexus 7000 supervisor modules to meet demanding data center requirements follow:

- Active and standby supervisor.

- In-Service Software Upgrade (ISSU) with dual supervisor modules.

- Virtual output queuing (VoQ), which is a quality of service (QoS)-aware lossless fabric, avoids the problems associated with head-of-line blocking.

- USB interfaces that enable access to USB flash memory devices for software image loading and recovery.

- Central arbitration that provides symmetrical control of the flow of traffic through the switch fabric helps ensure transparent switchover with no losses.

- Segmented and redundant out-of-band provisioning and management paths.

- Virtualization of the management plane via Virtual Device Contexts (vDC).

- Integrated diagnostics and protocol decoding with an embedded control plane packet analyzer; this is based on the Wireshark open source. (No additional licenses are required.)

- Fully decoupled control plane and data plane with no hardware forwarding on the module.

- Distributed forwarding architecture, enabling independent upgrades of the supervisor and fabric.

- With Central arbitration and VoQ, this enables for Unified Fabric.

- Transparent upgrade capacity and capability; designed to support 40-Gigabit and 100-Gigabit Ethernet.

- System locator and beacon LEDs for simplified operations.

- Dedicated out-of-band management processor for "lights out" management.

Connectivity Management Processor (CMP)

The supervisor incorporates an innovative dedicated connectivity management processor (CMP) to support remote management and troubleshooting of the complete system. The CMP provides a complete out-of-band management and monitoring capability independent from the primary operating system. The CMP enables *lights out* management of the supervisor module, all modules, and the Cisco Nexus 7000 Series system without the need for separate terminal servers with the associated additional complexity and cost. The CMP delivers the remote control through its own dedicated processor, memory, and boot flash memory and a separate Ethernet management port. The CMP can reset all system components, including power supplies; it can also reset the host supervisor module to which it is attached, enabling a complete system restart.

The CMP offer many benefits, including the following:

- Dedicated processor and memory, and boot flash.

- The CMP interface can reset all the system components, which include power, supervisor module, and system restart.

- An independent remote system management and monitoring capability enables *lights out* management of the system.

- Remote monitoring of supervisor status and initiation of resets that removes the need for separate terminal server devices for out-of-band management.

- System reset while retaining out-of-band Ethernet connectivity, which reduces the need for onsite support during system maintenance.

- Capability to remotely view boot-time messages during the entire boot process.

- Capability to initiate a complete system power shutdown and restart, which eliminates the need for local operator intervention to reset power for devices.

- Login authentication, which provides secure access to the out-of-band management environment.

- Access to supervisor logs that enables rapid detection and prevention of potential system problems.

- Capability to take full console control of the supervisor.

- Complete control is delivered to the operating environment.

Example 1-5 shows how to connect to the CMP interface and the available **show** commands available from the CMP interface. Also, note the escape sequence of "~," to get back to the main NX-OS interface. You can also connect from the CMP back to the CP module.

Example 1-5 *Connecting to the CMP Interface, Displaying Available show Commands*

```
N7010-1# attach cmp
Connected
Escape character is '~,' [tilde comma]

N7010-1-cmp5 login: admin
Password:
Last login: Tue Aug 11 23:58:12 2009 on ttyS1

N7010-1-cmp5# attach cp
This command will disconnect the front-panel console on this supervisor, and will
clear all console attach sessions on the CP - proceed(y/n)? y
N7010-1#

N7010-1# attach cmp
Connected
Escape character is '~,' [tilde comma]

N7010-1-cmp5 login: admin
Password:
Last login: Wed Aug 12 00:06:12 2009 on ttyS1
```

```
N7010-1-cmp5# show ?
  attach          Serial attach/monitor processes
  clock           Display current date
  cores           Show all core dumps for CMP
  cp              Show CP status information
  hardware        Show cmp hardware information
  interface       Display interface information
  line            Show cmp line information
  logging         Show logging configuration and contents of logfile
  logs            Show all log files for CMP
  processes       Show cmp processes information
  running-config  Current operating configuration
  sprom           Show SPROM contents
  ssh             SSH information
  system          Show system information
  users           Show the current users logged in the system
  version         Show cmp boot information
```

Telnet

NX-OS enables for Telnet server and client. The Telnet protocol enables TCP/IP terminal connections to a host. Telnet enables a user at one site to establish a TCP connection to a login server at another site and then passes the keystrokes from one device to the other. Telnet can accept either an IP address or a domain name as the remote device address.

Note   Remember that the Telnet server is disabled by default in NX-OS.

The Telnet server is disabled by default on an NX-OS device. Example 1-6 demonstrates how to enable a Telnet server in NX-OS.

Example 1-6   *Enabling a Telnet Server in NX-OS*

```
N7010-1# conf t
Enter configuration commands, one per line. End with CNTL/Z.
N7010-1(config)# feature telnet
N7010-1(config)# show telnet server
telnet service enabled
N7010-1(config)# copy running-config startup-config
[######################################] 100%
```

SSH

NX-OS supports SSH Server and SSH Client. Use SSH server to enable an SSH client to make a secure, encrypted connection to a Cisco NX-OS device; SSH uses strong encryption for authentication. The SSH server in Cisco NX-OS Software can interoperate with publicly and commercially available SSH clients. The user authentication mechanisms supported for SSH are Remote Authentication Dial-In User Service (RADIUS), Terminal Access Controller Access Control System Plus (TACACS+), and the use of locally stored usernames and passwords.

The SSH client application enables the SSH protocol to provide device authentication and encryption. The SSH client enables a Cisco NX-OS device to make a secure, encrypted connection to another Cisco NX-OS device or to any other device that runs the SSH server.

SSH requires server keys for secure communications to the Cisco NX-OS device. You can use SSH server keys for the following SSH options:

- SSH version 2 using Rivest, Shamir, and Adelman (RSA) public-key cryptography
- SSH version 2 using the Digital System Algorithm (DSA)

Be sure to have an SSH server key-pair with the appropriate version before allowing the SSH service. You can generate the SSH server key-pair according to the SSH client version used. The SSH service accepts two types of key-pairs for use by SSH version 2:

- The *dsa* option generates the DSA key-pair for the SSH version 2 protocol.
- The *rsa* option generates the RSA key-pair for the SSH version 2 protocol.

By default, Cisco NX-OS Software generates an RSA key using 1024 bits.

SSH supports the following public key formats:

- OpenSSH
- IETF Secure Shell (SECSH)

Example 1-7 demonstrates how to enable SSH server and configure the SSH server keys.

Example 1-7 *Enabling SSH Server and Configuring SSH Server Keys*

```
N7010-1# conf t
Enter configuration commands, one per line. End with CNTL/Z.
N7010-1(config)# no feature ssh
XML interface to system may become unavailable since ssh is disabled
N7010-1(config)# ssh key rsa 2048
generating rsa key(2048 bits).....
```

```
..
generated rsa key
N7010-1(config)# feature ssh
N7010-1(config)# exit
N7010-1# show ssh key
**************************************
rsa Keys generated:Thu Aug 13 23:33:41 2009
ssh-rsa AAAAB3NzaC1yc2EAAAABIwAAAQEA6+TdX+ABH/mq1gQbfhhsjBmm65ksgfQb3Mb3qbwUbNlc
Aa6fjJCGdHuf3kJox/hjgPDChJOdkUXHjESlV59OhZP/NHlBrBq0TGRr+hfdAssD3wG5oPkywgM4+bR/
ssCzoj6jVG41tGmfPip4pr3dqsMzR21DXSKK/tdj7bipWKy1wSkYQzZwatIVPIXRqTJY7L9a+JqVIJEA
0QlJM1l0wZ5YbxccB2GKNKCM2x2BZl4okVgl80CCJg7vmn+8RqIOQ5jNAPNeb9kFw9nsPj/r5xFC1RcS
KeQbdYAjItU6cX1TslRnKjlWewCgIa26dEaGdawMVuftgu0uM97VCOxZPQ==

bitcount:2048
fingerprint:
1f:b7:a3:3b:f5:ca:a6:36:19:93:98:c7:37:ba:27:db
**************************************
could not retrieve dsa key information
**************************************
N7010-1# show ssh server
ssh version 2 is enabled
N7010-1(config)# username nxos-admin password C1sc0123!

N7010-1(config)# username nxos-admin sshkey ssh-rsa
AAAAB3NzaC1yc2EAAAABIwAAAQEA6+TdX+ABH/mq1gQbfhhsjBmm65ksgfQb3Mb3qbwUbNlcAa6fjJCGdHu
f3kJox/hjgP
DChJOd-
kUXHjESlV59OhZP/NHlBrBq0TGRr+hfdAssD3wG5oPkywgM4+bR/ssCzoj6jVG41tGmfPip4pr3dqsMzR21
DXSKK/tdj7b
ip-
WKy1wSkYQzZwatIVPIXRqTJY7L9a+JqVIJEA0QlJM1l0wZ5YbxccB2GKNKCM2x2BZl4okVgl80CCJg7vmn+
8RqIOQ5jNAP
Neb9kFw9nsPj/r5xFC1RcSKeQbdYAjItU6cX1TslRnKjlWewCgIa26dEaGdawMVuftgu0uM97VCOxZPQ==
N7010-1(config)# show user-account
user:admin
        this user account has no expiry date
        roles:network-admin
user:nxos-admin
        this user account has no expiry date
        roles:network-operator
        ssh public key: ssh-rsa
AAAAB3NzaC1yc2EAAAABIwAAAQEA6+TdX+ABH/mq1gQbfhhsjBmm65ksgfQb3Mb3qbwUbNlcAa6fjJCGdHu
f3kJox/hjgP
DChJOd-
kUXHjESlV59OhZP/NHlBrBq0TGRr+hfdAssD3wG5oPkywgM4+bR/ssCzoj6jVG41tGmfPip4pr3dqsMzR21
DXSKK/tdj7b
```

```
ip-
WKy1wSkYQzZwatIVPIXRqTJY7L9a+JqVIJEA0QlJM1l0wZ5YbxccB2GKNKCM2x2BZl4okVgl80CCJg7vmn+
8RqIOQ5jNAP
Neb9kFw9nsPj/r5xFC1RcSKeQbdYAjItU6cX1TslRnKjlWewCgIa26dEaGdawMVuftgu0uM97VCOxZPQ==
N7010-1(config)#
N7010-1# copy running-config startup-config
[####################################] 100%
N7010-1#
```

XML

NX-OS has a robust XML management interface, which can be used to configure the entire switch. The interface uses the XML-based Network Configuration Protocol (NET-CONF) that enables you to manage devices and communicate over the interface with an XML management tool or a program. NETCONF is based on RFC 4741 and the NX-OS implementation requires you to use a Secure Shell (SSH) session for communication with the device.

NETCONF is implemented with an XML Schema (XSD) that enables you to enclose device configuration elements within a remote procedure call (RPC) message. From within an RPC message, you select one of the NETCONF operations that matches the type of command that you want the device to execute. You can configure the entire set of CLI commands on the device with NETCONF.

The XML management interface does not require any additional licensing. XML management is included with no additional charge.

XML/NETCONF can be enabled via a web2.0/ajax browser application that uses XML/NETCONF to pull all statistics off all interfaces on the Nexus 7000 running NX-OS in a dynamically updating table.

Figures 1-2, 1-3, and 1-4 demonstrate sample output from the XML/NETCONF interface.

SNMP

The Simple Network Management Protocol (SNMP) is an application-layer protocol that provides a message format for communication between SNMP managers and agents. SNMP provides a standardized framework and a common language used for the monitoring and management of devices in a network.

SNMP has different versions such as SNMPv1, v2, and v3. Each SNMP version has different security models or levels. Most Enterprise customers are looking to implement SNMPv3 because it offers encryption to pass management information (or traffic) across the network. The security level determines if an SNMP message needs to be protected and authenticated. Various security levels exist within a security model:

■ **noAuthNoPriv:** Security level that does not provide authentication or encryption.

■ **authNoPriv:** Security level that provides authentication but does not provide encryption.

■ **authPriv:** Security level that provides both authentication and encryption.

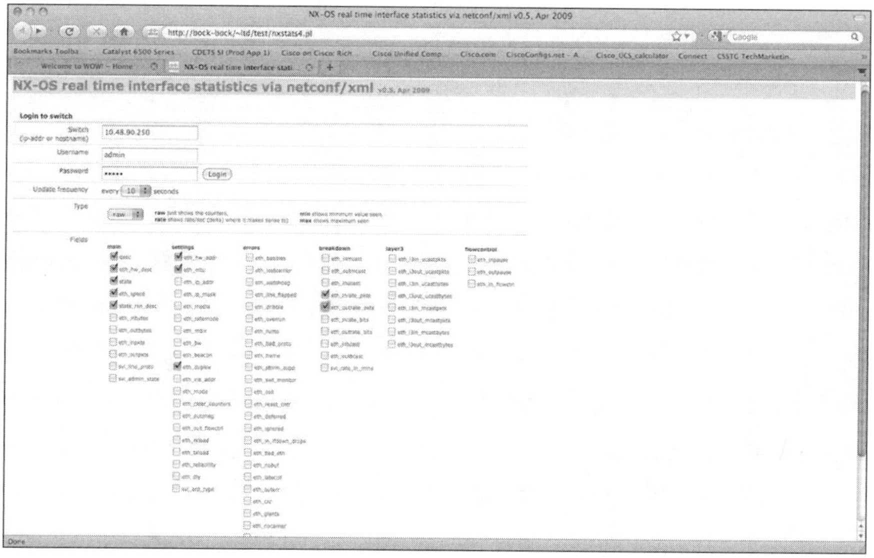

Figure 1-2   *Obtaining NX-OS Real-Time Interface Statistics via NETCONF/XML. The IP Address Entered Is the NX-OS mgmt0 Interface.*

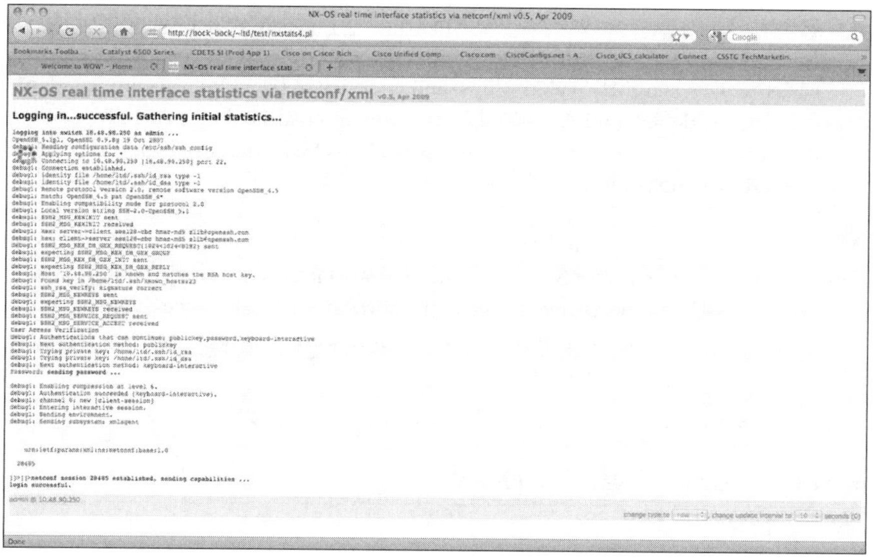

Figure 1-3   *Login Results to the NX-OS Devices via NETCONF/XML*

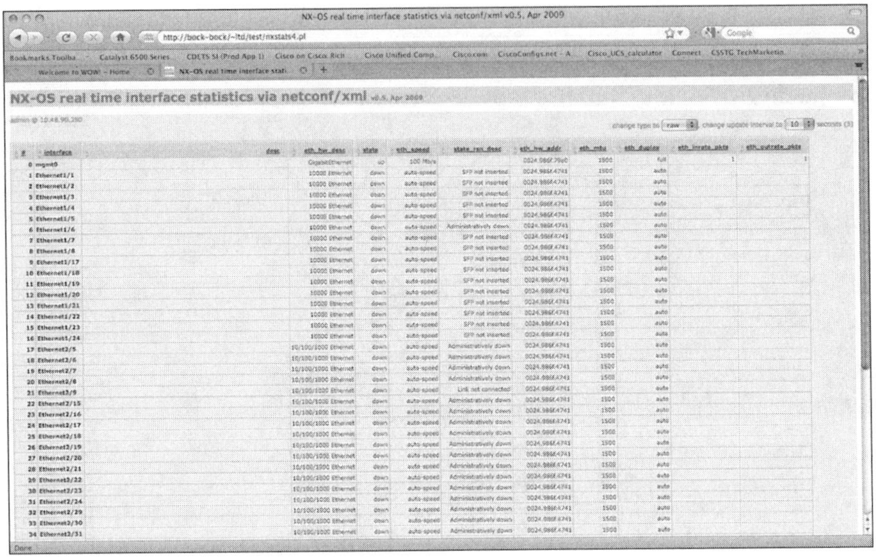

Figure 1-4   *Results of the Selected Attributes, Such as Speed, Duplex, Errors, Counters, MAC Address. The Page Refreshes Every 10 Seconds.*

Cisco NX-OS supports the following SNMP standards:

- **SNMPv1:** Simple community-string based access.

- **SNMPv2c:** RFC 2575-based group access that can be tied into RBAC model.

- **SNMPv3:** Enables for two independent security mechanisms, authentication (Hashed Message Authentication leveraging either Secure Hash Algorithm [SHA-1] or Message Digest 5 [MD5] algorithms) and encryption (Data Encryption Standard [DES] as the default and Advanced Encryption Standard [AES]) to ensure secure communication between NMS station and N7K/NX-OS. Both mechanisms are implemented as demonstrated in Example 1-8.

As NX-OS is truly modular and highly available, the NX-OS implementation of SNMP supports stateless restarts for SNMP. NX-OS has also implemented virtualization support for SNMP; NX-OS supports one instance of SNMP per virtual device context (VDC). SNMP is also VRF-aware, which allows you to configure SNMP to use a particular VRF to reach the network management host.

Example 1-8 demonstrates how to enable SNMPv3 on NX-OS.

Example 1-8   *Enabling SNMPv3 on NX-OS*

```
N7010-1# conf t
Enter configuration commands, one per line. End with CNTL/Z.
N7010-1(config)# snmp-server user NMS auth sha Cisc0123! priv Cisc0123! engineID
```

```
00:00:00:63:00:01:00:10:20:15:10:03
N7010-1(config)# snmp-server host 10.100.22.254 informs version 3 auth NMS
N7010-1(config)# snmp-server community public ro
N7010-1(config)# snmp-server community nxos rw
N7010-1(config)# show snmp
sys contact:
sys location:
0 SNMP packets input
        0 Bad SNMP versions
        0 Unknown community name
        0 Illegal operation for community name supplied
        0 Encoding errors
        0 Number of requested variables
        0 Number of altered variables
        0 Get-request PDUs
        0 Get-next PDUs
        0 Set-request PDUs
        0 No such name PDU
        0 Bad value PDU
        0 Read Only PDU
        0 General errors
        0 Get Responses
45 SNMP packets output
        45 Trap PDU
        0 Too big errors
        0 No such name errors
        0 Bad values errors
        0 General errors
        0 Get Requests
        0 Get Next Requests
        0 Set Requests
        0 Get Responses
        0 Silent drops
Community           Group / Access        context    acl_filter
---------           --------------        -------    ----------
nxos                   network-admin
public                 network-operator


                    SNMP USERS


User                      Auth  Priv(enforce) Groups
----                      ----  ------------- ------
admin                     md5   des(no)       network-admin
```

```
nxos-admin                sha   des(no)       network-operator


  NOTIFICATION TARGET USERS (configured  for sending V3 Inform)


User                        Auth  Priv


NMS                         sha   des
(EngineID 0:0:0:63:0:1:0:10:20:15:10:3)
SNMP Tcp Authentication Flag : Enabled.
-------------------------------------------------------------------
Port Monitor : enabled
-------------------------------------------------------------------
Policy Name  : default
Admin status : Not Active
Oper status  : Not Active
Port type    : All Ports
-------------------------------------------------------------------
Counter        Threshold  Interval Rising Threshold event Falling Threshold
event In Use
-------        ---------  -------- ---------------- ----- ------------------- --
Link Loss      Delta      60       5                4     1                   4
Yes
Sync Loss      Delta      60       5                4     1                   4
Yes
Protocol Error Delta      60       1                4     0                   4
Yes
Signal Loss    Delta      60       5                4     1                   4
Yes
Invalid Words  Delta      60       1                4     0                   4
Yes
Invalid CRC's  Delta      60       5                4     1                   4
Yes
RX Performance Delta      60       2147483648       4     524288000           4
Yes
TX Performance Delta      60       2147483648       4     524288000           4
Yes
-------------------------------------------------------------------
SNMP protocol : Enabled
-------------------------------------------------------------------
Context                       [Protocol instance, VRF, Topology]

N7010-1# show snmp user
```

```
                   SNMP USERS
   _____

   User                     Auth  Priv(enforce) Groups
   ____                     ____  _____  _____
   admin                    md5   des(no)       network-admin

   nxos-admin               sha   des(no)       network-operator


   _____
    NOTIFICATION TARGET USERS (configured  for sending V3 Inform)
   _____

   User                     Auth  Priv
   ____                     ____  ____
   NMS                      sha   des
   (EngineID 0:0:0:63:0:1:0:10:20:15:10:3)
   N7010-1(config)# exit
   N7010-1# copy running-config  startup-config
   [#######################################] 100%
   N7010-1#
```

DCNM

Cisco Data Center Network Manager (DCNM) is a management solution that supports NX-OS devices. DCNM maximizes the overall data center infrastructure uptime and reliability, which improves service levels. Focused on the operational management requirements of the data center, DCNM provides a robust framework and rich feature set that fulfills the switching, application, automation, provisioning, and services needs of today's data centers and tomorrow's data center requirements.

DCNM is a client-server application supporting a Java-based client-server application. The DCNM client communicates with the DCNM server only, never directly with managed Cisco NX-OS devices. The DCNM server uses the XML management interface of Cisco NX-OS devices to manage and monitor them. The XML management interface is a programmatic method based on the NETCONF protocol that complements the CLI functionality.

DCNM has a robust configuration and feature support on the NX-OS platform. The following features can be configured, provisioned, and monitored through DCNM enterprise management:

■ Physical ports

■ Port channels and virtual port channels (vPC)

■ Loopback and management interfaces

- VLAN network interfaces (sometimes referred to as switched virtual interfaces [SVI])

- VLAN and private VLAN (PVLAN)

- Spanning Tree Protocol, including Rapid Spanning Tree (RST) and Multi-Instance Spanning Tree Protocol (MST)

- Virtual Device Contexts

- Gateway Load Balancing Protocol (GLBP) and object tracking

- Hot Standby Router Protocol (HSRP)

- Access control lists

- IEEE 802.1X

- Authentication, authorization, and accounting (AAA)

- Role-based access control

- Dynamic Host Configuration Protocol (DHCP) snooping

- Dynamic Address Resolution Protocol (ARP) inspection

- IP Source Guard

- Traffic storm control

- Port security

- Hardware resource utilization with Ternary Content Addressable Memory (TCAM) statistics

- Switched Port Analyzer (SPAN)

DCNM also includes end-end enterprise visibility including topology views, event browsers, configuration change management, device operating system management, hardware asset inventory, logging, and statistical data collection management.

Managing System Files

Directories can be created on bootflash: and external flash memory (slot0:, usb1:, and usb2:); you can also navigate through these directories and use them for files. Files can be created and accessed on bootflash:, volatile:, slot0:, usb1:, and usb2: file systems. Files can be accessed only on the system: file systems. Debug file system can be used for debug log files specified in the **debug** *logfile* command. System image files, from remote servers using FTP, Secure Copy (SCP), Secure Shell FTP (SFTP), and TFTP can also be downloaded.

File Systems

Table 1-1 outlines the parameters for the syntax for specifying a local file system, which is:

```
filesystem:[//module/]
```

Example 1-9 demonstrates some file system commands and how to copy a file.

Table 1-1   *Syntax for Specifying a Local File System*

File System Name	Module	Description
Bootflash	sup-active sup-local	Internal CompactFlash memory located on the active supervisor module used for storing image files, configuration files, and other miscellaneous files. The initial default directory is bootflash.
Bootflash	sup-standby sup-remote	Internal CompactFlash memory located on the standby supervisor module used for storing image files, configuration files, and other miscellaneous files.
slot0	Not applicable	External CompactFlash memory installed in a supervisor module used for storing system images, configuration files, and other miscellaneous files.
volatile	Not applicable	Volatile random-access memory (VRAM) located on a supervisor module used for temporary or pending changes.
Nvram	Not applicable	Nonvolatile random-access memory (NVRAM) located on a supervisor module used for storing the startup-configuration file.
Log	Not applicable	Memory on the active supervisor that stores logging file statistics.
system	Not applicable	Memory on a supervisor module used for storing the running-configuration file.
debug	Not applicable	Memory on a supervisor module used for debug logs.
usb1	Not applicable	External USB flash memory installed in a supervisor module used for storing image files, configuration files, and other miscellaneous files.
usb2	Not applicable	External USB flash memory installed in a supervisor module used for storing image files, configuration files, and other miscellaneous files.

Example 1-9   *File System Commands/Copying a File*

```
N7010-1# dir bootflash:
        311       Jun 20 05:15:05 2009  MDS20090619155920643.lic
        309       Jun 20 05:15:56 2009  MDS20090619155929839.lic
    2470887       Aug 01 08:13:35 2009  dp42
    8533440       Apr 17 23:17:14 2009  lacp_tech_all.log
     308249       Aug 01 09:08:39 2009  libcmd.so
        134       Jun 19 23:06:53 2009  libglbp.log
        175       Jun 20 04:14:22 2009  libotm.log
      49152       Jun 19 22:50:53 2009  lost+found/
   87081184       Jan 02 06:21:20 2008  congo-s1-dk9.4.0.2.bin
   87755113       Dec 11 13:35:25 2008  congo-s1-dk9.4.0.4.bin
   92000595       Apr 16 21:55:19 2009  congo-s1-dk9.4.1.4.bin
   92645614       Apr 08 06:08:35 2009  congo-s1-dk9.4.1.5.bin
   92004757       Jun 02 04:29:19 2009  congo-s1-dk9.4.1.5E2.bin
   99851395       Aug 03 05:17:46 2009  congo-s1-dk9.4.2.0.601.bin
  100122301       Aug 12 04:42:13 2009  congo-s1-dk9.4.2.1.bin
    9905740       Jan 02 06:21:29 2008  congo-s1-epld.4.0.2.img
    9730124       Dec 11 13:42:30 2008  congo-s1-epld.4.0.4.img
   23584768       Jan 02 06:21:26 2008  congo-s1-kickstart.4.0.2.bin
   23785984       Dec 11 13:34:37 2008  congo-s1-kickstart.4.0.4.bin
   24718848       Apr 16 21:52:40 2009  congo-s1-kickstart.4.1.4.bin
   25173504       Apr 08 06:00:57 2009  congo-s1-kickstart.4.1.5.bin
   23936512       Aug 03 05:03:13 2009  congo-s1-kickstart.4.1.5E2.bin
   25333248       Aug 03 05:18:37 2009  congo-s1-kickstart.4.2.0.601.bin
   25234944       Aug 12 04:40:52 2009  congo-s1-kickstart.4.2.1.bin
      12558       Aug 01 08:51:22 2009  shrun
     916893       Apr 17 23:23:03 2009  stp_tech.og
       4096       Dec 11 14:04:50 2008  vdc_2/
       4096       Dec 11 14:04:50 2008  vdc_3/
       4096       Dec 11 14:04:50 2008  vdc_4/
     592649       Apr 17 23:18:16 2009  vpc_tech.log
        942       Jul 10 09:45:27 2009  wireshark
Usage for bootflash://sup-local
  982306816 bytes used
  827592704 bytes free
 1809899520 bytes total
N7010-1# dir bootflash://sup-remote
      12349       Dec 05 02:15:33 2008  7k-1-vdc-all.run
       4096       Apr 04 06:45:28 2009  eem/
      18180       Apr 02 23:47:26 2009  eem_script.cfg
   99851395       Aug 03 05:20:20 2009  congo-s1-dk9.4.2.0.601.bin
  100122301       Aug 12 04:46:18 2009  congo-s1-dk9.4.2.1.bin
```

```
    19021      Apr 03 21:04:50 2009   eem_script_counters.cfg
    19781      Apr 05 23:30:51 2009   eem_script_iptrack.cfg
    29104      Jun 19 22:44:51 2009   ethpm_act_logs.log
        0      Jun 19 22:44:51 2009   ethpm_syslogs.log
      175      Jun 20 04:14:37 2009   libotm.log
    49152      Jun 19 22:38:45 2009   lost+found/
 87755113      Apr 07 23:54:07 2009   congo-s1-dk9.4.0.4.bin
 92000595      Apr 16 21:55:19 2009   congo-s1-dk9.4.1.4.bin
 92645614      Apr 08 06:08:35 2009   congo-s1-dk9.4.1.5.bin
 92004757      Jun 02 04:29:19 2009   congo-s1-dk9.4.1.5E2.bin
 10993389      Mar 22 04:55:13 2009   congo-s1-epld.4.1.3.33.img
 23785984      Apr 07 23:47:43 2009   congo-s1-kickstart.4.0.4.bin
 24718848      Apr 16 21:52:40 2009   congo-s1-kickstart.4.1.4.bin
 25173504      Apr 08 06:00:57 2009   congo-s1-kickstart.4.1.5.bin
 23936512      Jun 02 04:26:35 2009   congo-s1-kickstart.4.1.5E2.bin
 25333248      Aug 03 05:19:26 2009   congo-s1-kickstart.4.2.0.601.bin
 25234944      Aug 12 04:45:24 2009   congo-s1-kickstart.4.2.1.bin
      310      Sep 19 03:58:55 2008   n7k-rhs-1.lic
    12699      Jan 23 14:02:52 2009   run_vpc_jan22
    11562      Mar 13 07:52:42 2009   startup-robert-cfg
    16008      Mar 12 02:02:40 2009   startup-vss-cfg
    17315      Mar 19 06:24:32 2009   startup-vss-cfg_roberto_mar18
       99      Apr 04 06:51:15 2009   test1
     9991      Jun 19 23:12:48 2009   vdc.cfg
     4096      Jan 22 13:37:57 2009   vdc_2/
     4096      Jan 22 00:40:57 2009   vdc_3/

     4096      Sep 11 12:54:10 2008   vdc_4/
   111096      Dec 20 04:40:17 2008   vpc.cap
        0      Feb 03 08:02:14 2009   vpc_hw_check_disable
    18166      Apr 03 03:24:22 2009   vpc_vss_apr02
    18223      Apr 02 22:40:57 2009   vss_vpc_apr2

Usage for bootflash://sup-remote
  863535104 bytes used
  946364416 bytes free
 1809899520 bytes total
N7010-1# copy bootflash://sup
bootflash://sup-1/        bootflash://sup-active/    bootflash://sup-remote/
bootflash://sup-2/        bootflash://sup-local/     bootflash://sup-standby/

N7010-1# copy bootflash://sup-local/congo-s1-epld.4.0.4.img bootflash://sup-
remote/congo-s1-epld.4.0.4.img
N7010-1# dir bootflash://sup-remote
```

```
     12349    Dec 05 02:15:33 2008  7k-1-vdc-all.run
      4096    Apr 04 06:45:28 2009  eem/
     18180    Apr 02 23:47:26 2009  eem_script.cfg
     19021    Apr 03 21:04:50 2009  eem_script_counters.cfg
     19781    Apr 05 23:30:51 2009  eem_script_iptrack.cfg
     29104    Jun 19 22:44:51 2009  ethpm_act_logs.log
         0    Jun 19 22:44:51 2009  ethpm_syslogs.log
       175    Jun 20 04:14:37 2009  libotm.log
     49152    Jun 19 22:38:45 2009  lost+found/
  87755113    Apr 07 23:54:07 2009  congo-s1-dk9.4.0.4.bin
  92000595    Apr 16 21:55:19 2009  congo-s1-dk9.4.1.4.bin
  92645614    Apr 08 06:08:35 2009  congo-s1-dk9.4.1.5.bin
  92004757    Jun 02 04:29:19 2009  congo-s1-dk9.4.1.5E2.bin
  99851395    Aug 03 05:20:20 2009  congo-s1-dk9.4.2.0.601.bin
 100122301    Aug 12 04:46:18 2009  congo-s1-dk9.4.2.1.bin
   9730124    Aug 12 22:02:57 2009  congo-s1-epld.4.0.4.img
  10993389    Mar 22 04:55:13 2009  congo-s1-epld.4.1.3.33.img
  23785984    Apr 07 23:47:43 2009  congo-s1-kickstart.4.0.4.bin
  24718848    Apr 16 21:52:40 2009  congo-s1-kickstart.4.1.4.bin
  25173504    Apr 08 06:00:57 2009  congo-s1-kickstart.4.1.5.bin
  23936512    Jun 02 04:26:35 2009  congo-s1-kickstart.4.1.5E2.bin
  25333248    Aug 03 05:19:26 2009  congo-s1-kickstart.4.2.0.601.bin
  25234944    Aug 12 04:45:24 2009  congo-s1-kickstart.4.2.1.bin
       310    Sep 19 03:58:55 2008  n7k-rhs-1.lic
     12699    Jan 23 14:02:52 2009  run_vpc_jan22
     11562    Mar 13 07:52:42 2009  startup-robert-cfg
     16008    Mar 12 02:02:40 2009  startup-vss-cfg
     17315    Mar 19 06:24:32 2009  startup-vss-cfg_roberto_mar18
        99    Apr 04 06:51:15 2009  test1

      9991    Jun 19 23:12:48 2009  vdc.cfg
      4096    Jan 22 13:37:57 2009  vdc_2/
      4096    Jan 22 00:40:57 2009  vdc_3/
      4096    Sep 11 12:54:10 2008  vdc_4/
    111096    Dec 20 04:40:17 2008  vpc.cap
         0    Feb 03 08:02:14 2009  vpc_hw_check_disable
     18166    Apr 03 03:24:22 2009  vpc_vss_apr02
     18223    Apr 02 22:40:57 2009  vss_vpc_apr2

Usage for bootflash://sup-remote
 873283584 bytes used
 936615936 bytes free
1809899520 bytes total
N7010-1#
```

Configuration Files: Configuration Rollback

The configuration rollback feature enables you to take a snapshot, or *checkpoint*, of the Cisco NX-OS configuration and then reapply that configuration to your device at any point without having to reload the device. Rollback allows any authorized administrator to apply this checkpoint configuration without requiring expert knowledge of the features configured in the checkpoint.

You can create a checkpoint copy of the current running configuration at any time. Cisco NX-OS saves this checkpoint as an ASCII file that you can use to roll back the running configuration to the checkpoint configuration at a future time. You can create multiple checkpoints to save different versions of your running configuration.

When you roll back the running configuration, you can trigger the following rollback types:

- **Atomic:** Implement the rollback only if no errors occur. This is the default rollback type.

- **Best-effort:** Implement a rollback and skip any errors.

- **Stop-at-first-failure:** Implement a rollback that stops if an error occurs.

When you are ready to roll back to a checkpoint configuration, you can view the changes that will be applied to your current running configuration before committing to the rollback operation. If an error occurs during the rollback operation, you can choose to cancel the operation or ignore the error and proceed with the rollback. If you cancel the operation, Cisco NX-OS provides a list of changes already applied before the error occurred. You need to clean up these changes manually.

Configuration rollback limitations are as follows:

- Allowed to create up to ten checkpoint copies per VDC.

- You are not allowed to apply a checkpoint file of one VDC into another VDC.

- You are not allowed to apply a checkpoint configuration in a nondefault VDC if there is a change in the global configuration portion of the running configuration compared to the checkpoint configuration.

- The checkpoint filenames must be 75 characters or less.

- You are not allowed to start a checkpoint filename with the word *auto*.

- You cannot name a checkpoint file with *summary* or any abbreviation of the word *summary*.

- Only one user can perform a checkpoint, rollback, or copy the running configuration to the startup configuration at the same time in a VDC.

- After execution of **write erase** and **reload** commands, checkpoints are deleted. You can use the **clear checkpoint database** command to clear out all checkpoint files.

- Rollback fails for NetFlow if during rollback you try to modify a record that is programmed in the hardware.

- Although rollback is not supported for checkpoints across software versions, users can perform rollback at their own discretion and can use the best-effort mode to recover from errors.

- When checkpoints are created on bootflash, differences with the running-system configuration cannot be performed before performing the rollback, and the system reports "No Changes."

Example 1-10 demonstrates how to create a configuration rollback.

Note   You need to make sure you are in the correct VDC. If you need to change VDCs, use the **switchto vdc** syntax.

Example 1-10   *Creating a Configuration Rollback*

```
N7010-1# checkpoint changes
..........Done
N7010-1# show diff rollback-patch checkpoint changes running-config
Collecting Running-Config
Generating Rollback Patch
Rollback Patch is Empty
N7010-1# conf t
Enter configuration commands, one per line. End with CNTL/Z.
N7010-1(config)# no snmp-server user nxos-admin
N7010-1(config)# exit
N7010-1# show diff rollback-patch checkpoint changes running-config
Collecting Running-Config
Generating Rollback Patch
!!
no username nxos-admin sshkey ssh-rsa
AAAAB3NzaC1yc2EAAAABIwAAAQEA6+TdX+ABH/mq1gQbfhhsjBmm65ksgfQb3Mb3qbwUbNlcAa6fjJCGdHu
f3kJ
ox/hjgPDChJOd-
kUXHjESlV59OhZP/NHlBrBq0TGRr+hfdAssD3wG5oPkywgM4+bR/ssCzoj6jVG41tGmfPip4pr3dqsMzR21
DXSK
K/tdj7bipWKy1wSkYQzZwatIVPIXRqTJY7L9a+JqVIJEA0QlJM1l0wZ5YbxccB2GKNKCM2x2BZ14okVgl80
CCJg
7vmn+8RqIOQ5jNAPNeb9kFw9nsPj/r5xFC1RcSKeQbdYAjItU6cX1TslRnKjlWewCgIa26dEaGdawMVuftg
u0uM
97VCOxZPQ==
no username nxos-admin
N7010-1# rollback running-config checkpoint changes
Note: Applying config in parallel may fail Rollback verification
Collecting Running-Config
Generating Rollback Patch
Executing Rollback Patch
```

```
Generating Running-config for verification
Generating Patch for verification
N7010-1# show snmp user nxos-admin


                SNMP USER


User                          Auth  Priv(enforce) Groups
____                          ____  _____  _____
nxos-admin            .        sha   des(no)       network-operator

You can also enable specific SNMP traps:
N7010-1(config)# snmp-server enable traps eigrp
N7010-1(config)# snmp-server enable traps callhome
N7010-1(config)# snmp-server enable traps link
N7010-1(config)# exit
N7010-1#
```

Operating System Files

Cisco NX-OS Software consists of three images:

- The kickstart image, contains the Linux kernel, basic drivers, and initial file system.

- The system image contains the system software, infrastructure, Layers 4 through 7.

- The *Erasable Programmable Logic Device (EPLD)* image: EPLDs are found on the Nexus 7000 currently shipping I/O modules. EPLD images are not released frequently,\; even if an EPLD image is released, the network administrator is not forced to upgrade to the new image. EPLD image upgrades for I/O modules disrupt traffic going through the I/O module. The I/O module powers down briefly during the upgrade. The EPLD image upgrades are performed one module at a time.

On the Nexus 7000 with dual-supervisor modules installed, NX-OS supports in-service software upgrades (ISSU). NX-OS ISSU upgrades are performed without disrupting data traffic. If the upgrade requires EPLD to be installed onto the line cards that causes a disruption of data traffic, the NX-OS software warns you before proceeding so that you can stop the upgrade and reschedule it to a time that minimizes the impact on your network.

NX-OS ISSU updates the following images:

- Kickstart image
- System image
- Supervisor module BIOS
- Data module image

- Data module BIOS

- Connectivity management processor (CMP) image

- CMP BIOS

The ISSU process performs a certain sequence of events, as outlined here:

Step 1. Upgrade the BIOS on the active and standby supervisor modules and the line cards (data cards/nonsupervisor modules).

Step 2. Bring up the standby supervisor module with the new kickstart and system images.

Step 3. Switch over from the active supervisor module to the upgraded standby supervisor module.

Step 4. Bring up the old active supervisor module with the new kickstart image and the new system image.

Step 5. Upgrade the CMP on both supervisor modules.

Step 6. Perform nondisruptive image upgrade for line card (data cards/nonsupervisor modules), one at a time.

Step 7. ISSU upgrade is complete.

Virtual Device Contexts (VDCs)

The Nexus 7000 NX-OS software supports Virtual Device Contexts (VDCs), VDC(s) allow the partitioning of a single physical Nexus 7000 device into multiple logical devices. This logical separation provides the following benefits:

- Administrative and management separation

- Change and failure domain isolation from other VDCs

- Address, VLAN, VRF, and vPC isolation

Each VDC appears as a unique device and allows for separate Roles-Based Access Control Management (RBAC) per VDC. This enables VDCs to be administered by different administrators while still maintaining a rich, granular RBAC capability. With this functionalit, each administrator can define virtual routing and forwarding instance (VRF) names and VLAN IDs independent of those used in other VDCs safely with the knowledge that VDCs maintain their own unique software processes, configuration, and data-plane forwarding tables.

Each VDC also maintains an individual high-availability (HA) policy that defines the action that the system will take when a failure occurs within a VDC. Depending on the hardware configuration of the system, there are various actions that can be performed. In a single supervisor system, the VDC can be shut down, restarted, or the supervisor can be reloaded. In a redundant supervisor configuration, the VDC can be shut down, restarted, or a supervisor switchover can be initiated.

Note   Refer to Chapter 6, "High Availability," for additional details.

There are components that are shared between VDC(s), which include the following:

- A single instance of the kernel which supports all of the processes and VDCs.
- Supervisor modules
- Fabric modules
- Power supplies
- Fan trays
- System fan trays
- CMP
- CoPP
- Hardware SPAN resources

Figure 1-5 shows the logical segmentation with VDCs on the Nexus 7000. A common use case is horizontal consolidation to reduce the quantity of physical switches at the data center aggregation layer. In Figure 1-5, there are two physical Nexus 7000 chassis; the logical VDC layout is also shown.

VDC Configuration

This section shows the required steps to creating a VDC; once the VDC is created, you will assign resources to the VDC. VDC(s) are always created from the default admin VDC context, VDC context 1.

Note   The maximum number of VDCs that can be configured per Nexus 7000 chassis is four; the default VDC (VDC 1) and three additional VDC(s).

Example 1-11 shows how to configure the VDC core on Egypt.

Example 1-11   *Creating VDC "core" on Egypt*

```
egypt(config)# vdc core
Note:  Creating VDC, one moment please ...
egypt# show vdc
vdc_id  vdc_name                      state           mac
```

```
------   --------                          -----            ----------
1       egypt                              active           00:1b:54:c2:38:c1
2       core                               active           00:1b:54:c2:38:c2

egypt# show vdc core detail
vdc id: 2
vdc name: core
vdc state: active
vdc mac address: 00:1b:54:c2:38:c2
vdc ha policy: RESTART
vdc dual-sup ha policy: SWITCHOVER
vdc boot Order: 2
vdc create time: Mon Feb 22 13:11:59 2010
vdc reload count: 1
vdc restart count: 0
egypt#
```

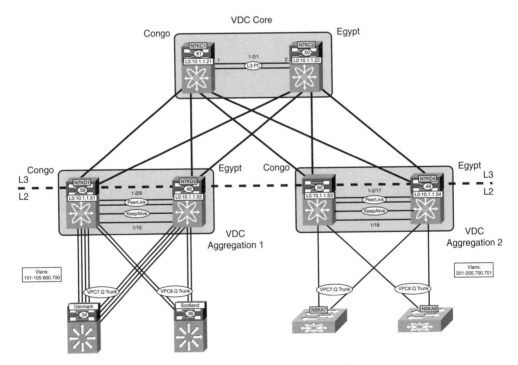

Figure 1-5 *Logical Segmentation with VDCs on the Nexus 7000*

Once the VDC is created, you now have to assign physical interfaces to the VDC. Depending on the Ethernet modules installed in the switch, interface allocation is supported as follows:

The 32-port 10-Gigabit Ethernet Module (N7K-M132XP-12), interfaces can be allocated on a per port-group basis; there are eight port-groups. For example, port-group 1 are interfaces e1, e3, e5, e7; port-group 2 are interfaces e2, e4, e6, e8.

The 48-port 10/100/1000 I/O Module (N7K-M148GT-11) can be allocated on a per-port basis.

The 48-port 1000BaseX I/O Module (N7K-M148GS-11) can be allocated on a per-port basis.

A future module, N7K-D132XP-15, interfaces will be allocated per 2 ports per VDC.

Note It is not possible to virtualize a physical interface and associate the resulting logical interfaces to different VDCs. A supported configuration is to virtualize a physical interface and associate the resulting logical interfaces with different VRFs or VLANs. By default, all physical ports belong to the default VDC.

Example 1-12 demonstrates how to allocate interfaces to a VDC.

Example 1-12 *Allocating Interfaces to a VDC*

```
egypt(config)# vdc core
eqypt(config-vdc)# allocate interface Ethernet1/17
egypt(config-vdc)# allocate interface Ethernet1/18
```

To verify the interfaces allocation, enter the show vdc membership command as demonstrated in Example 1-13.

Example 1-13 *Verifying Interface Allocation to a VDC*

```
egypt(config-vdc)# show vdc membership

vdc_id: 1 vdc_name: egypt interfaces:
        Ethernet1/26           Ethernet1/28           Ethernet1/30
        Ethernet1/32           Ethernet2/2            Ethernet2/4
        Ethernet2/6            Ethernet2/8            Ethernet2/26
        Ethernet2/28           Ethernet2/30           Ethernet2/32
        Ethernet3/4            Ethernet3/5            Ethernet3/6
        Ethernet3/7            Ethernet3/8            Ethernet3/9
```

```
        Ethernet3/11          Ethernet3/12          Ethernet3/13
        Ethernet3/14          Ethernet3/15          Ethernet3/16
        Ethernet3/17          Ethernet3/18          Ethernet3/19
        Ethernet3/20          Ethernet3/21          Ethernet3/22
        Ethernet3/23          Ethernet3/24          Ethernet3/25
        Ethernet3/26          Ethernet3/27          Ethernet3/28
        Ethernet3/29          Ethernet3/30          Ethernet3/31
        Ethernet3/32          Ethernet3/33          Ethernet3/34
        Ethernet3/35          Ethernet3/36          Ethernet3/39
        Ethernet3/40          Ethernet3/41          Ethernet3/42
        Ethernet3/43          Ethernet3/44          Ethernet3/45
        Ethernet3/46          Ethernet3/47          Ethernet3/48

vdc_id: 2 vdc_name: core interfaces:
        Ethernet1/17          Ethernet1/18          Ethernet1/19
        Ethernet1/20          Ethernet1/21          Ethernet1/22
        Ethernet1/23          Ethernet1/24          Ethernet1/25
        Ethernet1/27          Ethernet1/29          Ethernet1/31
        Ethernet2/17          Ethernet2/18          Ethernet2/19
        Ethernet2/20          Ethernet2/21          Ethernet2/22
        Ethernet2/23          Ethernet2/24          Ethernet2/25
        Ethernet2/27          Ethernet2/29          Ethernet2/31
        Ethernet3/1           Ethernet3/2           Ethernet3/3
        Ethernet3/10
```

In addition to interfaces, other physical resources can be allocated to an individual VDC, including IPv4 route memory, IPv6 route memory, port-channels, and SPAN sessions. Configuring these values prevents a single VDC from monopolizing system resources. Example 1-14 demonstrates how to accomplish this.

Example 1-14   *Allocating System Resources*

```
egypt(config)# vdc core
egypt(config-vdc)# limit-resource port-channel minimum 32 maximum equal-to-min
egypt(config-vdc)# limit-resource u4route-mem minimum 32 maximum equal-to-min
egypt(config-vdc)# limit-resource u6route-mem minimum 32 maximum equal-to-min
egypt(config-vdc)# limit-resource vlan minimum 32 maximum equal-to-min
egypt(config-vdc)# limit-resource vrf minimum 32 maximum equal-to-min
```

Defining the VDC HA policy is also done within the VDC configuration sub-mode. Use the ha-policy command to define the HA policy for a VDC as demonstrated in Example 1-15.

Example 1-15 *Changing the HA Policy for a VDC*

```
egypt(config)# vdc core
eqypt(config-vdc)# ha-policy dual-sup bringdown
```

The HA policy will depend based on the use-case or VDC role. For example, if you have dual-supervisor modules in the Nexus 7000 chassis or if the VDC role is development/test, the VDC HA policy may be to just shut down the VDC. If the VDC role is for the core and aggregation use case the HA policy would be switchover.

Troubleshooting

The troubleshooting sections introduce basic concepts, methodology, and general troubleshooting guidelines for problems that might occur when configuring and using Cisco NX-OS.

show Commands

Table 1-2 lists sample EXEC commands showing the differences between IOS and NX-OS.

Table 1-2 *Sample EXEC Commands Showing the Differences Between IOS and NX-OS*

Operation	IOS	NX-OS
Displays the running configuration	show running-config	show running-config
Displays the startup configuration	show startup-config	show startup-config
Displays the status of a specified port-channel interface	show etherchannel #	show port channel #
Displays the current boot variables	show boot	show boot
Displays all environmental parameters	show environment	show environment
Displays the percentage of fabric utilized per module	show fabric utilization	show hardware fabric-utilization [detail]
Displays the supervisors high-availability status	show redundancy	show system redundancy status
Displays CPU and memory usage data	show process cpu	show system resources
Displays specific VRF information	show ip vrf *name*	show vrf *name*

debug Commands

Cisco NX-OS supports an extensive debugging feature set for actively troubleshooting a network. Using the CLI, you can enable debugging modes for each feature and view a real-time updated activity log of the control protocol exchanges. Each log entry has a timestamp and is listed chronologically. You can limit access to the debug feature through the CLI roles mechanism to partition access on a per-role basis. Although the **debug** commands show real-time information, you can use the **show** commands to list historical and real-time information.

> **Caution**   Use the **debug** commands only under the guidance of your Cisco technical support representative because **debug** commands can impact your network/device performance.
>
> Save **debug** messages to a special log file, which is more secure and easier to process than sending the **debug** output to the console.

By using the **?** option, you can see the options that are available for any feature. A log entry is created for each entered command in addition to the actual **debug** output. The **debug** output shows a timestamped account of the activity that occurred between the local device and other adjacent devices.

You can use the **debug** facility to track events, internal messages, and protocol errors. However, you should be careful when using the **debug** utility in a production environment because some options might prevent access to the device by generating too many messages to the console or creating CPU-intensive events that could seriously affect network performance.

You can filter out unwanted **debug** information by using the **debug-filter** command. The **debug-filter** command enables you to limit the **debug** information produced by related **debug** commands.

Example 1-16 limits EIGRP hello packet **debug** information to Ethernet interface 1/1.

Example 1-16   *Filtering debug Information*

```
switch# debug-filter ip eigrp interface ethernet 1/1
switch# debug eigrp packets hello</code>
```

Topology

Throughout the book, you see a common topology for demonstration purposes. Figure 1-6 depicts the physical topology.

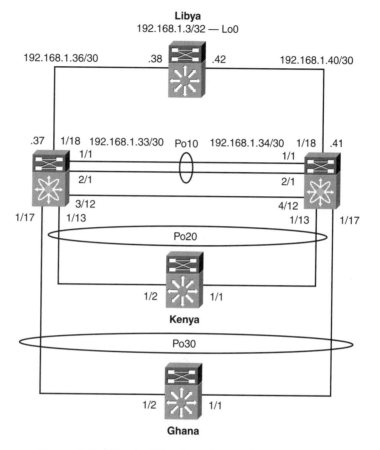

Figure 1-6 *Physical Topology for Book Demonstration Purposes*

Further Reading

NX-OS Feature Navigator: http://tinyurl.com/2btvax

NX-OS Nexus 7000 Supported MIB List: http://tinyurl.com/pzh4gg

NX-OS Nexus 5000 Supported MIB List: http://tinyurl.com/q4pqp5

NX-OS Nexus 1000V Supported MIB List: http://tinyurl.com/nu22mx

Chapter 2

Layer 2 Support and Configurations

The Nexus line of switches provides a robust Layer 2 feature set. This chapter covers common implementations and syntax for Layer 2 features such as virtual local-area networks (VLANS), Private VLANs (PVLANS), Spanning Tree Protocol (STP), Unidirectional Link Detection (UDLD), and Virtual Port Channel (vPC).

This chapter covers the following topics, as they relate to the Nexus family of switches:

- **Layer 2 overview:** Describes the functionality of layer 2 features and interfaces for the Nexus family of switches

- **VLANs and Private VLANs:** Describes VLAN and Private VLAN support available within the Nexus family of switches

- **Spanning Tree Protocol:** Outlines the different STP options available within the Nexus switches and the configuration parameters

- **Virtual Port Channel:** Describes the functionality of configuring Virtual Port Channels between a pair of Nexus switches and provides configuration examples and best practices

- **Unidirectional Link Detection:** Describes how to use Unidirectional Link Detection to prevent undesirable conditions in a Layer 2 environment

Layer 2 Overview

Although NX-OS is a single operating system for the Nexus line of switches, the hardware architecture of the switches might differ slightly. This section begins by reviewing some basic switching concepts and then discuss the forwarding behavior of both the Nexus 5000 and Nexus 7000 switches.

Layer 2 forwarding deals with the capability to build and maintain Media Access Control (MAC) address tables that are stored in a Content Addressable Memory (CAM) table. MAC tables are built by learning the MAC address of the stations that are plugged into them. The process of learning MAC addresses is done in large part dynamically; however, in certain cases, it might be necessary for a network administrator to create static MAC entries that are prepopulated into the CAM table. When populated, the CAM tables are used to make forwarding decisions at Layer 2 by analyzing the destination MAC (DMAC) address of the frame. When this table lookup occurs and any other decisions such as dropping the frame or flooding the frame, it determines whether the switch is said to implement a store-and-forward or cut-through method.

Store-and-Forward Switching

Store-and-forward switching waits until the entire frame has been received and then compares the last portion of the frame against the frame check sequence (FCS) to ensure that no errors have been introduced during physical transmission. If the frame is determined to be corrupt, it is immediately dropped. Store-and-forward switching also inherently addresses any issues that might arise when a packet's ingress and egress ports have dissimilar underlying physical characteristics, that is, 100 Mbps versus 1 Gbps versus 10 Gbps. Latency measurements in a store-and-forward switch are typically measured on a Last In First Out (LIFO) basis. The Nexus 7000 series of switches implements store-and-forward switching.

Cut-Through Switching

Although store-and-forward switches wait for the entire frame to be received into a buffer, cut-through switches can perform the L2 lookup as soon as the DMAC is received in the first 6 bytes of the frame. Historically, cut-through switching provided a method for forwarding frames at high speeds while relying on another station to discard invalid frames. The latency of cut-through switching platforms is typically measured on a First In First Out (FIFO) basis. As application-specific integrated circuit (ASIC) process technology matured, cut-through switches gained the capability to look further into the frame without the performance penalty associated with store-and-forward switches. Additionally, over time, physical mediums have become more reliable than in the past. With the maturity of both ASIC process technology and physical transmission reliability, the industry has seen a reemergence of cut-through switching technology. The Nexus 5000 series of switches uses the cut-through switching method, except in the case in which there is dissimilar transmission speeds between the ingress and egress ports.

Fabric Extension via the Nexus 2000

The Nexus 5000 offers a unique capability by combining with the Nexus 2000 Fabric Extenders. The Nexus 2000 operates as a line card for the Nexus 5000, without being constrained to a physical chassis as is the case with most modular switch platforms. To continue this analogy, the Nexus 5000 operates as a supervisor module for the *virtual chassis*. Although physically separate, the Nexus 5000 and 2000 are managed as a single entity from a software image, configuration, and spanning-tree perspective. This functionality enables data center engineers to gain the cabling benefits of an in-rack switching solution, with the simplicity of management of a centralized or end-of-row topology. The first product within the Nexus 2000 family is the 2148T that supports 48 fixed ports of Gigabit Ethernet, and four 10 Gigabit interfaces to connect to the Nexus 5000. You need to understand that the Nexus 2000 does not perform any local switching functions, and all traffic is switched in a centralized fashion by the Nexus 5000. The front panel ports on a Nexus 2000 do not operate the same way that a normal switch port would and should only be used for host connectivity. One of the most apparent differences in operations between the Nexus 2000 and other switches is the implementation of BPDUGuard on all front-panel ports. BPDUGuard is covered in depth later in this chapter.

The initial configuration of the Nexus 2000 is quite simple and when configured can then be treated as additional ports configurable on the Nexus 5000. The Nexus 2000 can be connected to the 5000 in one of two distinct modes:

- **Static pinning:** This configuration creates a direct relationship between front panel ports and their uplinks. The pinning is based on the number of uplinks available. For example, if one uplink is active, all front panel ports are mapped. Static pinning is a good option in which tight control over the bandwidth and oversubscription is desirable. The drawback of static pinning is that if uplinks are added or removed, the host ports are bounced to repin the hosts across the uplinks. One to four uplinks are supported in this configuration.

- **Etherchannel:** This configuration aggregates the uplink ports into a single logical interface that all front-panel ports are mapped to. As discussed later in the chapter, in an Etherchannel configuration only 1, 2, or 4 uplinks should be used. In this configuration hosts' ports remain up if uplinks are added or removed. The uplink port-channel can also be a VPC to two different Nexus 5000s.

Virtual Port channels can be used to connect Nexus 2000s to Nexus 5000s or to connect hosts to Nexus 2000; however, these two connectivity scenarios cannot be used together. Figure 2-1 illustrates the supported VPC topologies.

Configuring Nexus 2000 Using Static Pinning

This section demonstrates a basic Nexus 2000 configuration using the topology shown in Figure 2-2.

Example 2-1 demonstrates how to configure Nexus 2000 to 5000 connectivity using two uplinks in static pinning mode.

Supported VPC Topologies

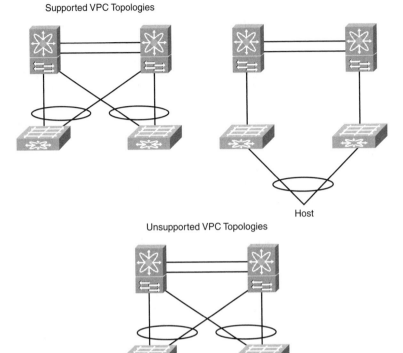

Unsupported VPC Topologies

Host

Figure 2-1   *Nexus 2000 Supported VPC Topologies*

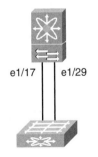

e1/17   e1/29

Figure 2-2   *Network Topology for Nexus 2000 Configuration*

Example 2-1 *Nexus 2000 Static Pinning Configuration*

```
NX5000(config)# fex 100
NX5000(config-fex)# pinning max-links 2
Change in Max-links will cause traffic disruption.
NX5000(config-fex)# description FEX100
NX5000(config-fex)# exit
NX5000(config)#


NX5000# conf t
NX5000(config)# interface ethernet 1/17
NX5000(config-if)# switchport mode fex-fabric
NX5000(config-if)# fex associate 100
NX5000(config-if)# no shutdown
NX5000(config-if)# exit
NX5000(config)# interface ethernet 1/29
NX5000(config-if)# switchport mode fex-fabric
NX5000(config-if)# fex associate 100
NX5000(config-if)# no shutdown
NX5000(config-if)# exit
NX5000(config)# exit
```

Nexus 2000 Static Pinning Verification

You can monitor the Nexus 2000 using the following commands:

- **show fex:** Displays a list of fabric extension (FEX) units, their description, state, model, and serial number.

- **show fex** *fex-id* **detail:** Provides verbose status information about a particular Nexus 2000. The output of this command provides details as to the software versions, operational configuration, uplink status, and much more.

- **show interface status fex** *fex-id*: Displays the status of front-panel host ports on a particular FEX.

- **show interface ethernet** *mod/slot* **fex-intf:** Displays front-panel hosts' ports pinned to a particular Nexus 5000 interface.

Example 2-2 shows sample output from the previous commands.

Example 2-2 *Nexus 2000 Static Pinning Verification*

```
NX5000# show fex
  FEX             FEX             FEX                    FEX
 Number       Description        State     Model             Serial
---------------------------------------------------------------------
  100            FEX100          Online    N2K-C2148T-1GE   JAF1318AALS
```

```
NX5000# show fex 100 detail
FEX: 100 Description: FEX100    state: Online
  FEX version: 4.0(1a)N2(1a) [Switch version: 4.0(1a)N2(1a)]
  FEX Interim version: 4.0(1a)N2(1a)
  Switch Interim version: 4.0(1a)N2(1a)
  Extender Model: N2K-C2148T-1GE, Extender Serial: JAF1318AALS
  Part No: 73-12009-05
  Card Id: 70, Mac Addr: 00:0d:ec:cd:26:c2, Num Macs: 64
  Module Sw Gen: 19 [Switch Sw Gen: 19]
 pinning-mode: static    Max-links: 2
  Fabric port for control traffic: Eth1/17
  Fabric interface state:
    Eth1/17 - Interface Up. State: Active
    Eth1/29 - Interface Up. State: Active
  Fex Port        State  Fabric Port  Primary Fabric
       Eth100/1/1   Up      Eth1/17      Eth1/17
       Eth100/1/2   Up      Eth1/17      Eth1/17
       Eth100/1/3   Up      Eth1/17      Eth1/17
       Eth100/1/4  Down     Eth1/17      Eth1/17
       Eth100/1/5  Down     Eth1/17      Eth1/17
       Eth100/1/6  Down     Eth1/17      Eth1/17
       Eth100/1/7  Down     Eth1/17      Eth1/17
       Eth100/1/8  Down     Eth1/17      Eth1/17
       Eth100/1/9  Down     Eth1/17      Eth1/17
      Eth100/1/10   Up      Eth1/17      Eth1/17
      Eth100/1/11   Up      Eth1/17      Eth1/17
      Eth100/1/12   Up      Eth1/17      Eth1/17
      Eth100/1/13   Up      Eth1/17      Eth1/17
      Eth100/1/14  Down     Eth1/17      Eth1/17
      Eth100/1/15  Down     Eth1/17      Eth1/17
      Eth100/1/16  Down     Eth1/17      Eth1/17
      Eth100/1/17  Down     Eth1/17      Eth1/17
      Eth100/1/18  Down     Eth1/17      Eth1/17
      Eth100/1/19  Down     Eth1/17      Eth1/17
      Eth100/1/20  Down     Eth1/17      Eth1/17
      Eth100/1/21  Down     Eth1/17      Eth1/17
      Eth100/1/22  Down     Eth1/17      Eth1/17
      Eth100/1/23  Down     Eth1/17      Eth1/17
      Eth100/1/24  Down     Eth1/17      Eth1/17
      Eth100/1/25  Down     Eth1/29      Eth1/29
      Eth100/1/26  Down     Eth1/29      Eth1/29
      Eth100/1/27  Down     Eth1/29      Eth1/29
      Eth100/1/28  Down     Eth1/29      Eth1/29
      Eth100/1/29  Down     Eth1/29      Eth1/29
```

```
        Eth100/1/30   Down     Eth1/29     Eth1/29
        Eth100/1/31   Down     Eth1/29     Eth1/29
        Eth100/1/32   Down     Eth1/29     Eth1/29
        Eth100/1/33   Down     Eth1/29     Eth1/29
        Eth100/1/34   Down     Eth1/29     Eth1/29
        Eth100/1/35   Down     Eth1/29     Eth1/29
        Eth100/1/36   Down     Eth1/29     Eth1/29
        Eth100/1/37   Down     Eth1/29     Eth1/29
        Eth100/1/38   Down     Eth1/29     Eth1/29
        Eth100/1/39   Down     Eth1/29     Eth1/29
        Eth100/1/40   Down     Eth1/29     Eth1/29
        Eth100/1/41   Down     Eth1/29     Eth1/29
        Eth100/1/42   Down     Eth1/29     Eth1/29
        Eth100/1/43   Down     Eth1/29     Eth1/29
        Eth100/1/44    Up      Eth1/29     Eth1/29
        Eth100/1/45    Up      Eth1/29     Eth1/29
        Eth100/1/46    Up      Eth1/29     Eth1/29
        Eth100/1/47    Up      Eth1/29     Eth1/29
        Eth100/1/48    Up      Eth1/29     Eth1/29
Logs:
[02/08/2010 18:26:44.953152] Module register received
[02/08/2010 18:26:44.954622] Registration response sent
[02/08/2010 18:26:44.989224] Module Online Sequence
[02/08/2010 18:26:46.868753] Module Online
NX5000# sho interface status fex 100
--------------------------------------------------------------------
Port          Name            Status  Vlan    Duplex  Speed  Type
--------------------------------------------------------------------
Eth100/1/1    --              up      trunk   full    1000   --
Eth100/1/2    --              up      trunk   full    1000   --
Eth100/1/3    --              up      trunk   full    1000   --
Eth100/1/4    --              down    1       full    1000   --
Eth100/1/5    --              down    1       full    1000   --
Eth100/1/6    --              down    1       full    1000   --
Eth100/1/7    --              down    1       full    1000   --
Eth100/1/8    --              down    1       full    1000   --
Eth100/1/9    --              down    1       full    1000   --
Eth100/1/10   --              up      89      full    1000   --
Eth100/1/11   --              up      trunk   full    1000   --
Eth100/1/12   --              up      trunk   full    1000   --
Eth100/1/13   --              up      trunk   full    1000   --
Eth100/1/14   --              down    1       full    1000   --
Eth100/1/15   --              down    1       full    1000   --
Eth100/1/16   --              down    1       full    1000   --
```

```
Eth100/1/17    --              down    1       full    1000    --
Eth100/1/18    --              down    1       full    1000    --
Eth100/1/19    --              down    1       full    1000    --
Eth100/1/20    --              down    1       full    1000    --
Eth100/1/21    --              down    1       full    1000    --
Eth100/1/22    --              down    1       full    1000    --
Eth100/1/23    --              down    89      full    1000    --
Eth100/1/24    --              down    89      full    1000    --
Eth100/1/25    --              down    100     full    1000    --
Eth100/1/26    --              down    100     full    1000    --
Eth100/1/27    --              down    1       full    1000    --
Eth100/1/28    --              down    1       full    1000    --
Eth100/1/29    --              down    1       full    1000    --
Eth100/1/30    --              down    1       full    1000    --
Eth100/1/31    --              down    1       full    1000    --
Eth100/1/32    --              down    1       full    1000    --
Eth100/1/33    --              down    1       full    1000    --
Eth100/1/34    --              down    1       full    1000    --
Eth100/1/35    --              down    1       full    1000    --
Eth100/1/36    --              down    1       full    1000    --
Eth100/1/37    --              down    89      full    1000    --
Eth100/1/38    --              down    89      full    1000    --
Eth100/1/39    --              down    89      full    1000    --
Eth100/1/40    --              down    89      full    1000    --
Eth100/1/41    --              down    89      full    1000    --
Eth100/1/42    --              down    89      full    1000    --
Eth100/1/43    --              down    89      full    1000    --
Eth100/1/44    --              up      89      full    1000    --
Eth100/1/45    --              up      89      full    1000    --
Eth100/1/46    --              up      89      full    1000    --
Eth100/1/47    --              up      89      full    1000    --
Eth100/1/48    --              up      89      full    1000    --
NX5000#


NX5000# show interface ethernet 1/17 fex-intf
Fabric          FEX
Interface       Interfaces
-------------------------------------------------
 Eth1/17        Eth100/1/24    Eth100/1/23    Eth100/1/22    Eth100/1/21
                Eth100/1/20    Eth100/1/19    Eth100/1/18    Eth100/1/17
                Eth100/1/16    Eth100/1/15    Eth100/1/14    Eth100/1/10
                Eth100/1/9     Eth100/1/8     Eth100/1/7     Eth100/1/6
                Eth100/1/5     Eth100/1/4     Eth100/1/13    Eth100/1/12
                Eth100/1/11    Eth100/1/3     Eth100/1/2     Eth100/1/1
```

```
NX5000# show interface ethernet 1/29 fex-intf
Fabric          FEX
Interface       Interfaces
--------------------------------------------------
  Eth1/29       Eth100/1/48   Eth100/1/47   Eth100/1/46   Eth100/1/45
                Eth100/1/44   Eth100/1/43   Eth100/1/42   Eth100/1/41
                Eth100/1/40   Eth100/1/39   Eth100/1/38   Eth100/1/37
                Eth100/1/36   Eth100/1/35   Eth100/1/34   Eth100/1/33
                Eth100/1/32   Eth100/1/31   Eth100/1/30   Eth100/1/29
                Eth100/1/28   Eth100/1/27   Eth100/1/26   Eth100/1/25
```

Configuring Nexus 2000 Using Port-Channels

This section demonstrates the configuration of the Nexus 2000 for the topology in Figure 2-3, using port-channels instead of static pinning.

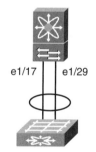

e1/17   e1/29

Figure 2-3 *Nexus 2000 Port-Channel Topology*

In the next example, we configure a similar topology using port-channels instead of static pinning. The configuration in Example 2-3 is similar to that of Example 2-1; however, in this method the **pinning max-links** parameter is set to one, and the individual interfaces are configured for a Port-Channel.

Example 2-3 *Nexus 2000 Port-Channel Configuration*

```
NX5000# config t
NX5000(config)# fex 100
NX5000(config-fex)# pinning max-links 1
Change in Max-links will cause traffic disruption.
NX5000(config-fex)# exit
NX5000(config)# interface port-channel 100
NX5000(config-if)# switchport mode fex-fabric
NX5000(config-if)# fex associate 100
```

```
NX5000(config-if)# no shutdown
NX5000(config-if)# exit
NX5000(config)# int e1/17,e1/29
NX5000(config-if-range)# channel-group 100 mode on
NX5000(config-if-range)# no shutdown
NX5000(config-if-range)# exit
```

Nexus 2000 Static Pinning Verification

Verification of the Nexus 2000 is similar whether port-channels or static pinning is used; however, all ports will now be pinned to the logical port-channel interface, as shown in Example 2-4.

Example 2-4 *Nexus 2000 Port-Channel Verification*

```
NX5000# sho fex
  FEX           FEX             FEX                   FEX
Number      Description       State    Model          Serial
----------------------------------------------------------------
  100           FEX100        Online    N2K-C2148T-1GE  JAF1318AALS
NX5000# sho fex 100 det
FEX: 100 Description: FEX100    state: Online
  FEX version: 4.0(1a)N2(1a) [Switch version: 4.0(1a)N2(1a)]
  FEX Interim version: 4.0(1a)N2(1a)
  Switch Interim version: 4.0(1a)N2(1a)
  Extender Model: N2K-C2148T-1GE, Extender Serial: JAF1318AALS
  Part No: 73-12009-05
  Card Id: 70, Mac Addr: 00:0d:ec:cd:26:c2, Num Macs: 64
  Module Sw Gen: 19 [Switch Sw Gen: 19]
 pinning-mode: static    Max-links: 1
  Fabric port for control traffic: Eth1/29
  Fabric interface state:
    Po100 - Interface Up. State: Active
    Eth1/17 - Interface Up. State: Active
    Eth1/29 - Interface Up. State: Active
  Fex Port        State  Fabric Port  Primary Fabric
      Eth100/1/1   Up      Po100        Po100
      Eth100/1/2   Up      Po100        Po100
      Eth100/1/3   Up      Po100        Po100
      Eth100/1/4  Down     Po100        Po100
      Eth100/1/5  Down     Po100        Po100
      Eth100/1/6  Down     Po100        Po100
      Eth100/1/7  Down     Po100        Po100
      Eth100/1/8  Down     Po100        Po100
      Eth100/1/9  Down     Po100        Po100
     Eth100/1/10   Up      Po100        Po100
```

```
    Eth100/1/11    Up      Po100      Po100
    Eth100/1/12    Up      Po100      Po100
    Eth100/1/13    Up      Po100      Po100
    Eth100/1/14    Down    Po100      Po100
    Eth100/1/15    Down    Po100      Po100
    Eth100/1/16    Down    Po100      Po100
    Eth100/1/17    Down    Po100      Po100
    Eth100/1/18    Down    Po100      Po100
    Eth100/1/19    Down    Po100      Po100
    Eth100/1/20    Down    Po100      Po100
    Eth100/1/21    Down    Po100      Po100
    Eth100/1/22    Down    Po100      Po100
    Eth100/1/23    Down    Po100      Po100
    Eth100/1/24    Down    Po100      Po100
    Eth100/1/25    Down    Po100      Po100
    Eth100/1/26    Down    Po100      Po100
    Eth100/1/27    Down    Po100      Po100
    Eth100/1/28    Down    Po100      Po100
    Eth100/1/29    Down    Po100      Po100
    Eth100/1/30    Down    Po100      Po100
    Eth100/1/31    Down    Po100      Po100
    Eth100/1/32    Down    Po100      Po100
    Eth100/1/33    Down    Po100      Po100
    Eth100/1/34    Down    Po100      Po100
    Eth100/1/35    Down    Po100      Po100
    Eth100/1/36    Down    Po100      Po100
    Eth100/1/37    Down    Po100      Po100
    Eth100/1/38    Down    Po100      Po100
    Eth100/1/39    Down    Po100      Po100
    Eth100/1/40    Down    Po100      Po100
    Eth100/1/41    Down    Po100      Po100
    Eth100/1/42    Down    Po100      Po100
    Eth100/1/43    Down    Po100      Po100
------------------------------------------------------------------
    Eth100/1/44    Up      Po100      Po100
    Eth100/1/45    Up      Po100      Po100
    Eth100/1/46    Up      Po100      Po100
    Eth100/1/47    Up      Po100      Po100
    Eth100/1/48    Up      Po100      Po100
Logs:
[02/08/2010 18:26:44.953152] Module register received
[02/08/2010 18:26:44.954622] Registration response sent
[02/08/2010 18:26:44.989224] Module Online Sequence
[02/08/2010 18:26:46.868753] Module Online
[02/08/2010 19:15:20.492760] Module disconnected
```

```
[02/08/2010 19:15:20.493584] Offlining Module
[02/08/2010 19:15:20.494099] Module Offline Sequence
[02/08/2010 19:15:20.905145] Module Offline
[02/08/2010 19:15:57.354031] Module register received
[02/08/2010 19:15:57.355002] Registration response sent
[02/08/2010 19:15:57.383437] Module Online Sequence
[02/08/2010 19:15:59.212748] Module Online
NX5000#
```

Layer 2 Forwarding on a Nexus 7000

The Nexus 7000 is an entirely distributed Layer 2 forwarding platform. This means that every module in the system contains its own forwarding table. When a packet is received on a port, the ingress module performs both an ingress L2 lookup and an initial egress L2 lookup. When the packet arrives at the egress module, a second egress lookup is performed to ensure that the table has not changed. Each module is also responsible for learning MAC addresses in the local hardware. MAC addresses learned by an individual module are flooded across the fabric to all other modules in the system, and an additional software process ensures that MAC addresses are properly synchronized across the hardware modules. Aging of MAC addresses is also done locally by each line card but only for primary entries (entries learned locally). When a module ages a MAC address, it also notifies the supervisors so that the address can be removed from the other modules. MAC address aging is configurable on a per-VLAN basis, with a limit of 14 unique aging values per system.

To configure the MAC address aging timer, enter the following command:

```
switch(config)# mac address-table aging-time 600
```

To create a static MAC entry, enter the following command:

```
Congo(config)# mac address-table static 12ab.47dd.ff89 vlan 1 interface ethernet 2/1
```

L2 Forwarding Verification

During the normal operation of a switched infrastructure, certain tasks are required to validate the L2 forwarding process. These tasks include displaying the MAC address table to identify connected nodes or validate switching paths. In certain cases, it might also be necessary to clear the MAC address table, forcing the switch to repopulate with the latest information. The following examples clear the MAC table, create a static MAC entry, validate that the entry is inserted into the MAC table, and finally validate that it is synchronized across all modules within the system. Example 2-5 shows how to clear the MAC address table.

Example 2-5 *Clearing MAC Address Table*

```
Congo# clear mac address-table dynamic
Congo(config)# sho mac address-table aging-time
Vlan    Aging Time
----    ----------
1       600
```

Example 2-6 shows how to display the MAC address table.

Example 2-6 *Displaying the MAC Address Table*

```
Congo# show mac address-table static
Legend:
        * - primary entry, G - Gateway MAC, (R) - Routed MAC
        age - seconds since last seen,+ - primary entry using vPC Peer-Link
    VLAN     MAC Address     Type      age     Secure NTFY   Ports
---------+-----------------+--------+---------+------+----+-----------------
G    -     001b.54c2.bbc1   static      -        F     F   sup-eth1(R)
*  1       12ab.47dd.ff89   static      -        F     F   Eth2/1
```

Due to the distributed forwarding nature of the Nexus 7000, each line card maintains its own forwarding table, which is synchronized across all cards. To verify the synchronization of tables, use the **show forwarding consistency l2 command**, as demonstrated in Example 2-7.

Example 2-7 *Checking Forwarding Table Consistency*

```
Congo# sho forwarding consistency l2 1
Legend:
        * - primary entry, G - Gateway MAC, (R) - Routed MAC
        age - seconds since last seen,+ - primary entry using vPC Peer-Link
Missing entries in the MAC Table
    VLAN     MAC Address     Type      age     Secure NTFY   Ports
---------+-----------------+--------+---------+------+----+-----------------

Extra and Discrepant entries in the MAC Table
    VLAN     MAC Address     Type      age     Secure NTFY   Ports
---------+-----------------+--------+---------+------+----+-----------------
Congo#
```

If there were any discrepancies between the two line cards, they would appear in the preceding output. Under normal circumstances, the two line cards should always be consistent and thus produce no output.

VLANs

VLANs provide a mechanism to segment traffic on a single switch into isolated networks. VLANs can be used to segment a switch for many reasons including security, business unit, or application/function. VLANs are configured on each switch in a given topology but can span multiple physical switches using 802.1Q trunks.

The Nexus 7000 switch supports 4096 VLANs per Virtual Device Context (VDC) for a system total of ~16k VLANs. Some of these VLANs are used by system-level functions and are not user-configurable. You can display the internal VLANs by using the **show vlan internal usage** command, as demonstrated in Example 2-8.

Example 2-8   *Internal VLAN Usage*

```
Congo# show vlan internal usage
VLAN        DESCRIPTION
- - - - - - - - -    - - - - - - - - - - - - - - - - - - - - - - - - - - - - - - - - - - - - - - - - - -
3968-4031   Multicast
4032        Online diagnostics vlan1
4033        Online diagnostics vlan2
4034        Online diagnostics vlan3
4035        Online diagnostics vlan4
4036-4047   Reserved
4094        Reserved
```

Configuring VLANs

VLANs are configured in global configuration mode with the **vlan** *vlan-id configuration command.*

Example 2-9 shows how to add a VLAN to the local database.

Example 2-9   *Creating a New VLAN*

```
Congo# config t
Enter configuration commands, one per line. End with CNTL/Z.
Congo(config)# vlan 10
Congo(config-vlan)# name newvlan
```

Example 2-10 shows how you can create multiple VLANs by specifying a range using the **vlan** *vlan-range* command.

Example 2-10   *Creating Multiple VLANs*

```
Congo# config t
Enter configuration commands, one per line. End with CNTL/Z.
Congo(config)# vlan 10-15
```

```
Congo(config-vlan)# exit
```

VLAN Trunking Protocol

In large switched networks, VLAN Trunking Protocol (VTP) is sometimes used to allow the dissemination of VLAN definition across a large number of switches.

Note   At press time, VTP is supported only on the Nexus 7000, and only transparent mode is supported.

With VTP, devices can operate in one of four distinct modes:

- **Off:** By default, NX-OS devices do not run VTP. Devices that are not running VTP will not send or receive VTP advertisements and will break the flow of VTP advertisements when inserted between two VTP devices.

- **VTP server mode:** In VTP server mode, VLANs can be created, modified, and deleted. VTP servers also define domainwide parameters such as a version and whether VTP pruning will be in effect. VTP servers send VTP advertisements to other devices within the VTP domain and update the VLAN database with advertisements received from other devices in the domain.

- **VTP Client mode:** VTP clients send and receive VTP advertisements and update their local VLAN database based on these advertisements; however, you cannot create, modify, or delete VLANs locally on the device.

- **VTP transparent mode:** Devices operating in VTP transparent mode relay messages received from other devices but do not advertise changes made to the devices' local database, nor will they modify the local database based on information received from other devices.

To configure VTP transparent mode, the code base must be loaded into memory by using the **feature** command, as demonstrated in Example 2-11.

Example 2-11   *Enabling the VTP Feature*

```
Congo# config t
Enter configuration commands, one per line. End with CNTL/Z.
Congo(config)# feature vtp
```

Example 2-12 shows how to specify VTP parameters in global configuration mode.

Example 2-12   *Specifying VTP Parameters*

```
Congo# config t
```

```
Enter configuration commands, one per line. End with CNTL/Z.
Congo(config)# vtp domain cisco
Congo(config)# vtp mode transparent
```

Assigning VLAN Membership

After the VLAN database has been created, ports can now be added to the VLAN based on the requirements of the devices connected to the switch. Additionally, links between switches might be required to carry multiple VLANs.

Example 2-13 shows how to add a port to a VLAN.

Example 2-13   *Adding a Port to a VLAN*

```
Kenya# conf t
Enter configuration commands, one per line. End with CNTL/Z.
Kenya(config)# interface ethernet 2/20
Kenya(config-if)# switchport
Kenya(config-if)# switchport mode access
Kenya(config-if)# switchport access vlan 10
Kenya(config-if)#
```

Example 2-14 shows how to create a trunk interface.

Example 2-14   *Configuring a Trunk Interface*

```
Kenya# conf t
Enter configuration commands, one per line. End with CNTL/Z.
Kenya(config)# interface ethernet 2/11
Kenya(config-if)# switchport
Kenya(config-if)# switchport mode trunk
Kenya(config-if)#
```

With this configuration, the trunk port carries all VLANs that are active in the local VLAN database. It is best practice to manually prune unnecessary trunk ports, limiting the VLANs carried to only those necessary using the following syntax:

```
Kenya\(config-if)# switchport trunk allowed vlan 10-20
```

As requirements change, it might be necessary to add or remove VLANs from a trunk port, using the **add** or **remove** keywords to the **switchport trunk allowed** command, as demonstrated in Example 2-15.

Example 2-15   *Adding and Removing VLANs from a Trunk*

```
Kenya(config-if)# switchport trunk allowed vlan add 5
Kenya(config-if)# switchport trunk allowed vlan remove 15
Kenya(config-if)# sho run interface ethernet 2/11
!Command: show running-config interface Ethernet2/11
!Time: Thu Oct 29 18:27:10 2009
version 4.2(2a)
interface Ethernet2/11
  switchport
  switchport mode trunk
  switchport trunk allowed vlan 5,10-14,16-20
  spanning-tree port type network
  no shutdown
```

Verifying VLAN Configuration

You can view the configured VLANs and the interfaces assigned to them with the **show vlan** command, as demonstrated in Example 2-16.

Example 2-16   *View Configured LANs and Interfaces*

```
Kenya# show vlan
VLAN Name                             Status    Ports
---- -------------------------------- --------- -------------------------------
1    default                          active    Eth2/12, Eth2/40
2    VLAN0002                         active    Eth2/12
3    VLAN0003                         active    Eth2/12
4    VLAN0004                         active    Eth2/12
5    VLAN0005                         active    Eth2/11, Eth2/12
6    VLAN0006                         active    Eth2/12
7    VLAN0007                         active    Eth2/12
8    VLAN0008                         active    Eth2/12
9    VLAN0009                         active    Eth2/12
10   VLAN0010                         active    Eth2/11, Eth2/12, Eth2/20
11   VLAN0011                         active    Eth2/11, Eth2/12
12   VLAN0012                         active    Eth2/11, Eth2/12
13   VLAN0013                         active    Eth2/11, Eth2/12
14   VLAN0014                         active    Eth2/11, Eth2/12
15   VLAN0015                         active    Eth2/12
16   VLAN0016                         active    Eth2/11, Eth2/12
17   VLAN0017                         active    Eth2/11, Eth2/12
18   VLAN0018                         active    Eth2/11, Eth2/12
19   VLAN0019                         active    Eth2/11, Eth2/12
20   VLAN0020                         active    Eth2/11, Eth2/12
VLAN Type
```

```
---- -----
1     enet
2     enet
3     enet
4     enet
5     enet
6     enet
7     enet
8     enet
9     enet
10    enet
11    enet
12    enet
13    enet
14    enet
15    enet
16    enet
17    enet
18    enet
19    enet
20    enet
Remote SPAN VLANs

------------------------------------------------------------------

Primary  Secondary  Type          Ports

-------  ---------  --------------  ----------------------------------
```

Private VLANs

Private VLANs (PVLAN) offer a mechanism to divide a single VLAN into multiple isolated Layer 2 networks. PVLANs can be configured on a single Nexus switch or extended
across multiple devices by trunking all the primary, isolated, and community VLANs to
any other devices that need to participate in the PVLAN domain. Private VLANs are useful in several scenarios:

- **IP address management:** Typically speaking, a one-to-one relationship exists between a VLAN and an IP subnet. In situations in which many VLANs are required
  with a relatively small number of hosts per subnet, PVLANs can be used to configure
  aggregation layer with a larger subnet, and configure each isolated group of hosts
  into isolated VLANs, thus not requiring an IP address or subnet mask change if the
  host is moved from one isolated VLAN to another.

- **Security:** PVLANs offer an additional level of security at Layer 2. Isolated VLANs
  are allowed to communicate only at Layer 2 with other members of the same isolated
  VLAN. If communication between isolated VLANs is required, the communication

must flow through an upstream router or firewall, making it possible to apply security policy on hosts within the same broadcast domain.

■ **Broadcast suppression:** PVLANs can also be used to control the propagation of broadcast traffic only to those devices that can benefit from receiving certain broadcasts.

Within a PVLAN domain, the two major types of VLANs follow:

■ **Primary:** The primary VLAN is where the broadcast domain is defined. Promiscuous ports are part of the primary VLAN and can communicate with all other ports in the primary VLAN, and all isolated and community VLAN ports.

■ **Secondary:** Subdomains that share IP address space with the primary VLAN but are isolated from each other in one of two ways:

   ■ **Isolated VLANs:** Each port within an isolated VLAN is restricted such that it can communicate only with promiscuous ports in the primary VLAN. Ports within the isolated VLANs cannot receive broadcasts from any other devices.

   ■ **Community VLANs:** Community VLAN ports are restricted from communicating with other community VLANs but might communicate with other ports in the same community VLAN and promiscuous ports belonging to the primary VLAN.

Multiple secondary VLANs can be associated with a single primary VLAN. These associations define a PVLAN domain.

Configuring PVLANs

In the following examples, you see the configuration of six hosts to meet the following requirements:

■ **Host1(192.168.100.21):** Communicates only with Host2 and its default gateway

■ **Host2(192.168.100.22):** Communicates only with Host1 and its default gateway

■ **Host3(192.168.100.23):** Communicates only with Host4 and its default gateway

■ **Host4(192.168.100.24):** Communicates only with Host3 and its default gateway

■ **Host5(192.168.100.25):** Sends traffic only to its default gateway

■ **Host6(192.168.100.26):** Sends traffic only to its default gateway

Figure 2-4 provides a visual representation of the configuration in the following examples.

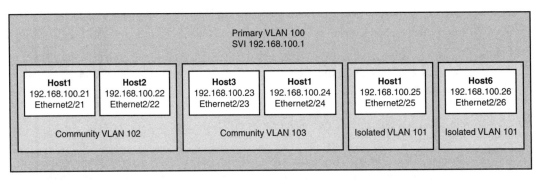

Figure 2-4 *Network Topology for PVLAN Configuration*

First, activate the code base for private VLANs by using the **feature** command as demonstrated in Example 2-17.

Example 2-17 *Enable Private VLANs*

```
Congo# config t
Enter configuration commands, one per line. End with CNTL/Z.
Congo(config)# feature private-vlan
```

Example 2-18 demonstrates how to configure the primary VLAN, isolated, and community VLANs and define their relationship.

Example 2-18 *Defining Private VLANs*

```
Congo(config)# vlan 101
Congo(config-vlan)# name VLAN100-ISOLATED
Congo(config-vlan)# private-vlan isolated
Congo(config-vlan)# vlan 102
Congo(config-vlan)# name VLAN100-COMMUNITY1
Congo(config-vlan)# private-vlan community
Congo(config-vlan)# vlan 103
Congo(config-vlan)# name VLAN100-COMMUNITY2
Congo(config-vlan)# private-vlan community
Congo(config-vlan)#
Congo(config)# vlan 100
Congo(config-vlan)# name VLAN100-PRIMARY
Congo(config-vlan)# private-vlan primary
Congo(config-vlan)# private-vlan association add 101-103
Congo(config-vlan)# exit
```

Example 2-19 shows how to define a Layer 3 switched virtual interface (SVI) and associate secondary Layer 2 VLANs.

Example 2-19 *Creating an SVI for the Primary VLAN*

```
Congo(config)# interface vlan 100
Congo(config-if)# ip address 192.168.100.1/24
Congo(config-if)# private-vlan mapping add 101-103
Congo(config-if)# exit
Congo(config)#
```

Example 2-20 shows how to define the PVLAN configuration on the access switch and assign the host ports into the appropriate secondary VLANs.

Example 2-20 *Private VLAN Access Switch Configuration*

```
Kenya(config)# feature private-vlan
Kenya(config)# vlan 101
Kenya(config-vlan)# name VLAN100-ISOLATED
Kenya(config-vlan)# private-vlan isolated
Kenya(config-vlan)# vlan 102
Kenya(config-vlan)# name VLAN100-COMMUNITY1
Kenya(config-vlan)# private-vlan community
Kenya(config-vlan)# vlan 103
Kenya(config-vlan)# name VLAN100-COMMUNITY2
Kenya(config-vlan)# private-vlan community
Kenya(config-vlan)# vlan 100
Kenya(config-vlan)# name VLAN100-PRIMARY
Kenya(config-vlan)# private-vlan primary
Kenya(config-vlan)# private-vlan association add 101-103
Kenya(config-vlan)#
Kenya(config)# interface ethernet2/21
Kenya(config-if)# description HOST1
Kenya(config-if)# switchport
Kenya(config-if)# switchport mode private-vlan host
Kenya(config-if)# switchport private-vlan host-association 100 102
Kenya(config-if)# exit
Kenya(config)# interface ethernet2/22
Kenya(config-if)# description HOST2
Kenya(config-if)# switchport
Kenya(config-if)# switchport mode private-vlan host
Kenya(config-if)# switchport private-vlan host-association 100 102
Kenya(config-if)# exit
Kenya(config)# interface ethernet2/23
Kenya(config-if)# description HOST3
```

```
Kenya(config-if)# switchport
Kenya(config-if)# switchport mode private-vlan host
Kenya(config-if)# switchport private-vlan host-association 100 103
Kenya(config-if)# exit
Kenya(config)# interface ethernet2/24
Kenya(config-if)# description HOST4
Kenya(config-if)# switchport
Kenya(config-if)# switchport private-vlan host-association 100 103
Kenya(config-if)# exit
Kenya(config)# interface ethernet2/25
Kenya(config-if)# description HOST5
Kenya(config-if)# switchport mode private-vlan host
Kenya(config-if)# switchport
Kenya(config-if)# switchport mode private-vlan host
Kenya(config-if)# switchport private-vlan host-association 100 101
Kenya(config-if)# exit
Kenya(config)# interface ethernet2/26
Kenya(config-if)# description HOST6
Kenya(config-if)# switchport
Kenya(config-if)# switchport mode private-vlan host
Kenya(config-if)# switchport private-vlan host-association 100 101
Kenya(config-if)# exit
```

Verifying PVLAN Configuration

Example 2-21 shows how to verify the mapping of the SVI for the primary VLAN and
associated secondary VLANs.

Example 2-21 *Verifying Layer 3 SVI PVLAN Mapping*

```
Congo# show interface private-vlan mapping
Interface Secondary VLAN Type
--------- -------------- ----------------
vlan100   101            isolated
vlan100   102            community
vlan100   103            community
```

Example 2-22 shows how to verify the mapping of the primary VLANs, the associated
secondary VLANs, and the host ports that belong to each on the access switch Kenya.

Example 2-22 *Verifying PVLAN Mapping*

```
Kenya# show vlan private-vlan
Primary  Secondary  Type        Ports
```

```
-------  ---------  ---------------  --------------------------------------------
100    101        isolated         Eth2/25, Eth2/26
100    102        community        Eth2/21, Eth2/22
100    103        community        Eth2/23, Eth2/24
```

Spanning Tree Protocol

The Spanning Tree Protocol provides a mechanism for physically redundant network topologies to remain logically loop free. All devices in a bridging domain run spanning-tree calculations to discover the topology and calculate the best path to the root bridge. Through the spanning-tree process, redundant network links are placed into a blocking state preventing loops from occurring at Layer 2.

The Nexus series of switches implements two forms of standards-based Spanning Tree Protocols:

- **Rapid Per-VLAN Spanning Tree (Rapid-PVST/802.1w):** Rapid-PVST is the default spanning-tree mode on Nexus 7000 switches. As the name implies, in Rapid-PVST, each VLAN elects a single root bridge, and all other devices determine the lowest cost path to the root bridge. With Rapid-PVST topology, changes are isolated to that particular VLAN. One additional characteristic worth noting is that 802.1w is backward compatible with standard Per-VLAN Spanning Tree (PVST/802.1d) for migration or interoperability purposes.

- **Multiple Spanning Tree (MST/802.1s):** In large Layer 2 environments, MST can be used to provide a much simpler configuration with lower control plane overhead than Rapid-PVST. When MST is leveraged, VLANs with similar topologies share a single spanning-tree instance. MST instances with identical names, revision numbers, and VLAN mappings create a construct called an MST region. For further simplification of complex Layer 2 domains, each MST region is presented to the network as a single bridge. It is also worth noting that MST is backward compatible with Rapid-PVST.

For the following common data center configuration examples, refer to the topology illustrated in Figure 2-5.

In Figure 2-5, Congo and Egypt are redundant data center aggregation switches. First, the aggregation switches will be configured for Rapid-PVST+ with Congo configured as the root bridge for VLANs 1 to 10 (depicted in Figure 2-6) and Egypt as root for VLANs 11 to 20 (depicted in Figure 2-7) in the aggregation block. This type of *root staggering* is often desirable to maximize the amount of bandwidth that is available by reducing the number of blocking links within the spanning tree.

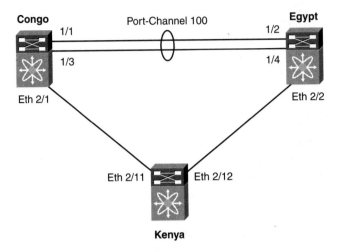

Figure 2-5   *Common Data Center Topology*

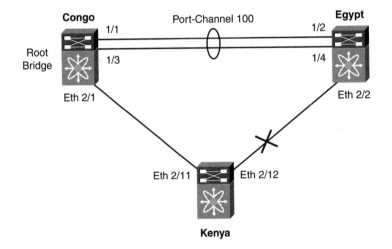

Figure 2-6   *STP Topology for VLANs 1 to 10*

Rapid-PVST+ Configuration

Typically, root bridge placement is influenced by modifying the priority. On NX-OS and most IOS devices, the default bridge priority is 32768, so you will be configuring considerably lower values on the aggregation switches.

Example 2-23 shows how to configure the spanning-tree priority on a range of VLANs.

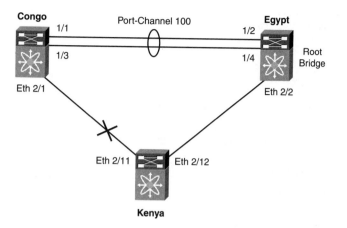

Figure 2-7   *STP Topology for VLANs 11 to 20*

Example 2-23   *Configuring Spanning Tree Bridge Priority*

```
Congo# conf t
Enter configuration commands, one per line. End with CNTL/Z.
Congo(config)# spanning-tree mode rapid-pvst
Congo(config)# vlan 1-20
Congo(config-vlan)# exit
Congo(config)# spanning-tree vlan 1-10 priority 4096
Congo(config)# spanning-tree vlan 11-20 priority 8192
Congo(config)#
--------------------------------------------------------------------
Egypt# conf t
Enter configuration commands, one per line. End with CNTL/Z.
Egypt(config)# spanning-tree mode rapid-pvst
Egypt(config)# vlan 1-20
Egypt(config-vlan)# exit
Egypt(config)# spanning-tree vlan 1-10 priority 8192
Egypt(config)# spanning-tree vlan 11-20 priority 4096
Egypt(config)#
```

Alternatively, you can manipulate the spanning-tree priority values using the **root** keyword, as demonstrated in Example 2-24.

Example 2-24   *Using the spanning-tree root Keyword*

```
Configuration on Congo
Congo(config)#spanning-tree vlan 1-10 root primary
Congo(config)#spanning-tree vlan 11-20 root secondary
--------------------------------------------------------------------
Egypt(config)#spanning-tree vlan 1-10 root secondary
```

```
Egypt(config)#spanning-tree vlan 11-20 root primary
```

Verifying Spanning-Tree State for a VLAN

Understanding the spanning-tree topology on a specific VLAN is important to ensure that the topology behaves as expected if a link or bridge failure occurs. Inconsistent spanning-tree configurations can lead to unexpected outages or slower reconvergence. Example 2-25 shows how to verify the spanning-tree state for a particular VLAN.

Example 2-25 *Displaying Spanning-Tree Information for a Specific VLAN*

```
Congo# show spanning-tree vlan 10
VLAN0010
  Spanning tree enabled protocol rstp
  Root ID    Priority    4106
             Address     001b.54c2.bbc1
             This bridge is the root
             Hello Time  2  sec  Max Age 12 sec  Forward Delay 9  sec
  Bridge ID  Priority    4106   (priority 4096 sys-id-ext 10)
             Address     001b.54c2.bbc1
             Hello Time  2  sec  Max Age 12 sec  Forward Delay 9  sec
Interface        Role Sts Cost      Prio.Nbr Type
---------------- ---- --- --------- -------- --------------------------------
Po100            Desg FWD 1         128.4195 Network P2p
Eth2/1           Desg FWD 4         128.257  Network P2p
```

Example 2-26 shows how to verify that Kenya has selected the best path to root; in this case, Ethernet 2/11 is blocking the redundant connection to Egypt.

Example 2-26 *Confirming Spanning Tree Bridge Priority*

```
Kenya# show spanning-tree vlan 10
VLAN0010
  Spanning tree enabled protocol rstp
  Root ID    Priority    4106
             Address     001b.54c2.bbc1
             Cost        4
             Port        267 (Ethernet2/11)
             Hello Time  2  sec  Max Age 12 sec  Forward Delay 9  sec
  Bridge ID  Priority    32778  (priority 32768 sys-id-ext 10)
             Address     001b.54c2.bbc3
             Hello Time  2  sec  Max Age 20 sec  Forward Delay 15 sec
Interface        Role Sts Cost      Prio.Nbr Type
---------------- ---- --- --------- -------- --------------------------------
Eth2/11          Root FWD 4         128.267  Network P2p
```

```
Eth2/12          Altn BLK 4        128.268  Network P2p
Kenya#
```

Spanning-Tree Timers

The hello, forward-delay, and max-age timers determine the operational characteristics of the spanning-tree bridge.

The hello timer defines how often the bridge sends Bridge Protocol Data Units (BPDU) to connected devices. On NX-OS, the default is 2 seconds but can be configured for 1 to 10 seconds.

The forward-delay timer specifies how long the bridge stays in the listening and learning states before transitioning into a forwarding state. By default, NX-OS waits 15 seconds before transitioning the port from listening to learning, and from learning to forwarding. The forward-delay timer is configurable from 15 to 30 seconds.

The max-age timer ensures backward compatibility with traditional 802.1D spanning-tree environments by specifying the length of time a BPDU received on a given port is stored. The default NX-OS max-age time is 20 seconds and can be configured from 6 to 40 seconds.

Example 2-27 shows how to verify the spanning-tree timers for a specific VLAN.

Example 2-27 *Default Spanning-Tree Timers*

```
Congo# show spanning-tree vlan 10
VLAN0010
  Spanning tree enabled protocol rstp
  Root ID    Priority    4106
             Address     001b.54c2.bbc1
             This bridge is the root
             Hello Time  2  sec  Max Age 20 sec  Forward Delay 15 sec
  Bridge ID  Priority    4106    (priority 4096 sys-id-ext 10)
             Address     001b.54c2.bbc1
             Hello Time  2  sec  Max Age 20 sec  Forward Delay 15 sec
Interface        Role Sts Cost        Prio.Nbr Type
---------------- ---- --- --------- -------- --------------------------------
Po100            Desg FWD 1           128.4195 (vPC peer-link) Network P2p
```

In smaller L2 domains, faster reconvergence can be achieved by manipulating these timers. Example 2-28 shows how to manually adjust the hello, forward-delay, and max-age timers.

Caution   Although it might be desirable to manipulate spanning-tree timers for faster reconvergence, these timers and the Layer 2 topology should be well understood. Incorrect spanning-tree timers can produce undesirable results.

Example 2-28   *Modifying Spanning Tree Timers*

```
Congo(config)# spanning-tree mode rapid-pvst
Congo(config)# spanning-tree vlan 10 hello-time 1
Congo(config)# spanning-tree vlan 10 forward-time 10
Congo(config)# spanning-tree vlan 10 max-age 15
Congo(config)#
Congo(config)# sho spanning-tree vlan 10
VLAN0010
  Spanning tree enabled protocol rstp
  Root ID     Priority    4106
              Address     001b.54c2.bbc1
              This bridge is the root
              Hello Time  1  sec  Max Age 15 sec  Forward Delay 10 sec
  Bridge ID   Priority    4106    (priority 4096 sys-id-ext 10)
              Address     001b.54c2.bbc1
              Hello Time  1  sec  Max Age 15 sec  Forward Delay 10 sec
Interface         Role Sts Cost      Prio.Nbr Type
---------------- ---- --- --------- -------- --------------------------------
Po100             Desg FWD 1         128.4195 (vPC peer-link) Network P2p
```

To mitigate some of the risk associated with the manual manipulation of spanning-tree timers, NX-OS provides the **diameter** keyword, and if needed, adjusts these timers according to best practices. In this topology, a single-tier Layer 2 design is implemented with access switches connecting to both aggregation switches; therefore, the maximum number of bridges between any two stations (diameter) is 3. If no diameter is specified, the default of 7 applies. By specifying the diameter of the spanning-tree domain, hello, forward-delay, and max-age timers are adjusted for optimal reconvergence in the event that a spanning-tree recalculation occurs.

Example 2-29 demonstrates how the **diameter** keyword is used to manipulate spanning-tree timers.

Example 2-29   *Specifying the Spanning-Tree Diameter*

```
Congo(config)#spanning-tree mode rapid-pvst
Congo(config)#spanning-tree vlan 1-10 root primary diameter 3
Congo(config)#spanning-tree vlan 11-20 root secondary diameter 3
-----------------------------------------------------------------------------
Egypt(config)# spanning-tree vlan 1-10 root primary diameter 3
```

```
Egypt(config)# spanning-tree vlan 11-20 root secondary diameter 3
Egypt(config)# sho spanning-tree vlan 10
VLAN0010
  Spanning tree enabled protocol rstp
  Root ID    Priority    4106
             Address     001b.54c2.bbc1
             This bridge is the root
             Hello Time   2  sec  Max Age 12 sec  Forward Delay 9  sec
  Bridge ID  Priority    4106    (priority 4096 sys-id-ext 10)
             Address     001b.54c2.bbc1
             Hello Time   2  sec  Max Age 12 sec  Forward Delay 9  sec
Interface          Role Sts Cost        Prio.Nbr Type
---------------- ---- --- --------- -------- --------------------------------
Po100              Desg FWD 1           128.4195 (vPC peer-link) Network P2p
Egypt(config)# spanning-tree vlan 1-10 root primary diameter 3
Egypt(config)# spanning-tree vlan 11-20 root secondary diameter 3
Egypt(config)# sho spanning-tree vlan 10
VLAN0010
  Spanning tree enabled protocol rstp
  Root ID    Priority    4106
             Address     001b.54c2.bbc1
             This bridge is the root
             Hello Time   2  sec  Max Age 12 sec  Forward Delay 9  sec
  Bridge ID  Priority    4106    (priority 4096 sys-id-ext 10)
             Address     001b.54c2.bbc1
             Hello Time   2  sec  Max Age 12 sec  Forward Delay 9  sec
Interface          Role Sts Cost        Prio.Nbr Type
---------------- ---- --- --------- -------- --------------------------------
Po100              Desg FWD 1           128.4195 (vPC peer-link) Network P2p
```

As you can see in the previous example, the hello time, max age, and forward delay have been adjusted based on the STP diameter keyword.

MST Configuration

The examples in this section demonstrate the same configuration as the previous section using MST instead of Rapid-PVST. The configuration steps are similar; however, you see the additional steps of creating an instance, defining a revision number, and associating VLANs with an instance. These steps are required to define which VLANs share the same spanning-tree topology within MST.

Example 2-30 demonstrates basic MST configuration.

Example 2-30 *Basic MST Configuration*

```
Congo# conf t
Enter configuration commands, one per line. End with CNTL/Z.
Congo(config)# spanning-tree mode mst
Congo(config)# spanning-tree mst configuration
Congo(config-mst)# name AGG1
Congo(config-mst)# revision 10
Congo(config-mst)# instance 1 vlan 1-10
Congo(config-mst)# instance 2 vlan 11-20
Congo(config-mst)#
```

Prior to exiting from MST configuration mode, it is recommended to review the changes being proposed. *Existing MST mode commits all changes prior to exiting.*

Example 2-31 shows MST verification.

Example 2-31 *MST Verification*

```
Congo(config-mst)# show pending
Pending MST Configuration
Name      [AGG1]
Revision  10    Instances configured 3
Instance  Vlans mapped
--------  -----------------------------------------------------------------
0         21-4094
1         1-10
2         11-20
--------------------------------------------------------------------------
Congo(config-mst)# exit
Congo(config)#
```

Because MST changes are not committed until you exit MST configuration mode, the administrator has the ability to back out of the configuration without committing the changes. During the configuration of Egypt, we misconfigure the instance mapping, abort the changes, and reconfigure appropriately.

Example 2-32 shows how to abort pending MST changes.

Example 2-32 *MST Misconfiguration*

```
Egypt(config)# spanning-tree mode mst
Egypt(config)# spanning-tree mst configuration
Egypt(config)# name AGG1
Egypt(config-mst)# revision 10
Egypt(config-mst)# instance 1 vlan 1-9
Egypt(config-mst)# instance 2 vlan 11-20
```

```
Egypt(config-mst)# show pending
Pending MST Configuration
Name      [AGG1]
Revision  10    Instances configured 3
Instance  Vlans mapped
--------  --------------------------------------------------------------------
0         10,21-4094
1         1-9
2         11-20
--------------------------------------------------------------------------------
Egypt(config-mst)# abort
Aborting and exiting region configuration mode
Egypt(config)# spanning-tree mst configuration
Egypt(config-mst)# spanning-tree mst configuration
Egypt(config-mst)# name AGG1
Egypt(config-mst)# revision 10
Egypt(config-mst)# instance 1 vlan 1-10
Egypt(config-mst)# instance 2 vlan 11-20
Egypt(config-mst)# show pending
Pending MST Configuration
Name      [AGG1]
Revision  10    Instances configured 3
Instance  Vlans mapped
--------  --------------------------------------------------------------------
0         21-4094
1         1-10
2         11-20
--------------------------------------------------------------------------------
Egypt(config-mst)# exit
Egypt(config)#
```

Because the instance 1 VLAN mapping was input incorrectly, the pending changes were aborted, and reconfigured correctly before exiting/committing.

If PVLANs are used within the environment, it is required that all secondary VLANs share the same MST instance as their associated primary VLAN. MST provides a mechanism to automatically enforce this.

Example 2-33 shows VLAN synchronization for MST.

Example 2-33   *Private VLAN Synchronization*

```
Congo(config)# spanning-tree mst configuration
Congo(config-mst)#private-vlan synchronize
```

Example 2-34 shows how to verify the spanning-tree configuration with the **show running-config spanning-tree** command.

Example 2-34 *Verifying MST Configuration*

```
Egypt(config)# sho run spanning-tree
spanning-tree mode mst
spanning-tree port type edge bpduguard default
spanning-tree port type edge bpdufilter default
spanning-tree mst configuration
  name AGG1
  revision 10
  instance 1 vlan 1-10
  instance 2 vlan 11-20
interface port-channel1
  spanning-tree port type network
  spanning-tree guard root
interface port-channel100
  spanning-tree port type network
interface Ethernet2/2
  spanning-tree port type network
```

Like Rapid-PVST+, the spanning-tree root placement can be influenced by modifying the priority for each bridge; however, instead of configuring the priority on a per-VLAN basis, MST switches are configured with a priority per-instance.

Example 2-35 shows how to adjust the priority for an MST instance.

Example 2-35 *MST Priority Configuration*

```
Congo(config)# spanning-tree mst 1 priority 4096
Congo(config)# spanning-tree mst 2 priority 8192
-----------------------------------------------------------------------
Egypt(config)# spanning-tree mst 1 priority 8192
Egypt(config)# spanning-tree mst 2 priority 4096
```

Alternatively, Example 2-36 shows how to use the **root** keyword as done previously in the Rapid-PVST section.

Example 2-36 *MST Root Configuration*

```
Configuration on Congo
Congo(config)#spanning-tree mst 1 root primary
Congo(config)#spanning-tree mst 2 root secondary
```

Example 2-37 shows how to verify the configuration of an MST instance.

Example 2-37 *MST Verification*

```
Congo# show spanning-tree mst 1
##### MST1     vlans mapped:   1-10
Bridge         address 001b.54c2.bbc1  priority      4097   (4096 sysid 1)
Root           this switch for MST1
Interface        Role Sts Cost      Prio.Nbr Type
---------------- ---- --- --------- -------- --------------------------------
Po100            Desg FWD 1000      128.4195 Network P2p
Eth2/1           Desg FWD 20000     128.257  Network P2p Bound(PVST)
Congo#
```

The example shows that Congo is the root bridge for MST instance 1, which has VLANs 1 to 10 mapped to it.

Additional Spanning-Tree Configuration

The sections that follow cover the configuration required to manipulate some additional spanning-tree parameters.

Port Cost

Port cost is used to calculate the shortest path to the root bridge. By default, port costs are automatically calculated by the device based on the transmission speed of the physical link. Table 2-1 illustrates the default port costs.

From time to time, it might be necessary to statically define port costs; an example of this is with port-channels in which the cost might change depending on the number of links active within the bundle.

Example 2-38 shows the root ports on Kenya prior to change to port cost.

Table 2-1 *Default Spanning Tree Costs*

Link Speed	Default Spanning Tree Cost
10 Mbps	100
100 Mbps	19
1000 Mbps	4
10,000 Mbps	2

Example 2-38 *MST Verification*

```
Kenya# show spanning-tree root
                              Root   Hello Max Fwd
```

```
Vlan                   Root ID          Cost  Time  Age Dly  Root Port
----------------       ----------------- ------- ----- --- ---  ----------------
VLAN0001         4097 001b.54c2.bbc1       4     2   12   9    Ethernet2/11
VLAN0002         4098 001b.54c2.bbc1       4     2   12   9    Ethernet2/11
VLAN0003         4099 001b.54c2.bbc1       4     2   12   9    Ethernet2/11
VLAN0004         4100 001b.54c2.bbc1       4     2   12   9    Ethernet2/11
VLAN0005         4101 001b.54c2.bbc1       4     2   12   9    Ethernet2/11
VLAN0006         4102 001b.54c2.bbc1       4     2   12   9    Ethernet2/11
VLAN0007         4103 001b.54c2.bbc1       4     2   12   9    Ethernet2/11
VLAN0008         4104 001b.54c2.bbc1       4     2   12   9    Ethernet2/11
VLAN0009         4105 001b.54c2.bbc1       4     2   12   9    Ethernet2/11
VLAN0010         4106 001b.54c2.bbc1       4     2   12   9    Ethernet2/11
VLAN0011         4107 001b.54c2.bbc2       4     2   12   9    Ethernet2/12
VLAN0012         4108 001b.54c2.bbc2       4     2   12   9    Ethernet2/12
VLAN0013         4109 001b.54c2.bbc2       4     2   12   9    Ethernet2/12
VLAN0014         4110 001b.54c2.bbc2       4     2   12   9    Ethernet2/12
VLAN0015         4111 001b.54c2.bbc2       4     2   12   9    Ethernet2/12
VLAN0016         4112 001b.54c2.bbc2       4     2   12   9    Ethernet2/12
VLAN0017         4113 001b.54c2.bbc2       4     2   12   9    Ethernet2/12
VLAN0018         4114 001b.54c2.bbc2       4     2   12   9    Ethernet2/12
VLAN0019         4115 001b.54c2.bbc2       4     2   12   9    Ethernet2/12
VLAN0020         4116 001b.54c2.bbc2       4     2   12   9    Ethernet2/12
Kenya#
```

Example 2-39 shows the configuration of port cost on a link.

Example 2-39 *Configuring Port Cost*

```
Kenya# conf t
Enter configuration commands, one per line. End with CNTL/Z.
Kenya(config)# interface ethernet 2/11
Kenya(config-if)# spanning-tree cost 128
Kenya(config-if)# exit
Kenya(config)# exit
```

Example 2-40 shows the output after adjusting the port cost. Now Ethernet 2/12 is the root port for all VLANs.

Example 2-40 *Spanning Tree Root Verification*

```
Kenya# show spanning-tree root
                              Root  Hello Max Fwd
Vlan                   Root ID          Cost  Time  Age Dly  Root Port
----------------       ----------------- ------- ----- --- ---  ----------------
```

```
VLAN0001       4097 001b.54c2.bbc1      5    2   12   9      Ethernet2/12
VLAN0002       4098 001b.54c2.bbc1      5    2   12   9      Ethernet2/12
VLAN0003       4099 001b.54c2.bbc1      5    2   12   9      Ethernet2/12
VLAN0004       4100 001b.54c2.bbc1      5    2   12   9      Ethernet2/12
VLAN0005       4101 001b.54c2.bbc1      5    2   12   9      Ethernet2/12
VLAN0006       4102 001b.54c2.bbc1      5    2   12   9      Ethernet2/12
VLAN0007       4103 001b.54c2.bbc1      5    2   12   9      Ethernet2/12
VLAN0008       4104 001b.54c2.bbc1      5    2   12   9      Ethernet2/12
VLAN0009       4105 001b.54c2.bbc1      5    2   12   9      Ethernet2/12
VLAN0010       4106 001b.54c2.bbc1      5    2   12   9      Ethernet2/12
VLAN0011       4107 001b.54c2.bbc2      4    2   12   9      Ethernet2/12
VLAN0012       4108 001b.54c2.bbc2      4    2   12   9      Ethernet2/12
VLAN0013       4109 001b.54c2.bbc2      4    2   12   9      Ethernet2/12
VLAN0014       4110 001b.54c2.bbc2      4    2   12   9      Ethernet2/12
VLAN0015       4111 001b.54c2.bbc2      4    2   12   9      Ethernet2/12
VLAN0016       4112 001b.54c2.bbc2      4    2   12   9      Ethernet2/12
VLAN0017       4113 001b.54c2.bbc2      4    2   12   9      Ethernet2/12
VLAN0018       4114 001b.54c2.bbc2      4    2   12   9      Ethernet2/12
VLAN0019       4115 001b.54c2.bbc2      4    2   12   9      Ethernet2/12
VLAN0020       4116 001b.54c2.bbc2      4    2   12   9      Ethernet2/12
Kenya#
```

Example 2-41 shows the configuration of port cost on a per VLAN basis.

Example 2-41 *Per VLAN Cost Configuration*

```
Kenya(config)# interface ethernet 2/11
Kenya(config-if)# spanning-tree vlan 1,3,5,7,9 cost 4
Kenya(config-if)# exit
```

Example 2-42 shows the result of the changes in the previous example. Ethernet2/11 is now root for VLANs 1, 3, 5, 6, and 9.

Example 2-42 *Spanning Tree Root Verification*

```
Kenya# show spanning-tree root

                                  Root  Hello Max Fwd
Vlan                  Root ID     Cost  Time  Age Dly  Root Port
--------------- ------------------- ------- ----- --- --- ----------------
VLAN0001       4097 001b.54c2.bbc1      4    2   12   9      Ethernet2/11
VLAN0002       4098 001b.54c2.bbc1      5    2   12   9      Ethernet2/12
VLAN0003       4099 001b.54c2.bbc1      4    2   12   9      Ethernet2/11
VLAN0004       4100 001b.54c2.bbc1      5    2   12   9      Ethernet2/12
VLAN0005       4101 001b.54c2.bbc1      4    2   12   9      Ethernet2/11
```

VLAN0006	4102 001b.54c2.bbc1	5	2	12	9	Ethernet2/12
VLAN0007	4103 001b.54c2.bbc1	4	2	12	9	Ethernet2/11
VLAN0008	4104 001b.54c2.bbc1	5	2	12	9	Ethernet2/12
VLAN0009	4105 001b.54c2.bbc1	4	2	12	9	Ethernet2/11
VLAN0010	4106 001b.54c2.bbc1	5	2	12	9	Ethernet2/12
VLAN0011	4107 001b.54c2.bbc2	4	2	12	9	Ethernet2/12
VLAN0012	4108 001b.54c2.bbc2	4	2	12	9	Ethernet2/12
VLAN0013	4109 001b.54c2.bbc2	4	2	12	9	Ethernet2/12
VLAN0014	4110 001b.54c2.bbc2	4	2	12	9	Ethernet2/12
VLAN0015	4111 001b.54c2.bbc2	4	2	12	9	Ethernet2/12
VLAN0016	4112 001b.54c2.bbc2	4	2	12	9	Ethernet2/12
VLAN0017	4113 001b.54c2.bbc2	4	2	12	9	Ethernet2/12
VLAN0018	4114 001b.54c2.bbc2	4	2	12	9	Ethernet2/12
VLAN0019	4115 001b.54c2.bbc2	4	2	12	9	Ethernet2/12
VLAN0020	4116 001b.54c2.bbc2	4	2	12	9	Ethernet2/12
VLAN0100	32868 001b.54c2.bbc1	5	2	20	15	Ethernet2/12
Kenya#						

Port Priority

With a well-planned root placement in the aggregation switches, manipulation of other spanning-tree parameters is seldom needed; however, in certain cases it might be necessary to manipulate port-priority to influence the forwarding path. With VLAN access ports, the port-priority applies to the VLAN to which the port belongs. For interfaces that are carrying multiple VLANs using 802.1Q trunking, a port-priority can be specified on a per-VLAN basis. The default port priority is 128.

Example 2-43 shows the configuration of port-priority on an interface.

Example 2-43 *Spanning Tree Port Priority Configuration*

```
Kenya# conf t
Enter configuration commands, one per line. End with CNTL/Z.
Kenya(config)# interface ethernet 2/12
Kenya(config-if)# spanning-tree port-priority 64
Kenya(config-if)# exit
Kenya(config)# exit
```

Spanning-Tree Toolkit

NX-OS provides many extensions to the operation of spanning tree. When used properly these extensions can improve the resiliency, performance, and security of spanning tree. The following sections take a look at some of the specific enhancements and then discuss some basic spanning-tree port types. We conclude by combining the techniques covered in this section with some sample port-profiles for various configurations.

BPDUFilter

BPDUFilter prevents the port from sending or receiving BPDUs. A BPDUFilter is usually used with BPDUGuard to prevent an inadvertent misconfiguration that can introduce loops into the environment. In the case where BPDUGuard is not enabled, BPDUFilter still provides some safeguard against accidental misconfiguration. A port configured with BPDUFilter initially sends a series of BPDUs, if the device receives BPDUs returns to the initial port state and transitions through the listening and learning phases.

To enable BPDUFilter on all edge ports, enter the following command:

```
Congo(config)# spanning-tree port type edge bpdufilter default
```

Example 2-44 shows how to enable BPDUFilter on a specific interface.

Example 2-44   *BPDU Interface Configuration*

```
Congo(config)# int ethernet 2/21
Congo(config-if)# spanning-tree bpdufilter enable
Congo(config-if)#
Congo(config-if)# exit
```

Example 2-45 shows how to disable BPDUFilter on a specific interface.

Example 2-45   *Disabling BPDUFilter*

```
Congo(config)# int ethernet 2/21
Congo(config-if)# spanning-tree bpdufilter disable
Congo(config-if)#
```

BPDUGuard

BPDUGuard shuts down an interface if a BPDU is received. This option protects the spanning tree from unauthorized switches being placed into the topology. BPDUGuard can also be useful in protecting against host misconfiguration that could introduce a loop into the environment.

To enable BPDUGuard on all edge ports, enter the following command:

```
Congo(config)# spanning-tree port type edge bpduguard default
```

Example 2-46 shows how to enable BPDUGuard on a specific interface.

Example 2-46   *Enabling BPDU Guard on a Specific Interface*

```
Congo(config)# int ethernet 2/1
Congo(config-if)# spanning-tree bpduguard enable
Congo(config-if)#
2009 Oct 28 14:45:20 Congo %STP-2-BLOCK_BPDUGUARD: Received BPDU on port
Ethernet2/1 with BPDU Guard enabled. Disabling port.
```

```
2009 Oct 28 14:45:21 Congo %ETHPORT-2-IF_DOWN_ERROR_DISABLED: Interface Ethernet
2/1 is down (Error disabled. Reason:BPDUGuard)
```

Example 2-47 shows how to disable BPDU guard on a specific interface.

Example 2-47 *Disabling BPDU Guard on a Specific Interface*

```
Congo(config)#
Congo(config)# interface ethernet 2/21
Congo(config-if)# spanning-tree bpduguard disable
Congo(config-if)# exit
```

To decrease administrative overhead, in a dynamic environment, it might be desirable to leverage the protection provided by BPDUGuard but undesirable to require manual intervention to enable ports that have been shut down. Ports that have been disabled due to BPDUGuard can be automatically enabled after a period of time by specifying an errdisable recovery time.

Example 2-48 shows how to configure errdisable recovery.

Example 2-48 *errdisable Recovery*

```
Congo(config)# errdisable recovery cause bpduguard
Congo(config)# errdisable recovery interval 60
```

RootGuard

RootGuard protects the root placement in the bridging domain. If a port configured with RootGuard receives a superior BPDU, the port is immediately placed into an inconsistent state. RootGuard is typically implemented in the data center aggregation layer to prevent misconfigured access switches from becoming the root bridge for the entire data center aggregation block. RootGuard can be implemented only on a port-by-port basis.

Example 2-49 shows how to enable RootGuard on a specific interface.

Example 2-49 *RootGuard Configuration*

```
Congo(config)# int ethernet 2/1
Congo(config-if)# spanning-tree guard root
Congo(config-if)#
```

Now, test RootGuard by changing the priority of a Kenya to a lower value.

Example 2-50 shows RootGuard in action.

Example 2-50 *RootGuard Verification*

```
Kenya(config)# spanning-tree vlan 1 priority 0
Output from Congo
Congo# 2009 Oct 28 14:50:24 Congo %STP-2-ROOTGUARD_BLOCK: Root guard blocking port
Ethernet2/1 on VLAN0001.
Congo#
! When we remove the priority command, port connectivity is restored.
Kenya(config)# no spanning-tree vlan 1 priority 0
Output from Congo
Congo# 2009 Oct 28 14:51:19 Congo %STP-2-ROOTGUARD_UNBLOCK: Root guard unblocking
port
Ethernet2/1 on VLAN0001.
Congo#
```

Example 2-51 shows how to remove RootGuard.

Example 2-51 *Disabling RootGuard*

```
Congo(config)# int ethernet 2/1
Congo(config-if)# no spanning-tree guard root
Congo(config-if)#
```

LoopGuard

LoopGuard prevents any alternative or root ports from becoming designated ports. This situation is typically caused by a unidirectional link.

To enable LoopGuard globally, enter the following command:

```
Egypt(config)# spanning-tree loopguard default
```

Example 2-52 shows how to enable LoopGuard on a specific interface.

Example 2-52 *Enabling LoopGuard on a Specific Interface*

```
Egypt# conf t
Enter configuration commands, one per line. End with CNTL/Z.
Egypt(config)# int port-channel 100
Egypt(config-if)# spanning-tree guard loop
```

To disable LoopGuard on a specific interface, the **no** form of this command should be used, as shown in Example 2-53.

Example 2-53 *Disabling LoopGuard on a Specific Interface*

```
Egypt# conf t
```

```
Enter configuration commands, one per line. End with CNTL/Z.
Egypt(config)# int port-channel 100
Egypt(config-if)# no spanning-tree guard loop
```

Dispute Mechanism

The 802.1D-2004 standard specifies a dispute mechanism that can prevent loops created for a variety of reasons. Two common cases in which the dispute mechanism helps are unidirectional links or port-channel misconfiguration. Dispute mechanism is enabled by default and cannot be disabled.

Bridge Assurance

Bridge Assurance is a new feature that can eliminate issues caused by a malfunctioning bridge. With Bridge Assurance, all ports send and receive BPDUs on all VLANs regardless of their state. This creates a bidirectional keepalive using BPDUs, and if a bridge stops receiving BPDUs, these ports are placed into an inconsistent state. This functionality can prevent loops that can be introduced as a result of a malfunctioning bridge. Bridge Assurance is enabled by default on any port that is configured with a spanning-tree port type network but can be disabled globally with the following command:

```
Congo(config)# no spanning-tree bridge assurance
```

To enable Bridge Assurance by setting the spanning-tree port type, enter the following commands:

```
Congo(config)# int port-channel 1
Congo(config-if)# spanning-tree port type network
```

An interesting side effect of Bridge Assurance is an automatic *pruning* function. In the topology from Figure 2-5, if a VLAN is defined on Congo but not on Egypt, Bridge Assurance puts that VLAN into a blocking state because it is not receiving BPDUs for that VLAN from Egypt. Example 2-54 demonstrates this functionality.

Example 2-54   *Bridge Assurance as a Pruning Mechanism*

```
Congo# conf t
Enter configuration commands, one per line. End with CNTL/Z.
Congo(config)# vlan 500
Congo(config-vlan)# exit
Congo(config)# 2009 Oct 28 14:06:53 Congo %STP-2-BRIDGE_ASSURANCE_BLOCK: Bridge
Assurance blocking port Ethernet2/1 VLAN0500.
2009 Oct 28 14:06:53 Congo %STP-2-BRIDGE_ASSURANCE_BLOCK: Bridge Assurance
  blocking port port-channel100 VLAN0500.
```

After the VLAN is defined on Egypt, Bridge Assurance can detect the presence of BPDUs for that VLAN and allow it to move into a forwarding state, as demonstrated in Example 2-55.

Example 2-55 *Detecting VLAN BPDUs and Advancing in State*

```
Egypt(config)# vlan 500
Egypt(config-vlan)# exit
Egypt(config)#
Congo#
Congo# 2009 Oct 28 14:10:42 Congo %STP-2-BRIDGE_ASSURANCE_UNBLOCK: Bridge
  Assurance unblocking port port-channel100 VLAN0500.
Congo#
```

Spanning-Tree Port Types

NX-OS provides three basic switch port types that ease the administrative burden of configuring STP extensions:

- **Normal ports:** By default, a switchport is a normal port for the purpose of spanning tree. Normal ports remain unmodified and operate as standard bridge ports.

- **Network ports:** Network ports define connections between two bridges. By default, Bridge Assurance is enabled on these ports.

- **Edge ports:** Previously known as PortFast, a port configured as a spanning-tree edge denotes that the port should transition immediately into a forwarding state, bypassing the listening and learning states. Only nonbridging Layer 2 devices should be configured as edge ports. This port type should be reserved for data center hosts that cannot create a Layer 2 loop; this includes single attached hosts, Layer 3 routers and firewalls, or multihomed devices that leverage some form of NIC teaming.

Example 2-56 shows how to specify the default spanning-tree port type.

Example 2-56 *Defining Default Spanning-Tree Port Type*

```
Congo(config)#
Congo(config)# spanning-tree port type edge default
Warning: this command enables edge port type (portfast) by default on all
interfaces.
You should now disable edge port type (portfast) explicitly on switched ports
leading to hubs, switches and bridges as they may create temporary bridging loops.
! -OR-
Congo(config)#
Congo(config)# spanning-tree port type network default
Congo(config)#
```

To define the spanning-tree port type on a specific interface, enter the following commands:

```
Kenya(config)# interface ethernet 2/11
Kenya(config-if)# spanning-tree port type network
```

Virtualization Hosts

Due to the recent trend of virtualization in the data center, a hybrid of the two interface types exists as well. Although historically, 802.1Q trunks were reserved for interconnecting network devices only, virtualization hosts often require 802.1Q trunk connectivity directly to hosts. Even though these hosts tag traffic with 802.1Q headers, they are typically not true bridges and therefore can be treated as hosts and bypass the listening and learning stages of spanning-tree initialization. This configuration is sometimes referred to as *TrunkFast*.

Example 2-57 shows how to enable TrunkFast on a specific interface.

Example 2-57   *Enabling TrunkFast*

```
Kenya(config)# interface ethernet 2/40
Kenya(config-if)# switchport
Kenya(config-if)# spanning-tree port type edge trunk
Warning: Edge port type (portfast) should only be enabled on ports connected to
a single host. Connecting hubs, concentrators, switches, bridges, etc... to this
 interface when edge port type (portfast) is enabled, can cause temporary bridging
loops.
 Use with CAUTION
Kenya(config-if)#
```

Caution   Virtualization techniques vary greatly; consult your vendor's documentation to determine whether this feature should be implemented.

Configuring Layer 2 Interfaces

Now that the initial spanning-tree configurations are complete, you can begin adding additional interfaces into the switching environment. The following examples discuss three different types of switchports; edge, trunk, and an edge trunk port.

Trunk Ports

Example 2-58 shows a sample configuration that would be used for access to aggregation links where multiple VLANs exist.

Example 2-58 *Standard Trunk Port Configuration*

```
interface Ethernet 2/9
switchport
switchport mode trunk
switchport trunk allowed vlan 100-103
spanning-tree port type network
```

Standard Host

Example 2-59 shows a sample configuration that would be used for standard Linux/Windows hosts that belong to a single VLAN.

Example 2-59 *Sample Access Port Configuration*

```
interface Ethernet1/7
  no shutdown
  switchport
  switchport mode access
  switchport access vlan 10
  spanning-tree port type edge
  spanning-tree bpduguard enable
  spanning-tree bpdufilter enable
```

Link to Virtualization Host

Virtualization has changed the way that network administrators must think about edge and trunk ports. In the past, physical hosts typically hosted a single MAC/IP pair, which mapped to a single VLAN. With virtualization, internal software provides some level of switching function making it possible for a virtualized host to contain many different MAC/IP pairs that might map to more than one VLAN. To perform optimally, special consideration should be made for these hosts at the physical network edge. Example 2-60 shows a sample configuration used for a virtualization host that uses an internal softswitch and guests that reside on multiple VLANs.

Example 2-60 *Sample Virtualization Host Port Configuration*

```
Kenya(config-if)# interface Ethernet1/7
Kenya(config-if)# no shutdown
Kenya(config-if)# switchport mode trunk
Kenya(config-if)# switchport trunk allowed vlan 101-103
Kenya(config-if)# spanning-tree port type edge trunk
Kenya(config-if)# spanning-tree bpduguard enable
```

Port-Profiles

Beginning in NX-OS 4.2(2), port-profiles can simplify the configuration of multiple ports that share common configuration components.

Example 2-61 shows a sample configuration of a port profile and how it is applied and verified.

Example 2-61   *Port Profiles*

```
Kenya(config)# port-profile COMMUNITY1
Kenya(config-ppm)# switchport
Kenya(config-ppm)# switchport mode access
Kenya(config-ppm)# switchport private-vlan host-association 100 102
Kenya(config-ppm)# spanning-tree port type edge
Kenya(config-ppm)# spanning-tree bpdufilter enable
Kenya(config-ppm)# spanning-tree bpduguard enable
Kenya(config-ppm)# no shutdown
Kenya(config-ppm)# state enabled


Kenya# conf t
Enter configuration commands, one per line. End with CNTL/Z.
Kenya(config)# interface ethernet 2/28
Kenya(config-if)# inherit port-profile COMMUNITY1
Kenya(config-if)# exit
Kenya(config)# exit
Kenya# sho run int ethernet 2/28
!Command: show running-config interface Ethernet2/28
!Time: Fri Oct 30 08:52:29 2009
version 4.2(2a)
interface Ethernet2/28
  inherit port-profile COMMUNITY1
Kenya#
Kenya# sho port-profile
port-profile COMMUNITY1
 type: Ethernet
 description:
 status: enabled
 max-ports: 512
 inherit:
 config attributes:
  switchport
  switchport mode access
```

```
   switchport private-vlan host-association 100 102
   spanning-tree port type edge
   spanning-tree bpdufilter enable
   spanning-tree bpduguard enable
   no shutdown
 evaluated config attributes:
   switchport
   switchport mode access
   switchport private-vlan host-association 100 102
   spanning-tree port type edge
   spanning-tree bpdufilter enable
   spanning-tree bpduguard enable
   no shutdown
  assigned interfaces:
   Ethernet2/21
   Ethernet2/28
Kenya#
```

Port-Channels

Where multiple links exist between two switches, it is often desirable to treat them as a single link from a spanning-tree perspective. The benefit of this logical bundling is that redundant physical connectivity is not blocked by spanning tree, making more bandwidth available for data traffic. Port-channels also create a level of redundancy as the failure of a physical link can no longer cause spanning tree to reconverge. The Nexus 7000 enables up to eight links to be aggregated in a port-channel. For optimal performance, it is recommended that the number of links be a power of 2 (for example, 2, 4, or 8 links). Members of a port-channel can be on the same line card, or to protect against line card failure, can be distributed across multiple modules in the system. Port-channels use various algorithms to hash frames as they arrive and load balance traffic across the physical interfaces, where any given flow always hashes to the same physical interface. A common misconception regarding port-channels is that the logical interface is a 20/40/80-Gbps link. For 10-Gbps member links, however, no single flow would exceed the transmission speed of the physical links which are members. An analogy here would be that port-channels add new lanes to the highway but do not increase the speed limit. A port-channel can be configured as either a Layer 2 or Layer 3 link depending on the requirements.

The hashing used to load balance traffic across the links is user-configurable, and the following options are available on the Nexus 7000:

■ Source IP

■ Destination IP

■ Source MAC

■ Destination MAC

- Source port

- Destination port

- Source and destination IP

- Source and destination MAC

- Source and destination port

You can configure these options globally, or because of the distributed nature of the Nexus 7000, on a line card-by-line card basis. If Virtual Device Contexts are used, these parameters are defined in the default VDC.

Example 2-62 shows how to configure and verify the load balancing algorithm.

Example 2-62   *Port-Channel Load Balancing Algorithm*

```
Congo(config)# port-channel load-balance ethernet source-dest-ip-vlan
Congo(config)# show port-channel load-balance
Port Channel Load-Balancing Configuration:
System: source-dest-ip-vlan
Port Channel Load-Balancing Addresses Used Per-Protocol:
Non-IP: source-dest-mac
IP: source-dest-ip-vlan
```

Assigning Physical Ports to a Port-Channel

Two options exist for assigning members to the logical interface:

- Configure member links to run the industry standard 802.3ad Link Aggregation Control Protocol (LACP).

- Statically configure the port as a member of the port channel. This mode is on, and no aggregation protocol information is exchanged between the devices.

There is no right or wrong method to use, and implementations vary based on personal preference. Some administrators like the environment to be deterministic and opt for the static configuration, whereas others might want to take advantage of some of the enhanced features that LACP offers. One of the benefits offered by LACP is a level of protection against misconfigured ports inadvertently becoming a member of the channel that could lead to Layer 2 loops, or black-holing data traffic. This level of protection is especially desirable in Virtual Port Channel configurations, which are discussed later in this chapter.

The **channel-group** command associates member interfaces with the port-channel. If an existing configuration is applied to the interface that makes it incompatible with the port-channel, the channel-group might be rejected from time to time. In these instances, channel compatibility can be ensured by adding the **force** command.

To assign a physical port to a port-channel without LACP, enter the following commands:

```
Egypt(config)# interface ethernet 1/4
Egypt(config-if)# channel-group 100 mode on
```

LACP is a modular process within NX-OS and must be explicitly enabled before configuration can begin. This is accomplished with the **feature** command.

When enabled, ports can be negotiated into a channel by specifying one of two modes:

- **Active:** This mode actively tries to negotiate channel membership by sending LACP packets.

- **Passive:** This mode listens for LACP packets and responds to them but does not send LACP negotiation packets.

For a link to bundle between two devices, the ports must be configured in either an active/active or active/passive fashion. If both sides of the link are configured for passive, they will not be bundled.

Example 2-63 shows how to assign a physical port to a port-channel with LACP.

Example 2-63 *LACP Configuration*

```
Congo(config)# feature lacp
Congo(config)# sho feature | inc lacp
lacp                  1             enabled

Congo(config)# interface ethernet 1/1,ethernet1/3
Congo(config-if-range)# channel-group 100 mode active
Congo(config-if-range)#
-------------------------------------------------------------------------
Egypt(config)# interface ethernet 1/2, ethernet 1/4
Egypt(config-if-range)# channel-group 100 mode active
Egypt(config-if-range)#
```

During the negotiation phase, many parameters are verified to ensure that the port is compatible with the port-channel.

Example 2-64 shows the compatibility parameters that must match for a port to bundle.

Example 2-64 *Channel Compatibility*

```
Egypt# show port-channel compatibility-parameters
* port mode
Members must have the same port mode configured, either E,F or AUTO. If
they are configured in AUTO port mode, they have to negotiate E or F mode
when they come up. If a member negotiates a different mode, it will be
```

```
suspended.
* speed
Members must have the same speed configured. If they are configured in AUTO
speed, they have to negotiate the same speed when they come up. If a member
negotiates a different speed, it will be suspended.
* MTU
Members have to have the same MTU configured. This only applies to ethernet
port-channel.
* MEDIUM
Members have to have the same medium type configured. This only applies to
ethernet port-channel.
* Span mode
Members must have the same span mode.
* load interval
Member must have same load interval configured.
* sub interfaces
Members must not have sub-interfaces.
* Duplex Mode
Members must have same Duplex Mode configured.
* Ethernet Layer
Members must have same Ethernet Layer (switchport/no-switchport) configured.
* Span Port
Members cannot be SPAN ports.
* Storm Control
Members must have same storm-control configured.
* Flow Control
Members must have same flowctrl configured.
* Capabilities
Members must have common capabilities.
* Capabilities speed
Members must have common speed capabilities.
* Capabilities duplex
Members must have common speed duplex capabilities.
* rate mode
Members must have the same rate mode configured.
* 1G port is not capable of acting as peer-link
Members must be 10G to become part of a vPC peer-link.
* port
Members port VLAN info.
* port
Members port does not exist.
* switching port
Members must be switching port, Layer 2.
* port access VLAN
```

```
Members must have the same port access VLAN.
* port native VLAN
Members must have the same port native VLAN.
* port allowed VLAN list
Members must have the same port allowed VLAN list.
* port egress queuing policy
10G port-channel members must have the same egress queuing policy as the
port-channel.
* Port Security policy
Members must have the same port-security enable status as port-channel
Egypt#
```

Example 2-65 shows how to quickly verify the channel configuration with the **show port-channel summary** command.

Example 2-65 *LACP Configuration*

```
Egypt# show port-channel summary
Flags:  D - Down        P - Up in port-channel (members)
        I - Individual  H - Hot-standby (LACP only)
        s - Suspended   r - Module-removed
        S - Switched    R - Routed
        U - Up (port-channel)
--------------------------------------------------------------------------------
Group Port-      Type      Protocol  Member Ports
      Channel
--------------------------------------------------------------------------------
100   Po100(SU)  Eth       LACP      Eth1/2(P)   Eth1/4(P)
```

Logical interfaces parameters apply to all the member links, giving the administrator an easy way to manipulate multiple ports.

Note In IOS devices, port-channel interfaces are initially put into an administratively down state, whereas, in NX-OS newly created port-channels are active as soon as they are created.

Port Channel Flow Control

Flow control is supported on port-channel interfaces as well. For flow control to work properly, both sides of the port-channel must be configured. By default, the port-channel flow control is desired. Flow control can be statically configured for on or off and for each direction.

Example 2-66 shows how to configure and verify port-channel flow control.

Example 2-66   *Port Channel Flow Control*

```
Congo(config)# interface port-channel 100
Congo(config-if)# flowcontrol send on
Congo(config-if)# flowcontrol receive on
Congo# show interface port-channel 100 flowcontrol
----------------------------------------------------------------------
Port      Send FlowControl  Receive FlowControl  RxPause TxPause
          admin    oper      admin    oper
----------------------------------------------------------------------
Po100     on       on        on       on          0       0
Congo#
```

Verifying Load Distribution Across a Port-Channel

Unequal traffic distribution across physical ports can be caused for a variety of reasons, including configuration of a suboptimal load balancing algorithm, or a nonpower of 2 number of links, (for example, 3). From time to time, it is good to verify that traffic is load-balanced across all of the available members. A useful command to get a quick snapshot of these statistics is **show port-channel traffic**. Example 2-67 shows example output from this command.

Example 2-67   *Verifying Load Distribution*

```
Congo# show port-channel rbh-distribution
  ChanId    Member port    RBH values         Num of buckets
  --------  -------------  ------------------  ------------------
  11        Eth2/17        4,5,6,7             4
  11        Eth1/17        0,1,2,3             4
  --------  -------------  ------------------  ------------------
  13        Eth2/18        4,5,6,7             4
  13        Eth1/18        0,1,2,3             4
  --------  -------------  ------------------  ------------------
  15        Eth2/25        4,5,6,7             4
  15        Eth1/25        0,1,2,3             4
francevdc1#
Congo(config)# show port-channel traffic
ChanId      Port Rx-Ucst Tx-Ucst Rx-Mcst Tx-Mcst Rx-Bcst Tx-Bcst
------  ---------  -------  -------  -------  -------  -------  -------
  100       Eth1/1    53.67%   46.32%   97.39%   97.27%   0.0%     0.0%
  100       Eth1/3    46.32%   53.67%   2.60%    2.72%    0.0%     0.0%
```

In the previous output, the first command shows the number of hash buckets that each member link is assigned to, and the second shows the amount of traffic each link has forwarded. When troubleshooting port-channels, one additional task is to determine which link a particular flow will be hashed to. As shown in Example 2-68, the **show port-channel loadbalance forwarding-path** command can be used to gather this information.

Example 2-68 *Determining Which Link a Particular Flow Will Use*

```
francevdc1# show port-channel load-balance forwarding-path interface port-channel 11
src-ip 172.16.30.25 dst-ip 192.168.10.236 module 2
Missing params will be substituted by 0's.
Module 2: Load-balance Algorithm: source-dest-ip-vlan
RBH: 0x2          Outgoing port id: Ethernet1/17
francevdc1# show port-channel load-balance forwarding-path interface port-channel 11
src-ip 172.16.30.25 dst-ip 192.168.10.235 module 2
Missing params will be substituted by 0's.
Module 2: Load-balance Algorithm: source-dest-ip-vlan
RBH: 0x5          Outgoing port id: Ethernet2/17
```

By specifying inputting in the required values based on the hash algorithm in use, you've identified that for traffic from 172.16.30.25 destined for 192.168.10.236 interface, Ethernet1/17 forwards traffic, and traffic destined for 172.16.30.25 selects Ethernet2/17 to forward traffic.

Virtual Port Channels

The Nexus 7000 and 5000 series switches take port-channel functionality to the next level by enabling links that are connected to different devices to be aggregated into a single, logical link. This technology was introduced in NX-OS version 4.1(4) and is called Virtual Port Channel (vPC). In addition to link redundancy provided by port-channels, vPC's offer some additional benefits:

■ Device level redundancy with faster convergence than multiple port-channels using traditional Spanning Tree

■ Further elimination of spanning-tree blocked ports by providing a loop-free topology

■ Better bandwidth utilization

Caution Port-channels configured as vPCs can be used only as Layer 2 links, and no dynamic routing protocol should be used across the link.

vPCs are configured by associating two Nexus devices into a vPC domain. Within the vPC domain, information is exchanged between vPC peers across two special links:

■ **vPC peer-keepalive link:** Provides heartbeating between vPC peers to ensure that both devices are online, and also to avoid active/active or split-brain scenarios that could introduce loops into the vPC topology. The vPC peer-keepalive link can be either 1 Gbps or 10 Gbps.

- **vPC peer link:** Used to exchange state information between the vPC peers and also provides additional mechanisms that can detect and prevent split-brain scenarios.

Note The mgmt0 interface can be used as the vPC peer-keepalive link but should be avoided if at all possible. On the Nexus 7000, the mgmt0 is actually a logical interface representing the physical management port of the active supervisor. During processes such as supervisor switchover during hardware failure or In-Service Software Upgrades (ISSU), the physical link supporting the mgmt0 interface might change, causing a disruption of the keepalive messages. By using normal switch interfaces, additional levels of redundnancy in the port-channels can be used. If the mgmt0 interface is used as the peer-keepalive link, it is critical to ensure that all physical management ports are connected to an external device, such as a management switch.

The remainder of this section demonstrates configuration based on the topology illustrated in Figure 2-8.

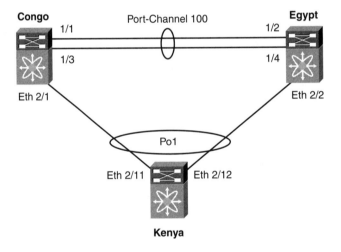

Figure 2-8   *VPC Topology*

To configure vPC, perform the following steps.

Step 1.   Enable the vPC feature on each vPC peer:

```
! Congo
Congo# conf t
Enter configuration commands, one per line. End with CNTL/Z.
Congo
Congo(config)# feature vpc
```

```
Congo(config)# exit
! Egypt
Egypt(config)# feature vpc
Egypt(config)# exit
```

Step 2.   Create VRF for the VPC keepalive link:

```
! Congo
Congo(config-if)# vrf context vpc-keepalive
Congo(config-vrf)# exit
! Egypt
Egypt(config)# vrf context vpc-keepalive
Egypt(config-vrf)# exit
! Congo
Congo(config)# int ethernet 2/47
Congo(config-if)# vrf member vpc-keepalive
Congo(config-if)# ip address 1.1.1.1 255.255.255.252
Congo(config-if)# no shutdown
Congo(config-if)# exit
Congo(config)# exit
! Egypt
Egypt(config)# interface ethernet 2/48
Egypt(config-if)# no switchport
Egypt(config-if)# vrf member vpc-keepalive
Egypt(config-if)# ip address 1.1.1.2 255.255.255.252
Egypt(config-if)# no shutdown
Egypt(config-if)# exit
Egypt(config)# exit
! Congo
Congo(config-if)# vrf context vpc-keepalive
Congo(config-vrf)# exit
! Egypt
Egypt(config)# vrf context vpc-keepalive
Egypt(config-vrf)# exit
! Congo
Congo(config)# int ethernet 2/47
Congo(config-if)# vrf member vpc-keepalive
Congo(config-if)# ip address 1.1.1.1 255.255.255.252
Congo(config-if)# no shutdown
Congo(config-if)# exit
Congo(config)# exit
! Egypt
Egypt(config)# interface ethernet 2/48
Egypt(config-if)# no switchport
Egypt(config-if)# vrf member vpc-keepalive
Egypt(config-if)# ip address 1.1.1.2 255.255.255.252
```

```
Egypt(config-if)# no shutdown
Egypt(config-if)# exit
```

Step 3.   Verify connectivity of the VPC peer keepalive link:

```
Congo# ping 1.1.1.2 vrf vpc-keepalive
PING 1.1.1.2 (1.1.1.2): 56 data bytes
64 bytes from 1.1.1.2: icmp_seq=0 ttl=254 time=0.958 ms
64 bytes from 1.1.1.2: icmp_seq=1 ttl=254 time=0.617 ms
64 bytes from 1.1.1.2: icmp_seq=2 ttl=254 time=0.595 ms
64 bytes from 1.1.1.2: icmp_seq=3 ttl=254 time=0.603 ms
64 bytes from 1.1.1.2: icmp_seq=4 ttl=254 time=0.645 ms
--- 1.1.1.2 ping statistics ---
5 packets transmitted, 5 packets received, 0.00% packet loss
round-trip min/avg/max = 0.595/0.683/0.958 ms


Congo(config)# vpc domain 1
Congo(config-vpc-domain)# peer-keepalive destination 1.1.1.2 source
1.1.1.1 vrf vpc-
keepalive
Congo(config-vpc-domain)# exit
Egypt(config)# vpc domain 1
Egypt(config-vpc-domain)# peer-keepalive destination 1.1.1.1 source
1.1.1.
  2 vrf vpc-keepalive
Egypt(config-vpc-domain)# exit
```

Step 4.   Verify that VPC peer keepalive link is working:

```
Congo# sho vpc
Legend:
                (*) - local vPC is down, forwarding via vPC peer-link
vPC domain id                 : 1
Peer status                   : peer link not configured
vPC keep-alive status         : peer is alive
Configuration consistency status: failed
Configuration consistency reason: vPC peer-link does not exists
vPC role                      : none established
Number of vPCs configured     : 0
Peer Gateway                  : Disabled
Dual-active excluded VLANs     : -
Congo#
```

Step 5.   Configure the vPC peer-link:

```
! Congo
Congo# conf t
```

```
Enter configuration commands, one per line. End with CNTL/Z.
Congo(config)# interface port-channel 100
Congo(config-if)# vpc peer-link
Please note that spanning tree port type is changed to "network" port
type on vPC peer-
link.
This will enable spanning tree Bridge Assurance on vPC peer-link
provided the STP
Bridge Assurance (which is enabled by default) is not disabled.
Congo(config-if)#
! Egypt
Egypt# conf t
Enter configuration commands, one per line. End with CNTL/Z.
Egypt(config-if)# switchport mode trunk
Egypt(config)# interface port-channel 100
Egypt(config-if)# vpc peer-link
Please note that spanning tree port type is changed to "network" port
type on vPC peer-link.
This will enable spanning tree Bridge Assurance on vPC peer-link
provided the STP Bridge Assurance.(which is enabled by default) is not
disabled.
Egypt(config-if)#
```

Note   Interfaces that are members of the VPC peer-link must be 10 GbE ports, and it is recommended that they are in dedicated rate-mde.

Step 6.   Verify configuration consistency checks pass, and you have an active VPC configuration:

```
Egypt# show vpc
Legend:
                (*) - local vPC is down, forwarding via vPC peer-link
vPC domain id                   : 1
Peer status                     : peer adjacency formed ok
vPC keep-alive status           : peer is alive
Configuration consistency status: success
vPC role                        : secondary
Number of vPCs configured       : 0
Peer Gateway                    : Disabled
Dual-active excluded VLANs       : -
vPC Peer-link status
---------------------------------------------------------------------
id   Port    Status Active vlans
--   ----    ------ ---------------------------------------------------
1    Po100   up     1-20,100
```

If the configuration consistency status returns anything other than success, additional information about the inconsistencies can be derived with the following command:

```
Congo# show vpc consistency-parameters global


    Legend:
        Type 1 : vPC will be suspended in case of mismatch

Name                        Type  Local Value            Peer Value
-------------               ----  ---------------------  --------------
---------
STP Mode                    1     Rapid-PVST             Rapid-PVST
STP Disabled                1     VLANs 91               VLANs 91
STP MST Region Name         1     customer               customer
STP MST Region Revision     1     1                      1
STP MST Region Instance to  1
 VLAN Mapping
STP Loopguard               1     Disabled               Disabled
STP Bridge Assurance        1     Enabled                Enabled
STP Port Type, Edge         1     Normal, Disabled,      Normal,
Disabled,
BPDUFilter, Edge BPDUGuard        Disabled               Disabled
STP MST Simulate PVST       1     Enabled                Enabled
Interface-vlan admin up     2     40-43,50,60,70-71,91,1 40-
43,50,60,70-71,91,1
                                  00-103                 00-103
Allowed VLANs               -     40-43,50,60,91,100-103 9,40-
43,50,60,91,100-1
                                  ,1000                  03,1000
Local suspended VLANs       -     -                      -
```

Step 7. Add port-channels to a VPC:

```
! Congo
Congo(config-if)# exit
Congo(config)# interface ethernet 2/1
Congo(config-if)# channel-group 1 mode active
Congo(config-if)# no shutdown
Congo(config-if)# exit
Congo(config)# interface port-channel 1
Congo(config-if)# switchport
Congo(config-if)# switchport mode trunk
Congo(config-if)# vpc 1
! Egypt
Egypt(config)# int ethernet 2/2
Egypt(config-if)# channel-group 1 mode active
```

```
Egypt(config-if)# no shutdown
Egypt(config-if)# exit
Egypt(config)# int port-channel 1
Egypt(config-if)# switchport
Egypt(config-if)# switchport mode trunk
Egypt(config-if)# vpc 1
! Kenya
Kenya(config)# interface ethernet 2/11-12
Kenya(config-if-range)# switchport
Kenya(config-if-range)# channel-group 1 mode active
Kenya(config-if-range)# no shutdown
Kenya(config-if-range)# exit
Kenya(config)# exit
Kenya(config)# int port-channel 1
Kenya(config-if)# switchport
Kenya(config-if)# switchport mode trunk
Kenya(config-if)#
```

Step 8.   Verify that the vPC is operational:

```
Congo# show vpc
Legend:
                (*) - local vPC is down, forwarding via vPC peer-link
vPC domain id                   : 1
Peer status                     : peer adjacency formed ok
vPC keep-alive status           : peer is alive
Configuration consistency status: success
vPC role                        : primary
Number of vPCs configured       : 1
Peer Gateway                    : Disabled
Dual-active excluded VLANs       : -
vPC Peer-link status
---------------------------------------------------------------------
id   Port   Status Active vlans
--   ----   ------ ----------------------------------------------
1    Po100  up     1-20,100
vPC status
---------------------------------------------------------------------
id   Port   Status Consistency Reason                     Active vlans
--   ----   ------ ----------- ------------------------- -----------
1    Po1    up     success     success                    1-20,100
```

VPC Peer-Gateway

The VPC Peer-Gateway feature was introduced in NX-OS 4.2(1). This feature is designed to enable certain storage, application servers or load balancers to implement *fast-path functionality*. This causes nodes to send return traffic to a specific MAC address of the sender rather than HSRP address. By default, this traffic might be dropped as VPC loop avoidance does not allow traffic received on a VPC peer-link to be forwarded out a VPC interface (loop avoidance). A VPC Peer-Gateway enables the VPC peer device to forward packets destined for its peer router MAC locally.

To enable the peer-gateway, enter the following command:

```
Congo(config-vpc-domain)# peer-gateway
```

Unidirectional Link Detection

Full-duplex communication creates a situation in which a node can receive traffic but cannot transmit or vice versa; this condition is known as a *unidirectional link* and can be problematic for protocols that require a bidirectional exchange of information. This condition is most often attributed to fiber optic cabling as the physical medium. It is also possible for unidirectional link conditions to exist in other mediums such as twisted-pair copper cabling. Although upper layer protocols can overcome this scenario easily, this scenario can produce unexpected results at Layer 2. For these Layer 2 protocols, Cisco provides a mechanism for detecting and disabling links where bidirectional traffic flow is not possible. Cisco developed Unidirectional Link Detection (UDLD) to eliminate any negative behavior associated with the failure of bidirectional communication. UDLD enables each device to send packets to the directly connected device at periodic intervals (15 seconds by default); the sending and receiving of these packets ensures that traffic flow is bi-directional. The Cisco UDLD implementation defines two modes that devices can operate:

- **Aggressive mode:** Typically used for copper-based mediums such as twisted pair copper

- **Nonaggressive mode:** Typically used for fiber-based networks

Example 2-69 shows the configuration and verification of UDLD.

Example 2-69   *UDLD Configuration*

```
! Enabling UDLD
Congo(config)# feature udld
Congo(config)#
! Verifying UDLD global status
Congo# show udld global
UDLD global configuration mode: enabled
UDLD global message interval: 15
```

```
Congo# show udld
Interface Ethernet1/1
--------------------------------
Port enable administrative configuration setting: device-default
Port enable operational state: enabled
Current bidirectional state: bidirectional
Current operational state:  advertisement - Single neighbor detected
Message interval: 7
Timeout interval: 5
        Entry 1
        ---------------
        Expiration time: 20
        Cache Device index: 1
        Current neighbor state: unknown
        Device ID: TBM12224047
        Port ID: Ethernet1/2
        Neighbor echo 1 devices: TBM12224047
        Neighbor echo 1 port: Ethernet1/1
        Message interval: 7
        Timeout interval: 5
        CDP Device name: Egypt(TBM12224047)
! Enabling UDLD aggressive mode
Congo(config-if)# udld aggressive
Congo(config-if)# exit
Congo(config)# sho udld ethernet 1/1
Interface Ethernet1/1
--------------------------------
Port enable administrative configuration setting: enabled-aggressive
Port enable operational state: enabled-aggressive
Current bidirectional state: bidirectional
Current operational state:  advertisement - Single neighbor detected
Message interval: 15
Timeout interval: 5
        Entry 1
        ---------------
        Expiration time: 44
        Cache Device index: 1
        Current neighbor state: bidirectional
        Device ID: TBM12224047
        Port ID: Ethernet1/2
        Neighbor echo 1 devices: TBM12224047
        Neighbor echo 1 port: Ethernet1/1
        Message interval: 15
        Timeout interval: 5
```

```
        CDP Device name: Egypt(TBM12224047)


Congo# show udld neighbors
Port            Device Name    Device ID   Port ID          Neighbor State
- - - - - - - - - - - - - - - - - - - - - - - - - - - - - - - - - - - - - - - - - -
Ethernet1/1     TBM12224047    1           Ethernet1/2      bidirectional
Ethernet1/3     TBM12224047    1           Ethernet1/4      bidirectional
```

Summary

The Layer 2 switching capabilities of NX-OS provide a scalable, resilient foundation for your data center. This chapter covered the following topics:

- VLANs segment traffic at Layer 2 to address security concerns or define failure domains.

- PVLANs provide an additional level of security by enabling administrators to subdivide VLANs.

- Spanning Tree provides a mechanism to ensure that physically redundant networks are logically loop-free. You learned how to configure and tune Rapid-PVST+ and MST.

- Enhancements to Spanning Tree such as BPDUGuard, BPDUFilter, RootGuard, and LoopGuard.

- Links can be aggregated through the use of port-channels and vPCs to simplify Spanning Tree topologies while making additional bandwidth available for data traffic.

With NX-OS on the Nexus 7000 and 5000, Cisco provides a highly available implementation of standards-based Layer 2 technology and builds upon it with new innovation required to meet the specific demands within today's data centers.

Chapter 3

Layer 3 Support and Configurations

The Nexus line of switches provides a robust Layer 3 feature set. This chapter features common implementations and syntax for Layer 3 features such as EIGRP, OSPF, BGP, and FHRPs such as HSRP, VRRP, and GLBP, and covers the following topics:

- **EIGRP:** Describes the configuration and operations of EIGRP on Nexus 7000 series switches

- **OSPF:** Describes the configuration and operations of OSPF on Nexus 7000 series switches

- **BGP:** Describes the configuration and operations of BGP on Nexus 7000 series switches

- **HSRP:** Describes the configuration and operations of HSRP on Nexus 7000 series switches

- **VRRP:** Describes the configuration and operations of VRRP on Nexus 7000 series switches

- **GLBP:** Describes the configuration and operations of GLBP on Nexus 7000 series switches

EIGRP

Cisco NX-OS on the Nexus 7000 series switches support Layer 3 routing using dynamic routing protocols, static routing, and policy-based routing. NX-OS also provides advanced virtualization capabilities using Virtual Routing and Forwarding instances (VRF). Supporting industry leading protocols such as Enhanced Interior Gateway Routing Protocol (EIGRP), Open Shortest Path First (OSPF), Border Gateway Protocol (BGP), and Intermediate System-to-Intermediate System (IS-IS), and Routing Information Protocol (RIP) and static routing, the Nexus 7000 enables significant flexibility and options to interconnect multiple topologies. The Route Policy Manager supports complex configurations, tight routing control, and migrations from one protocol to another. This chapter covers common implementations and syntax for EIGRP, OSPF, and BGP and First Hop Redundancy Protocols (FHRP) such as Hot Standby Router Protocol (HSRP), Virtual Router Redundancy Protocol (VRRP), and Gateway Load Balancing Protocol (GLBP).

EIGRP was developed by Cisco and runs only on Cisco devices. EIGRP is a highly scalable, flexible, and robust routing protocol considered a hybrid of distance vector and link-state protocols. Considered a hybrid routing protocol, EIGRP implements the best characteristics of both distance vector and link-state protocols such as the hello mechanism and incremental updates.

EIGRP Operation

EIGRP calculates routes based on metrics received from neighbors and uses an algorithm called the Diffusing Update Algorithm (DUAL). The primary advantage that DUAL provides over other routing algorithms is the capability to provide loop-free topologies at every stage of network convergence. When joined with the other capabilities of EIGRP, such as its multiprotocol nature; WAN friendly neighboring and updating capabilities; and flexible summarization and quick convergence, it makes for a powerful routing protocol.

EIGRP forms adjacencies with its directly connected neighbors to exchange routing updates similar to a link state protocol. During the initial neighbor formation, attributes such as smooth round trip time (SRTT), hold time, retry timeout, IP address, and interface on which the hello was received are negotiated and recorded in a neighbor table, as demonstrated in Example 3-1.

Example 3-1   *EIGRP Neighbors*

```
Congo# show ip eigrp ne
IP-EIGRP neighbors for process 100 VRF default
H    Address                    Interface       Hold  Uptime   SRTT   RTO  Q   Seq
                                                 (sec)          (ms)       Cnt Num
1    10.10.10.3                 Vlan10          11    01:42:49  44     264  0   128
0    192.168.1.38               Eth1/18         14    01:52:06  414    2484 0   221
```

The hellos between the EIGRP neighbors are the mechanism for maintaining the adjacency. Within the hello is a hold timer that tells EIGRP the maximum time before the next hello should be received. By default, the hold timer is three times the hello interval. If the hold timer is exceeded before another hello is received, EIGRP considers the neighbor unreachable and informs DUAL. The network's topology is recalculated and bounded, partial updates are sent to the remaining neighbors, and the network begins to converge.

Configuring EIGRP

EIGRP within NX-OS is compatible with EIGRP on IOS devices enabling a smooth integration of Nexus equipment with existing gear. Configuring EIGRP within NX-OS will be similar, yet distinctly different in some aspects to traditional IOS configuration. These differences will be highlighted throughout the section.

Enabling EIGRP is a multistep process that will be covered in detail. The following is a quick listing of steps to enable a basic configuration of EIGRP:

Step 1.   Enable EIGRP.

Step 2.   Configure the EIGRP routing process.

Step 3.   Assign interfaces to the instance tag.

Step 4.   Configure passive interfaces if necessary.

Step 5.   Configure network summarization.

Step 6.   Configure the redistribution of other protocols if necessary.

Step 7.   Verify EIGRP operation.

The first step to configure EIGRP is to enable it in global configuration mode using the **feature** command, as demonstrated in Example 3-2. With the modular nature of NX-OS, using the **feature** command loads the EIGRP modular code into memory for execution. Without the feature enabled, it would not be resident in memory.

Example 3-2   *Enabling EIGRP*

```
Congo# confi t
Enter configuration commands, one per line. End with CNTL/Z.
Congo(config)# feature eigrp
Congo(config)# end
Congo# show run eigrp
!Command: show running-config eigrp
!Time: Tue Sep 29 16:03:10 2009
version 4.2(2a)
feature eigrp
```

As with IOS-based EIGRP configuration, the next step is to configure the EIGRP routing process, as demonstrated in Example 3-3. In NX-OS, you configure an instance tag for the process. Traditionally in IOS this would be the autonomous system (AS) number. In NX-OS the instance tag can be the AS, but additionally the instance tag can be up to 20 case-sensitive alphanumeric characters.

Example 3-3   *Creating an EIGRP Instance with a Numeric Tag*

```
Congo# confi t
```

```
Enter configuration commands, one per line. End with CNTL/Z.
Congo(config)# router eigrp 200
Congo(config-router)# exit
Congo(config)# show run eigrp
!Command: show running-config eigrp
!Time: Tue Sep 29 16:05:21 2009

version 4.2(2a)
feature eigrp
router eigrp 200
```

Example 3-4 shows an alphanumeric string for the tag.

Example 3-4   *Creating an EIGRP Instance with an Alphanumeric String*

```
Congo# confi t
Enter configuration commands, one per line. End with CNTL/Z.
Congo(config)# router eigrp DataCenter1
Congo(config)# show run eigrp
!Command: show running-config eigrp
!Time: Tue Sep 29 16:11:05 2009

version 4.2(2a)
feature eigrp
router eigrp DataCenter1
```

Note that when using an instance tag that cannot qualify as an AS number, use the **autonomous-system** *as-number* command to configure the AS; otherwise, EIGRP remains shut down.

Example 3-5 shows how to configure an AS number under an EIGRP process that uses an alphanumeric tag.

Example 3-5   *Configuring EIGRP with an Autonomous System Number*

```
Congo# confi t
Enter configuration commands, one per line. End with CNTL/Z.
Congo(config)# router eigrp DataCenter1
Congo(config-router)# autonomous-system 100
Congo(config-router)# exit
Congo(config)# show run eigrp
!Command: show running-config eigrp
!Time: Tue Sep 29 16:11:05 2009

version 4.2(2a)
```

```
feature eigrp
router eigrp DataCenter1
  autonomous-system 100
```

With EIGRP configured as a feature and assigned an autonomous system ID, the next step is to assign interfaces to the instance tag, as demonstrated in Example 3-6. This advertises the IP subnet in EIGRP and enables the capability for neighbor adjacencies to be formed.

Note that this is different from traditional IOS configuration where you configure a **network** statement under the routing process, and then, in turn, any interface on the router that fell within that network range was advertised. The approach taken in NX-OS is much more granular and enables additional levels of control over which networks are advertised.

Example 3-6   *Adding an SVI to EIGRP with a Numeric Tag*

```
Congo# confi t
Enter configuration commands, one per line. End with CNTL/Z.
Congo(config)# int vlan 10
Congo(config-if)# ip router eigrp 200
Congo(config-if)# show ip eigrp int vlan 10
IP-EIGRP interfaces for process 200 VRF default
                        Xmit Queue    Mean    Pacing Time   Multicast    Pending
Interface       Peers   Un/Reliable   SRTT    Un/Reliable   Flow Timer   Routes
Vlan10            0         0/0         0         0/10          0            0
   Hello interval is 5 sec
   Holdtime interval is 15 sec
   Next xmit serial <none>
   Un/reliable mcasts: 0/0  Un/reliable ucasts: 0/0
   Mcast exceptions: 0  CR packets: 0  ACKs suppressed: 0
   Retransmissions sent: 0  Out-of-sequence rcvd: 0
   Authentication mode is not set
```

Example 3-7 shows how to add an SVI to EIGRP when using an alphanumeric tag.

Example 3-7   *Adding an SVI to EIGRP with an Alphanumeric Tag*

```
Congo# confi t
Enter configuration commands, one per line. End with CNTL/Z.
Congo(config)# int vlan 10
Congo(config-if)# ip router eigrp DataCenter1
Congo(config-if)# show ip eigrp int vlan 10
IP-EIGRP interfaces for process 100 VRF default
                        Xmit Queue    Mean    Pacing Time   Multicast    Pending
```

```
Interface         Peers  Un/Reliable  SRTT   Un/Reliable   Flow Timer   Routes
Vlan10             1        0/0         44       0/10          208          0
  Hello interval is 5 sec
  Holdtime interval is 15 sec
  Next xmit serial <none>
  Un/reliable mcasts: 0/1  Un/reliable ucasts: 2/2
  Mcast exceptions: 0  CR packets: 0  ACKs suppressed: 1
  Retransmissions sent: 0  Out-of-sequence rcvd: 0
  Authentication mode is not set
```

In a data center's distribution/aggregation layer, it is common to have multiple VLAN interfaces that, in turn, need to be advertised to the network at large. By default, when EIGRP is enabled on the VLAN interface, it sends and receives hellos. If a neighbor is detected, EIGRP attempts to form an adjacency. Although this default setup is wanted, there might be designs in which forming multiple EIGRP adjacencies between the same pair of switches is not wanted due to the potential impact of network convergence time and unnecessary duplicate next hops. In configurations such as this, use the **passive-interface** command, as demonstrated in Example 3-8. A passive interface accomplishes the requirement of advertising the subnet via EIGRP, but also instructing the EIGRP process to not listen to hellos on the interfaces configured to be passive.

Example 3-8   *Configuring a Passive Interface in EIGRP with a Numeric Tag*

```
Congo# config t
Congo(config)# int vlan100
Congo(config-if)# ip passive-interface eigrp 200
Congo(config-if)# end
```

Example 3-9 shows how to configure a passive interface in EIGRP when using an alphanumeric tag.

Example 3-9   *Configuring a Passive Interface in EIGRP with an Alphanumeric Tag*

```
Congo# config t
Congo(config)# int vlan100
Congo(config-if)# ip passive-interface eigrp DataCenter1
Congo(config-if)# exit
Congo(config)# show run int vlan 100
!Command: show running-config interface Vlan100
!Time: Tue Sep 29 16:30:02 2009
version 4.2(2a)
interface Vlan100
  no shutdown
  description Server Subnet1
```

```
ip address 10.10.100.2/24
ip router eigrp DataCenter1
ip passive-interface eigrp DataCenter1
```

EIGRP Summarization

EIGRP has the capability to summarize routes in a flexible manner, per interface. This enables network designers to summarize their networks for maximum efficiency without the constraints of specific borders or other topological designations. When a network is summarized, a single entry with a shorter prefix (commonly called a supernet) is created and added to the routing table as a representation of the longer prefix subnets. The examples that follow show how to create a summary for 192.168.128.0 /20 that is advertised out interface e1/18.

> **Note** Note with this summary, the following networks are represented: 192.168.128.0/24 through 192.168.143.0/24.

Example 3-10 shows EIGRP summarization between the Congo and Libya networks, as illustrated in Figure 3-1.

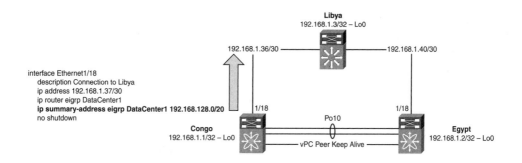

Figure 3-1 *EIGRP Summarization*

Example 3-10 *Summarizing Networks in EIGRP Using Numeric Tags*

```
Congo# confi t
Congo(config)# interface e1/18
Congo(config-if)# ip summary-address eigrp 200 192.168.128.0/20
Congo(config-if)# end
```

Example 3-11 shows how to summarize a network when EIGRP uses an alphanumeric tag.

Example 3-11   *Summarizing Networks in EIGRP Using Alphanumeric Tags*

```
Congo# config t
Congo(config)# int e1/18
Congo(config-if)# ip summary-address eigrp DataCenter1 192.168.128.0/20
```

As highlighted in Example 3-12, you can see the resulting summary address in the routing table on Congo.

Example 3-12   *Reviewing the Network Summarization in NX-OS*

```
Congo(config-if)# show ip ro
IP Route Table for VRF "default"
'*' denotes best ucast next-hop
'**' denotes best mcast next-hop
'[x/y]' denotes [preference/metric]
10.10.10.0/24, ubest/mbest: 1/0, attached
    *via 10.10.10.2, Vlan10, [0/0], 2d22h, direct
10.10.10.1/32, ubest/mbest: 1/0
    *via 10.10.10.1, Vlan10, [0/0], 2d22h, hsrp
10.10.10.2/32, ubest/mbest: 1/0, attached
    *via 10.10.10.2, Vlan10, [0/0], 2d22h, local
10.10.100.0/24, ubest/mbest: 1/0, attached
    *via 10.10.100.2, Vlan100, [0/0], 01:33:23, direct
10.10.100.1/32, ubest/mbest: 1/0
    *via 10.10.100.1, Vlan100, [0/0], 01:33:03, hsrp
10.10.100.2/32, ubest/mbest: 1/0, attached
    *via 10.10.100.2, Vlan100, [0/0], 01:33:23, local
192.168.1.1/32, ubest/mbest: 2/0, attached
    *via 192.168.1.1, Lo0, [0/0], 2d22h, local
    *via 192.168.1.1, Lo0, [0/0], 2d22h, direct
192.168.1.2/32, ubest/mbest: 1/0
    *via 192.168.1.38, Eth1/18, [90/128832], 02:22:00, eigrp-DataCenter1, internal
192.168.1.3/32, ubest/mbest: 1/0
    *via 192.168.1.38, Eth1/18, [90/128512], 02:29:54, eigrp-DataCenter1, internal
192.168.1.32/30, ubest/mbest: 1/0, attached
    *via 192.168.1.33, Vlan5, [0/0], 2d22h, direct
192.168.1.33/32, ubest/mbest: 1/0, attached
    *via 192.168.1.33, Vlan5, [0/0], 2d22h, local
192.168.1.36/30, ubest/mbest: 1/0, attached
    *via 192.168.1.37, Eth1/18, [0/0], 2d22h, direct
192.168.1.37/32, ubest/mbest: 1/0, attached
    *via 192.168.1.37, Eth1/18, [0/0], 2d22h, local
192.168.1.40/30, ubest/mbest: 1/0
    *via 192.168.1.38, Eth1/18, [90/768], 02:29:54, eigrp-DataCenter1, internal
```

```
192.168.128.0/20, ubest/mbest: 1/0

   *via Null0, [5/128320], 00:01:54, eigrp-DataCenter1, discard

192.168.128.1/32, ubest/mbest: 2/0, attached
   *via 192.168.128.1, Lo2, [0/0], 00:02:04, local
   *via 192.168.128.1, Lo2, [0/0], 00:02:04, direct
```

As Example 3-13 demonstrates, the summary address is propagated to an IOS speaking EIGRP neighbor, Libya, and that it is summarizing the /32 route for Loopback2 as expected.

Example 3-13 *Reviewing the Network Summarization in IOS*

```
Libya#show ip ro
Codes: C - connected, S - static, R - RIP, M - mobile, B - BGP
       D - EIGRP, EX - EIGRP external, O - OSPF, IA - OSPF inter area
       N1 - OSPF NSSA external type 1, N2 - OSPF NSSA external type 2
       E1 - OSPF external type 1, E2 - OSPF external type 2
       i - IS-IS, su - IS-IS summary, L1 - IS-IS level-1, L2 - IS-IS level-2
       ia - IS-IS inter area, * - candidate default, U - per-user static route
       o - ODR, P - periodic downloaded static route
Gateway of last resort is not set
     192.168.128.0/32 is subnetted, 1 subnets
D       192.168.128.1
           [90/131072] via 192.168.1.41, 00:05:38, TenGigabitEthernet1/49
     172.26.0.0/16 is variably subnetted, 2 subnets, 2 masks
S       172.26.2.0/23 [1/0] via 172.26.32.33
C       172.26.32.32/27 is directly connected, GigabitEthernet1/48
     10.0.0.0/24 is subnetted, 2 subnets
D       10.10.10.0
           [90/3072] via 192.168.1.41, 02:24:25, TenGigabitEthernet1/49
           [90/3072] via 192.168.1.37, 02:24:25, TenGigabitEthernet1/50
D       10.10.100.0
           [90/3072] via 192.168.1.41, 01:36:59, TenGigabitEthernet1/49
           [90/3072] via 192.168.1.37, 01:36:59, TenGigabitEthernet1/50
     192.168.1.0/24 is variably subnetted, 5 subnets, 2 masks
C       192.168.1.40/30 is directly connected, TenGigabitEthernet1/49
C       192.168.1.36/30 is directly connected, TenGigabitEthernet1/50
D       192.168.1.1/32
           [90/128576] via 192.168.1.37, 00:07:51, TenGigabitEthernet1/50
C       192.168.1.3/32 is directly connected, Loopback0
D       192.168.1.2/32
           [90/128576] via 192.168.1.41, 02:25:45, TenGigabitEthernet1/49
```

```
D      192.168.128.0/20

            [90/128576] via 192.168.1.37, 00:05:38, TenGigabitEthernet1/50
```

EIGRP Stub Routing

One of EIGRP's scalability features is stub routing. When EIGRP stub routing is enabled, the router advertises a smaller subset of networks dependent on the configuration. An EIGRP stub router informs its neighbors that it is a stub and responds to queries with **INACCESSIBLE**. Although not commonly deployed in the data center, there are use cases for the EIGRP stub. An example would be to define the data center as an EIGRP stub to minimize updates and queries from the WAN. Another example that could leverage the EIGRP stub would be when a merger or acquisition is made and complex routing can be simplified with the EIGRP stub.

Stub routing is configured under the address-family mode in the routing process, as demonstrated in Example 3-14, for the network topology shown in Figure 3-2.

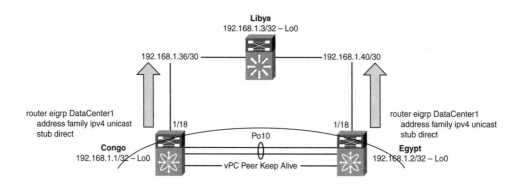

Figure 3-2   *EIGRP Stub Routing*

Example 3-14   *Configuring EIGRP Stub Routing with Numeric Tags*

```
Congo(config-if)#
Congo# confi t
Congo(config)# router eigrp 200
Congo(config-router)# address-family ipv4 unicast
Congo(config-router)# stub direct
Congo(config-router)# end
```

Example 3-15 shows how to configure EIGRP stub when using an alphanumeric tag.

Example 3-15 *Configuring EIGRP Stub Routing with Alphanumeric Tags*

```
Congo# config t
Congo(config)# router eigrp DataCenter1
Congo(config-router)# address-family ipv4 unicast
Congo(config-router)# stub
Congo(config-router)# end
```

The stub status of a neighbor can be identified in the detail output from **show ip eigrp neighbor detail**, as demonstrated in Example 3-16.

Example 3-16 *Verification of EIGRP Stub Neighbor*

```
Congo# show ip eigrp ne det
IP-EIGRP neighbors for process 100 VRF default
H    Address                  Interface        Hold  Uptime   SRTT    RTO   Q    Seq
                                               (sec)          (ms)        Cnt Num
1    10.10.10.3               Vlan10           13    00:00:19 38      228   0    149
     Version 12.4/1.2, Retrans: 0, Retries: 0, Prefixes: 3
     Stub Peer Advertising ( CONNECTED/DIRECT SUMMARY ) Routes

     Suppressing queries

0    192.168.1.38             Eth1/18          12    02:40:32 36      216   0    245
     Restart time 00:14:10
     Version 12.2/3.0, Retrans: 0, Retries: 0, Prefixes: 3
```

Securing EIGRP

Securing EIGRP routing updates is also possible by using authentication between EIGRP neighbors. EIGRP authentication is enabled either at the routing process level or per-interface allowing for flexible deployment options.

Note Note that interface-level authentication overrides the process-level configuration.

Configuring EIGRP authentication involves a multistep process. You must first define a key chain that contains attributes such as the password to be used to authenticate the connection, and the lifetime of the key chain for both sending and receiving, as demonstrated in the configuration in Example 3-17, for the network topology in Figure 3-3.

Example 3-17 *Configuring a Key Chain*

```
Congo(config)# key chain nexus
Congo(config-keychain)# key 1
Congo(config-keychain-key)# key-string nexus
```

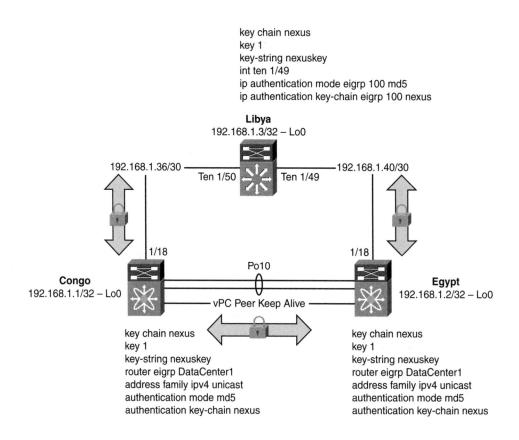

key chain nexus
key 1
key-string nexuskey
int ten 1/49
ip authentication mode eigrp 100 md5
ip authentication key-chain eigrp 100 nexus

Libya
192.168.1.3/32 – Lo0

192.168.1.36/30 ——— Ten 1/50   Ten 1/49 ———192.168.1.40/30

1/18   1/18
Po10

Congo   **Egypt**
192.168.1.1/32 – Lo0 ——— vPC Peer Keep Alive ———192.168.1.2/32 – Lo0

key chain nexus   key chain nexus
key 1   key 1
key-string nexuskey   key-string nexuskey
router eigrp DataCenter1   router eigrp DataCenter1
address family ipv4 unicast   address family ipv4 unicast
authentication mode md5   authentication mode md5
authentication key-chain nexus   authentication key-chain nexus

Figure 3-3   *EIGRP Authentication*

Now that a key exists, the next step is to configure the routing protocol, EIGRP in this case, to enable authentication and to use the key chain, as demonstrated in Example 3-18. This step is completed under the address-family configuration. It is necessary to specify an encryption mechanism, MD5, and configure the key chain to use.

Note   Note that the use of **address-family** commands provides the ability to group protocol-specific attributes such as stub, authentication, and redistribution. This flexibility allows for complex routing scenarios with a fine level of control.

Example 3-18   *Configuring EIGRP Authentication*

```
Congo(config-router)# router eigrp DataCenter1
Congo(config-router)# address-family ipv4 unicast
Congo(config-router-af)# authentication mode md5
Congo(config-router-af)# authentication key-chain nexus
```

It is important to note that the values specified under the address-family configuration are for all EIGRP neighbors. These values can be overridden by an interface-specific configuration that might be helpful when multiple keys are used on different devices in the internetwork, as demonstrated in Example 3-19.

Example 3-19 *Configuring EIGRP Authentication on an Interface*

```
Congo# config t
Congo(config)# interface e1/18
Congo(config-if)# ip authentication mode eigrp DataCenter1 md5
Congo(config-if)# ip authentication key-chain eigrp DataCenter1 newkey
```

Example 3-20 demonstrates how to verify the authentication configuration.

Example 3-20 *Verification of EIGRP Authentication*

```
Congo# show ip eigrp DataCenter1 vrf default
IP-EIGRP AS 100 ID 192.168.1.1 VRF default
  Process-tag: DataCenter1
  Status: running
  Authentication mode: md5
  Authentication key-chain: nexus
  Metric weights: K1=1 K2=0 K3=1 K4=0 K5=0
  IP proto: 88 Multicast group: 224.0.0.10
  Int distance: 90 Ext distance: 170
  Max paths: 8
  Number of EIGRP interfaces: 4 (2 loopbacks)
  Number of EIGRP passive interfaces: 1
  Number of EIGRP peers: 2
  Graceful-Restat: Enabled
  Stub-Routing: Disabled
  NSF converge time limit/expiries: 120/0
  NSF route-hold time limit/expiries: 240/7
  NSF signal time limit/expiries: 20/0
  Redistributed max-prefix: Disabled
```

EIGRP Redistribution

It is a common requirement to redistribute routes learned from other routing protocols or for directly connected interfaces into EIGRP. With the exception of the default route, this is accomplished in a similar manner to traditional IOS redistribution with a few minor differences that are highlighted in the sample configurations.

Starting with the default route, the methodology to redistribute it into the routing table uses the **default-information originate** command.

As demonstrated in Example 3-21, the process begins by defining a prefix list, which is then used by a route map referenced by the **default-information originate** command (see Figure 3-4).

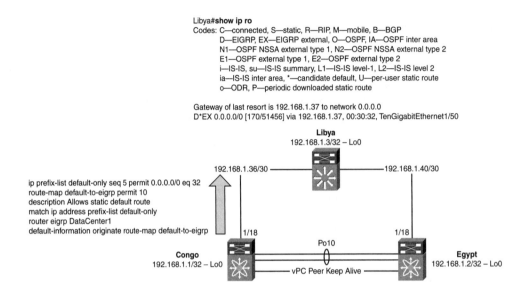

Figure 3-4   *EIGRP Redistribution of the Default Route*

> **Note**   NX-OS does not have the capability to do "wide-open" or "uncontrolled" redistribution. NX-OS enforces the use of a route map to define routes that should be redistributed.

Example 3-21   *Defining a Prefix List*

```
Congo# config t
Enter configuration commands, one per line. End with CNTL/Z.
Congo(config)# ip prefix-list default-only seq 5 permit 0.0.0.0/0 eq 32
Congo(config)#
```

> **Note**   Three operators can be used in a prefix list—**eq**, **le**, and **ge**. The **eq** operator is an *exact* match of the prefix. The **le** operator specifies less than or equal to the matching prefix. Finally the **ge** operator specifies greater than or equal to the matching prefix.

The next step is to define a route map, called **default-to-eigrp**, which uses the prefix list named **default-only** to bring in only the 0/0 route, as demonstrated in Example 3-22.

Example 3-22 *Defining a Route Map*

```
Congo(config)# route-map default-to-eigrp permit 10
Congo(config-route-map)# description Allows static default route
Congo(config-route-map)# match ip address prefix-list default-only
```

Finally, you configure EIGRP to use the route map **default-to-eigrp** as part of the **default-information originate** command, as demonstrated in Example 3-23.

Example 3-23 *Redistribution of the Default Route into EIGRP*

```
Congo(config)# router eigrp DataCenter1
Congo(config-router)# default-information originate route-map default-to-eigrp
```

Now the default route shows up in the neighboring routers, as highlighted in Example 3-24.

Example 3-24 *Verification of the Redistribution of the Default Route into EIGRP in NX-OS*

```
Egypt# show ip ro
IP Route Table for VRF "default"
'*' denotes best ucast next-hop
'**' denotes best mcast next-hop
'[x/y]' denotes [preference/metric]
0.0.0.0/0, ubest/mbest: 1/0

    *via 10.10.10.2, Vlan10, [170/51456], 00:28:57, eigrp-DataCenter1, external
```

On an IOS router, you see the default is learned as well but displayed a bit differently, as demonstrated in Example 3-25.

Example 3-25 *Verification of the Redistribution of the Default Route into EIGRP in IOS*

```
Libya#show ip ro
Codes: C - connected, S - static, R - RIP, M - mobile, B - BGP
       D - EIGRP, EX - EIGRP external, O - OSPF, IA - OSPF inter area
       N1 - OSPF NSSA external type 1, N2 - OSPF NSSA external type 2
       E1 - OSPF external type 1, E2 - OSPF external type 2
       i - IS-IS, su - IS-IS summary, L1 - IS-IS level-1, L2 - IS-IS level-2
       ia - IS-IS inter area, * - candidate default, U - per-user static route
       o - ODR, P - periodic downloaded static route
Gateway of last resort is 192.168.1.37 to network 0.0.0.0
     172.26.0.0/16 is variably subnetted, 2 subnets, 2 masks
S       172.26.2.0/23 [1/0] via 172.26.32.33
C       172.26.32.32/27 is directly connected, GigabitEthernet1/48
     10.0.0.0/24 is subnetted, 2 subnets
```

```
D        10.10.10.0
             [90/3072] via 192.168.1.41, 01:00:41, TenGigabitEthernet1/49
             [90/3072] via 192.168.1.37, 01:00:41, TenGigabitEthernet1/50
D        10.10.100.0
             [90/3072] via 192.168.1.41, 01:00:41, TenGigabitEthernet1/49
             [90/3072] via 192.168.1.37, 01:00:41, TenGigabitEthernet1/50
      192.168.1.0/24 is variably subnetted, 5 subnets, 2 masks
C        192.168.1.40/30 is directly connected, TenGigabitEthernet1/49
C        192.168.1.36/30 is directly connected, TenGigabitEthernet1/50
D        192.168.1.1/32
             [90/128576] via 192.168.1.37, 01:15:04, TenGigabitEthernet1/50
C        192.168.1.3/32 is directly connected, Loopback0
D        192.168.1.2/32
             [90/128576] via 192.168.1.41, 01:00:41, TenGigabitEthernet1/49
D*EX 0.0.0.0/0 [170/51456] via 192.168.1.37, 00:30:32, TenGigabitEthernet1/50
```

NX-OS also has a feature that enables network administrators to control the number of routes redistributed into EIGRP. You need to consider three options based on the specific requirement of the network:

- **Fixed Limit:** Allows network administrators to specify a number of routes between 1 and 65,535. This can be used as a safety mechanism to prevent a problem or misconfiguration elsewhere in the network where too many routes are flooded, preventing propagation into EIGRP. You can configure a warning threshold to create a syslog message as the number of routes redistributed approaches a percentage of the configured limit. When the maximum limit is reached, EIGRP no longer accepts additional routes.

- **Warning:** Creates a syslog warning when the maximum number of routes is exceeded. However it is important to note that EIGRP continues to process and accept routes that exceed the maximum limit.

- **Withdraw:** Starts a timer and withdraws all redistributed routes when the maximum limit is exceeded. The number of routes must be brought below the maximum before they are redistributed back into EIGRP.

Example 3-26 specifies the maximum number of prefixes to a fixed limit of 100 routes to be redistributed into EIGRP with a warning message logged when the number of routes exceeds 75 percent.

Example 3-26   *Limiting the Number of Prefixes Redistributed into EIGRP*

```
Congo# confi t
Enter configuration commands, one per line. End with CNTL/Z.
Congo(config)# router eigrp DataCenter1
Congo(config-router)# redistribute maximum-prefix 100 75
```

On IOS devices, network administrators are used to using the **show ip protocol** command to review system values for their routing protocols. Similarly in NX-OS, a concise source of information regarding the EIGRP configuration can be found using the syntax shown in Example 3-27.

Example 3-27 *EIGRP Routing Detail*

```
Congo# show ip eigrp DataCenter1 vrf default
IP-EIGRP AS 100 ID 192.168.1.1 VRF default
  Process-tag: DataCenter1
  Status: running
  Authentication mode: md5
  Authentication key-chain: nexus
  Metric weights: K1=1 K2=0 K3=1 K4=0 K5=0
  IP proto: 88 Multicast group: 224.0.0.10
  Int distance: 90 Ext distance: 170
  Max paths: 8
  Number of EIGRP interfaces: 4 (2 loopbacks)
  Number of EIGRP passive interfaces: 1
  Number of EIGRP peers: 2
  Graceful-Restart: Enabled
  Stub-Routing: Disabled
  NSF converge time limit/expiries: 120/0
  NSF route-hold time limit/expiries: 240/7
  NSF signal time limit/expiries: 20/0
  Redistributed max-prefix: Enabled
  Redistributed max-prefix mode: Not specified
  Redistributed prefix count/max: 1/100
  Redistributed max-prefix warning threshold: 75%
  Redistributed max-prefix retries attempted/allowed: 0/1
  Redistributed max-prefix timer left: 0.000000 (300s total)
```

With the output in Example 3-27, a network administrator can discern multiple key attributes about the configuration such as the number of interfaces configured in the routing protocol, how many interfaces are passive, authentication, and more. This information is extremely valuable when troubleshooting network issues.

With the modular nature of NX-OS, it is now possible to display the relevant EIGRP configuration by using the **show run eigrp** command, as demonstrated in Example 3-28.

Example 3-28 *Reviewing the Entire EIGRP Configuration*

```
Congo# show run eigrp
!Command: show running-config eigrp
!Time: Tue Sep 29 19:06:34 2009
version 4.2(2a)
```

```
feature eigrp
router eigrp DataCenter1
  autonomous-system 100
  redistribute maximum-prefix 100 75
  default-information originate route-map default-to-eigrp
  address-family ipv4 unicast
    authentication mode md5
    authentication key-chain nexus
interface Vlan10
  ip router eigrp DataCenter1
interface Vlan100
  ip router eigrp DataCenter1
  ip passive-interface eigrp DataCenter1
interface loopback0
  ip router eigrp DataCenter1
interface loopback2
  ip router eigrp DataCenter1
interface Ethernet1/18
  ip router eigrp DataCenter1
  ip summary-address eigrp DataCenter1 192.168.128.0/20
```

With the output in Example 3-28, a network administrator can quickly review the entire
EIGRP configuration and speed resolution of configuration issues. This information is
extremely valuable when troubleshooting network issues.

OSPF

OSPF is a dynamic link-state routing protocol based on the Internet Engineering Task
Force (IETF) Requests for Comments (RFC). OSPF uses the concept of areas to provide
scalability and administrative control for IP routes. Following are three versions of OSPF:

- OSPFv1, which has been replaced by OSPFv2.

- OSPFv2, which routes IPv4.

- OSPFv3, which introduces significant changes to OSPFv2 and is designed to route
  IPv6. This chapter will not cover OSPFv3.

OSPFv2 Configuration

OSPF within NX-OS is compatible with OSPF on IOS and other IETF-compliant devices
enabling a smooth integration of Nexus equipment. Configuring OSPF within NX-OS
will be similar, yet distinctly different in some aspects to traditional IOS configuration.
These differences will be highlighted throughout the section.

Enabling OSPF is a multistep process that is covered in detail. The following is a quick listing of steps to enable a basic configuration of OSPF:

Step 1.   Enable OSPF.

Step 2.   Configure the OSPF routing process.

Step 3.   Assign interfaces to the OSPF instance.

Step 4.   Configure passive-interfaces if necessary.

Step 5.   Configure network summarization.

Step 6.   Configure redistribution of other protocols if necessary.

Step 7.   Verify the OSPF operation.

The first step to configure OSPF is to enable it in global configuration mode using the **feature** command, as demonstrated in Example 3-29. With the modular nature of NX-OS, using the **feature** command loads the OSPF modular code into memory for execution. Without the feature enabled, it would not be resident in memory. Figure 3-5 illustrates the topology used in Examples 3-29 through 3-37 where OSPF is enabled and a basic configuration applied.

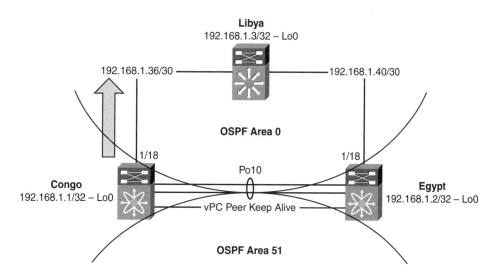

Figure 3-5   *Network Topology for OSPFv2 Configuration*

Example 3-29   *Enabling the OSPF Feature*

```
Congo# confi t
Enter configuration commands, one per line. End with CNTL/Z.
Congo(config)# feature ospf
Congo(config)# end
```

```
Congo# show run ospf
!Command: show running-config ospf
!Time: Tue Sep 29 19:52:55 2009
version 4.2(2a)
feature ospf
```

As with IOS-based OSPF configuration, the next step is to configure the OSPF routing process, as demonstrated in Example 3-30. NX-OS requires an instance tag configured for the process. Traditionally in IOS this would be a device-specific instance tag. The instance tag can be a device-specific tag, or the instance tag can be up to 20 case-sensitive alphanumeric characters. This helps document the network configuration and can simplify device identification.

Example 3-30   *Configuring OSPF with a Numeric Process ID*

```
Congo# confi t
Enter configuration commands, one per line. End with CNTL/Z.
Congo(config)# router ospf 100
Congo(config-router)# end
Congo# show run ospf
!Command: show running-config ospf
!Time: Tue Sep 29 20:04:59 2009
version 4.2(2a)
feature ospf
router ospf 100
```

Example 3-31 demonstrates how to configure an alphanumeric string for the tag.

Example 3-31   *Configuring OSPF with an Alphanumeric Process ID*

```
Congo# confi t
Enter configuration commands, one per line. End with CNTL/Z.
Congo(config)# router ospf DataCenter1
Congo(config-router)# end
Congo# show run ospf
!Command: show running-config ospf
!Time: Tue Sep 29 20:05:46 2009
version 4.2(2a)
feature ospf
router ospf DataCenter1
```

Note   The *preference* in IOS was to configure a router ID, whereas in NX-OS, it is a *requirement* for OSPF to obtain an IP address to use as a router ID, or a router ID must be configured, as demonstrated in Example 3-32. A router ID is used to uniquely identify an OSPF router on an internetwork and is included in every hello packet.

Example 3-32 *Configuring an OSPF Router ID*

```
Congo# confi t
Enter configuration commands, one per line. End with CNTL/Z.
Congo(config)# router ospf DataCenter1
Congo(config-router)# router-id 192.168.1.1
Congo(config-router)# end
Congo# show run ospf
!Command: show running-config ospf
!Time: Tue Sep 29 20:10:10 2009
version 4.2(2a)
feature ospf
router ospf DataCenter1
  router-id 192.168.1.1
```

With OSPF configured as a feature and assigned a router ID, the next step is to assign interfaces to the instance tag, as demonstrated in Example 3-33. This advertises the IP subnet in OSPF and enables the capability for neighbor adjacencies to be formed.

Note This is different from traditional IOS configuration in which you configured a **network** and **area** statement under the routing process and then, in turn, any interface on the router that fell within that network range was advertised. The approach taken in NX-OS is much more granular and enables additional levels of control over which networks are advertised.

Example 3-33 *Advertising Networks in OSPF Using a Numeric Process ID*

```
Congo# confi t
Enter configuration commands, one per line. End with CNTL/Z.
Congo(config)# int vlan 10
Congo(config-if)# ip router ospf 100 area 0
Congo(config-if)# show ip ospf int vlan 10
 Vlan10 is up, line protocol is up
    IP address 10.10.10.2/24, Process ID 100 VRF default, area 0.0.0.0
    Enabled by interface configuration
    State WAITING, Network type BROADCAST, cost 40
    Index 1, Transmit delay 1 sec, Router Priority 1
    No designated router on this network
    No backup designated router on this network
```

```
   0 Neighbors, flooding to 0, adjacent with 0
   Timer intervals: Hello 10, Dead 40, Wait 40, Retransmit 5
     Hello timer due in 00:00:05
     Wait timer due in 00:00:35
   No authentication
   Number of opaque link LSAs: 0, checksum sum 0
```

Example 3-34 demonstrates how to configure an alphanumeric process ID.

Example 3-34   *Advertising Networks in OSPF Using an Alphanumeric Process ID*

```
Congo# confi t
Enter configuration commands, one per line. End with CNTL/Z.
Congo(config)# int vlan 10
Congo(config-if)# ip router ospf DataCenter1 area 0
Congo(config-if)# show ip ospf int vlan 10
 Vlan10 is up, line protocol is up
    IP address 10.10.10.2/24, Process ID DataCenter1 VRF default, area 0.0.0.0
    Enabled by interface configuration
    State BDR, Network type BROADCAST, cost 40
    Index 1, Transmit delay 1 sec, Router Priority 1
    Designated Router ID: 192.168.1.2, address: 10.10.10.3
    Backup Designated Router ID: 192.168.1.1, address: 10.10.10.2
    1 Neighbors, flooding to 1, adjacent with 1
    Timer intervals: Hello 10, Dead 40, Wait 40, Retransmit 5
      Hello timer due in 00:00:03
    No authentication
    Number of opaque link LSAs: 0, checksum sum 0
```

Another difference between IOS and NX-OS behavior can be seen in the way OSPF shows the area number. In the preceding examples, the area designator is entered as **area 0**; however, this shows up as area 0.0.0.0 in the output. As demonstrated in Example 3-35, this behavior does not impact the actual functionality of OSPF as shown between an OSPF router running IOS and a router running NX-OS.

Example 3-35   *OSPF Areas in IOS Compared to NX-OS*

```
Libya#show ip ospf ne det
 Neighbor 192.168.1.2, interface address 192.168.1.41
    In the area 0 via interface TenGigabitEthernet1/49
    Neighbor priority is 1, State is FULL, 6 state changes
    DR is 192.168.1.42 BDR is 192.168.1.41
    Options is 0x42
    Dead timer due in 00:00:37
```

```
    Neighbor is up for 00:00:38
    Index 1/1, retransmission queue length 0, number of retransmission 1
    First 0x0(0)/0x0(0) Next 0x0(0)/0x0(0)
    Last retransmission scan length is 1, maximum is 1
    Last retransmission scan time is 0 msec, maximum is 0 msec
! The output from NX-OS shows that the area is area 0.0.0.0
Egypt# show ip ospf ne detail
 Neighbor 192.168.1.3, interface address 192.168.1.42
    Process ID DataCenter1 VRF default, in area 0.0.0.0 via interface
Ethernet1/18
    State is FULL, 5 state changes, last change 00:05:49
    Neighbor priority is 1
    DR is 192.168.1.42 BDR is 192.168.1.41
    Hello options 0x12, dbd options 0x52
    Last non-hello packet received 00:01:46
      Dead timer due in 00:00:33
```

In a data center's distribution/aggregation layer, it is common to have multiple VLAN interfaces that, in turn, need to be advertised to the network at large. By default, when OSPF is enabled on the VLAN interface, it sends and receives hellos. If a neighbor is detected, OSPF attempts to form an adjacency. Although this default behavior is wanted, there might be designs where forming multiple OSPF adjacencies between the same pair of switches is not wanted due to the potential impact of network convergence time and unnecessary duplicate next hops. In configurations such as this, you can use the **passive-interface** command, as demonstrated in Example 3-36. A passive interface accomplishes the requirement of advertising the subnet via OSPF but also instructs the OSPF process to not listen to hellos on the interfaces configured to be passive.

Example 3-36   *OSPF Passive Interface with a Numeric Process ID*

```
Congo# config t
Congo(config)# int vlan100
Congo(config-if)# ip ospf passive-interface ospf 100
Congo(config-if)# end
```

Example 3-37 demonstrates how to configure an OSPF passive interface with an alphanumeric process ID.

Example 3-37   *OSPF Passive Interface with an Alphanumeric Process ID*

```
Congo# confi t
Enter configuration commands, one per line. End with CNTL/Z.
Congo(config)# int vlan 100
Congo(config-if)# ip ospf passive-interface
```

```
Congo(config-if)# show ip ospf int vlan 100
 Vlan100 is up, line protocol is up
    IP address 10.10.100.2/24, Process ID DataCenter1 VRF default, area 0.0.0.51
    Enabled by interface configuration
    State DR, Network type BROADCAST, cost 40
    Index 2, Passive interface
Congo(config-if)# show run int vlan 100
!Command: show running-config interface Vlan100
!Time: Tue Sep 29 23:35:42 2009
version 4.2(2a)
interface Vlan100
  no shutdown
  description Server Subnet1
  ip address 10.10.100.2/24
  ip ospf passive-interface
  ip router ospf DataCenter1 area 0.0.0.51
```

OSPF Summarization

The capability of OSPF to summarize routes is restricted to area boundary routers (ABR) or autonomous system boundary routers (ASBR). When a network is summarized, a single entry with a shorter prefix (commonly called a *supernet*) is created and added to the routing table as a representation of the longer prefix subnets. In Example 3-38, a summary for 192.168.128.0 /20 is created and advertised out interface e1/18 for the network topology illustrated in Figure 3-6.

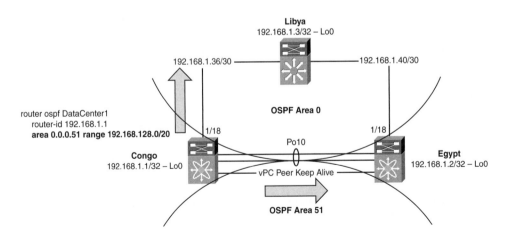

Figure 3-6 *OSPF Summarization*

Note   With this summary, the following networks are represented: 192.168.128.0/24 through 192.168.143.0/24.

Example 3-38   *OSPF Summarization with a Numeric Process ID*

```
Congo(config)# router ospf 100
Congo(config-router)# area 52 range 192.168.128.0/20
Congo(config-router)# end
```

Example 3-39 demonstrates how to configure OSPF summarization with an alphanumeric process ID.

Example 3-39   *OSPF Summarization with an Alphanumeric Process ID*

```
config t
Congo(config)# router ospf DataCenter1
Congo(config-router)# area 52 range 192.168.128.0/20
Congo(config-router)# end
```

You can see the resulting summary address in the routing table on Congo as highlighted in Example 3-40.

Example 3-40   *Verification of the OSPF Summary Address in NX-OS*

```
Congo# show ip ro
IP Route Table for VRF "default"
'*' denotes best ucast next-hop
'**' denotes best mcast next-hop
'[x/y]' denotes [preference/metric]
0.0.0.0/0, ubest/mbest: 1/0
    *via 192.168.1.38, Eth1/18, [1/0], 00:20:40, static
10.10.10.0/24, ubest/mbest: 1/0, attached
    *via 10.10.10.2, Vlan10, [0/0], 01:02:21, direct
10.10.10.1/32, ubest/mbest: 1/0
    *via 10.10.10.1, Vlan10, [0/0], 01:02:21, hsrp
10.10.10.2/32, ubest/mbest: 1/0, attached
    *via 10.10.10.2, Vlan10, [0/0], 01:02:21, local
10.10.100.0/24, ubest/mbest: 1/0, attached
    *via 10.10.100.2, Vlan100, [0/0], 01:02:21, direct
10.10.100.1/32, ubest/mbest: 1/0
    *via 10.10.100.1, Vlan100, [0/0], 01:02:21, hsrp
10.10.100.2/32, ubest/mbest: 1/0, attached
    *via 10.10.100.2, Vlan100, [0/0], 01:02:21, local
192.168.1.1/32, ubest/mbest: 2/0, attached
```

```
     *via 192.168.1.1, Lo0, [0/0], 01:02:21, local
     *via 192.168.1.1, Lo0, [0/0], 01:02:21, direct
192.168.1.2/32, ubest/mbest: 1/0
     *via 192.168.1.38, Eth1/18, [110/6], 00:12:39, ospf-DataCenter1, intra
192.168.1.3/32, ubest/mbest: 1/0
     *via 192.168.1.38, Eth1/18, [110/5], 00:12:00, ospf-DataCenter1, intra
192.168.1.32/30, ubest/mbest: 1/0, attached
     *via 192.168.1.33, Vlan5, [0/0], 01:02:21, direct
192.168.1.33/32, ubest/mbest: 1/0, attached
     *via 192.168.1.33, Vlan5, [0/0], 01:02:21, local
192.168.1.36/30, ubest/mbest: 1/0, attached
     *via 192.168.1.37, Eth1/18, [0/0], 00:20:40, direct
192.168.1.37/32, ubest/mbest: 1/0, attached
     *via 192.168.1.37, Eth1/18, [0/0], 00:20:40, local
192.168.1.40/30, ubest/mbest: 1/0
     *via 192.168.1.38, Eth1/18, [110/5], 00:18:56, ospf-DataCenter1, intra
192.168.128.0/20, ubest/mbest: 1/0
     *via Null0, [220/1], 00:03:46, ospf-DataCenter1, discard
192.168.128.1/32, ubest/mbest: 2/0, attached
     *via 192.168.128.1, Lo2, [0/0], 01:02:21, local
     *via 192.168.128.1, Lo2, [0/0], 01:02:21, direct
```

As Example 3-41 demonstrates, you also see that the summary address is propagated to
an IOS speaking OSPF neighbor, Libya, and that it is summarizing the /32 route for
Loopback2 as expected.

Example 3-41 *Verification of the OSPF Summary Address in IOS*

```
Libya# show ip ro
Codes: C - connected, S - static, R - RIP, M - mobile, B - BGP
       D - EIGRP, EX - EIGRP external, O - OSPF, IA - OSPF inter area
       N1 - OSPF NSSA external type 1, N2 - OSPF NSSA external type 2
       E1 - OSPF external type 1, E2 - OSPF external type 2
       i - IS-IS, su - IS-IS summary, L1 - IS-IS level-1, L2 - IS-IS level-2
       ia - IS-IS inter area, * - candidate default, U - per-user static route
       o - ODR, P - periodic downloaded static route
Gateway of last resort is not set
     172.26.0.0/16 is variably subnetted, 2 subnets, 2 masks
S        172.26.2.0/23 [1/0] via 172.26.32.33
C        172.26.32.32/27 is directly connected, GigabitEthernet1/48
     10.0.0.0/24 is subnetted, 2 subnets
O        10.10.10.0 [110/41] via 192.168.1.41, 00:07:23, TenGigabitEthernet1/49
                    [110/41] via 192.168.1.37, 00:07:23, TenGigabitEthernet1/50
O IA     10.10.100.0
```

```
             [110/41] via 192.168.1.41, 00:07:23, TenGigabitEthernet1/49
             [110/41] via 192.168.1.37, 00:07:23, TenGigabitEthernet1/50
        192.168.1.0/24 is variably subnetted, 5 subnets, 2 masks
C          192.168.1.40/30 is directly connected, TenGigabitEthernet1/49
C          192.168.1.36/30 is directly connected, TenGigabitEthernet1/50
O          192.168.1.1/32
             [110/2] via 192.168.1.37, 00:07:23, TenGigabitEthernet1/50
C          192.168.1.3/32 is directly connected, Loopback0
O          192.168.1.2/32
             [110/2] via 192.168.1.41, 00:07:23, TenGigabitEthernet1/49
O IA 192.168.128.0/20
             [110/2] via 192.168.1.37, 00:04:56, TenGigabitEthernet1/50
```

OSPF Stub Routing

One of OSPF's scalability features is stub routing. When OSPF stub routing is enabled, the ABR no longer floods Type 5 LSAs into the area, minimizing the routing table and SPF churn. Following are two forms of stub routing:

■ **Not-so-stubby routing:** Permits external routes.

■ **Totally stub routing:** Does not enable external routes.

Stub routing enables intra-area routes to be learned and flooded throughout the area and all external routes. A not-so-stubby-area (NSSA) behaves in much the same way as a stub area with the exception that you can configure the NSSA to allow redistribution of external routes as Type 7 LSAs. Although not commonly deployed in the data center, there are use cases for the OSPF stub. A common model for environments is where end-host systems such as servers or mainframes are capable of routing via multiple interfaces via OSPF benefit from stub routing to minimize the amount of routing table state maintained. Another example that could leverage the OSPF stub would be when a merger or acquisition is made and complex routing can be simplified with the OSPF stub.

Stub routing is configured under the main routing process, as demonstrated in Example 3-42 for the network topology illustrated in Figure 3-7.

Example 3-42 *OSPF Stub Routing Using a Numeric Process ID*

```
Congo# confi t
Enter configuration commands, one per line. End with CNTL/Z.
Congo(config)# router ospf 100
Congo(config-router)# area 51 stub
```

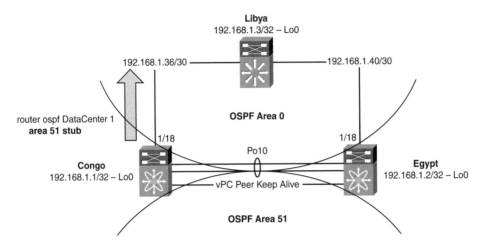

Figure 3-7   *OSPF Stub*

Example 3-43 demonstrates configuring OSPF stub routing using an alphanumeric tag.

Example 3-43   *OSPF Stub Routing Using an Alphanumeric Process ID*

```
Congo# confi t
Enter configuration commands, one per line. End with CNTL/Z.
Congo(config)# router ospf DataCenter1
Congo(config-router)# area 51 stub
```

You can identify the stub status of a neighbor from the **show ip ospf detail** command output, as demonstrated in Example 3-44.

Example 3-44   *Verification of OSPF Stub Neighbor*

```
Congo#show ip ospf
 Routing Process DataCenter1 with ID 192.168.1.1 VRF default
 Stateful High Availability enabled
 Graceful-restart is configured
   Grace period: 60 state: Inactive
   Last graceful restart exit status: None
 Supports only single TOS(TOS0) routes
 Supports opaque LSA
 This router is an area border
 Administrative distance 110
 Reference Bandwidth is 40000 Mbps
 Initial SPF schedule delay 200.000 msecs,
   minimum inter SPF delay of 1000.000 msecs,
   maximum inter SPF delay of 5000.000 msecs
 Initial LSA generation delay 0.000 msecs,
   minimum inter LSA delay of 5000.000 msecs,
```

```
     maximum inter LSA delay of 5000.000 msecs
  Minimum LSA arrival 1000.000 msec
  Maximum paths to destination 8
 Number of external LSAs 0, checksum sum 0
  Number of opaque AS LSAs 0, checksum sum 0
  Number of areas is 2, 1 normal, 1 stub, 0 nssa
  Number of active areas is 2, 1 normal, 1 stub, 0 nssa
     Area BACKBONE(0.0.0.0)
          Area has existed for 00:03:13
          Interfaces in this area: 2 Active interfaces: 2
          Passive interfaces: 0  Loopback interfaces: 0
          No authentication available
          SPF calculation has run 5 times
           Last SPF ran for 0.000502s
          Area ranges are
          Number of LSAs: 6, checksum sum 0x33cd3
    Area (0.0.0.51) (Inactive)
          Area has existed for 00:03:13
          Interfaces in this area: 1 Active interfaces: 1
          Passive interfaces: 1  Loopback interfaces: 0
          This area is a STUB area
          Generates stub default route with cost 1
          No authentication available
          SPF calculation has run 5 times
           Last SPF ran for 0.000076s
          Area ranges are
            192.168.128.0/20 Passive (Num nets: 0) Advertise
          Number of LSAs: 7, checksum sum 0x446f2
```

Example 3-45 demonstrates the syntax for configuring a totally stubby area.

Example 3-45 *Configuration of a Totally Stub Area Using a Numeric Process ID*

```
Congo# confi t
Enter configuration commands, one per line. End with CNTL/Z.
Congo(config)# router ospf 100
Congo(config-router)# area 51 stub no-summary
```

Example 3-46 demonstrates configuring a totally stubby area using an alphanumeric tag for the routing process ID.

Example 3-46 *Configuration of a Totally Stub Area Using an Alphanumeric Process ID*

```
Congo# confi t
```

```
Enter configuration commands, one per line. End with CNTL/Z.
Congo(config)# router ospf DataCenter1
Congo(config-router)# area 51 stub no-summary
```

You can identify the stub status of a neighbor from the **show ip ospf detail** command output, as demonstrated in Example 3-47. You can notice an additional line that indicates **Summarization is disabled** to reflect the totally stub area status.

Example 3-47   *Verification of Totally Stub Status on a Neighbor*

```
Congo(config-router)# show ip ospf
 Routing Process DataCenter1 with ID 192.168.1.1 VRF default
 Stateful High Availability enabled
 Graceful-restart is configured
   Grace period: 60 state: Inactive
   Last graceful restart exit status: None
 Supports only single TOS(TOS0) routes
 Supports opaque LSA
 This router is an area border
 Administrative distance 110
 Reference Bandwidth is 40000 Mbps
 Initial SPF schedule delay 200.000 msecs,
   minimum inter SPF delay of 1000.000 msecs,
   maximum inter SPF delay of 5000.000 msecs
 Initial LSA generation delay 0.000 msecs,
   minimum inter LSA delay of 5000.000 msecs,
   maximum inter LSA delay of 5000.000 msecs
 Minimum LSA arrival 1000.000 msec
Maximum paths to destination 8
Number of external LSAs 0, checksum sum 0
 Number of opaque AS LSAs 0, checksum sum 0
 Number of areas is 2, 1 normal, 1 stub, 0 nssa
 Number of active areas is 2, 1 normal, 1 stub, 0 nssa
    Area BACKBONE(0.0.0.0)
        Area has existed for 00:15:47
        Interfaces in this area: 2 Active interfaces: 2
        Passive interfaces: 0  Loopback interfaces: 0
        No authentication available
        SPF calculation has run 7 times
         Last SPF ran for 0.000484s
        Area ranges are
        Number of LSAs: 6, checksum sum 0x33ad4
    Area (0.0.0.51) (Inactive)
        Area has existed for 00:15:47
```

```
            Interfaces in this area: 1 Active interfaces: 1
            Passive interfaces: 1  Loopback interfaces: 0
            This area is a STUB area
            Generates stub default route with cost 1
            Summarization is disabled
            No authentication available
            SPF calculation has run 7 times
             Last SPF ran for 0.000074s
            Area ranges are
              192.168.128.0/20 Passive (Num nets: 0) Advertise
            Number of LSAs: 2, checksum sum 0x17359
```

Securing OSPF

You can secure OSPF routing updates by using authentication between OSPF neighbors. OSPF authentication is enabled either at the routing process level or per-interface, allowing for flexible deployment options.

Note   Interface-level authentication overrides the process-level configuration.

Configuring OSPF authentication is a multistep process. You must first define a key chain that contains attributes such as the password to be used to authenticate the connection and the lifetime of the key chain for both sending and receiving, as demonstrated in Example 3-48, for the network topology illustrated in Figure 3-8.

Example 3-48   *Configuring a Key Chain*

```
Congo(config)# key chain nexus
Congo(config-keychain)# key 1
Congo(config-keychain-key)# key-string nexus
```

Now that a key exists, the next step is to configure the routing protocol, OSPF in this case, to enable authentication and configure the interface to utilize the key chain. This step is completed under the OSPF routing process configuration. It is necessary to specify an encryption mechanism, MD5, and configure the key chain to use, as demonstrated in Example 3-49.

Example 3-49   *Configuring OSPF MD5 Authentication*

```
Congo# confi t
Enter configuration commands, one per line. End with CNTL/Z.
Congo(config)# router ospf DataCenter1
Congo(config-router)# area 0 authentication message-digest
```

```
Congo(config-router)# int vlan 10
Congo(config-if)# ip ospf authentication key-chain nexus
```

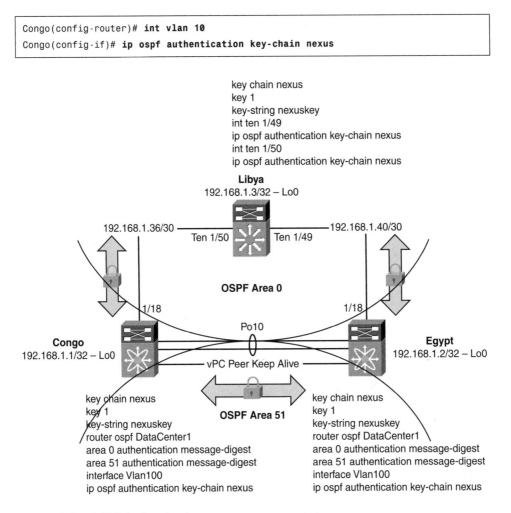

Figure 3-8 *OSPF Authentication*

The values specified under the address-family configuration are for all OSPF neighbors in the area configured for authentication, as demonstrated in Example 3-50. These values can be overridden by interface-specific configuration that can be helpful when multiple keys are used on different devices in the internetwork.

Example 3-50 *Configuration of OSPF Authentication on an SVI*

```
Congo#config t
Congo(config)# router ospf DataCenter1
Congo(config-router)# area 0 authentication message-digest
Congo(config-if)# int vlan 10
Congo(config-if)# ip ospf authentication-key 7 newkey
```

Example 3-51 demonstrates how to verify authentication configuration.

Example 3-51   *Verification of OSPF Authentication*

```
Congo# show ip ospf int vlan 10
 Vlan10 is up, line protocol is up
    IP address 10.10.10.2/24, Process ID DataCenter1 VRF default, area 0.0.0.0
    Enabled by interface configuration
    State BDR, Network type BROADCAST, cost 40
    Index 1, Transmit delay 1 sec, Router Priority 1
    Designated Router ID: 192.168.1.2, address: 10.10.10.3
    Backup Designated Router ID: 192.168.1.1, address: 10.10.10.2
    1 Neighbors, flooding to 1, adjacent with 1
    Timer intervals: Hello 10, Dead 40, Wait 40, Retransmit 5
      Hello timer due in 00:00:01
    Message-digest authentication, using keychain nexus (ready)

    Number of opaque link LSAs: 0, checksum sum 0
```

OSPF Redistribution

It is a common requirement to redistribute routes learned from other routing protocols or for directly connected interfaces into OSPF. With the exception of the default route, this is accomplished in a similar manner to traditional IOS redistribution with a few minor differences that are highlighted in the sample configurations.

Starting with the default route, the methodology to redistribute it into the routing table is similar to IOS in that the **default-information originate** command is used.

The process begins by defining a prefix list, as demonstrated in Example 3-52, which is then used by a route map referenced by the **default-information originate** command.

Figure 3-9 illustrates the topology used for Examples 3-52 through 3-64.

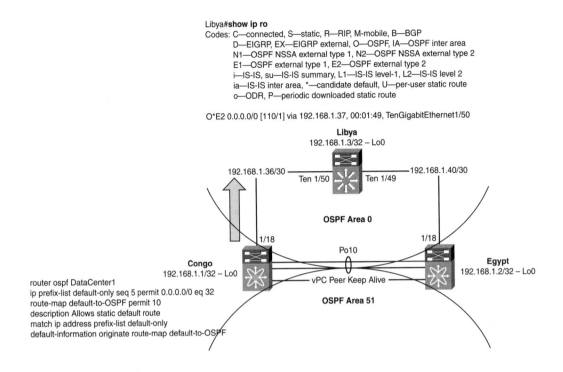

Figure 3-9 *Network Topology for OSPF Redistribution*

Example 3-52 *Defining a Prefix List for the Default Route*

```
Congo# config t
Enter configuration commands, one per line. End with CNTL/Z.
Congo(config)# ip prefix-list default-only seq 5 permit 0.0.0.0/0 eq 32
Congo(config)#
```

Next, you define a route map, called **default-to-ospf**, which uses the prefix list named **default-only**, to bring in only the 0/0 route, as demonstrated in Example 3-53.

Example 3-53 *Defining a Route Map for the Default Route*

```
Congo(config)# route-map default-to-OSPF permit 10
Congo(config-route-map)# description Allows static default route
Congo(config-route-map)# match ip address prefix-list default-only
```

Finally, configure OSPF to use the route map default-**to-ospf** as part of the **default-information originate** command, as demonstrated in Example 3-54.

Example 3-54   *Configuring OSPF to Redistribute the Default Route*

```
Congo(config)# router ospf DataCenter1
Congo(config-router)# default-information originate route-map default-to-OSPF
```

Now the default route shows up in the neighboring routers, as highlighted in Example 3-55. In NX-OS, you see the 0/0 route as an OSPF route and know that it is external because of the type-2 designation.

Example 3-55   *Verification of the Default Route in OSPF in NX-OS*

```
Egypt# show ip ro
IP Route Table for VRF "default"
'*' denotes best ucast next-hop
'**' denotes best mcast next-hop
'[x/y]' denotes [preference/metric]
0.0.0.0/0, ubest/mbest: 1/0
    *via 192.168.1.42, Eth1/18, [110/1], 00:00:19, ospf-DataCenter1, type-2
```

On an IOS router, you see the default is learned as well, but displayed a bit differently. The route is learned as an External Type 2 route, as demonstrated in Example 3-56.

Example 3-56   *Verification of the Default Route in OSPF in IOS*

```
Libya# show ip ro
Codes: C - connected, S - static, R - RIP, M - mobile, B - BGP
       D - EIGRP, EX - EIGRP external, O - OSPF, IA - OSPF inter area
       N1 - OSPF NSSA external type 1, N2 - OSPF NSSA external type 2
       E1 - OSPF external type 1, E2 - OSPF external type 2
       i - IS-IS, su - IS-IS summary, L1 - IS-IS level-1, L2 - IS-IS level-2
       ia - IS-IS inter area, * - candidate default, U - per-user static route
       o - ODR, P - periodic downloaded static route
Gateway of last resort is 192.168.1.37 to network 0.0.0.0

     172.26.0.0/16 is variably subnetted, 2 subnets, 2 masks
S       172.26.2.0/23 [1/0] via 172.26.32.33
C       172.26.32.32/27 is directly connected, GigabitEthernet1/48
     10.0.0.0/24 is subnetted, 2 subnets
O       10.10.10.0 [110/41] via 192.168.1.41, 00:01:49, TenGigabitEthernet1/49
                   [110/41] via 192.168.1.37, 00:01:49, TenGigabitEthernet1/50
O IA    10.10.100.0
           [110/41] via 192.168.1.41, 00:01:49, TenGigabitEthernet1/49
           [110/41] via 192.168.1.37, 00:01:49, TenGigabitEthernet1/50
     192.168.1.0/24 is variably subnetted, 4 subnets, 2 masks
C       192.168.1.40/30 is directly connected, TenGigabitEthernet1/49
C       192.168.1.36/30 is directly connected, TenGigabitEthernet1/50
```

```
C       192.168.1.3/32 is directly connected, Loopback0
O       192.168.1.2/32
            [110/2] via 192.168.1.41, 00:01:49, TenGigabitEthernet1/49
O*E2 0.0.0.0/0 [110/1] via 192.168.1.37, 00:01:49, TenGigabitEthernet1/50
```

Redistribution of routes other than the default follows a similar sequence of steps in that you create a prefix list, use it in a route map, and then enable the redistribution.

Note   NX-OS does not have the capability to do "wide-open" or "uncontrolled" redistribution. NX-OS enforces the use of a route map to define routes that should be redistributed.

NX-OS does not require a default metric to be specified on the **redistribution** command or under the routing protocol configuration as it sets the default metric to 0. This can be changed by using the **default-metric** command that applies a metric to any redistributed routes where a metric is not applied on the **redistribution** command as demonstrated here:

```
router ospf DataCenter1
    default-metric 100
```

The process begins by defining a prefix list, as demonstrated in Example 3-57, which is then used by a route map referenced by the **default-information originate** command.

Example 3-57   *Defining a Prefix List for Redistribution*

```
Egypt# config t
Enter configuration commands, one per line. End with CNTL/Z.
Egypt(config)# ip prefix-list connected-interfaces seq 15 permit 10.100.0.0/16 ge
17
Egypt(config)#
```

Next, define a route map, called **connected-to-OSPF**, which uses the prefix list named **connected-interfaces**, to bring in only the 10.100.0.0/16 or longer routes, as demonstrated in Example 3-58.

Example 3-58   *Defining a Route Map for Redistribution*

```
Egypt(config)# route-map connected-to-OSPF permit 10
Egypt(config-route-map)# description allows local interfaces
Egypt(config-route-map)# match ip address prefix-list connected-interfaces
```

Finally, configure OSPF to use the route map **connected-to-OSPF** as part of the **redistribute direct** command, as demonstrated in Example 3-59.

Example 3-59 *Configuring Redistribution into OSPF*

```
Egypt(config)# router ospf DataCenter1
Egypt(config-router)# redistribute direct route-map connected-to-OSPF
```

Now the new routes show up in the neighboring routers, as highlighted in Example 3-60. In NX-OS, you see the 10.100.0.0/16 routes as OSPF routes and know that they are external because of the type-2 designation.

Example 3-60 *Verification of the Redistributed Routes in NX-OS*

```
Congo# show ip route ospf
IP Route Table for VRF "default"
'*' denotes best ucast next-hop
'**' denotes best mcast next-hop
'[x/y]' denotes [preference/metric]
10.100.100.0/24, ubest/mbest: 1/0
    *via 192.168.1.38, Eth1/18, [110/20], 00:26:53, ospf-DataCenter1, type-2
10.100.200.0/24, ubest/mbest: 1/0
    *via 192.168.1.38, Eth1/18, [110/20], 00:26:53, ospf-DataCenter1, type-2
10.100.201.0/24, ubest/mbest: 1/0
    *via 192.168.1.38, Eth1/18, [110/20], 00:26:53, ospf-DataCenter1, type-2
10.100.202.0/24, ubest/mbest: 1/0
    *via 192.168.1.38, Eth1/18, [110/20], 00:26:53, ospf-DataCenter1, type-2
192.168.1.2/32, ubest/mbest: 1/0
    *via 192.168.1.38, Eth1/18, [110/6], 00:26:53, ospf-DataCenter1, intra
192.168.1.3/32, ubest/mbest: 1/0
    *via 192.168.1.38, Eth1/18, [110/5], 15:24:13, ospf-DataCenter1, intra
192.168.1.40/30, ubest/mbest: 1/0
    *via 192.168.1.38, Eth1/18, [110/5], 00:27:01, ospf-DataCenter1, intra
```

On an IOS router, you see the 10.100.0.0/16 routes are learned as well but displayed a bit differently. The routes are learned as an External Type 2 route, as demonstrated in Example 3-61.

Example 3-61 *Verification of the Redistributed Routes in IOS*

```
Libya# show ip ro
Codes: C - connected, S - static, R - RIP, M - mobile, B - BGP
       D - EIGRP, EX - EIGRP external, O - OSPF, IA - OSPF inter area
       N1 - OSPF NSSA external type 1, N2 - OSPF NSSA external type 2
       E1 - OSPF external type 1, E2 - OSPF external type 2
       i - IS-IS, su - IS-IS summary, L1 - IS-IS level-1, L2 - IS-IS level-2
       ia - IS-IS inter area, * - candidate default, U - per-user static route
       o - ODR, P - periodic downloaded static route
```

```
Gateway of last resort is 192.168.1.37 to network 0.0.0.0
     172.26.0.0/16 is variably subnetted, 2 subnets, 2 masks
S        172.26.2.0/23 [1/0] via 172.26.32.33
C        172.26.32.32/27 is directly connected, GigabitEthernet1/48
     10.0.0.0/24 is subnetted, 6 subnets
O E2     10.100.100.0
             [110/20] via 192.168.1.41, 00:16:20, TenGigabitEthernet1/49
O        10.10.10.0 [110/41] via 192.168.1.41, 00:16:20, TenGigabitEthernet1/49
                        [110/41] via 192.168.1.37, 00:16:20, TenGigabitEthernet1/50
O IA     10.10.100.0
             [110/41] via 192.168.1.41, 00:16:20, TenGigabitEthernet1/49
             [110/41] via 192.168.1.37, 00:16:20, TenGigabitEthernet1/50
O E2     10.100.202.0
             [110/20] via 192.168.1.41, 00:16:20, TenGigabitEthernet1/49
O E2     10.100.200.0
             [110/20] via 192.168.1.41, 00:16:20, TenGigabitEthernet1/49
O E2     10.100.201.0
             [110/20] via 192.168.1.41, 00:16:20, TenGigabitEthernet1/49
     192.168.1.0/24 is variably subnetted, 5 subnets, 2 masks
C        192.168.1.40/30 is directly connected, TenGigabitEthernet1/49
O IA     192.168.1.32/30
             [110/41] via 192.168.1.41, 00:16:20, TenGigabitEthernet1/49
             [110/41] via 192.168.1.37, 00:16:20, TenGigabitEthernet1/50
C        192.168.1.36/30 is directly connected, TenGigabitEthernet1/50
C        192.168.1.3/32 is directly connected, Loopback0
O        192.168.1.2/32
             [110/2] via 192.168.1.41, 00:16:20, TenGigabitEthernet1/49
O*E2 0.0.0.0/0 [110/1] via 192.168.1.37, 00:16:20, TenGigabitEthernet1/50
```

NX-OS also has a feature that enables network administrators to control the number of routes redistributed into OSPF. Following are three options to consider based on the specific requirement of the network:

- **Fixed limit:** Allows network administrators to specify a number of routes between 1 and 65,535. This can be used as a safety mechanism to prevent a problem or misconfiguration elsewhere in the network where too many routes are flooded and prevent propagation into OSPF. A warning threshold can be configured to create a syslog message as the number of routes redistributed approaches a percentage of the configured limit. When the maximum limit is reached, OSPF no longer accepts additional routes.

- **Warning:** Creates a syslog warning when the maximum number of routes is exceeded. However it is important to note that OSPF continues to process and accept routes that exceed the maximum limit.

■ **Withdraw:** Starts a timer and withdraws all redistributed routes when the maximum limit is exceeded. The number of routes must be brought below the maximum before they are redistributed back into OSPF.

In Example 3-62, a fixed limit of 100 routes is specified to be redistributed into OSPF with a warning message logged when the number of routes exceeds 75 percent.

Example 3-62 *Limiting the Number of Redistributed Routes in OSPF*

```
Congo# confi t
Enter configuration commands, one per line. End with CNTL/Z.
Congo(config)# router ospf DataCenter1
Congo(config-router)# redistribute maximum-prefix 100 75
```

On IOS devices, network administrators are accustomed to using the **show ip protocol** command to review system values for their routing protocols. Similarly in NX-OS, a concise source of information for the OSPF configuration can be found, as demonstrated in Example 3-63. This information is extremely valuable when troubleshooting network issues.

Example 3-63 *Reviewing Detailed OSPF Information*

```
Congo# show ip ospf
 Routing Process DataCenter1 with ID 192.168.1.1 VRF default
 Stateful High Availability enabled
 Graceful-restart is configured
   Grace period: 60 state: Inactive
   Last graceful restart exit status: None
 Supports only single TOS(TOS0) routes
 Supports opaque LSA
 This router is an area border and autonomous system boundary.
 Administrative distance 110
 Reference Bandwidth is 40000 Mbps
 Initial SPF schedule delay 200.000 msecs,
   minimum inter SPF delay of 1000.000 msecs,
   maximum inter SPF delay of 5000.000 msecs
Initial LSA generation delay 0.000 msecs,
   minimum inter LSA delay of 5000.000 msecs,
   maximum inter LSA delay of 5000.000 msecs
 Minimum LSA arrival 1000.000 msec
 Maximum paths to destination 8
 Number of external LSAs 1, checksum sum 0xd193
 Number of opaque AS LSAs 0, checksum sum 0
 Number of areas is 2, 1 normal, 1 stub, 0 nssa
Number of active areas is 2, 1 normal, 1 stub, 0 nssa
```

```
Area BACKBONE(0.0.0.0)
      Area has existed for 00:49:34
      Interfaces in this area: 2 Active interfaces: 2
      Passive interfaces: 0  Loopback interfaces: 0
      Message-digest authentication
      SPF calculation has run 15 times
       Last SPF ran for 0.000501s
      Area ranges are
      Number of LSAs: 6, checksum sum 0x31cde
 Area (0.0.0.51) (Inactive)
      Area has existed for 00:49:34
      Interfaces in this area: 1 Active interfaces: 1
      Passive interfaces: 1  Loopback interfaces: 0
      This area is a STUB area
      Generates stub default route with cost 1
      Summarization is disabled
      No authentication available
      SPF calculation has run 15 times
       Last SPF ran for 0.000074s
      Area ranges are
        192.168.128.0/20 Passive (Num nets: 0) Advertise
      Number of LSAs: 2, checksum sum 0x16f5b
```

With the modular nature of NX-OS, you can now display the relevant OSPF configuration by using the **show run ospf** command, as demonstrated in Example 3-64.

Example 3-64   *Viewing the OSPF-Only Configuration*

```
Congo# show run ospf
!Command: show running-config ospf
!Time: Wed Sep 30 01:25:45 2009
version 4.2(2a)
feature ospf
router ospf DataCenter1
  router-id 192.168.1.1
  area 0.0.0.51 stub no-summary
  default-information originate route-map default-to-OSPF
  area 0.0.0.51 range 192.168.128.0/20
  redistribute maximum-prefix 100 75
  area 0.0.0.0 authentication message-digest
  default-metric 100
interface Vlan10
  ip ospf authentication key-chain nexus
  ip router ospf DataCenter1 area 0.0.0.0
```

```
interface Vlan100
  ip ospf passive-interface
  ip router ospf DataCenter1 area 0.0.0.51
interface loopback0
  ip router ospf DataCenter area 0.0.0.0
interface loopback2
  ip router ospf DataCenter area 0.0.0.51
interface Ethernet1/18
  ip ospf network point-to-point
  ip router ospf DataCenter1 area 0.0.0.0
```

With the output in Example 3-64, a network administrator can quickly review the entire OSPF configuration and speed resolution of configuration issues. This information is extremely valuable when troubleshooting network issues.

BGP

The Border Gateway Protocol (BGP) is an Internet Engineering Task Force (IETF) standard protocol that traditionally has been used as the routing protocol of the Internet. BGP has attributes such as timers and administrative routing controls designed to meet the scale of large networks. Many network administrators choose to leverage BGP for scaling challenges as their IP networks grow. Another common option is for mergers and acquisitions in which disparate networks are required to interconnect and share routing information but lack a common administrative control.

BGP uses the concept of autonomous systems (AS) as a delineation between networks. An AS is a collection of routers under a common administrative control. Neighbor relationships are manually configured between autonomous systems to exchange routing tables and apply routing policy.

BGP Configuration

BGP within NX-OS is compatible with BGP on IOS and other IETF-compliant devices enabling a smooth integration of Nexus equipment. Configuring BGP within NX-OS will be similar, yet distinctly different in some aspects to traditional IOS configuration. These differences will be highlighted throughout the section.

Enabling BPG is a multistep process covered in detail. The following is a quick listing of steps to enable a basic configuration of BGP:

Step 1.   Enable BGP.

Step 2.   Configure BGP routing process with the AS identification.

Step 3.   Configure address families.

Step 4.   Configure BGP neighbors.

Step 5.   Configure network routing policy.

Step 6.   Configure redistribution of other protocols if necessary.

Step 7.   Verify BGP operation.

The first step to configure BGP is to enable it on global configuration mode using the **feature** command, as demonstrated in Example 3-65. With the modular nature of NX-OS, using the **feature** command loads the BGP modular code into memory for execution. Without the feature enabled, it would not be resident in memory. Figure 3-10 illustrates the topology used for Examples 3-65 through 3-87.

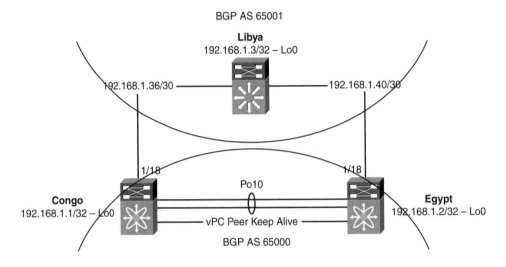

Figure 3-10   *Network Topology for Basic BGP Configuration*

Example 3-65   *Enabling the BGP Feature*

```
Congo# confi t
Enter configuration commands, one per line. End with CNTL/Z.
Congo(config)# feature bgp
Congo(config)# end
Congo# show run bgp
!Command: show running-config bgp
!Time: Wed Sep 30 18:47:51 2009
version 4.2(2a)
feature bgp
```

Similar to IOS-based BGP configuration, the next step is to configure the BGP routing process with the AS identification, as demonstrated in Example 3-66.

Note NX-OS does not support the use of an alphanumeric tag for BGP like it does for IGPs such as EIGRP and OSPF.

Example 3-66 *Configuring the BGP Process*

```
Congo# config t
Enter configuration commands, one per line. End with CNTL/Z.
Congo(config)# router bgp 65000
Congo# show run bgp
!Command: show running-config bgp
!Time: Wed Sep 30 18:51:45 2009
version 4.2(2a)
feature bgp
router bgp 65000
```

NX-OS also supports the capability to use 4-byte AS numbers as of NX-OS release 4.2(1). This 4-byte support can be configured using either plain text notation or in dotted-decimal notation. This is important for companies with newer Internet AS number registration that can utilize the new 4-byte AS assignments.

Example 3-67 demonstrates the use of plain text notation.

Example 3-67 *Configuring BGP with 4-Byte AS Numbers Using Plain Text*

```
Congo# config t
Congo(config)# router bgp 4200000088
Congo# show run bgp
!Command: show running-config bgp
!Time: Sun Oct 11 15:32:42 2009
version 4.2(2a)
feature bgp
router bgp 4200000088
```

Example 3-68 demonstrates the use of dotted-decimal notation.

Example 3-68 *Configuring BGP with 4-Byte AS Numbers Using Dotted-Decimal Notation*

```
Congo# config t
Congo(config)# router bgp 65000.65088
Congo# show run bgp
!Command: show running-config bgp
!Time: Sun Oct 11 15:31:05 2009
version 4.2(2a)
```

```
feature bgp
router bgp 65000.65088
```

In IOS, it was *preferred* to configure a router ID, whereas in NX-OS it is a *requirement* that BGP can obtain an IP address to use as a router ID or one must be configured, as demonstrated in Example 3-69.

Example 3-69 *Configuring the BGP Router ID*

```
Congo# confi t
Enter configuration commands, one per line. End with CNTL/Z.
Congo(config)# router bgp 65000
Congo(config-router)# router-id 192.168.1.1
Congo# show run bgp
!Command: show running-config bgp
!Time: Wed Sep 30 19:17:36 2009
version 4.2(2a)
feature bgp
router bgp 65000
  router-id 192.168.1.1
```

With BGP configured as a feature and assigned a router ID, the next step is to configure address families, as demonstrated in Example 3-70. Address families are subcomponents of the global BGP configuration, and while not mandatory for basic BGP configurations, address families are required for use with advanced features such as route redistribution, load balancing, and route aggregation.

Example 3-70 *Configuring BGP Address Families*

```
Congo# confi t
Enter configuration commands, one per line. End with CNTL/Z.
Congo(config)# router bgp 65000
Congo(config-router)# address-family ipv4 unicast
Congo# show run bgp
!Command: show running-config bgp
!Time: Wed Sep 30 20:15:12 2009
version 4.2(2a)
feature bgp
router bgp 65000
  router-id 192.168.1.1
  address-family ipv4 unicast
```

BGP Neighbors

After the address family is configured, the next step would be to configure the iBGP and eBGP peers using the **neighbor** commands. iBGP is used between BGP speakers in the same autonomous system where eBGP is used between BGP speakers in different autonomous systems. Example 3-71 notes the update source as Loopback 0 to make peering simpler by using the loopback 0 IP address as the source IP for a peering session.

Example 3-71 *Configuring an iBGP Neighbor*

```
Congo# confi t
Enter configuration commands, one per line. End with CNTL/Z.
Congo(config)# router bgp 65000
Congo(config-router-af)# neighbor 192.168.1.2 remote-as 65000
Congo(config-router-neighbor)# description Egypt
Congo(config-router-neighbor)# update-source loopback0
Congo(config-router-neighbor)# address-family ipv4 unicast
Congo(config-router-neighbor-af)# end
```

You can verify the peering session by looking at the output from the **show ip bgp neighbor 192.168.1.2** command, as demonstrated in Example 3-72.

Example 3-72 *Verification of an iBGP Neighbor*

```
Congo# show ip bgp neighbors 192.168.1.2
BGP neighbor is 192.168.1.2,  remote AS 65000, ibgp link,  Peer index 1
  Description: Egypt
  BGP version 4, remote router ID 192.168.1.2
  BGP state = Established, up for 4d14h
  Using loopback0 as update source for this peer
  Last read 00:00:31, hold time = 180, keepalive interval is 60 seconds
  Last written 00:00:32, keepalive timer expiry due 00:00:27
  Received 6610 messages, 0 notifications, 0 bytes in queue
  Sent 6628 messages, 0 notifications, 0 bytes in queue
  Connections established 1, dropped 0
  Last reset by us 4d14h, due to session closed
  Last reset by peer never, due to process restart

  Neighbor capabilities:
  Dynamic capability: advertised (mp, refresh, gr) received (mp, refresh, gr)
  Dynamic capability (old): advertised received
  Route refresh capability (new): advertised received
  Route refresh capability (old): advertised received
  4-Byte AS capability: advertised received
  Address family IPv4 Unicast: advertised received
```

```
Graceful Restart capability: advertised received
Graceful Restart Parameters:
Address families advertised to peer:
  IPv4 Unicast
Address families received from peer:
  IPv4 Unicast
Forwarding state preserved by peer for:
Restart time advertised to peer: 120 seconds
Stale time for routes advertised by peer: 300 seconds
Restart time advertised by peer: 120 seconds
Message statistics:
                             Sent               Rcvd
Opens:                        19                  1
Notifications:                 0                  0
Updates:                       1                  1
Keepalives:                 6608               6608
Route Refresh:                 0                  0
Capability:                    0                  0
Total:                      6628               6610
Total bytes:              125556             125556
Bytes in queue:                0                  0
For address family: IPv4 Unicast
BGP table version 3, neighbor version 3
0 accepted paths consume 0 bytes of memory
0 sent paths
Third-party Nexthop will not be computed.
Local host: 192.168.1.1, Local port: 58042
Foreign host: 192.168.1.2, Foreign port: 179
fd = 37
```

Establishing an external BGP (eBGP) session is similar to an internal BGP (iBGP) session with the primary difference the remote-as number used. For an iBGP session, the AS number is the same as the AS number used on the BGP process, whereas with eBGP it is a different AS number. Example 3-73 demonstrates the configuration of an eBGP session.

Example 3-73 *Configuring an eBGP Neighbor*

```
Congo# confi t
Enter configuration commands, one per line. End with CNTL/Z.
Congo(config)# router bgp 65000
Congo(config-router)#
Congo(config-router)# neighbor 192.168.1.38 remote-as 65001
Congo(config-router-neighbor)# description Libya
Congo(config-router-neighbor)# address-family ipv4 unicast
Congo(config-router-neighbor-af)# end
```

You can verify the peering session by looking at the output from **show ip bgp neighbor 192.168.1.38**, as demonstrated in Example 3-74.

Example 3-74 *Verification of an eBGP Neighbor*

```
Congo# show ip bgp neighbor 192.168.1.38
BGP neighbor is 192.168.1.38,  remote AS 65001, ebgp link,  Peer index 2
  Description: Libya
  BGP version 4, remote router ID 192.168.1.3
  BGP state = Established, up for 00:01:13
  Peer is directly attached, interface Ethernet1/18
  Last read 00:00:11, hold time = 180, keepalive interval is 60 seconds
  Last written 00:00:12, keepalive timer expiry due 00:00:47
  Received 4 messages, 0 notifications, 0 bytes in queue
  Sent 5 messages, 0 notifications, 0 bytes in queue
  Connections established 1, dropped 0
  Last reset by us never, due to process restart
  Last reset by peer never, due to process restart
  Neighbor capabilities:
  Dynamic capability: advertised (mp, refresh, gr)
  Dynamic capability (old): advertised
  Route refresh capability (new): advertised received
  Route refresh capability (old): advertised received
  4-Byte AS capability: advertised
  Address family IPv4 Unicast: advertised received
  Graceful Restart capability: advertised
  Graceful Restart Parameters:
  Address families advertised to peer:
    IPv4 Unicast
  Address families received from peer:
  Forwarding state preserved by peer for:
  Restart time advertised to peer: 120 seconds
  Stale time for routes advertised by peer: 300 seconds
  Message statistics:
                          Sent               Rcvd
  Opens:                    1                  1
  Notifications:            0                  0
  Updates:                  1                  0
  Keepalives:               3                  3
  Route Refresh:            0                  0
  Capability:               0                  0
  Total:                    5                  4
```

```
Total bytes:                    61              38
Bytes in queue:                 0               0
For address family: IPv4 Unicast
BGP table version 4, neighbor version 4
0 accepted paths consume 0 bytes of memory
0 sent paths
Local host: 192.168.1.37, Local port: 179
Foreign host: 192.168.1.38, Foreign port: 38354
fd = 42
```

Securing BGP

You can secure BGP routing updates through authentication between BGP neighbors. BGP authentication is enabled on a per-neighbor basis and uses MD5 hashing.

Note   The BGP password *must* match on both BGP peers to establish a session. This is particularly important when peering with external organizations, such as an ISP in which the peering router might not be under your direct control.

Configuring BGP authentication simply requires the password to be enabled on the neighbor, as shown in Example 3-75.

Example 3-75   *Configuring BGP Authentication*

```
Congo# confi t
Enter configuration commands, one per line. End with CNTL/Z.
Congo(config)# router bgp 65000
Congo(config-router)# neighbor 192.168.1.38
Congo(config-router-neighbor)# password bgppassword
Congo(config-router-neighbor)# end
```

You can verify the authentication on the peer session by using the **show ip bgp neighbor** command, as demonstrated in Example 3-76.

Example 3-76   *Verification of BGP Authentication*

```
Congo# show ip bgp neighbor 192.168.1.38
BGP neighbor is 192.168.1.38,  remote AS 65001, ebgp link,  Peer index 2
  Description: Libya
  BGP version 4, remote router ID 192.168.1.3
  BGP state = Established, up for 00:05:16
  Peer is directly attached, interface Ethernet1/18
  TCP MD5 authentication is enabled
```

```
Last read 00:00:14, hold time = 180, keepalive interval is 60 seconds
Last written 00:00:15, keepalive timer expiry due 00:00:44
Received 31 messages, 0 notifications, 0 bytes in queue
Sent 37 messages, 1 notifications, 0 bytes in queue
Connections established 2, dropped 1
Last reset by us 00:05:36, due to holdtimer expired error
Last reset by peer never, due to process restart
Neighbor capabilities:
Dynamic capability: advertised (mp, refresh, gr)
Dynamic capability (old): advertised
Route refresh capability (new): advertised received
Route refresh capability (old): advertised received
4-Byte AS capability: advertised
Address family IPv4 Unicast: advertised received
Graceful Restart capability: advertised
Graceful Restart Parameters:
Address families advertised to peer:
  IPv4 Unicast
Address families received from peer:
Forwarding state preserved by peer for:
Restart time advertised to peer: 120 seconds
Stale time for routes advertised by peer: 300 seconds
Message statistics:
                         Sent               Rcvd
Opens:                     2                  2
Notifications:             1                  0
Updates:                   2                  0
Keepalives:               32                 29
Route Refresh:             0                  0
Capability:                0                  0
Total:                    37                 31
Total bytes:             637                513
Bytes in queue:            0                  0
For address family: IPv4 Unicast
BGP table version 6, neighbor version 6
0 accepted paths consume 0 bytes of memory
0 sent paths
Local host: 192.168.1.37, Local port: 60095
Foreign host: 192.168.1.38, Foreign port: 179
fd = 42
```

BGP Peer Templates

When configuring BGP, it is common to find that many of the commands required to establish a baseline for consistent network policy are repetitive. NX-OS features a capability for creating BGP peering templates that are convenient time-saving tools. These templates enable the network administrator to configure attributes that will be used among multiple peers once and apply them when a new peer is configured.

BGP peer templates support multiple attributes including multihop Time-To-Live (TTL), timers, next-hop self, password, remote-as, and maximum prefix. In Example 3-77, a BGP peer template named iBGP-Peers is created and applied to an iBGP session.

> **Note**   You can find a full listing of template options on Cisco.com:
> http://www.cisco.com/en/US/docs/switches/datacenter/sw/4_2/nx-os/unicast/command/reference/l3_cmds_t.html#wp1547869.

Example 3-77   *Configuring BGP Peer Templates*

```
Egypt# confi t
Enter configuration commands, one per line. End with CNTL/Z.
Egypt(config)# router bgp 65000
Egypt(config-router)# template peer iBGP-Peers
Egypt(config-router-neighbor)# remote-as 65000
Egypt(config-router-neighbor)# password 3 cd87a249cfe3fb9aefc4f7f321a18044
Egypt(config-router-neighbor)# update-source loopback0
Egypt(config-router-neighbor)# timers 45 120
Egypt(config-router-neighbor)# neighbor 192.168.1.1
Egypt(config-router-neighbor)# inherit peer iBGP-Peers
Egypt(config-router-neighbor)# end
```

You can verify the peer using the peer template, as demonstrated in Example 3-78.

Example 3-78   *Verification of BGP Peer Using the Peer Template*

```
Egypt# show ip bgp neighbor 192.168.1.1
BGP neighbor is 192.168.1.1,  remote AS 65000, ibgp link,  Peer index 1
  Inherits peer configuration from peer-template iBGP-Peers
  Description: Congo
  BGP version 4, remote router ID 192.168.1.1
  BGP state = Established, up for 00:02:05
  Using loopback0 as update source for this peer
  TCP MD5 authentication is enabled
  Last read 00:00:04, hold time = 120, keepalive interval is 45 seconds
  Last written 00:00:34, keepalive timer expiry due 00:00:10
  Received 6672 messages, 1 notifications, 0 bytes in queue
```

```
   Sent 6689 messages, 1 notifications, 0 bytes in queue
   Connections established 3, dropped 2
   Last reset by us 00:02:23, due to session cleared
   Last reset by peer 00:24:09, due to administratively shutdown
   Neighbor capabilities:
   Dynamic capability: advertised (mp, refresh, gr) received (mp, refresh, gr)
   Dynamic capability (old): advertised received
   Route refresh capability (new): advertised received
   Route refresh capability (old): advertised received
   4-Byte AS capability: advertised received
   Address family IPv4 Unicast: advertised received
   Graceful Restart capability: advertised received
   Graceful Restart Parameters:
   Address families advertised to peer:
     IPv4 Unicast
   Address families received from peer:
     IPv4 Unicast
   Forwarding state preserved by peer for:
     IPv4 Unicast
   Restart time advertised to peer: 120 seconds
   Stale time for routes advertised by peer: 300 seconds
   Restart time advertised by peer: 120 seconds
   Message statistics:
                            Sent              Rcvd
   Opens:                    21                 3
   Notifications:             1                 1
   Updates:                   3                 3
   Keepalives:             6664              6665
   Route Refresh:             0                 0
   Capability:                0                 0
   Total:                  6689              6672
   Total bytes:          126649            126668
   Bytes in queue:            0                 0
   For address family: IPv4 Unicast
   BGP table version 8, neighbor version 8
   0 accepted paths consume 0 bytes of memory
   0 sent paths
   Third-party Nexthop will not be computed.
   Local host: 192.168.1.2, Local port: 54942
   Foreign host: 192.168.1.1, Foreign port: 179
   fd = 42
```

Advertising BGP Networks

When BGP neighbor relationships are defined, secured, and simplified using templates, the next step is to advertise networks. The NX-OS implementation of BGP is flexible and enables entries to be added to the routing table through multiple mechanisms. The two most common are **network** statements and redistribution from an IGP.

In Example 3-79, the network 10.100.100.0/24 is advertised via BGP to Libya using the **network** command.

Example 3-79 *Advertising Networks in BGP*

```
Congo# confi t
Enter configuration commands, one per line. End with CNTL/Z.
Congo(config)# router bgp 65000
Congo(config-router)# address-family ipv4 unicast
Congo(config-router-af)# network 10.100.100.0 mask 255.255.255.0
```

On the IOS router Libya, the route shows as an eBGP route with an administrative distance of 20, as demonstrated in Example 3-80.

Example 3-80 *Verification of Advertised Network in IOS*

```
Libya# show ip route
Codes: C - connected, S - static, R - RIP, M - mobile, B - BGP
       D - EIGRP, EX - EIGRP external, O - OSPF, IA - OSPF inter area
       N1 - OSPF NSSA external type 1, N2 - OSPF NSSA external type 2
       E1 - OSPF external type 1, E2 - OSPF external type 2
       i - IS-IS, su - IS-IS summary, L1 - IS-IS level-1, L2 - IS-IS level-2
       ia - IS-IS inter area, * - candidate default, U - per-user static route
       o - ODR, P - periodic downloaded static route
Gateway of last resort is not set
     172.26.0.0/16 is variably subnetted, 2 subnets, 2 masks
S       172.26.2.0/23 [1/0] via 172.26.32.33
C       172.26.32.32/27 is directly connected, GigabitEthernet1/48
C    192.168.200.0/24 is directly connected, Loopback10
C    192.168.201.0/24 is directly connected, Loopback11
     10.0.0.0/24 is subnetted, 1 subnets
B       10.100.100.0 [20/0] via 192.168.1.37, 00:10:20
     192.168.1.0/24 is variably subnetted, 3 subnets, 2 masks
C       192.168.1.40/30 is directly connected, TenGigabitEthernet1/49
C       192.168.1.36/30 is directly connected, TenGigabitEthernet1/50
C       192.168.1.3/32 is directly connected, Loopback0
```

Advertising routes via the **network** command might not be desirable for all situations or designs. With this in mind, NX-OS supports the redistribution of routes into BGP from other protocols or topologies such as directly connected or static routes.

In Example 3-81, the OSPF process DataCenter1 will be redistributed into BGP. Any subnets that are in the 192.168.0.0/16 range and the 10.100.0.0/16 range will be advertised into BGP.

> **Note**   By default, a prefix list is designed to make an exact match. With the addition of the **le** (less than or equal to) argument, you can instruct the prefix list to match subnets less than or equal to 192.168.0.0/16 and 10.100.0.0/16.

The process begins by defining a prefix list to define subnets you either want to permit or deny into BGP.

Example 3-81   *Defining a Prefix List for BGP Redistribution*

```
Congo(config)# ip prefix-list OSPFtoBGP description Defines routes from OSPF to be
redistributed into BGP
Congo(config)# ip prefix-list OSPFtoBGP permit 192.168.0.0/16 le 32
Congo(config)# ip prefix-list OSPFtoBGP permit 10.100.0.0/16 le 32
```

Next, you define a route map, called **OSPFtoBGP**, which uses the prefix list named **OSPFtoBGP**, to only bring in the 192.168.0.0/16 10.100.0.0/16 or longer routes, as demonstrated in Example 3-82.

Example 3-82   *Defining a Route Map for BGP Redistribution*

```
Congo(config)# route-map OSPFtoBGP permit
Congo(config-route-map)# match ip address prefix-list OSPFtoBGP
```

Finally, you configure BGP to use the route map **OSPFtoBGP** as part of the **redistribute bgp** command, as demonstrated in Example 3-83.

Example 3-83   *Configuring BGP Redistribution*

```
Congo(config-route-map)# router bgp 65000
Congo(config-router)# address-family ipv4 unicast
Congo(config-router-af)# redistribute ospf DataCenter1 route-map OSPFtoBGP
```

On a neighboring IOS router, the subnets have been added to the routing table via BGP and display an administrative distance of 20, which is one of the metrics used by the router to determine a route's viability in the routing table, as Example 3-84 shows.

Example 3-84 *Verification of Redistribution in IOS*

```
Libya# show ip route
Codes: C - connected, S - static, R - RIP, M - mobile, B - BGP
       D - EIGRP, EX - EIGRP external, O - OSPF, IA - OSPF inter area
       N1 - OSPF NSSA external type 1, N2 - OSPF NSSA external type 2
       E1 - OSPF external type 1, E2 - OSPF external type 2
       i - IS-IS, su - IS-IS summary, L1 - IS-IS level-1, L2 - IS-IS level-2
       ia - IS-IS inter area, * - candidate default, U - per-user static route
       o - ODR, P - periodic downloaded static route
Gateway of last resort is not set
      172.26.0.0/16 is variably subnetted, 2 subnets, 2 masks
S        172.26.2.0/23 [1/0] via 172.26.32.33
C        172.26.32.32/27 is directly connected, GigabitEthernet1/48
C     192.168.200.0/24 is directly connected, Loopback10
C     192.168.201.0/24 is directly connected, Loopback11
      10.0.0.0/24 is subnetted, 4 subnets
B        10.100.100.0 [20/0] via 192.168.1.37, 6d01h
B        10.100.202.0 [20/100] via 192.168.1.37, 00:33:43
B        10.100.200.0 [20/100] via 192.168.1.37, 00:33:43
B        10.100.201.0 [20/100] via 192.168.1.37, 00:33:43
      192.168.1.0/24 is variably subnetted, 4 subnets, 2 masks
C        192.168.1.40/30 is directly connected, TenGigabitEthernet1/49
C        192.168.1.36/30 is directly connected, TenGigabitEthernet1/50
C        192.168.1.3/32 is directly connected, Loopback0
B        192.168.1.2/32 [20/41] via 192.168.1.37, 00:34:37
```

Note NX-OS does not have the capability to do "wide-open" or "uncontrolled" redistribution. NX-OS enforces the use of a route-map to define routes that should be redistributed.

Modifying BGP Routing Metrics

BGP administrators frequently require flexibility in the manipulation of the multitude of BGP metrics that can influence routing policy. NX-OS supports administration of metrics such as AS-Path, weight, local preference, and more. These metrics can be applied in a granular nature using prefix lists to define the desired metric.

Example 3-85 shows the weight and local preference set to nondefault values.

Example 3-85 *Changing Weight and Local Preference in BGP*

```
Congo# confi t
Enter configuration commands, one per line. End with CNTL/Z.
Congo(config)# route-map OSPFtoBGP permit 10
```

```
Congo(config-route-map)# match ip address prefix-list OSPFtoBGP
Congo(config-route-map)# set weight 200
Congo(config-route-map)# set local-preference 2500
```

You can verify the changes to the weight and local preference through the **show ip bgp** command, as demonstrated in Example 3-86.

Example 3-86   *Verification of Weight and Local Preference in BGP*

```
Congo# confi t
Enter configuration commands, one per line. End with CNTL/Z.
Congo(config)# route-map OSPFtoBGP permit 10
Congo(config-route-map)# match ip address prefix-list OSPFtoBGP
Congo(config-route-map)# set weight 200
Congo(config-route-map)# set local-preference 2500
Congo# show ip bgp
BGP routing table information for VRF default, address family IPv4 Unicast
BGP table version is 12, local router ID is 192.168.1.1
Status: s-suppressed, x-deleted, S-stale, d-dampened, h-history, *-valid, >-best
Path type: i-internal, e-external, c-confed, l-local, a-aggregate, r-redist
Origin codes: i - IGP, e - EGP, ? - incomplete, | - multipath

   Network           Next Hop           Metric      LocPrf     Weight Path
*  r10.100.100.0/24  0.0.0.0               100        2500        200 ?
*>l                  0.0.0.0                          100      32768 i
*>r10.100.200.0/24   0.0.0.0               100        2500        200 ?
*>r10.100.201.0/24   0.0.0.0               100        2500        200 ?
*>r10.100.202.0/24   0.0.0.0               100        2500        200 ?
*>r192.168.1.2/32    0.0.0.0                41        2500        200 ?
*>r192.168.1.40/30   0.0.0.0                44        2500        200 ?
```

Verifying BGP-Specific Configuration

With the modular nature of NX-OS, you can now show the relevant BGP configuration by using the **show run bgp** command, as demonstrated in Example 3-87.

Example 3-87   *Viewing the BGP-Only Configuration*

```
Congo# show run bgp
!Command: show running-config bgp
!Time: Sun Oct 11 15:18:30 2009
version 4.2(2a)
feature bgp
router bgp 65000
  router-id 192.168.1.1
```

```
address-family ipv4 unicast
  network 10.100.100.0/24
  redistribute ospf DataCenter1 route-map OSPFtoBGP
template peer iBGP-Peers
  remote-as 65000
  password 3 cd87a249cfe3fb9aefc4f7f321a18044
  update-source loopback0
  timers 45 120
neighbor 192.168.1.2 remote-as 65000
  inherit peer iBGP-Peers
  description Egypt
  address-family ipv4 unicast
neighbor 192.168.1.38 remote-as 65001
  description Libya
  password 3 cd87a249cfe3fb9aefc4f7f321a18044
  address-family ipv4 unicast
```

First Hop Redundancy Protocols (FHRP)

Data center network designs frequently call for maximum redundancy to support the 24x7x365 operation mode called for in high availability environments. A component of these designs is the use of a First Hop Redundancy Protocol (FHRP). FHRPs provide a mechanism for maintaining an active default IP gateway at all times. This section covers three FHRPs and their associated configuration, including the following

- Hot Standby Router Protocol (HSRP)

- Virtual Router Redundancy Protocol (VRRP)

- Gateway Load Balancing Protocol (GLBP)

HSRP

HSRP is a Cisco innovation introduced to the networking world in 1998 and described in RFC 2281. HSRP enables two or more routers to provide first hop redundancy services for IP traffic. In HSRP, a virtual IP address is configured and is "owned" by one of the routers participating in the HSRP group to represent the default gateway for a given subnet. If that router fails or is taken out of service, the second router assumes the role of the default gateway using the same Media Access Control (MAC) address. This prevents the hosts on the network from needing to send an Address Resolution Protocol (ARP) for the new gateway's MAC address, and traffic is passed with minimal to no disruption.

HSRP Configuration

The first step to configure HSRP is to enable it in global configuration mode using the **feature** command, as demonstrated in Example 3-88. With the modular nature of NX-OS, using the **feature** command loads the HSRP modular code into memory for execution. Without the feature enabled, it would not be resident in memory.

Figure 3-11 illustrates the topology used in Examples 3-88 through 3-97.

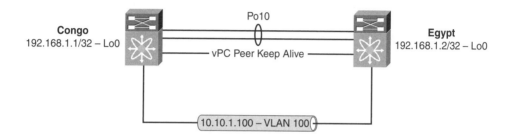

Figure 3-11   *Network Topology for HSRP Configuration*

Example 3-88   *Enabling the HSRP Feature*

```
Congo# confi t
Enter configuration commands, one per line. End with CNTL/Z.
Congo(config)# feature hsrp
Congo(config)# end
Congo# show run hsrp
!Command: show running-config hsrp
!Time: Sun Oct 11 21:44:42 2009
version 4.2(2a)
feature hsrp
```

Similar to IOS-based HSRP configuration, the next step is to configure the HSRP process under a VLAN interface, as demonstrated in Example 3-89.

Note   Recommended practice dictates that you should configure all HSRP options such as priority, preempt, authentication, and so on prior to adding the IP address to the group. This minimizes disruption and state change on the network.

Example 3-89   *Configuring HSRP on an SVI*

```
Congo# confi t
Enter configuration commands, one per line. End with CNTL/Z.
Congo(config)# int vlan 100
```

```
Congo(config-if)# hsrp 100
Congo(config-if-hsrp)# ip 10.10.100.1
Congo# show run hsrp
!Command: show running-config hsrp
!Time: Sun Oct 11 21:57:16 2009

version 4.2(2a)
feature hsrp

interface Vlan100
  hsrp 100
    ip 10.10.100.1
```

HSRP Priority and Preempt

NX-OS supports the capability to configure different HSRP priorities to help the network administrator define deterministic switching through the network. Similar to the HSRP implementation in IOS, a device with a higher priority will become the active gateway and the lower-priority device will become the standby. The default HSRP priority is 100, and it might be desirable to change the default to another value to align HSRP priorities with spanning-tree configuration to optimize traffic flows and provide deterministic switching. When two HSRP devices have the same priority, HSRP selects the device with the highest IP address to be active.

Additionally, when a priority is configured, it is typical to configure a **preempt** command to ensure that the active router is consistent after a network change. In Example 3-90, a priority of 200 is configured in addition to a preempt that uses the capability to wait a specified amount of time before preempting. This is preferable to minimize the potential of a flapping link or other inconsistent state in the network forcing HSRP changes.

Example 3-90 *Configuring HSRP Priority and Preemption*

```
Congo# config t
Enter configuration commands, one per line. End with CNTL/Z.
Congo(config)# int vlan 100
Congo(config-if)# hsrp 100
Congo(config-if-hsrp)# priority 200
Congo(config-if-hsrp)# preempt delay minimum 60
Congo(config-if-hsrp)# end
Congo# show run hsrp
!Command: show running-config hsrp
!Time: Sun Oct 11 22:07:18 2009

version 4.2(2a)
feature hsrp

interface Vlan100
```

```
hsrp 100
  preempt delay minimum 60
  priority 200
  ip 10.10.100.1
```

Verifying the HSRP Configuration

A quick method to use to see the current state of the HSRP configuration is to use the **show hsrp** command, as demonstrated in Example 3-91. All the parameters configured in Example 3-90 are reflected in the output such as priority, preempt, and IP address.

Example 3-91   *Verification of HSRP Status*

```
Congo# show hsrp
Vlan100 - Group 100 (HSRP-V1) (IPv4)
  Local state is Active, priority 200 (Cfged 200), may preempt
    Forwarding threshold(for VPC), lower: 1 upper: 200
  Preemption Delay (Seconds) Minimum:60
  Hellotime 3 sec, holdtime 10 sec
  Next hello sent in 2.539000 sec(s)
  Virtual IP address is 10.10.100.1 (Cfged)
  Active router is local
  Standby router is 10.10.100.3
  Virtual mac address is 0000.0c07.ac64 (Default MAC)
  2 state changes, last state change 00:01:00
  IP redundancy name is hsrp-Vlan100-100 (default)
```

Caution   HSRP is vPC-aware and as such the recommendation is made to NOT configure HSRP priority and preemption as vPC mechanisms are designed to work in an active/active methodology. vPC is covered in detail in Chapter 2, "Layer 2 Support and Configurations."

Securing HSRP

Securing HSRP is important in many environments to avoid a new router or device being added to the network and incorrectly assuming the role of the default gateway on a subnet. HSRP authentication can be configured to prevent such a situation. The implementation of HSRP authentication in NX-OS provides two forms of authentication:

■ **Plain text:** Has the password used for authentication in clear text and passes it as such on the network.

■ **MD5:** Uses the MD5 algorithm to hash the password before it is passed across the network.

Example 3-92 shows the configuration of plain text authentication.

Example 3-92 *Configuring HSRP Clear-Text Authentication*

```
Congo# confi t
Enter configuration commands, one per line. End with CNTL/Z.
Congo(config)# int vlan100
Congo(config-if)# hsrp 100
Congo(config-if-hsrp)# authentication text hsrp
```

You can see the addition of authentication to the HSRP configuration in the output of **show hsrp**, as illustrated in Example 3-93.

Example 3-93 *Verification of HSRP Clear-Text Authentication*

```
Congo# show hsrp
Vlan100 - Group 100 (HSRP-V1) (IPv4)
  Local state is Active, priority 200 (Cfged 200), may preempt
    Forwarding threshold(for VPC), lower: 1 upper: 200
  Preemption Delay (Seconds) Minimum:60
  Hellotime 3 sec, holdtime 10 sec
  Next hello sent in 0.069000 sec(s)
  Virtual IP address is 10.10.100.1 (Cfged)
  Active router is local
  Standby router is 10.10.100.3
  Authentication text "hsrp"
  Virtual mac address is 0000.0c07.ac64 (Default MAC)
  2 state changes, last state change 00:15:24
  IP redundancy name is hsrp-Vlan100-100 (default)
```

Configuration of MD5 authentication is a multistep process. You must first define a key chain that contains attributes such as the password to be used to authenticate the connection and the lifetime of the key chain for both sending and receiving, as demonstrated in Example 3-94.

Example 3-94 *Configuring a Key Chain*

```
Congo(config)# key chain nexus
Congo(config-keychain)# key 1
Congo(config-keychain-key)# key-string nexus
```

The next step is to enable authentication under the HSRP process, as illustrated in Example 3-95, and reference the key chain created in the previous step.

Example 3-95 *Configuring HSRP MD5 Authentication*

```
Congo# config t
```

```
Enter configuration commands, one per line. End with CNTL/Z.
Congo(config)# int vlan 100
Congo(config-if)# hsrp 100
Congo(config-if-hsrp)# authentication md5 key-chain nexus
```

You can verify that the MD5 authentication is in place from the output of the **show hsrp** command, as demonstrated in Example 3-96.

Example 3-96 *Verification of HSRP MD5 Authentication*

```
Congo(config-if-hsrp)# show hsrp
Vlan100 - Group 100 (HSRP-V1) (IPv4)
  Local state is Active, priority 200 (Cfged 200), may preempt
    Forwarding threshold(for VPC), lower: 1 upper: 200
  Preemption Delay (Seconds) Minimum:60
  Hellotime 3 sec, holdtime 10 sec
  Next hello sent in 1.059000 sec(s)
  Virtual IP address is 10.10.100.1 (Cfged)
  Active router is local
  Standby router is 10.10.100.3
  Authentication MD5, key-chain nexus
  Virtual mac address is 0000.0c07.ac64 (Default MAC)
  2 state changes, last state change 00:23:03
  IP redundancy name is hsrp-Vlan100-100 (default)
```

HSRP Secondary Support

The implementation of HSRP in NX-OS also supports secondary IP addressing. Secondary IP addresses are typically found in environments under transition to a new IP addressing scheme and usually temporary.

Example 3-97 shows HSRP configured to provide services to a secondary IP subnet, 172.16.1.0/24.

Example 3-97 *Configuring HSRP for Secondary Subnets*

```
Congo# confi t
Enter configuration commands, one per line. End with CNTL/Z.
Congo(config)# int vlan 100
Congo(config-if)# ip address 172.16.1.2/24 secondary
Congo(config-if)# hsrp 100
Congo(config-if-hsrp)# ip 172.16.1.1 secondary
Congo(config-if-hsrp)# end
Congo# show hsrp
Vlan100 - Group 100 (HSRP-V1) (IPv4)
```

```
Local state is Active, priority 200 (Cfged 200), may preempt
  Forwarding threshold(for VPC), lower: 1 upper: 200
Preemption Delay (Seconds) Minimum:60
Hellotime 3 sec, holdtime 10 sec
Next hello sent in 0.489000 sec(s)
Virtual IP address is 10.10.100.1 (Cfged)
   Secondary Virtual IP address is 172.16.1.1
Active router is local
Standby router is 10.10.100.3
Authentication MD5, key-chain nexus
Virtual mac address is 0000.0c07.ac64 (Default MAC)
2 state changes, last state change 00:40:20
IP redundancy name is hsrp-Vlan100-100 (default)
```

VRRP

Virtual Router Redundancy Protocol (VRRP) is an industry standard introduced to the networking world in 2004 and described in RFC 3768. VRRP enables two or more routers to provide first-hop redundancy services for IP traffic. In VRRP, a virtual IP address is configured and is "owned" by one of the routers participating in the VRRP group to represent the default gateway for a given subnet. If that router fails or is taken out of service, the second router assumes the role of the default gateway using the same MAC address. This prevents the hosts on the network from needing to send an ARP request for the new gateway's MAC address, and traffic is passed with minimal to no disruption.

VRRP Configuration

The first step to configure VRRP is to enable it in global configuration mode using the **feature** command, as demonstrated in Example 3-98. With the modular nature of NX-OS, using the **feature** command loads the VRRP modular code into memory for execution. Without the feature enabled, it would not be resident in memory.

Figure 3-12 illustrates the topology used in Examples 3-98 through 3-105.

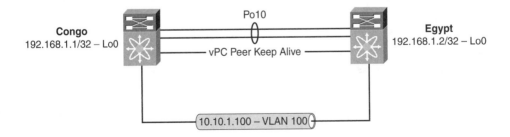

Figure 3-12 *Network Topology for VRRP Configuration*

Example 3-98 *Enabling the VRRP Feature*

```
Congo# config t
Enter configuration commands, one per line. End with CNTL/Z.
Congo(config)# feature vrrp
Congo(config)# end
Congo# show run vrrp
!Command: show running-config vrrp
!Time: Sun Oct 11 23:01:46 2009

version 4.2(2a)
feature vrrp
```

Similar to IOS-based VRRP configuration, the next step is to configure the VRRP process under a VLAN interface, as demonstrated in Example 3-99.

Caution   Recommended practice dictates that you should configure all VRRP options such as priority, preempt, authentication, and so on prior to adding the IP address to the group. This minimizes disruption and state change on the network.

Example 3-99 *Configuring VRRP on an SVI*

```
Congo# confi t
Enter configuration commands, one per line. End with CNTL/Z.
Congo(config)# int vlan 100
Congo(config-if)# vrrp 100
Congo(config-if-vrrp)# address 10.10.100.1
Congo(config-if-vrrp)# end
Congo# show run vrrp
!Command: show running-config vrrp
!Time: Sun Oct 11 23:04:13 2009

version 4.2(2a)
feature vrrp

interface Vlan100
  vrrp 100
    address 10.10.100.1
    no shutdown
```

Caution   Unlike HSRP, VRRP groups must be manually enabled before they begin operation.

VRRP Priority and Preempt

NX-OS supports the capability to configure different VRRP priorities to help the network administrator define deterministic switching through the network. Similar to the VRRP implementation in IOS, a device with a higher priority becomes the active gateway and the lower-priority device becomes the standby. The default VRRP priority is 100.

Additionally, when a priority is configured, it is typical to configure a **preempt** command to ensure that the active router is consistent after a network change. In Example 3-100, a priority of 200 is configured in addition to a preempt.

Caution   Preempt in VRRP does not support a delay mechanism similar to HSRP and also is enabled by default.

Example 3-100   *Configuring VRRP Priority*

```
Congo# config t
Enter configuration commands, one per line. End with CNTL/Z.
Congo(config)# int vlan 100
Congo(config-if)# vrrp 100
Congo(config-if-vrrp)# priority 200
Congo(config-if-vrrp)# end
Congo# show run vrrp
!Command: show running-config vrrp
!Time: Sun Oct 11 23:10:55 2009
version 4.2(2a)
feature vrrp

interface Vlan100
  vrrp 100
    priority 200
    address 10.10.100.1
    no shutdown
```

Verifying VRRP Configuration

A quick method to use to see the current state of the VRRP configuration is to use the **show vrrp** command, as demonstrated in Example 3-101. The output displays all the parameters configured in Example 3-100, such as priority, preempt, and IP address.

Example 3-101   *Viewing VRRP Status*

```
Congo# show vrrp
        Interface  VR IpVersion Pri   Time Pre State   VR IP addr
  _ _ _ _ _ _ _ _ _ _ _ _ _ _ _ _ _ _ _ _ _ _ _ _ _ _ _ _ _ _ _ _ _.
        Vlan100 100    IPV4     200   1 s  Y  Master  10.10.100.1
```

You can display additional details by reviewing the output from the **show vrrp detail** command, as demonstrated in Example 3-102.

Example 3-102 *Viewing VRRP Detail*

```
Congo# show vrrp detail
Vlan100 - Group 100 (IPV4)
     State is Master
     Virtual IP address is 10.10.100.1
     Priority 200, Configured 200
     Forwarding threshold(for VPC), lower: 1 upper: 200
     Advertisement interval 1
     Preemption enabled
     Virtual MAC address is 0000.5e00.0164
     Master router is 10.10.100.2
```

> **Caution**   VRRP is vPC-aware and as such the recommendation is made to NOT configure VRRP priority and preemption because vPC mechanisms are designed to work in an active/active methodology. vPC is covered in detail in Chapter 2.

Securing VRRP

Securing VRRP is important in many environments to avoid a new router or device that is added to the network from incorrectly assuming the role of the default gateway on a subnet. VRRP authentication can be configured to prevent such a situation. The current implementation of VRRP authentication in NX-OS provides one form of authentication—plain text. Plain text, as its name implies, has the password used for authentication in clear text and passes it as such on the network.

Example 3-103 shows the use of plain text authentication.

Example 3-103 *Configuring VRRP Authentication*

```
Congo# confi t
Enter configuration commands, one per line. End with CNTL/Z.
Congo(config)# int vlan 100
Congo(config-if)# vrrp 100
Congo(config-if-vrrp)# authentication text vrrp
```

You can see the addition of authentication to the VRRP configuration in the output of **show vrrp detailed**, as demonstrated in Example 3-104.

Example 3-104 *Verification of VRRP Authentication*

```
Egypt# show vrrp det
```

```
Vlan100 - Group 100 (IPV4)
     State is Backup
     Virtual IP address is 10.10.100.1
     Priority 100, Configured 100
     Forwarding threshold(for VPC), lower: 1 upper: 100
     Advertisement interval 1
     Preemption disabled
     Authentication text "vrrp"
     Virtual MAC address is 0000.5e00.0164
     Master router is 10.10.100.2
```

VRRP Secondary Support

The implementation of VRRP in NX-OS also supports secondary IP addressing. Secondary IP addresses are typically found in environments under transition to a new IP addressing scheme and usually temporary.

Example 3-105 shows VRRP configured to provide services to a secondary IP subnet, 172.16.1.0/24.

Example 3-105 *Configuring VRRP for Secondary Subnets*

```
Congo# confi t
Enter configuration commands, one per line. End with CNTL/Z.
Congo(config)# int vlan 100
Congo(config-if)# vrrp 100
Congo(config-if-vrrp)# address 172.16.1.1 secondary
Congo(config-if-vrrp)# end
Congo# show vrrp det
Vlan100 - Group 100 (IPV4)
     State is Master
     Virtual IP address is 10.10.100.1
     Secondary Virtual IP address(es):
        172.16.1.1
     Priority 200, Configured 200
     Forwarding threshold(for VPC), lower: 1 upper: 200
     Advertisement interval 1
     Preemption enabled
     Authentication text "vrrp"
     Virtual MAC address is 0000.5e00.0164
     Master router is 10.10.100.2
```

GLBP

Gateway Load Balancing Protocol (GLBP) is a Cisco innovation that, although similar to HSRP and VRRP, provides basic load-balancing capabilities. GLBP enables two or more routers to provide first-hop redundancy services for IP traffic. In GLBP, a virtual IP address is configured and is "owned" by one of the routers participating in the GLBP group to represent the default gateway for a given subnet. The owning router or active virtual gateway (AVG) in a GLBP environment responds to the sender with a unique MAC address to enable the distribution of traffic.

GLBP uses different load-balancing mechanisms to determine the distribution of traffic between the routers participating in the GLBP group.

GLBP Configuration

The first step to configure GLBP is to enable it in global configuration mode using the **feature** command, as demonstrated in Example 3-106. With the modular nature of NX-OS, using the **feature** command loads the GLBP modular code into memory for execution. Without the feature enabled, it would not be resident in memory.

Figure 3-13 illustrates the topology used in Examples 3-106 through 3-115.

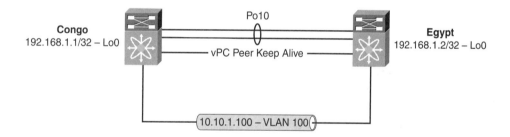

Figure 3-13 *Network Topology for GLBP Configuration*

Example 3-106 *Enabling the GLBP Feature*

```
Congo# confi t
Enter configuration commands, one per line. End with CNTL/Z.
Congo(config)# feature glbp
Congo(config)# end
Congo# show run glbp
!Command: show running-config glbp
!Time: Sun Oct 11 23:36:24 2009
version 4.2(2a)
feature glbp
```

Similar to IOS-based GLBP configuration, the next step is to configure the GLBP process under a VLAN interface, as demonstrated in Example 3-107.

Caution   Recommended practice dictates that you should configure all GLBP options such as priority, preempt, authentication, and so on prior to adding the IP address to the group. This minimizes disruption and state change on the network.

Example 3-107   *Configuring GLBP on an SVI*

```
Congo# confi t
Enter configuration commands, one per line. End with CNTL/Z.
Congo(config)# int vlan 100
Congo(config-if)# glbp 100
Congo(config-if-glbp)# ip 10.10.100.1
Congo# show run glbp
!Command: show running-config glbp
!Time: Sun Oct 11 23:38:42 2009

version 4.2(2a)
feature glbp

interface Vlan100
  glbp 100
    ip 10.10.100.1
```

GLBP Priority and Preempt

NX-OS supports the capability to configure different GLBP priorities. In GLBP, the priority determines the Active Virtual Gateway (AVG) for each group. The AVG is responsible for assigning virtual MAC addresses to each member of the GLBP group including itself. This enables each router to have an Active Virtual Forwarder (AVF) that is responsible for forwarding traffic directed to its virtual MAC address. The default priority is 100.

In Example 3-108, a priority of 200 is configured in addition to a preempt that uses the capability to wait a specified amount of time before preempting for the AVG role.

Example 3-108   *Configuring GLBP Priority and Preemption*

```
Congo# confi t
Enter configuration commands, one per line. End with CNTL/Z.
Congo(config)# int vlan 100
Congo(config-if)# glbp 100
Congo(config-if-glbp)# priority 200
Congo(config-if-glbp)# preempt
Congo(config-if-glbp)# end
Congo# show run glbp
```

```
!Command: show running-config glbp
!Time: Sun Oct 11 23:49:01 2009
version 4.2(2a)
feature glbp

interface Vlan100
  glbp 100
    ip 10.10.100.1
    priority 200
    preempt
```

Verifying GLBP Configuration

A quick method to use to see the current state of the GLBP configuration is to use the **show glbp** command, as demonstrated in Example 3-109. The output displays all the parameters configured in Example 3-108, such as priority, preempt, and IP address.

Example 3-109 *Verification of GLBP Priority and Preemption*

```
Congo# show glbp
Vlan100 - Group 100
    State is Active
       4 state change(s), last state change(s) 00:11:13
    Virtual IP address is 10.10.100.1
    Hello time 3 sec, hold time 10 sec
      Next hello sent in 2.480 sec
    Redirect time 600 sec, forwarder time-out 14400 sec
    Preemption enabled, min delay 0 sec
    Active is local
    Standby is 10.10.100.3, priority 100 (expires in 7.221 sec)
    Priority 200 (configured)
    Weighting 100 (default 100), thresholds: lower 1, upper 100
    Load balancing: round-robin
    Group members:
      001B.54C2.7641 (10.10.100.2) local
      001B.54C2.78C1 (10.10.100.3)
    There are 2 forwarders (1 active)
    Forwarder 1
     State is Active
        2 state change(s), last state change 00:11:03
     MAC address is 0007.B400.6401 (default)
     Owner ID is 001B.54C2.7641
     Preemption enabled, min delay 30 sec
     Active is local, weighting 100
    Forwarder 2
```

```
State is Listen
    1 state change(s), last state change 00:03:10
MAC address is 0007.B400.6402 (learnt)
Owner ID is 001B.54C2.78C1
Redirection enabled, 597.221 sec remaining (maximum 600 sec)
Time to live: 14397.221 sec (maximum 14400 sec)
Preemption enabled, min delay 30 sec
Active is 10.10.100.3 (primary), weighting 100 (expires in 7.221 sec)
```

Caution   GLBP is vPC-aware and as such the recommendation is made to not configure GLBP priority and preemption because vPC mechanisms are designed to work in an active/active methodology. vPC is covered in detail in Chapter 2.

Securing GLBP

Securing GLBP is important in many environments to avoid a new router or device that is added to the network from incorrectly assuming the role of the default gateway on a subnet. GLBP authentication can be configured to prevent such a situation. The implementation of GLBP authentication in NX-OS provides two forms of authentication:

- **Plain text:** Plain text, as its name implies, has the password used for authentication in clear text and passes it as such on the network.

- **MD5:** Uses the MD5 algorithm to hash the password before it is passed across the network.

Example 3-110 shows the configuration of plain text authentication.

Example 3-110   *Configuring GLBP Clear–Text Authentication*

```
Congo# confi t
Enter configuration commands, one per line. End with CNTL/Z.
Congo(config)# int vlan100
Congo(config-if)# glbp 100
Congo(config-if-hsrp)# authentication text glbp
```

You can confirm the addition of authentication to the GLBP configuration from the output of the **show glbp** command, as demonstrated in Example 3-111.

Example 3-111   *Verification of GLBP Clear-Text Authentication*

```
Congo# show glbp
Vlan100 - Group 100
    State is Active
      4 state change(s), last state change(s) 00:19:40
```

```
   Virtual IP address is 10.10.100.1
   Hello time 3 sec, hold time 10 sec
     Next hello sent in 2.890 sec
   Redirect time 600 sec, forwarder time-out 14400 sec
   Authentication text "glbp"
   Preemption enabled, min delay 0 sec
   Active is local
   Standby is 10.10.100.3, priority 100 (expires in 7.827 sec)
   Priority 200 (configured)
   Weighting 100 (default 100), thresholds: lower 1, upper 100
   Load balancing: round-robin
   Group members:
     001B.54C2.7641 (10.10.100.2) local
     001B.54C2.78C1 (10.10.100.3)
   There are 2 forwarders (1 active)
   Forwarder 1
    State is Active
       2 state change(s), last state change 00:19:30
    MAC address is 0007.B400.6401 (default)
    Owner ID is 001B.54C2.7641
    Preemption enabled, min delay 30 sec
    Active is local, weighting 100
   Forwarder 2
    State is Listen
       3 state change(s), last state change 00:00:54
    MAC address is 0007.B400.6402 (learnt)
    Owner ID is 001B.54C2.78C1
    Redirection enabled, 597.827 sec remaining (maximum 600 sec)
    Time to live: 14397.827 sec (maximum 14400 sec)
    Preemption enabled, min delay 30 sec
    Active is 10.10.100.3 (primary), weighting 100 (expires in 7.827 sec)
```

Configuring MD5 authentication is a multistep process. You must first define a key
chain that contains attributes like the password to be used to authenticate the connection and lifetime of the key chain for both sending and receiving, as demonstrated in
Example 3-112.

Example 3-112 *Configuring a Key Chain*

```
Congo(config)# key chain nexus
Congo(config-keychain)# key 1
Congo(config-keychain-key)# key-string nexus
```

The next step is to enable authentication under the GLBP process, as demonstrated in Example 3-113, and reference the key chain created in Example 3-112.

Example 3-113   *Configuring GLBP MD5 Authentication*

```
Congo# confi t
Enter configuration commands, one per line. End with CNTL/Z.
Congo(config)# int vlan 100
Congo(config-if)# glbp 100
Congo(config-if-glbp)# authentication md5 key-chain nexus
```

You can verify that the MD5 authentication is in place via the **show glbp** command, as demonstrated in Example 3-114.

Example 3-114   *Verification of GLBP MD5 Authentication*

```
Congo# show glbp
Vlan100 - Group 100
   State is Active
      4 state change(s), last state change(s) 00:21:30
   Virtual IP address is 10.10.100.1
   Hello time 3 sec, hold time 10 sec
      Next hello sent in 2.500 sec
   Redirect time 600 sec, forwarder time-out 14400 sec
   Authentication MD5, key-chain "nexus"
   Preemption enabled, min delay 0 sec
   Active is local
   Standby is 10.10.100.3, priority 100 (expires in 7.458 sec)
   Priority 200 (configured)
   Weighting 100 (default 100), thresholds: lower 1, upper 100
   Load balancing: round-robin
   Group members:
      001B.54C2.7641 (10.10.100.2) local
      001B.54C2.78C1 (10.10.100.3) authenticated
   There are 2 forwarders (1 active)
   Forwarder 1
    State is Active
       2 state change(s), last state change 00:21:20
    MAC address is 0007.B400.6401 (default)
    Owner ID is 001B.54C2.7641
    Preemption enabled, min delay 30 sec (00:00:08 secs remaining)
    Active is local, weighting 100
   Forwarder 2
    State is Listen
       5 state change(s), last state change 00:00:21
```

```
MAC address is 0007.B400.6402 (learnt)
Owner ID is 001B.54C2.78C1
Redirection enabled, 597.458 sec remaining (maximum 600 sec)
Time to live: 14397.458 sec (maximum 14400 sec)
Preemption enabled, min delay 30 sec
Active is 10.10.100.3 (primary), weighting 100 (expires in 7.458 sec)
```

GLBP Secondary Support

The implementation of GLBP in NX-OS also supports secondary IP addressing. Secondary IP addresses are typically found in environments that are under transition to a new IP addressing scheme and usually temporary.

Example 3-115 shows GLBP configured to provide services to a secondary IP subnet, 172.16.1.0/24.

Example 3-115 *Configuring GLBP for Secondary Subnets*

```
Congo# confi t
Enter configuration commands, one per line. End with CNTL/Z.
Congo(config)# int vlan 100
Congo(config-if)# ip address 172.16.1.2/24 secondary
Congo(config-if)# glbp 100
Congo(config-if-glbp)# ip 172.16.1.1 secondary
Congo(config-if-glbp)# show glbp
Vlan100 - Group 100
  State is Active
    4 state change(s), last state change(s) 00:23:27
  Virtual IP address is 10.10.100.1
    Secondary virtual IP address 172.16.1.1
  Hello time 3 sec, hold time 10 sec
    Next hello sent in 190 msec
  Redirect time 600 sec, forwarder time-out 14400 sec
  Authentication MD5, key-chain "nexus"
  Preemption enabled, min delay 0 sec
  Active is local
  Standby is 10.10.100.3, priority 100 (expires in 7.980 sec)
  Priority 200 (configured)
  Weighting 100 (default 100), thresholds: lower 1, upper 100
  Load balancing: round-robin
  Group members:
    001B.54C2.7641 (10.10.100.2) local
    001B.54C2.78C1 (10.10.100.3) authenticated
  There are 2 forwarders (1 active)
  Forwarder 1
```

```
  State is Active
      2 state change(s), last state change 00:23:17
  MAC address is 0007.B400.6401 (default)
  Owner ID is 001B.54C2.7641
  Preemption enabled, min delay 30 sec
  Active is local, weighting 100
Forwarder 2
  State is Listen
      5 state change(s), last state change 00:02:18
  MAC address is 0007.B400.6402 (learnt)
  Owner ID is 001B.54C2.78C1
  Redirection enabled, 597.980 sec remaining (maximum 600 sec)
  Time to live: 14397.980 sec (maximum 14400 sec)
  Preemption enabled, min delay 30 sec
  Active is 10.10.100.3 (primary), weighting 100 (expires in 7.980 sec)
```

Summary

The Layer 3 routing capabilities of NX-OS are flexible and support a wide range of IGPs in addition to BGP. Combining an underlying architecture focused on high availability with years of routing experience makes a compelling operating system. With VRF-aware features as a standard offering and support for both Cisco-innovated protocols in addition to industry-standard protocols enable the network administrator to develop and deploy flexible, scalable, and resilient data center architectures.

Chapter 4

IP Multicast Configuration

Cisco NX-OS was designed to be a data center-class operating system. A component of such an operating system includes support for a rich set of IP multicast features, including key capabilities such as Internet Group Management Protocol (IGMP), Protocol Independent Multicast (PIM) sparse mode, Source Specific Multicast (SSM), Multicast Source Discovery Protocol (MSDP), and Multiprotocol Border Gateway Protocol (MBGP). This chapter focuses on the following components:

- Multicast Operation

- PIM Configuration on Nexus 7000

- IGMP Operation

- IGMP Configuration on Nexus 7000

- IGMP Configuration on Nexus 5000

- IGMP Configuration on Nexus 1000V

- MSDP Configuration on Nexus 7000

Multicast Operation

As a technology, IP multicast enables a single flow of traffic to be received by multiple destinations in an efficient manner. This provides an optimal use of network bandwidth wherein destinations that do not want to receive the traffic do not have it sent to them. There are multiple methodologies utilized to provide this functionality that cover aspects such as discovery of sources and receivers and delivery mechanisms. Multicast is a network-centric technology and as such, the network equipment between the sender of multicast traffic and the receivers must be "multicast-aware" and understand the services and addressing used by multicast. In IPv4, multicast uses a block of addresses that has been set aside by the Internet Assigned Number Authority (IANA). This range of addresses is the Class D block 224.0.0.0 through 239.255.255.255, and within this block a range has been set aside for private intranet usage, similar to RFC 1918 addressing for unicast. RFC 2365, "Administratively Scoped IP Multicast," documents this usage and allocates addresses in the 239.0.0.0 through 239.255.255.255 range for private use. Each individual multicast address can represent a group that the receivers then request to join.

The network listens for receivers to signal their requirement to join a group. The network then begins to forward and replicate the data from the source to the receivers that join the group. This is significantly more efficient than generally flooding the traffic to all systems on a network to only have the traffic discarded.

Multicast Distribution Trees

Multiple methods can be used to control and optimize the learning and forwarding of multicast traffic through the network. A key concept to understand is that of a *distribution tree*, which represents the path that multicast data takes across the network between the sources of traffic and the receivers. NX-OS cam build different multicast distribution trees to support different multicast technologies such as Source Specific Multicast (SSM), Any Source Multicast (ASM), and Bidirectional (Bidir).

The first multicast distribution tree is the source tree, which represents the shortest path that multicast traffic follows through the network from the source that is transmitting to a group address and the receivers that request the traffic from the group. This is referred to as the Shortest Path Tree (SPT).

Figure 4-1 depicts a source tree for group 239.0.0.1 with a source on Host A and receivers on Hosts B and C.

The next multicast distribution tree is the *shared tree*. The shared tree represents a shared distribution path that multicast traffic follows through the network from a network-centric function called the *Rendezvous Point (RP)* to the receivers that request the traffic from the group. The RP creates a source tree, or SPT, to the source. The shared tree can also be referred to as the RP tree or RPT.

Figure 4-2 depicts a shared tree, or RPT, for group 239.0.0.10 with a source on Host A. Router C is the RP and the receivers are Hosts B and C.

The final multicast distribution tree is the bidirectional shared tree or *bidir*, which represents a shared distribution path that multicast traffic follows through the network from the RP or a shared root to the receivers that request the traffic from the group. The capability to send multicast traffic from the shared root can provide a more efficient method of traffic delivery and optimize the amount of state the network must maintain.

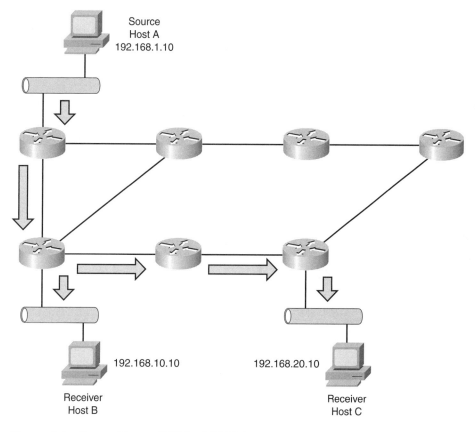

Figure 4-1 *Source Tree or SPT for 239.0.0.1*

Note You need to understand that one of the primary scalability considerations in a multicast design is the amount of information the network needs to maintain for the multicast traffic to work. This information is referred to as *state* and contains the multicast routing table, information on senders and receivers, and other metrics on the traffic.

Figure 4-3 depicts a shared tree, or RPT, for group 239.0.0.10 with a source on Host A. Router D is the RP and the receivers are Hosts B and C.

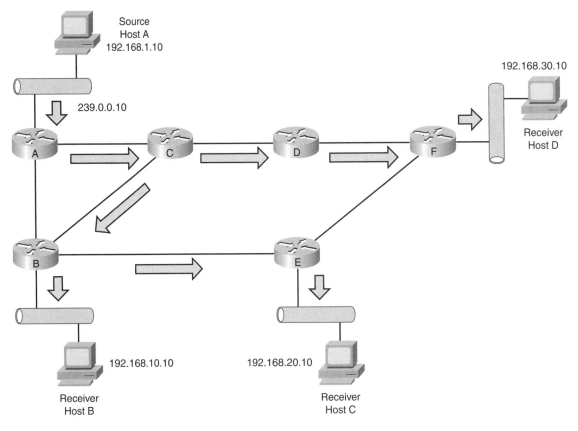

Figure 4-2   *Shared Tree or RPT for 239.0.0.10*

Reverse Path Forwarding

An additional concept beyond multicast distribution trees that is important for multicast is that of Reverse Path Forwarding (RPF). Multicast, by design, is traffic not intended for every system on a network but rather sent only to receivers that request it. Routers in the network must form a path toward the source or RP. The path from the source to the receivers flows in the reverse direction from which the path was created when the receiver requested to join the group. Each incoming multicast packet undergoes an RPF check to verify it was received on an interface leading to the source. If the packet passes the RPF check, it is forwarded; if not, the packet is discarded. The RPF check is done to minimize the potential for duplicated packets and source integrity.

Protocol Independent Multicast (PIM)

With a solid understanding of the multicast distribution tree modes and the RPF, the next concept is that of Protocol Independent Multicast (PIM), which is an industry standard protocol developed to leverage any existing underlying Interior Gateway Routing (IGP)

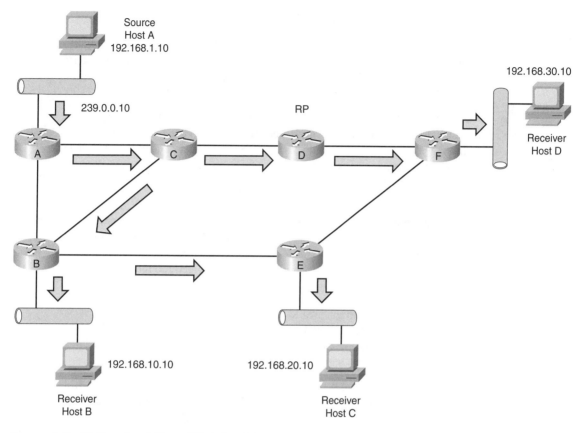

Figure 4-3   *Bidirectional Shared Tree for 239.0.0.25*

protocol, such as Enhanced Interior Gateway Routing Protocol (EIGRP), Open Shortest Path First (OSPF), or Routing Information Protocol (RIP), to determine the path of multicast packets in the network. PIM does not maintain its own routing table and as such has a much lower overhead when compared with other multicast routing technologies.

In general, PIM can operate in two modes: dense mode and sparse mode. NX-OS supports only sparse mode because most dense mode applications have been depreciated from networks, and the flood and prune behavior of dense mode is not efficient for modern data centers.

PIM sparse mode mechanics entail neighbor relationships between PIM-enabled devices. These neighbor relationships determine PIM-enabled paths in a network and enable the building of distribution trees through the network. As mentioned, PIM leverages the existing unicast routing table for path selection. This gives PIM a dynamic capability to adapt the multicast topology to match the unicast topology as the network changes due to link failures, system maintenance, or administrative policy.

NX-OS implementation of PIM supports three modes:

- **Any Source Multicast (ASM):** Uses RPs with a shared tree to discover sources and receivers. ASM also supports the capability for traffic to be switched from the shared tree to an SPT between the source and receiver if signaled to do so. ASM is the default mode when an RP is configured.

- **Source Specific Multicast (SSM):** Unlike ASM or Bidir, does not utilize RPs and instead builds SPTs between the source and receivers. SSM sends an immediate join to the source and reduces state in the network. SSM is also frequently used to facilitate communication between PIM domains where sources are not dynamically learned via MSDP or other mechanisms. SSM relies on the receivers to use IGMPv3 that is discussed in the next section.

- **Bidirectional shared trees (Bidir):** Similar to ASM in that it builds a shared tree between receivers and the RP, but unlike ASM does not support switching over to a SPT. With Bidir, routers closest to the receivers take on a role called *Designated Forwarder (DF)*. This allows the source to send traffic directly to the DF without passing through the RP that may be a significant benefit in some environments.

A final option would be to configure static RPF routes that would force multicast traffic to not follow the unicast table. As with most static routes, the opportunity for dynamic failover and changes to the multicast routing might be compromised, so you should give careful consideration to employing this option.

The ASM, Bidir, SSM, and static RPF modes are typically deployed within a single PIM domain. In cases where multicast traffic needs to cross multiple PIM domains and Border Gateway Protocol (BGP) is used to interconnect the networks, the Multicast Source Discovery Protocol (MSDP) is typically used. MSDP is used to advertise sources in each domain without needing to share domain-specific state and scales well.

RPs

Rendezvous Points (RP) are key to the successful forwarding of multicast traffic for ASM and Bidir configurations. Given this importance, there are multiple methods to configure RPs and learn about them in the network. RPs are routers that the network administrator selects to perform this role and are the shared root for RPTs. A network can have multiple RPs designated to service particular groups or have a single RP that services all groups.

Following are four primary methods to configure RPs in NX-OS:

- **Static RPs:** As their name implies, Static RPs are statically configured on every router in the PIM domain. This is the simplest method for RP configuration, though it requires configuration on every PIM device.

- **Bootstrap Routers (BSRs):** Distribute the same RP cache information to every router in the PIM domain. This is done by the BSR when it sends BSR messages out all PIM-enabled interfaces. These messages are flooded hop by hop to all routers in the network. The BSR candidate role is configured on the router, and an election is performed to determine the single BSR for the domain.

When the BSR is elected, messages from candidate RPs are received, via unicast, for each multicast group. The BSR sends these candidate RPs out in BSR messages, and every router in the PIM domain runs the same algorithm against the list of candidate RPs. Because each router gas the same list of candidate RPs and each router runs the same algorithm to determine the RP, every router selects the same RP.

Note   BSR is described in RFC 5059 and provides a nonproprietary method for RP definition.

Caution   Do not configure both Auto-RP and BSR protocols in the same network. Auto-RP is the Cisco propietary implementation of what was standardized as BSR, and they serve the same purpose. As such, only one is needed. Inconsistent multicast routing can be observed if both are configured.

- **Auto-RP:** A Cisco propietary protocol to define RPs in a network. Auto-RP was developed before BSR was standardized. Auto-RP uses candidate mapping agents and RPs to determine the RP for a group. A primary difference between Auto-RP and BSR is that Auto-RP uses multicast to deliver the candidate-RP group messages on multicast group 224.0.1.39. The mapping agent sends the group to the RP mapping table on multicast group 224.0.1.40.

- **Anycast-RP:** Another methdology to advertise RPs in a network. There are two implementations of Anycast-RP. One uses MSDP and the other is based on RFC 4610, PIM Anycast-RP. With Anycast-RP, the same IP address is configured on multiple routers, typically a loopback interface. Because PIM uses the underlying unicast routing table, the closest RP will be used. Anycast is the only RP method that enables more than one RP to be active, which enables load-balancing and additional fault tolerance options.

Note   Anycast-RP doesn't advertise the RP to the multicast table but rather the unicast table. The RP still needs to be dynamically discovered using technologies such as BSR or Auto-RP or statically defined to make a complete and working configuration.

PIM Configuration on Nexus 7000

PIM within NX-OS is compatible with PIM on IOS devices enabling a smooth integration of Nexus equipment with existing gear.

> **Note** PIM is a Layer 3 protocol and as such does not work on Nexus 5000, 2000, and 1000V switches because they are Layer 2 only.

The first step to configure PIM is to enable it on global configuration mode using the **feature** command. With the modular nature of NX-OS, using the **feature** command loads the PIM modular code into memory for execution. Without the feature enabled, it would not be resident in memory. In Example 4-1, PIM is enabled as a feature on Router Greed and sparse mode is configured on interface e1/25 and Port-Channel 10 per the topology depicted in Figure 4-4, which serves as the topology for all the following PIM configuration examples.

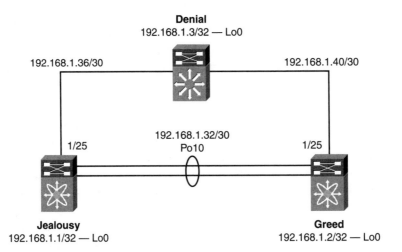

Figure 4-4 *Basic Multicast Topology*

Example 4-1 *Enabling the PIM Feature and Basic Interface Configuration*

```
Greed# confi t
Enter configuration commands, one per line.  End with CNTL/Z.
Greed(config)# feature pim
Greed(config)# int e1/25
Greed(config-if)# ip pim sparse-mode
Greed(config-if)# int port-channel10
Greed(config-if)# ip pim sparse-mode
Greed(config-if)# end
Greed# show run pim

!Command: show running-config pim
!Time: Sun Dec 20 20:01:34 2009
```

```
version 4.2(2a)
feature pim

ip pim ssm range 232.0.0.0/8

interface port-channel10
  ip pim sparse-mode

interface Ethernet1/25
  ip pim sparse-mode
```

Note   To add PIM to the configuration on an interface, it must be an L3 port. If L2 were selected as a default during intial setup, the **no switchport** command must be used before PIM can be configured.

With PIM sparse mode enabled, more options can be configured per interface including authentication, priority, hello interval border, and neighbor policy.

Note   You can find additional information about these options at Cisco.com at http://www.cisco.com/en/US/docs/switches/datacenter/sw/4_2/nx-os/multicast/command/reference/mcr_cmds_i.html.

In Example 4-2, the hello timers are reduced from the default of 30,000 milliseconds to 10,000 milliseconds to improve convergence, and authentication is enabled on the PIM hellos for interface Port-Channel10.

Note   Changing PIM hello timers might increase the load on the router's control plane, and you might see an increase in CPU utilization.

Example 4-2   *Configuration of PIM Hello Authentication and Tuning Hello Timers*

```
Enter configuration commands, one per line.  End with CNTL/Z.
Greed(config)# int po10
Greed(config-if)# ip pim hello-authentication ah-md5 cisco
Greed(config-if)# ip pim hello-interval 10000
Greed(config-if)# end
Greed# show ip pim ne
PIM Neighbor Status for VRF "default"
Neighbor          Interface          Uptime    Expires   DR        Bidir-
                                                         Priority  Capable
```

```
192.168.1.42     Ethernet1/25        00:24:16  00:01:37  1          no
192.168.1.33     port-channel10      00:00:11  00:00:32  1          yes
Greed# show ip pim int po10
PIM Interface Status for VRF "default"
port-channel10, Interface status: protocol-up/link-up/admin-up
  IP address: 192.168.1.34, IP subnet: 192.168.1.32/30
  PIM DR: 192.168.1.34, DR's priority: 1
  PIM neighbor count: 1
  PIM hello interval: 10 secs, next hello sent in: 00:00:06
  PIM neighbor holdtime: 35 secs
  PIM configured DR priority: 1
  PIM border interface: no
  PIM GenID sent in Hellos: 0x1f081512
  PIM Hello MD5-AH Authentication: enabled
  PIM Neighbor policy: none configured
  PIM Join-Prune policy: none configured
  PIM Interface Statistics, last reset: never
    General (sent/received):
      Hellos: 56/32, JPs: 0/0, Asserts: 0/0
      Grafts: 0/0, Graft-Acks: 0/0
      DF-Offers: 0/0, DF-Winners: 0/0, DF-Backoffs: 0/0, DF-Passes: 0/0
    Errors:
      Checksum errors: 0, Invalid packet types/DF subtypes: 0/0
      Authentication failed: 39
      Packet length errors: 0, Bad version packets: 0, Packets from self: 0
      Packets from non-neighbors: 0
      JPs received on RPF-interface: 0
      (*,G) Joins received with no/wrong RP: 0/0
      (*,G)/(S,G) JPs received for SSM/Bidir groups: 0/0
      JPs policy filtered: 0
Greed#
```

When PIM sparse mode is enabled on all interfaces that need to participate in multicast, the next step is to configure the RPs. As previously discussed, multiple methods of RP configuration exist.

Configuring Static RPs

The first configuration methodology for RPs is static RP. Example 4-3 illustrates the steps required to configure a static RP on Router Jealousy.

Example 4-3 *Configuration of a Static RP*

```
Jealousy# show ip pim rp
PIM RP Status Information for VRF "default"
BSR disabled
Auto-RP disabled
BSR RP Candidate policy: None
BSR RP policy: None
Auto-RP Announce policy: None
Auto-RP Discovery policy: None

Jealousy# confi t
Enter configuration commands, one per line.  End with CNTL/Z.
Jealousy(config)# ip pim rp-address 192.168.1.1
Jealousy(config)# end

Jealousy# show ip pim rp
PIM RP Status Information for VRF "default"
BSR disabled
Auto-RP disabled
BSR RP Candidate policy: None
BSR RP policy: None
Auto-RP Announce policy: None
Auto-RP Discovery policy: None

RP: 192.168.1.1*, (0), uptime: 00:00:05, expires: never,
  priority: 0, RP-source: (local), group ranges:
      224.0.0.0/4
Jealousy#
```

In the output in Example 4-3, the static RP configured supports all multicast traffic for 224.0.0.0/4. NX-OS enables the configuration of multiple RP addresses to service different group ranges. In Example 4-4, Jealousy's configuration is modified to use Denial as the RP for 239.0.0.0/8.

Example 4-4 *Configuring a Group Range Per RP*

```
Jealousy# confi t
Enter configuration commands, one per line.  End with CNTL/Z.
Jealousy(config)# ip pim rp-address 192.168.1.3 group-list 238.0.0.0/8
Jealousy# show ip pim rp
PIM RP Status Information for VRF "default"
BSR disabled
Auto-RP disabled
BSR RP Candidate policy: None
BSR RP policy: None
Auto-RP Announce policy: None
```

```
Auto-RP Discovery policy: None

RP: 192.168.1.1*, (0), uptime: 00:03:36, expires: never,
   priority: 0, RP-source: (local), group ranges:
        224.0.0.0/4
RP: 192.168.1.3, (0), uptime: 00:00:05, expires: never,
   priority: 0, RP-source: (local), group ranges:
        238.0.0.0/8
Jealousy#
Jealousy(config)# end
```

Configuring BSRs

The next RP configuration methodology is Bootstrap Router (BSR). In Example 4-5, Greed is configured with both a bsr-candidate and bsr rp-candidate policy for groups in the 239.0.0.0/8 range. This enables Greed to participate in BSR elections and, if elected as a RP, apply a policy determining which routes will be advertised. Jealousy is configured to listen to BSR messages as well.

Example 4-5   *BSR Base Configuration*

```
Greed# show ip pim rp
PIM RP Status Information for VRF "default"
BSR disabled
Auto-RP disabled
BSR RP Candidate policy: None
BSR RP policy: None
Auto-RP Announce policy: None
Auto-RP Discovery policy: None
Greed# config t
Enter configuration commands, one per line.  End with CNTL/Z.
Greed(config)# ip pim bsr bsr-candidate port-channel10
Greed(config)# ip pim bsr rp-candidate port-channel10 group-list 239.0.0.0/8
Greed(config)# end

Greed# show ip pim rp
PIM RP Status Information for VRF "default"
BSR: 192.168.1.34*, next Bootstrap message in: 00:00:54,
     priority: 64, hash-length: 30
Auto-RP disabled
BSR RP Candidate policy: None
BSR RP policy: None
Auto-RP Announce policy: None
Auto-RP Discovery policy: None
```

```
RP: 192.168.1.34*, (0), uptime: 00:00:05, expires: 00:02:24,
  priority: 192, RP-source: 192.168.1.34 (B), group ranges:
    239.0.0.0/8
Greed#
! On Jealousy, the configuration is modified to add BSR listen support.
Jealousy# show ip pim rp
PIM RP Status Information for VRF "default"
BSR forward-only mode
BSR: Not Operational
Auto-RP disabled
BSR RP Candidate policy: None
BSR RP policy: None
Auto-RP Announce policy: None
Auto-RP Discovery policy: None

Jealousy# confi t
Enter configuration commands, one per line.  End with CNTL/Z.
Jealousy(config)# ip pim bsr listen
Jealousy(config)# end

Jealousy# show ip pim rp
PIM RP Status Information for VRF "default"
BSR: 192.168.1.34, uptime: 0.033521, expires: 00:02:09,
    priority: 64, hash-length: 30
Auto-RP disabled
BSR RP Candidate policy: None
BSR RP policy: None
Auto-RP Announce policy: None
Auto-RP Discovery policy: None

RP: 192.168.1.34*, (0), uptime: 0.033667, expires: 00:02:29,
  priority: 192, RP-source: 192.168.1.34 (B), group ranges:
    239.0.0.0/8
Jealousy#
```

Configuring BSR for Bidir is simply a matter of adding bidir to the **rp-candidate** command. Example 4-6 illustrates this, and you can see the change on Jealousy.

Example 4-6 *Configuring BSR and Bidir*

```
Greed# config t
Enter configuration commands, one per line.  End with CNTL/Z.
Greed(config)# ip pim bsr bsr-candidate port-channel10
```

```
Greed(config)# ip pim bsr rp-candidate port-channel10 group-list 239.0.0.0/8 bidir
Greed(config)# end
Greed# show ip pim rp
PIM RP Status Information for VRF "default"
BSR: 192.168.1.34*, next Bootstrap message in: 00:00:56,
     priority: 64, hash-length: 30
Auto-RP disabled
BSR RP Candidate policy: None
BSR RP policy: None
Auto-RP Announce policy: None
Auto-RP Discovery policy: None
RP: 192.168.1.34*, (1), uptime: 00:00:06, expires: 00:02:23,
  priority: 192, RP-source: 192.168.1.34 (B), group ranges:
      239.0.0.0/8 (bidir)


Greed# show ip pim group
PIM Group-Range Configuration for VRF "default"
Group-range      Mode     RP-address      Shared-tree-only range
232.0.0.0/8      SSM      -               -
239.0.0.0/8      Bidir    192.168.1.34    -
- - - - - - - - - - - - - - - - - - - - - - - - - - - - - - - - - - - - - - - - -
! Jealousy is configured to listen to BSR messages.
Jealousy# confi t
Enter configuration commands, one per line.  End with CNTL/Z.
Jealousy(config)# ip pim bsr listen
Jealousy(config)# end

Jealousy# show ip pim group
PIM Group-Range Configuration for VRF "default"
Group-range      Mode     RP-address      Shared-tree-only range
232.0.0.0/8      SSM      -               -
239.0.0.0/8      Bidir    192.168.1.34    -
Jealousy#
```

Configuring Auto-RP

NX-OS also supports Auto-RP, a Cisco-specific precursor to BSR. In Example 4-7, Greed is configured as both a mapping agent and candidate RP. A mapping agent is a role a router can take in an Auto-RP network responsible for RP elections based on information sent from candidate RPs. A candidate RP in an Auto-RP network advertises its capability to serve as an RP to the mapping agent. This can be useful to help scale networks as they grow. Jealousy is configured to listen and forward Auto-RP messages.

Example 4-7   *Configuring an Auto-RP Mapping Agent and Candidate RP*

```
Greed# confi t
Enter configuration commands, one per line.  End with CNTL/Z.
Greed(config)# ip pim auto-rp listen forward
Greed(config)# ip pim auto-rp rp-candidate port-channel10 group-list 239.0.0.0/8
Greed(config)# ip pim auto-rp mapping-agent port-channel10
Greed(config)# end
Greed# show ip pim rp
PIM RP Status Information for VRF "default"
BSR disabled
Auto-RP RPA: 192.168.1.34*, next Discovery message in: 00:00:50
BSR RP Candidate policy: None
BSR RP policy: None
Auto-RP Announce policy: None
Auto-RP Discovery policy: None

RP: 192.168.1.34*, (0), uptime: 00:00:46, expires: 00:02:53,
  priority: 0, RP-source: 192.168.1.34 (A), group ranges:
      239.0.0.0/8
--------------------------------------------------------------------------
! Jealousy is configured to listen and forward Auto-RP messages.
Jealousy# confi t
Enter configuration commands, one per line.  End with CNTL/Z.
Jealousy(config)# ip pim auto-rp forward listen
Jealousy(config)# end

Jealousy# show ip pim rp
PIM RP Status Information for VRF "default"
BSR forward-only mode
BSR: Not Operational
Auto-RP RPA: 192.168.1.34, uptime: 00:04:22, expires: 00:02:06
BSR RP Candidate policy: None
BSR RP policy: None
Auto-RP Announce policy: None
Auto-RP Discovery policy: None

RP: 192.168.1.34*, (0), uptime: 00:03:28, expires: 00:02:06,
  priority: 0, RP-source: 192.168.1.34 (A), group ranges:
      239.0.0.0/8
Jealousy#
```

> **Note**   The commands **ip pim send-rp-announce** and **ip pim auto-rp rp-candidate** perform the same function and can be used as alternatives for each other with no impact to functionality.
>
> The commands **ip pim send-rp-discovery** and **ip pim auto-rp mapping agent** perform the same function and can be used as alterntates for each other with no impact to functionality.

Configuring Auto-RP for Bidir is simply a matter of adding **bidir** to the **rp-candidate** command. Example 4-8 illustrates this, and the change can be observed on Jealousy.

Example 4-8   *Configuring Auto-RP and Bidir*

```
Greed# confi t
Enter configuration commands, one per line.  End with CNTL/Z.
Greed(config)#
Greed(config)#
Greed(config)# ip pim auto-rp rp-candidate port-channel10 group-list 239.0.0.0/8
bidir
Greed(config)# end


Greed# show ip pim group
PIM Group-Range Configuration for VRF "default"
Group-range       Mode      RP-address       Shared-tree-only range
232.0.0.0/8       SSM       -                -
239.0.0.0/8       Bidir     192.168.1.34     -
```

Configuring Anycast-RP

An alternative configuration is PIM Anycast-RP in which the same IP address is configured on multiple devices. This capability enables receivers to follow the unicast routing table to find the best path to the RP. It is commonly used in large environments where the desire is to minimize the impact of being an RP on a device and provide rudimentary load-balancing. In Example 4-9, both Greed and Jealousy have Loopback1 added to their configuration and defined as the PIM Anycast-RP for the network shown in Figure 4-5. This additonal loopback is added to ease troubleshooting in the network and easily identify anycast traffic.

Example 4-9   *Configuring PIM Anycast-RP*

```
Greed# config t
Enter configuration commands, one per line.  End with CNTL/Z.
Greed(config)# int lo1
Greed(config-if)# Desc Loopback or PIM Anycast-RP
Greed(config-if)# ip address 192.168.1.100/32
Greed(config-if)# ip router eigrp 100
```

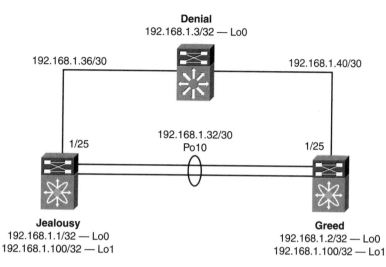

Denial
192.168.1.3/32 — Lo0

192.168.1.36/30   192.168.1.40/30

192.168.1.32/30
Po10

1/25   1/25

Jealousy   **Greed**
192.168.1.1/32 — Lo0   192.168.1.2/32 — Lo0
192.168.1.100/32 — Lo1   192.168.1.100/32 — Lo1

Figure 4-5   *PIM Anycast-RP Topology*

```
Greed(config-if)# no shut
Greed(config-if)# exit
Greed(config)# ip pim anycast-rp 192.168.1.100 192.168.1.33
Greed(config)# end

Greed# show ip pim rp
PIM RP Status Information for VRF "default"
BSR disabled
Auto-RP disabled
BSR RP Candidate policy: None
BSR RP policy: None
Auto-RP Announce policy: None
Auto-RP Discovery policy: None
-----------------------------------------------------------------------
Anycast-RP 192.168.1.100 members:
  192.168.1.33
! The same configuration is applied to Jealousy with the exception of the address
used by the pim anycast-rp command.
Jealousy# config t
Enter configuration commands, one per line.  End with CNTL/Z.
Jealousy(config)# int lo1
Jealousy(config-if)# Desc Loopback or PIM Anycast-RP
Jealousy(config-if)# ip address 192.168.1.100/32
Jealousy(config-if)# ip router eigrp 100
Jealousy(config-if)# no shut
Jealousy(config-if)# exit
```

```
Jealousy(config)# ip pim anycast-rp 192.168.1.100 192.168.1.34
Jealousy(config)# end
Jealousy# show ip pim rp
PIM RP Status Information for VRF "default"
BSR forward-only mode
BSR: Not Operational
Auto-RP disabled
BSR RP Candidate policy: None
BSR RP policy: None
Auto-RP Announce policy: None
Auto-RP Discovery policy: None

Anycast-RP 192.168.1.100 members:
  192.168.1.34
```

Configuring SSM and Static RPF

Two methods for configuring support of multicast traffic do not rely on an RP—Source Specific Multicast (SSM) and Static RPF entries. In Example 4-10, Greed is configured to support SSM on the 239.0.0.0/8 range of multicast addresses.

SSM has the advantage of not requiring an RP to function, and in some topologies this can lend itself to more efficient routing through the network. The main considerations for using SSM include the requirement for the receivers to use IGMPv3 and support for SSM by the Internet working equipment.

Static RPF, similar to static routing in unicast traffic, might be desirable where the topology is simple or lacks multiple paths where a dynamic routing protocol would be advantageous.

Example 4-10   *Configuration of SSM*

```
Greed# config t
Enter configuration commands, one per line.  End with CNTL/Z.
Greed(config)# ip pim ssm range 239.0.0.0/8
This command overwrites default SSM route
Greed(config)# end

Greed# show ip pim group
PIM Group-Range Configuration for VRF "default"
Group-range        Mode     RP-address       Shared-tree-only range
239.0.0.0/8        SSM      -                -
Greed#
```

> **Note**   NX-OS will display a warning about changing the default SSM configuration. NX-OS supports SSM on 232.0.0.0/8 by default.

Finally, configuration of static RPF entries enables the network administrator to define multicast routes through the network that do not follow the unicast routing table via PIM. In Example 4-11, a static RPF entry is created on Greed to send 192.168.1.1/32 traffic through Denial via 192.168.1.42. Using static RPF entries can be desirable in networks where per usage fees are associated or where extremely high latency might be masked by the unicast routing protocol, such as satellite networks.

Example 4-11   *Configuring a Static RPF Entry*

```
Greed# show ip route 192.168.1.1
IP Route Table for VRF "default"
'*' denotes best ucast next-hop
'**' denotes best mcast next-hop
'[x/y]' denotes [preference/metric]

192.168.1.1/32, ubest/mbest: 1/0
    *via 192.168.1.33, Po10, [90/128576], 03:25:55, eigrp-100, internal

Greed# config t
Enter configuration commands, one per line.  End with CNTL/Z.
Greed(config)# ip mroute 192.168.1.1/32 192.168.1.42
Greed(config)# end

Greed# show ip route 192.168.1.1
IP Route Table for VRF "default"
'*' denotes best ucast next-hop
'**' denotes best mcast next-hop
'[x/y]' denotes [preference/metric]

192.168.1.1/32, ubest/mbest: 1/1
    *via 192.168.1.33, Po10, [90/128576], 03:26:21, eigrp-100, internal
    **via 192.168.1.42, Eth1/25, [1/0], 00:00:06, mstatic
```

IGMP Operation

Internet Group Management Protocol (IGMP) is an important component of a multicast network. IGMP is the protocol used by a host to signal its desire to join a specific multicast group. The router that sees the IGMP join message begins to send the multicast traffic requested by the host to the receiver. IGMP has matured over time, and there currently are three versions specified, named appropriately enough: IGMPv1, IGMPv2, and IGMPv3.

IGMPv1 is defined in the Internet Engineering Task Force (IETF) Request for Comments (RFC) 1112, IGMPv2 is defined in RFC 2236, and IGMPv3 is defined in RFC 3376.

Note Most modern operating systems use IGMPv3, though there are legacy systems that do not yet support it.

IGMP works through membership reports, and at its most simple process, routers on a network receive an unsolicited membership report from hosts that want to receive multicast traffic. The router processes these requests and begins to send the multicast traffic to the host until either a timeout value or a leave message is received.

IGMPv3 adds support for SSM, previously described in the chapter. Additionally, IGMPv3 hosts do not perform report suppression like IGMPv1 and IGMPv2 hosts. IGMP report suppression is a methodology in which the switch sends only one IGMP report per multicast router query to avoid duplicate IGMP reports and preserve CPU resources.

IGMP works on routers that understand multicast traffic. In the case of switches that might operate only at Layer 2, a technology called *IGMP snooping* enables intelligent forwarding of multicast traffic without broadcast or flooding behaviors. IGMP snooping enables a Layer 2 switch to examine, or snoop, IGMP membership reports and send multicast traffic only to ports with hosts that ask for the specific groups. Without IGMP snooping, a typical Layer 2 switch would flood all multicast traffic to every port. This could be quite a lot of traffic and can negatively impact network performance.

IGMP Configuration on Nexus 7000

The Nexus 7000 is a Layer 3 switch and as such can do both full IGMP processing and IGMP snooping. By default, IGMP is enabled on an interface when the following conditions are met:

■ PIM is enabled on the interface.

■ A local multicast group is statically bound.

■ Link-local reports are enabled.

Note IGMPv2 is enabled by default, though IGMPv3 can be specified to change the default.

In Example 4-12, PIM is configured on interface VLAN10, and IGMP in turn is enabled for the network shown in Figure 4-6.

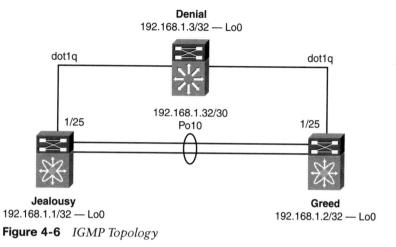

Figure 4-6 *IGMP Topology*

Example 4-12 *Enabling IGMP on an Interface*

```
Greed# show ip igmp int vlan 10
IGMP is disabled on Vlan10

Greed# confi t
Enter configuration commands, one per line.  End with CNTL/Z.
Greed(config)# int vlan 10
Greed(config-if)# ip pim sparse-mode
Greed(config-if)# end

Greed# show ip igmp int vlan 10
IGMP Interfaces for VRF "default"
Vlan10, Interface status: protocol-up/link-up/admin-up
  IP address: 192.168.10.2, IP subnet: 192.168.10.0/24
  Active querier: 192.168.10.2, version: 2, next query sent in: 00:00:22
  Membership count: 0
  Old Membership count 0
  Route-queue depth: 0
  IGMP version: 2, host version: 2
  IGMP query interval: 125 secs, configured value: 125 secs
  IGMP max response time: 10 secs, configured value: 10 secs
  IGMP startup query interval: 31 secs, configured value: 31 secs
  IGMP startup query count: 2
  IGMP last member mrt: 1 secs
  IGMP last member query count: 2
  IGMP group timeout: 260 secs, configured value: 260 secs
  IGMP querier timeout: 255 secs, configured value: 255 secs
  IGMP unsolicited report interval: 10 secs
  IGMP robustness variable: 2, configured value: 2
```

```
IGMP reporting for link-local groups: disabled
IGMP interface enable refcount: 1
IGMP interface immediate leave: disabled
IGMP Report Policy: None
IGMP State Limit: None
IGMP interface statistics:
  General (sent/received):
    v1-reports: 0/0
    v2-queries: 2/2, v2-reports: 0/0, v2-leaves: 0/0
    v3-queries: 0/0, v3-reports: 0/0
  Errors:
    General Queries received with invalid destination address; v2: 0, v3: 0
    Checksum errors: 0, Packet length errors: 0
    Packets with Local IP as source: 0, Source subnet check failures: 0
    Query from non-querier:0
    Report version mismatch: 0, Query version mismatch: 0
    Unknown IGMP message type: 0
    Invalid v1 reports: 0, Invalid v2 reports: 0, Invalid v3 reports: 0
  Packets dropped due to router-alert check: 0
Interface PIM DR: Yes
Interface vPC CFS statistics:
  DR queries sent: 0
  DR queries rcvd: 0
  DR queries fail: 0
  DR updates sent: 0
  DR updates rcvd: 0
  DR updates fail: 0
Greed#
```

In Example 4-13, the version of IGMP is changed from IGMPv2 to IGMPv3 to enable support for SSM.

Example 4-13 *Changing the IGMP Version*

```
Greed# confi t
Enter configuration commands, one per line.  End with CNTL/Z.
Greed(config)# int vlan 10
Greed(config-if)# ip igmp version 3
Greed(config-if)# end
Greed# show ip igmp int vlan 10
IGMP Interfaces for VRF "default"
Vlan10, Interface status: protocol-up/link-up/admin-up
  IP address: 192.168.10.2, IP subnet: 192.168.10.0/24
  Active querier: 192.168.10.2, version: 3, next query sent in: 00:00:36
```

```
   Membership count: 0
   Old Membership count 0
   Route-queue depth: 0
   IGMP version: 3, host version: 3
   IGMP query interval: 125 secs, configured value: 125 secs
   IGMP max response time: 10 secs, configured value: 10 secs
   IGMP startup query interval: 31 secs, configured value: 31 secs
   IGMP startup query count: 2
   IGMP last member mrt: 1 secs
   IGMP last member query count: 2
   IGMP group timeout: 260 secs, configured value: 260 secs
   IGMP querier timeout: 255 secs, configured value: 255 secs
   IGMP unsolicited report interval: 10 secs
   IGMP robustness variable: 2, configured value: 2
   IGMP reporting for link-local groups: disabled
   IGMP interface enable refcount: 1
   IGMP interface immediate leave: disabled
   IGMP Report Policy: None
   IGMP State Limit: None
   IGMP interface statistics:
     General (sent/received):
       v1-reports: 0/0
       v2-queries: 4/4, v2-reports: 0/0, v2-leaves: 0/0
       v3-queries: 0/0, v3-reports: 0/0
     Errors:
       General Queries received with invalid destination address; v2: 0, v3: 0
       Checksum errors: 0, Packet length errors: 0
       Packets with Local IP as source: 0, Source subnet check failures: 0
       Query from non-querier:0
       Report version mismatch: 0, Query version mismatch: 0
       Unknown IGMP message type: 0
       Invalid v1 reports: 0, Invalid v2 reports: 0, Invalid v3 reports: 0
     Packets dropped due to router-alert check: 0
   Interface PIM DR: Yes
   Interface vPC CFS statistics:
     DR queries sent: 0
     DR queries rcvd: 0
     DR queries fail: 0
     DR updates sent: 0
     DR updates rcvd: 0
     DR updates fail: 0
Greed#
```

In Example 4-14, IGMP snooping is enabled and the configuration is displayed.

Example 4-14   *IGMP Snooping on Nexus 7000*

```
Greed# show ip igmp snooping vlan 10
IGMP Snooping information for vlan 10
  IGMP snooping enabled
  IGMP querier present, address: 192.168.10.2, version: 3, interface Vlan10
  Querier interval: 125 secs
  Querier last member query interval: 1 secs
  Querier robustness: 2
  Switch-querier disabled
  IGMPv3 Explicit tracking enabled
  IGMPv2 Fast leave disabled
  IGMPv1/v2 Report suppression enabled
  IGMPv3 Report suppression disabled
  Link Local Groups suppression enabled
  Router port detection using PIM Hellos, IGMP Queries
  Number of router-ports: 1
  Number of groups: 0
  Active ports:
    Eth1/25
Greed#
```

Note   By default, IGMP snooping is enabled. Network administrators should carefully examine any requirements to disable IGMP snooping and the detrimental performance that might be experienced.

IGMP Configuration on Nexus 5000

The Nexus 5000 is a Layer 2 switch and fully supports IGMP snooping. By default, IGMP snooping is enabled, so no direct configuration is required for this feature to work. Example 4-15 reviews the IGMP snooping configuration for the network illustrated in Figure 4-7.

Example 4-15   *IGMP Snooping on Nexus 5000*

```
CMHLAB-N5K1# show ip igmp snooping vlan 100
IGMP Snooping information for vlan 100
  IGMP snooping enabled
  IGMP querier present, address: 10.2.1.1, version: 2, interface port-channel30
  Switch-querier disabled
  IGMPv3 Explicit tracking enabled
  IGMPv2 Fast leave disabled
```

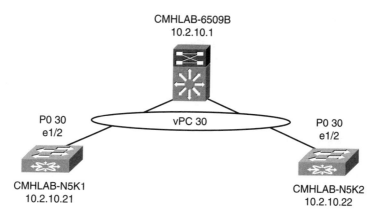

Figure 4-7   *IGMP Snooping Topology on Nexus 5000*

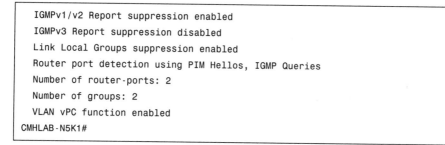

IGMP Configuration on Nexus 1000V

The Nexus 1000V is a Layer 2 switch and fully supports IGMP snooping. By default, IGMP snooping is enabled, so no direct configuration is required for this feature to work. Example 4-16 reviews the IGMP snooping configuration, as depicted in Figure 4-8.

Example 4-16   *IGMP Snooping on Nexus 1000V*

```
CMHLAB-DC2-VSM1# show ip igmp snooping vlan 100
IGMP Snooping information for vlan 100
  IGMP snooping enabled
  IGMP querier present, address: 10.2.1.1, version: 2, interface Ethernet4/2
  Switch-querier disabled
  IGMPv3 Explicit tracking enabled
  IGMPv2 Fast leave disabled
  IGMPv1/v2 Report suppression enabled
  IGMPv3 Report suppression disabled
  Router port detection using PIM Hellos, IGMP Queries
  Number of router-ports: 3
  Number of groups: 3
CMHLAB-DC2-VSM1#
```

The Nexus 1000V also supports IGMP snooping on vEthernet ports created for Guest Virtual Machines (VM). This provides the capability to better control IP multicast traffic in a VMware virtualized network to improve performance and reduce CPU load. Example 4-17 shows the IGMP snooping on vEthernet1 that maps to a Guest VM called CMHLAB-TestSrv3.

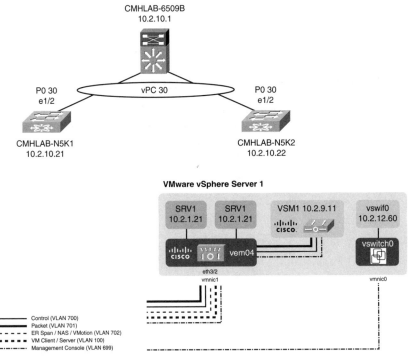

Figure 4-8   *Network Topology for IGMP Snooping Configuration*

Example 4-17   *IGMP Snooping on vEthernet1*

```
CMHLAB-DC2-VSM1# show ip igmp snooping groups vlan 100
Type: S - Static, D - Dynamic, R - Router port

Vlan   Group Address      Ver  Type  Port list
100    */*                v2   R     Eth6/2 Eth5/1 Eth4/2
100    224.0.1.24         v2   D     Veth8
100    239.0.0.10         v2   D     Veth1
100    239.255.255.254    v2   D     Veth8
CMHLAB-DC2-VSM1#
CMHLAB-DC2-VSM1# show int vether1
Vethernet1 is up
    Port description is CMHLAB-Testsrv3, Network Adapter 1
    Hardware is Virtual, address is 0050.5686.0a8d
    Owner is VM "CMHLAB-Testsrv3", adapter is Network Adapter 1
    Active on module 4
    VMware DVS port 66
    Port-Profile is DC2-N1K-VLAN100
    Port mode is access
    5 minute input rate 112 bits/second, 0 packets/second
    5 minute output rate 930872 bits/second, 818 packets/second
    Rx
    144716 Input Packets 128048 Unicast Packets
    19 Multicast Packets 16649 Broadcast Packets
    26634502 Bytes
    Tx
    1857975 Output Packets 158259 Unicast Packets
    540565 Multicast Packets 1159151 Broadcast Packets 529325 Flood Packets
    257965170 Bytes
    100 Input Packet Drops 0 Output Packet Drops

CMHLAB-DC2-VSM1#
```

MSDP Configuration on Nexus 7000

NX-OS on the Nexus 7000 supports MSDP to provide interdomain multicast capabilities. MSDP enables for multicast source information to be shared between PIM domains.

Note   MSDP requires BGP to be configured and working prior to successful implementation.

The first step to configure MSDP is to enable it in global configuration mode using the
feature command. With the modular nature of NX-OS, using the **feature** command loads
the MSDP modular code into memory for execution. The MSDP feature will not be resident in memory without first being enabled. This is advantageous because it preserves
memory resources in the router when a feature is not used. In Example 4-18, MSDP is
enabled as a feature on Router Jealousy, as depicted in Figure 4-9.

Example 4-18   *Enabling the MSDP Feature on the Jealousy Router*

```
Jealousy# confi t
Enter configuration commands, one per line.  End with CNTL/Z.
Jealousy(config)# feature msdp
Jealousy(config)# end
Jealousy# show run msdp

!Command: show running-config msdp
!Time: Mon Dec 21 06:48:46 2009


version 4.2(2a)
feature msdp
```

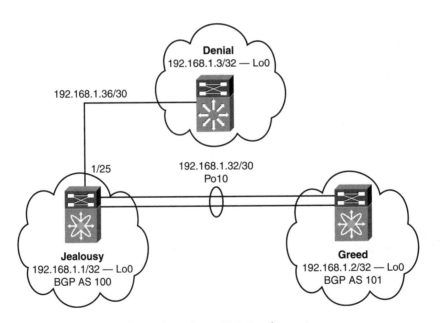

Figure 4-9   *Network Topology for MSDP Configuration*

In Example 4-19, MSDP is configured on Jealousy (AS 100) to provide an interdomain multicast connection between Greed (AS 101) and Denial (AS 102).

Example 4-19 *MSDP Peer Configuration*

```
Jealousy# confi t
Enter configuration commands, one per line.  End with CNTL/Z.
Jealousy(config)# ip msdp peer 192.168.1.34 connect-source port-channel10 remote-as
101
Jealousy(config)# ip msdp description 192.168.1.34 MSDP Peer to Greed
Jealousy(config)#
Jealousy(config)# ip msdp peer 192.168.1.38 connect-source Ethernet1/25 remote-as
103
Jealousy(config)# ip msdp description 192.168.1.38 MSDP Peer to Denial
Jealousy(config)#
Jealousy(config)# end

Jealousy# show ip msdp sum
MSDP Peer Status Summary for VRF "default"
Local ASN: 100, originator-id: 0.0.0.0


Number of configured peers:  2
Number of established peers: 2
Number of shutdown peers:    0


Peer            Peer        Connection    Uptime/    Last msg  (S,G)s
Address         ASN         State         Downtime   Received  Received
192.168.1.34    101         Established   00:00:08   00:00:07  0
192.168.1.38    103         Established   00:00:08   00:00:07  0
```

Summary

NX-OS has a rich set of multicast features embedded into the operating system to provide the options and support a modern network administrator requires. Support for PIM and its myriad of choices such as ASM, SSM, Bidir, and static RPF provide the capability to integrate into networks of most any size and topology.

Supporting key technologies such as IGMP and IGMP snooping empower NX-OS to scale to meet the demands of a modern multicast network. These tools also enable the network administrator to have the ability to filter and control the flow of multicast at Layer 2 with a comprehensive set of options in the Nexus 7000, 5000, and 1000V.

Finally, providing support for interdomain multicast through the use of MSDP enables network administrators to scale their networks with the use of BGP and still retain the ability to implement multicast. MSDP also enables multicast to be facilitated between autonomous systems and between PIM domains for significant flexibility and control.

Chapter 5

Security

This chapter covers the following topics:

- Configuring RADIUS
- Configuring TACACS+
- Configuring SSH
- Configuring Cisco TrustSec
- Configuring IP ACLs
- Configuring MAC ACLs
- Configuring VLAN ACLs
- Configuring Port Security
- Configuring DHCP Snooping
- Configuring Dynamic ARP Inspection
- Configuring IP Source Guard
- Configuring Keychain Management
- Configuring Traffic Storm Control
- Configuring Unicast RPF
- Configuring Control Plane Policing
- Configuring Rate Limits
- SNMPv3

Security is a common discussion and concern. Cisco NX-OS Software supports a pervasive security feature set that protects with NX-OS switches, protects the network against network degradation, protects the network against failure, and protects against data loss or compromise resulting from intentional attacks. This chapter discusses several security features to address a defense in-depth approach to provide a scaleable, robust, and secure data center solution set.

Configuring RADIUS

Authentication, Authorization, and Accounting (AAA) services enable verification of identity, granting of access, and tracking the actions of users managing a Cisco NX-OS device. Cisco NX-OS devices support Remote Access Dial-In User Service (RADIUS) or Terminal Access Controller Access Control device Plus (TACACS+) protocols.

Based on the user ID and password combination provided, Cisco NX-OS devices perform local authentication or authorization using the local database or remote authentication or authorization using one or more AAA servers. A preshared secret key provides security for communication between the Cisco NX-OS device and AAA servers. A common secret key can be configured for all AAA servers or for specific AAA server.

AAA security provides the following services:

- **Authentication:** Identifies users, including login and password dialog, challenge and response, messaging support, and, depending on the security protocol selected, encryption.

  Authentication is the process of verifying the identity of the person or device accessing the Cisco NX-OS device, which is based on the user ID and password combination provided by the entity trying to access the Cisco NX-OS device. Cisco NX-OS devices enable local authentication (using the local lookup database) or remote authentication (using one or more RADIUS or TACACS+ servers).

- **Authorization:** Provides access control. AAA authorization is the process of assembling a set of attributes that describe what the user is authorized to perform. Authorization in the Cisco NX-OS software is provided by attributes downloaded from AAA servers. Remote security servers, such as RADIUS and TACACS+, authorize users for specific rights by associating attribute-value (AV) pairs, which define those rights with the appropriate user.

- **Accounting:** Provides the method for collecting information, logging the information locally, and sending the information to the AAA server for billing, auditing, and reporting.

The accounting feature tracks and maintains a log of every management session used to access the Cisco NX-OS device. The logs can be used to generate reports for troubleshooting and auditing purposes. The accounting log can be stored locally or sent to remote AAA servers.

AAA services provides several benefits such as flexibility and control of access configuration, scalability, and centralized or distributed authentication methods, such as RADIUS and TACACS+.

Successful deployment of AAA services includes several prerequisites:

- Verification that the RADIUS or TACACS+ server is reachable through IP, such as a simple ping test.

- Verification that the Cisco NX-OS device is configured as a client of the AAA servers.

- Configuration of a secret key on the Cisco NX-OS device and the remote AAA servers.

- Verification that the remote server responds to AAA requests from the Cisco NX-OS device by specifying the correct source interface.

The TACACS+ protocol provides centralized validation of users attempting to gain access to a Cisco NX-OS device. TACACS+ services are maintained in a database on a TACACS+ daemon running on a Cisco ACS Linux appliance. TACACS+ provides for separate authentication, authorization, and accounting facilities. The TACACS+ protocol uses TCP port 49 for transport communication.

RADIUS is a client/server protocol through which remote access servers communicate with a central server to authenticate users and authorize their access to the requested system or service. RADIUS maintains user profiles in a central database that all remote servers can share. This model provides security, and the company can use it to set up a policy that is applied at a single administered network point. Cisco Secure ACS 5.0 accepts authentication requests on port 1645 and port 1812. For RADIUS accounting, Cisco Secure ACS accepts accounting packets on ports 1646 and 1813.

Example 5-1 shows how to configure the authentication methods for the console login with RADIUS authentication, based on the network topology shown in Figure 5-1.

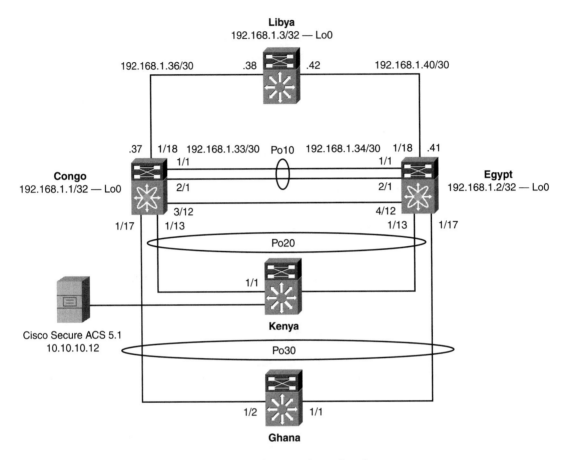

Figure 5-1   *Security Network Topology Used Throughout the Chapter*

> **Note**   Unless otherwise noted, refer to the network topology illustrated in Figure 5-1 for all remaining configuration examples throughout the chapter.

Example 5-1   *AAA RADIUS Configuration for Console Authentication*

```
Egypt#
Egypt# conf t
Egypt (config)# interface loopback0
Egypt (config)# ip address 192.168.1.2/32
Egypt (config)# ip radius source-interface loopback0
Egypt (config)# radius-server host 10.10.10.12 key 7 "QTSX123" authentication
accounting
Egypt (config)# aaa authentication login console group radius
Egypt (config)# interface loopback0
Egypt (config)# ip address 192.168.1.1/32
```

```
Egypt (config)# exit
Egypt# copy running-config startup-config
```

Example 5-2 shows the configuration of default login authentication methods.

Example 5-2   *AAA RADIUS Configuration for Default Telnet / SSH Authentication*

```
Egypt#
Egypt (config)# interface loopback0
Egypt (config)# ip address 192.168.1.2/32
Egypt (config)# ip radius source-interface loopback0
Egypt (config)# radius-server host 10.10.10.12 key 7 "QTSX123" authentication
accounting
Egypt (config)# aaa authentication login console group radius
Egypt (config)# exit
Egypt# copy running-config startup-config
```

Note   AAA configuration and operations are local to the virtual device context (VDC), except the default console methods and the AAA accounting log. The configuration and operation of the AAA authentication methods for the console login apply only to the default VDC.

RADIUS Configuration Distribution

Cisco Fabric Services (CFS) enables the Cisco NX-OS device to distribute the RADIUS configuration to other Cisco NX-OS devices in the network. When you enable CFS distribution for a feature on your device, the device belongs to a CFS region containing other devices in the network that you have also enabled for CFS distribution for the feature.

RADIUS CFS distribution is disabled by default. To enable RADIUS configuration distribution, use the following command:

```
Egypt (config)# radius distribute
```

To apply the RADIUS configuration changes in the temporary database to the running configuration and distribute RADIUS, use the following command:

```
Egypt (config)# radius commit
```

Note   Because RADIUS server and global keys are unique, they are not distributed through the CFS sessions. Also, CFS does not distribute the RADIUS server group or AAA commands.

Example 5-3 verifies that there is not any RADIUS configuration on Congo; this example demonstrates that CFS distributes the RADIUS configuration.

Example 5-3 *Verifying No RADIUS Configuration on Switch-1*

```
Congo#
before cfs:
Congo# show running-config radius
!Command: show running-config radius
!Time: Thu Oct  8 18:01:04 2009
version 4.2(2a)
Congo#
```

Example 5-4 verifies that there is not any RADIUS configuration on Egypt; this example demonstrates that CFS distributes the RADIUS configuration.

Example 5-4 *Verifying No RADIUS Configuration on Switch-2*

```
Egypt# show running-config radius
!Command: show running-config radius
!Time: Thu Oct  8 18:00:24 2009
version 4.2(2a)
```

Example 5-5 shows how to configure RADIUS on Egypt.

Example 5-5 *Configuring RADIUS on Switch-2*

```
Egypt#
Egypt# conf t
Egypt(config)# ip radius source-interface  loopback 0
Source-interface configuration is exempted from CFS distribution
Egypt(config)# radius-server host 10.10.10.12 key NXOS123
Egypt(config)# aaa authentication login console group radius
Egypt(config)# radius commit
```

Example 5-6 verifies the RADIUS configuration delivered via CFS distribution.

Example 5-6 *Verifying RADIUS CFS Distribution on Switch-2*

```
Egypt(config)# show running-config radius
!Command: show running-config radius
!Time: Thu Oct  8 18:09:31 2009
version 4.2(2a)
radius distribute
radius-server retransmit 0
```

```
radius-server host 10.10.10.12 authentication accounting
radius commit
Egypt(config)#
```

Example 5-7 shows how to verify the RADIUS CFS configuration.

Example 5-7 *Verifying RADIUS CFS Configuration*

```
Egypt# show radius-cfs
distribution : enabled
session ongoing: no
session db: does not exist
merge protocol status: merge activation done
Egypt#

Egypt# show radius-server
retransmission count:1
timeout value:5
deadtime value:0
source interface:loopback0
total number of servers:1

following RADIUS servers are configured:
        10.10.10.12:
                available for authentication on port:1812
                available for accounting on port:1813
Egypt#

Egypt# show cfs peers

Physical Fabric
Switch WWN              IP Address
-------------------------------------------------------------------------------
20:00:00:1b:54:c2:78:c1 172.26.32.39                      [Local]
 20:00:00:1b:54:c2:76:41 172.26.32.37
Total number of entries = 2

Egypt# show cf status
Distribution : Enabled
Distribution over IP : Enabled - mode IPv4
IPv4 multicast address : 239.255.70.83
IPv6 multicast address : ff15::efff:4653
Distribution over Ethernet : Enabled
```

```
Egypt# show cfs merge status
 Application      Scope            Vsan        Status
 radius           Physical-fc-ip    -          Success
Egypt# copy running-config startup-config
```

Note   If the RADIUS server becomes unavailable, the default behavior is to fallback to local NX-OS authentication.

Example 5-8 demonstrates the loss of communication to the Cisco Secure ACS 5.0 Virtual Machine. Manually shut down the interface to the Cisco Secure ACS 5.0 Linux Server, as shown in example. Cisco Secure ACS provides centralized management of access policies for device administration, access control management, and compliance.

Example 5-8   *Administratively Shut Down Interface Gigabit Ethernet1/1 Connected to Cisco ACS RADIUS Server*

```
Kenya# config t
Kenya(config)#int gi1/1
Kenya(config-if)#shutdown
Kenya(config-if)# exit
Kenya(config)# exit


Kenya#show interfaces gigabitEthernet 1/1
GigabitEthernet1/1 is administratively down, line protocol is down (disabled)
  Hardware is Gigabit Ethernet Port, address is 0018.73b1.e280 (bia 0018.73b1.e280)
  MTU 1500 bytes, BW 1000000 Kbit, DLY 10 usec,
     reliability 255/255, txload 1/255, rxload 1/255
  Encapsulation ARPA, loopback not set
  Keepalive set (10 sec)
  Auto-duplex, Auto-speed, link type is auto, media type is 10/100/1000-TX
  input flow-control is off, output flow-control is off
  ARP type: ARPA, ARP Timeout 04:00:00
  Last input 00:01:09, output never, output hang never
  Last clearing of "show interface" counters never
  Input queue: 0/2000/0/0 (size/max/drops/flushes); Total output drops: 0
  Queueing strategy: fifo
  Output queue: 0/40 (size/max)
  5 minute input rate 0 bits/sec, 0 packets/sec
  5 minute output rate 0 bits/sec, 0 packets/sec
     114119 packets input, 73777471 bytes, 0 no buffer
     Received 59680 broadcasts (48762 multicasts)
     0 runts, 0 giants, 0 throttles
```

```
        0 input errors, 0 CRC, 0 frame, 0 overrun, 0 ignored
        0 input packets with dribble condition detected
        3453776 packets output, 281211243 bytes, 0 underruns
        0 output errors, 0 collisions, 0 interface resets
        0 babbles, 0 late collision, 0 deferred
        0 lost carrier, 0 no carrier
        0 output buffer failures, 0 output buffers swapped out
Kenya#
```

Telnet to the Nexus 7000 NX-OS device and log in as admin, as shown in Example 5-9.

Example 5-9 *Local Authentication in the Event the RADIUS Server Is Not Available or Offline*

```
[hk@hk ~]$ telnet congo
Trying 172.26.32.37...
Connected to congo.
Escape character is '^]'.
User Access Verification
login: admin
Password:


Remote AAA servers unreachable; local authentication done



Cisco Nexus Operating System (NX-OS) Software
TAC support: http://www.cisco.com/tac
Copyright (c) 2002-2009, Cisco Systems, Inc. All rights reserved.
The copyrights to certain works contained in this software are
owned by other third parties and used and distributed under
license. Certain components of this software are licensed under
the GNU General Public License (GPL) version 2.0 or the GNU
Lesser General Public License (LGPL) Version 2.1. A copy of each
such license is available at
http://www.opensource.org/licenses/gpl-2.0.php and
http://www.opensource.org/licenses/lgpl-2.1.php
Congo# ping 10.10.10.12
PING 10.10.10.12 (10.10.10.12): 56 data bytes
Request 0 timed out
Request 1 timed out
Request 2 timed out
Request 3 timed out
Request 4 timed out
```

```
--- 10.10.10.12 ping statistics ---
5 packets transmitted, 0 packets received, 100.00% packet loss
Congo#
```

To finish the configuration, the Cisco Secure ACS 5.0 Server needs configuration as well. Figures 5-2 through 5-5 provide a series of screenshots to show the configuration steps from the Cisco Secure ACS GUI.

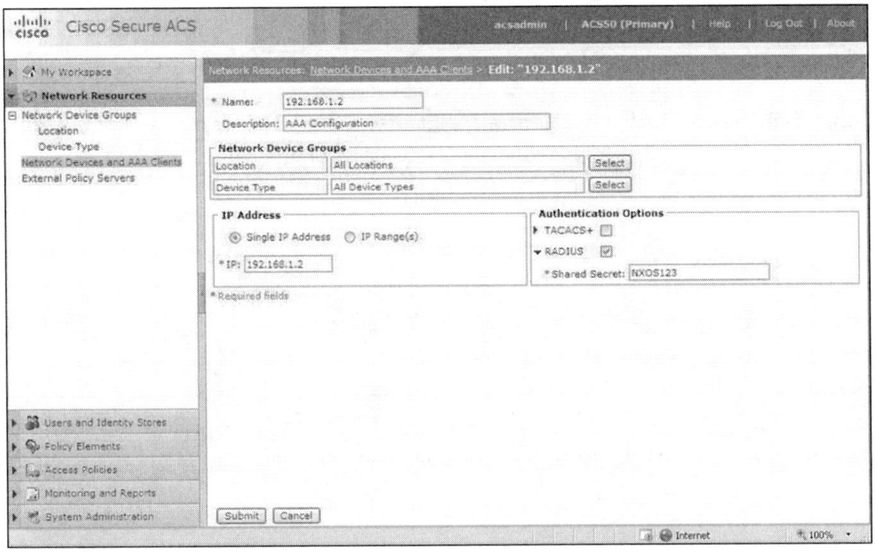

Figure 5-2 *Displaying the Specific Cisco Secure ACS RADIUS Configuration*

Figure 5-2 shows the Cisco Secure ACS RADIUS configuration that defines the loopback of the NX-OS device and the shared secret key that needs to match between both the NX-OS device and the Cisco Secure ACS Server.

Figure 5-3 shows how to add a user to the Cisco Secure Database; user **console1** is added to demonstrate console AAA RADIUS authentication.

Figure 5-4 demonstrates a successful authentication and login with user console1 via the Async console interface of the NX-OS device.

Figure 5-5 verifies the successful RADIUS Authentication report on the Cisco Secure ACS server.

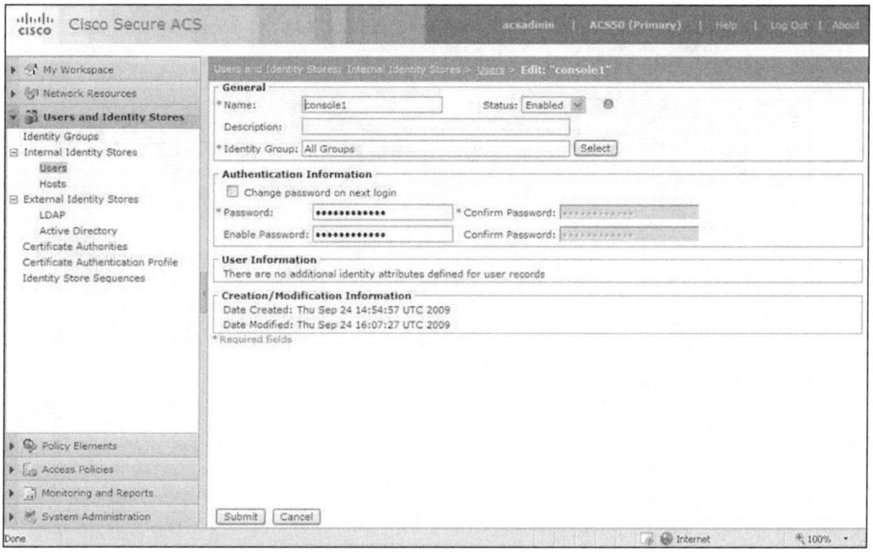

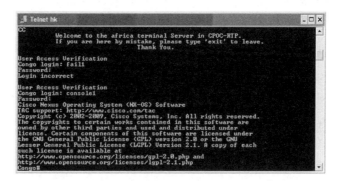

Figure 5-3 *Adding a User to the Cisco Secure RADIUS Database*

Figure 5-4 *A Successful Authentication for User console1 via the Console Interface*

Configuring TACACS+

The TACACS+ protocol provides centralized validation of users attempting to gain access to a Cisco NX-OS device. TACACS+ services are maintained in a database on a TACACS+ daemon running on a Cisco ACS Linux appliance. TACACS+ provides for separate authentication, authorization, and accounting facilities. The TACACS+ protocol uses TCP port 49 for transport communication.

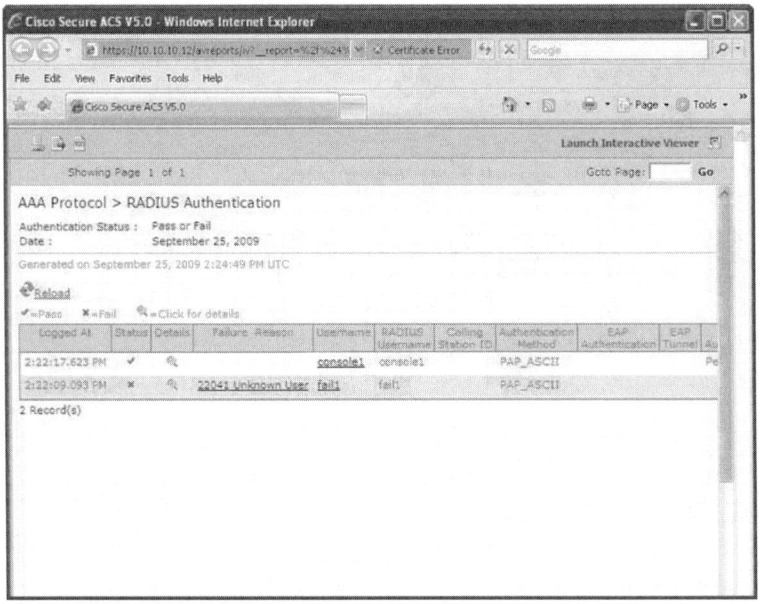

Figure 5-5   *Confirming That User console1 Successfully Authenticates via the RADIUS Protocol*

Enabling TACACS+

The TACACS+ feature is disabled by default. TACACS+ must explicitly enable the TACACS+ feature to access the configuration and verification commands for authentication.

To verify the default TACACS+ feature status, use the following command:

```
Egypt# show feature | i tacacs
tacacs                1          disabled
```

To enable the TACACS+ feature, enter the configuration as demonstrated in Example 5-10.

Example 5-10   *Enabling TACACS+ Feature/Process*

```
Egypt#
Egypt# conf t
Enter configuration commands, one per line. End with CNTL/Z.
Egypt(config)# feature tacacs+
Egypt(config)# show feature | i tacacs
tacacs                1          enabled
Egypt(config)# exit
Egypt# copy running-configuration startup=configuration
```

To verify that the TACACS+ feature is enabled, enter the following command:

```
Egypt# show feature | i tacacs+
tacacs                  1          enabled
Egypt#
```

TACACS+ Configuration Distribution

CFS enables the Cisco NX-OS device to distribute the TACACS+ configuration to other Cisco NX-OS devices in the network. When you enable CFS distribution for a feature on your device, the device belongs to a CFS region containing other devices in the network that you have also enabled for CFS distribution for the feature. CFS distribution for TACACS+ is disabled by default.

To enable TACACS+ CFS distribution, enter the following command:

```
Egypt(config)# tacacs+ distribute
```

To verify TACACS+ CFS distribution, enter the **show tacacs+ status** command, as demonstrated in Example 5-11.

Example 5-11   *Verifying TACACS+ CFS Distribution*

```
Egypt(config)# show tacacs+ status
distribution : enabled
session ongoing: no
session db: does not exist
merge protocol status: not yet initiated after enable

last operation: enable
last operation status: success
Egypt(config)#
```

Configuring the Global TACACS+ Keys

TACACS+ secret keys can be configured at the global level for all servers used by the NX-OS device. The secret key is a shared secret text string between the Cisco NX-OS device and the TACACS+ server hosts.

Note   Because TACACS+ server and global keys are unique, they are not distributed through the CFS sessions. Also, CFS does not distribute the RADIUS server group or aaa commands.

Example 5-12 shows how to configure the TACACS+ server keys.

Example 5-12 *Configuring the TACACS+ Server Keys*

```
Egypt(config)# tacacs-server key 0 NXOS123
Global key configuration is exempted from CFS distribution
Egypt(config)# show tacacs-server
Global TACACS+ shared secret:********
timeout value:5
deadtime value:0
source interface:any available
total number of servers:0
Egypt(config)#
```

Configuring the TACACS+ Server Hosts

To access a remote TACACS+ server, you must configure the IP address or the hostname for the TACACS+ server; in this example the TACACS+ server is 10.10.10.12.

Note   64 TACACS+ servers can be defined or configured.

Example 5-13 shows how to configure the TACACS+ server host; this is the IP address of the Cisco Secure ACS TACACS+ Server.

Example 5-13 *Configuring the TACACS Server Host*

```
Egypt(config)# tacacs-server host 10.10.10.12
Egypt(config)# show tacacs+ pend
pending         pending-diff
Egypt(config)# show tacacs+ pending
tacacs-server key 7 QTSX123
tacacs-server host 10.10.10.12
Egypt(config)# tacacs+ commit
Egypt(config)# show tacacs-server
Global TACACS+ shared secret:********
timeout value:5
deadtime value:0
source interface:any available
total number of servers:1

following TACACS+ servers are configured:
        10.10.10.12:
                available on port:49
Egypt(config)# show tacacs+ pending
No active CFS distribution session exist for TACACS+
Egypt(config)# copy running-config startup-config
[####################################] 100%
Egypt(config)#
```

> **Note** The **tacacs+ commit** command changes the temporary database configuration changes to the running configuration.

Configuring TACACS+ Server Groups

With NX-OS, you can specify one or more remote AAA servers to authenticate users using server groups; members of a group must belong to the TACACS+ protocol. The TACACS+ servers are tried in the same order in which they are configured.

Example 5-14 shows how to configure TACACS+ server groups.

Example 5-14 *Configuring the TACACS+ Server Group of TACACS+Server*

```
Egypt(config)# aaa group server tacacs+ TACACS+Server
Egypt(config-tacacs+)# server 10.10.10.12
Egypt(config-tacacs+)# show tacacs-server groups
total number of groups:1

following TACACS+ server groups are configured:
        group TACACS+Server:
                server 10.10.10.12 on port 49
                deadtime is 0
Egypt(config-tacacs+)#
```

Example 5-15 shows how to configure the default TACACS+ authentication method for Telnet and SSH.

Example 5-15 *Configuring the Default TACACS+ Authentication Method for Telnet and SSH*

```
Egypt(config)# aaa authentication login default group TACACS+Server
Egypt(config)# show tacacs-server
Global TACACS+ shared secret:********
timeout value:5
deadtime value:0
source interface:loopback0
total number of servers:1
following TACACS+ servers are configured:
        10.10.10.12:
                available on port:49
Egypt(config)#
Egypt#
```

Configuring TACACS+ Source Interface

Because you can have multiple Layer 3 interfaces, you can specify the global source interface for TACACS+ server groups to use when accessing TACACS+, because IP reachability is required between the NX-OS device and the Cisco Secure ACS Server:

```
Egypt(config)# ip tacacs source-interface loopback 0
```

Note   Different source interfaces can be specified for specific TACACS+ server groups; by default the NX-OS device picks any available Layer 3 interface.

Note   Note, with TACACS+ CFS enabled, the source-interface configuration is exempted from CFS distribution.

Example 5-16 verifies TACACS+ CFS configuration distribution on the second switch.

Example 5-16   *Verifying TACACS+ CFS Configuration Distribution on the Second Switch*

```
Congo(config)# ip tacacs source-interface loopback 0
Source-interface configuration is exempted from CFS distribution
Congo(config)#
Congo#


CFS on the second Switch
Congo(config)# show feature | i tacacs+
tacacs                   1           disabled
Congo(config)# feature tacacs+
Congo(config)# show feature | i tacacs+
tacacs                   1           enabled
Congo(config)# tacacs+ distribute
Congo(config)# show tacacs+ status
distribution : disabled
session ongoing: no
session db: does not exist
merge protocol status:

last operation: none
last operation status: none
Congo(config)# show running-config tacacs+
!Command: show running-config tacacs+
!Time: Thu Oct  1 14:15:42 2009
version 4.2(2a)
feature tacacs+
Congo(config)# tacacs+ distribute
```

```
Congo(config)# show tacacs+ status
distribution : enabled
session ongoing: no
session db: does not exist
merge protocol status: merge activation done

last operation: enable
last operation status: success
Congo(config)# show running-config tacacs+

!Command: show running-config tacacs+
!Time: Thu Oct  1 14:16:02 2009

version 4.2(2a)
feature tacacs+

tacacs+ distribute
tacacs-server host 10.10.10.12
tacacs+ commit

Congo(config)#
```

Example 5-17 shows successful Telnet authentication using TACACS+.

Example 5-17 *Verifying Successful Telnet Authentication Using TACACS+*

```
[hk@hk ~]$ telnet egypt
Trying 172.26.32.39...
Connected to egypt.
Escape character is '^]'.
User Access Verification
login: admin
Password:
Cisco Nexus Operating System (NX-OS) Software
TAC support: http://www.cisco.com/tac
Copyright (c) 2002-2009, Cisco Systems, Inc. All rights reserved.
The copyrights to certain works contained in this software are
owned by other third parties and used and distributed under
license. Certain components of this software are licensed under
the GNU General Public License (GPL) version 2.0 or the GNU
Lesser General Public License (LGPL) Version 2.1. A copy of each
such license is available at
http://www.opensource.org/licenses/gpl-2.0.php and
http://www.opensource.org/licenses/lgpl-2.1.php
Egypt#
```

In Example 5-18, NX-OS shows the default Local Fallback behavior, administratively shutting down interface gigabit ethernet 1/1 connected to Cisco Secure ACS TACACS+ Server. The ping test demonstrates loss of connectivity to the TACACS+ server. The local fallback is required in the event that the AAA server is unreachable; there is no additional configuration required in NX-OS.

Example 5-18 *Default Local Fallback Behavior, Administratively Shutting Down Interface Gigabit Ethernet 1/1 Connected to Cisco Secure ACS TACACS+ Server*

```
Kenya(config)#int gi1/1
Kenya(config-if)#shut
Kenya(config-if)#
----------------------------------------------------------------------
Egypt# ping 10.10.10.12
PING 10.10.10.12 (10.10.10.12): 56 data bytes
Request 0 timed out
Request 1 timed out
Request 2 timed out
Request 3 timed out
Request 4 timed out
--- 10.10.10.12 ping statistics ---

5 packets transmitted, 0 packets received, 100.00% packet loss
Egypt#
[hk@hk ~]$ telnet egypt
Trying 172.26.32.39...
Connected to egypt.
Escape character is '^]'.
User Access Verification
login: admin
Password:
Cisco Nexus Operating System (NX-OS) Software
TAC support: http://www.cisco.com/tac
Copyright (c) 2002-2009, Cisco Systems, Inc. All rights reserved.
The copyrights to certain works contained in this software are
owned by other third parties and used and distributed under
license. Certain components of this software are licensed under
the GNU General Public License (GPL) version 2.0 or the GNU
Lesser General Public License (LGPL) Version 2.1. A copy of each
such license is available at
http://www.opensource.org/licenses/gpl-2.0.php and
http://www.opensource.org/licenses/lgpl-2.1.php
```

```
Egypt#

2009 Oct  1 15:59:05 Egypt %TACACS-3-TACACS_ERROR_MESSAGE: All servers failed to
respond
2009 Oct  1 16:00:31 Egypt %TACACS-3-TACACS_ERROR_MESSAGE: All servers failed to
respond
Egypt#
```

Figure 5-6 shows the configuration of the Cisco Secure ACS TACACS+ configuration, which defines the loopback of the NX-OS device and shared secret key that needs to match between both the NX-OS device and the Cisco Secure ACS Server.

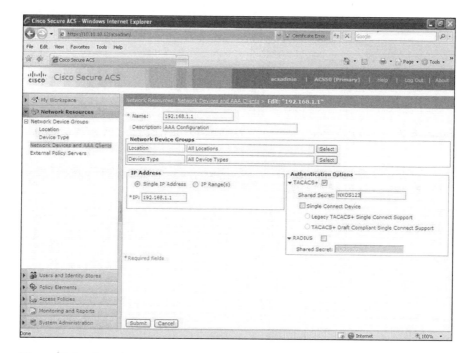

Figure 5-6 *Specific Cisco Secure ACS TACACS+ Configuration*

Figure 5-7 shows the configuration of the redundant NX-OS devices, both of which need to be defined.

Figure 5-8 show successful TACACS+ authentication of user **admin** for SSH access to the NX-OS device.

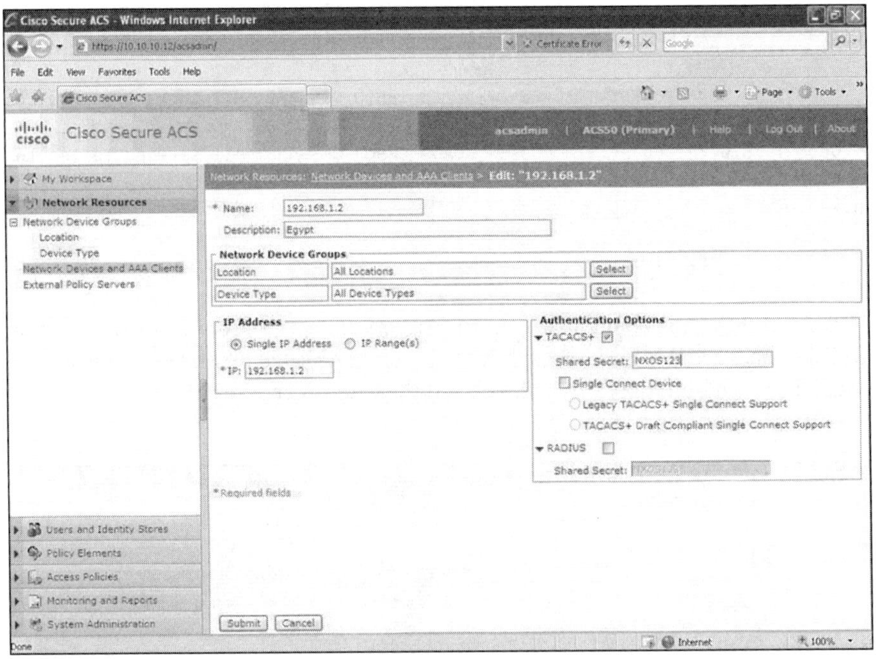

Figure 5-7   *Adding Redundant NX-OS Devices to the Cisco Secure ACS Database*

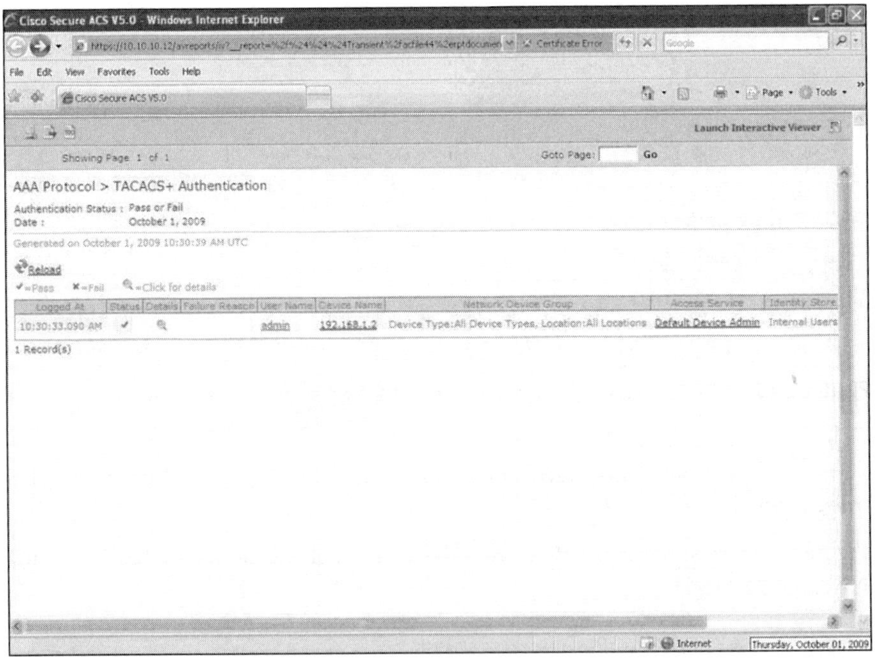

Figure 5-8   *Successful Authentication via TACACS+ for User "admin"*

Configuring SSH

Secure Shell (SSH) is composed of an SSH server, SSH client, and SSH server keys. SSH server is enabled on the NX-OS devices and a SSH client so as to make a secure, encrypted connection to a Cisco NX-OS device. SSH uses strong encryption for authentication; SSH user authentication mechanisms supported for SSH are RADIUS, TACACS+, and the default locally stored usernames and passwords.

The SSH client application runs over the SSH protocol to provide device authentication and encryption. The SSH client enables a Cisco NX-OS device to make a secure, encrypted connection to another Cisco NX-OS device or to any other device that runs the SSH server.

The NX-OS SSH server and SSH client implementation enables interoperability with publicly and commercially available implementations.

Cisco NX-OS supports the following SSH server keys:

- SSH requires server keys for secure communications to the Cisco NX-OS device. You can use SSH server keys for the following SSH options:

    - SSH version 2 using Rivest, Shamir, and Adelman (RSA) public-key cryptography

    - SSH version 2 using the Digital System Algorithm (DSA)

- Be sure to have an SSH Server key-pair with the appropriate version before enabling the SSH service. You can generate the SSH server key-pair according to the SSH Client version used. The SSH service accepts two types of key-pairs for use by SSH version 2:

    - The **dsa** option generates the DSA key-pair for the SSH version 2 protocol.

    - The **rsa** option generates the RSA key-pair for the SSH version 2 protocol.

- SSH supports the following public key formats:

    - OpenSSH

    - IETF Secure Shell (SECSH)

Note   Ensure that you are in the correct VDC (or use the **switchto vdc** command).

To enable the SSH modular process, enter the following commands:

```
Congo# conf t
Enter configuration commands, one per line. End with CNTL/Z.
Congo(config)# feature ssh
```

Example 5-19 shows how to generate SSH Server keys. The default SSH Server key is an RSA key generated using 1024 bits.

Example 5-19 *Generating a 2048-Bit SSH RSA Server Key*

```
Congo# conf t
Enter configuration commands, one per line. End with CNTL/Z.
Congo(config)# ssh key rsa 2048
rsa keys already present, use force option to overwrite them
Congo(config)# ssh key rsa 2048 force
deleting old rsa key.....
generating rsa key(2048 bits).....

generated rsa key
Congo(config)# feature ssh
Congo(config)# exit
```

Example 5-20 shows how to verify the SSH Server keys that were generated on the NX-OS device.

Example 5-20 *Verifying the SSH Server Keys That Were Generated on the NX-OS Device*

```
Congo# show ssh key
**************************************
rsa Keys generated:Wed Sep 30 14:38:37 2009

ssh-rsa AAAAB3NzaC1yc2EAAAABIwAAAQEAsxCDzRe9HzqwzWXSp5kQab2NlX9my68RdmFFsM0M+fAB
GNdwd5q01g5AKfuqvnrkAl7DR9n0d2v2Zde7JbZx2HCUjQFGEVAlK2a7I6pfCBschiRUf6j/7DBcCdHf
1SQrTTvQLhwEhFkbginXqlhuNjSbJj5uxMZYEInenxLswNe7Kc/Ovdw3lBbxdgHCKOSTrVs47PKshwST
PBcoqX/7Df5oCW8Um8ipJ0U3/7lnZlEE9Uz+ttT1zYf1ApqfsErAGT4wZo973Iza0Ub3lyWBnChQBN6n
ScxvYk/1wuqF4P0nS4ujnW9X+pxvBE1JedQDf6f0rj+Txt9L5AfqYnI+bQ==

bitcount:2048
fingerprint:
15:63:01:fc:9f:f7:66:35:3c:90:d3:f8:ed:f8:bb:16
**************************************
```

Example 5-21 shows how to verify SSH server communication to the NX-OS device.

Example 5-21 *Verifying SSH Server Communication to the NX-OS Device*

```
Congo# show int mgmt 0
mgmt0 is up
  Hardware: GigabitEthernet, address: 001b.54c1.b448 (bia 001b.54c1.b448)
  Internet Address is 172.26.32.37/27
  MTU 1500 bytes, BW 1000000 Kbit, DLY 10 usec,
     reliability 255/255, txload 1/255, rxload 1/255
  Encapsulation ARPA
```

```
 full-duplex, 1000 Mb/s
 Auto-Negotiation is turned on
 1 minute input rate 952 bits/sec, 1 packets/sec
 1 minute output rate 648 bits/sec, 0 packets/sec
 Rx
   12649 input packets 11178 unicast packets 951 multicast packets
   520 broadcast packets 1423807 bytes
 Tx
   7653 output packets 6642 unicast packets 953 multicast packets
   58 broadcast packets 943612 bytes

[hk@hk .ssh]$ ssh admin@172.26.32.37
User Access Verification
Password:
Cisco Nexus Operating System (NX-OS) Software
TAC support: http://www.cisco.com/tac
Copyright (c) 2002-2009, Cisco Systems, Inc. All rights reserved.
The copyrights to certain works contained in this software are
owned by other third parties and used and distributed under
license. Certain components of this software are licensed under
the GNU General Public License (GPL) version 2.0 or the GNU
Lesser General Public License (LGPL) Version 2.1. A copy of each
such license is available at
http://www.opensource.org/licenses/gpl-2.0.php and
http://www.opensource.org/licenses/lgpl-2.1.php
```

Example 5-22 shows how to verify SSH Server configuration on the NX-OS device.

Example 5-22 *Verifying SSH Server Configuration on the NX-OS Device*

```
Congo# show ssh server
ssh version 2 is enabled
Congo# show ssh key
**************************************
rsa Keys generated:Wed Sep 30 14:38:37 2009

ssh-rsa
AAAAB3NzaC1yc2EAAAABIwAAAQEAsxCDzRe9HzqwzWXSp5kQab2NlX9my68RdmFFsM0M+fABGNdwd5q01g5
AKfuqvnrkAl7DR9n0d2v2Zde7JbZx2HCUjQFGEVAlK2a7I6pfCBschiRUf6j/7DBcCdHf1SQrTTvQLhwEhF
kbginXqlhuNjSbJj5uxMZYEInenxLswNe7Kc/Ovdw3lBbxdgHCKOSTrVs47PKshwSTPBcoqX/7Df5oCW8Um
8ipJ0U3/7lnZlEE9Uz+ttT1zYf1ApqfsErAGT4wZo973Iza0Ub3lyWBnChQBN6nScxvYk/1wuqF4P0nS4uj
nW9X+pxvBE1JedQDf6f0rj+Txt9L5AfqYnI+bQ==

bitcount:2048
fingerprint:
15:63:01:fc:9f:f7:66:35:3c:90:d3:f8:ed:f8:bb:16
```

Configuring Cisco TrustSec

With the Cisco TrustSec security suite, Cisco NX-OS provides data confidentiality and integrity, supporting standard IEEE 802.1AE link-layer cryptography with 128-bit Advanced Encryption Standard (AES) cryptography. Link-layer cryptography helps ensure end-to-end data privacy while enabling the insertion of security service devices along the encrypted path. Today, the IEEE 802.1AE link-layer encryption is point-to-point. The Cisco TrustSec security architecture builds secure networks by establishing trusted network devices. Each device is authenticated by its neighbors. Communication on the links between devices in the cloud is secured with a combination of encryption, message integrity checks, and data-path replay protection mechanisms.

Refer to the network topology in Figure 5-9 for the configurations in this section.

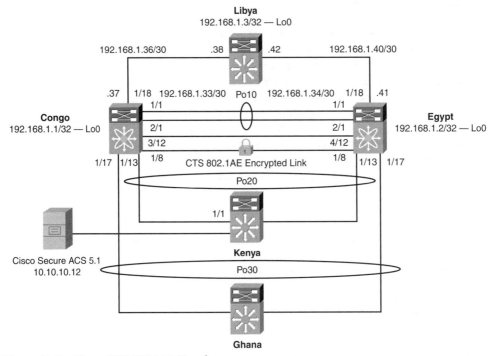

Figure 5-9 *Cisco CTS 802.1AE Topology*

To enable 802.1x and CTS features on the NX-OS device for CTS support, enter the following commands:

```
Egypt# conf t
Egypt (config)# feature dot1x
Egypt (config)# feature cts
```

To verify that 802.1x and CTS features are enabled, enter the following command:

```
Egypt# show run cts

feature dot1x

feature cts
```

Note The CTS unique device ID and password can have a maximum length of 32 characters and is case-sensitive.

Example 5-23 shows how to configure the CTS unique device ID.

Example 5-23 *Configuring the CTS Unique Device ID*

```
Egypt(config)# cts device-id egypt-cts password CTS_TrustSec123

Egypt(config) # interface Ethernet1/8
Egypt(config-if)# description to Congo
Egypt(config-if)# switchport
Egypt(config-if)# switchport access vlan 500
Egypt(config-if)# cts manual
Egypt(config-if-cts-manual)# sap pmk deadbeef modelist gcm-encrypt
Egypt(config-if)# mtu 9216
Egypt(config-if)# no shutdown

Egypt(config)# interface Vlan500
Egypt(config-if)# no shutdown
Egypt(config-if)# ip address 1.1.1.1/24
```

To enable 802.1x and CTS features on the NX-OS device for CTS support on Congo, enter the following commands:

```
Congo# conf t
Congo (config)# feature dot1x
Congo (config)# feature cts
```

To verify that 802.1x and CTS features are enabled, enter the following command:

```
Egypt# show run cts
feature dot1x
feature cts
```

Example 5-24 shows how to configure the CTS unique device ID on Congo.

Example 5-24 *Configuring the CTS Unique Device ID on Congo*

```
Congo(config)# cts device-id congo-cts password CTS_TrustSec123

Congo(config)# interface Ethernet1/8
Congo(config-if)# description to Egypt
Congo(config-if)# switchport
Congo(config-if)# switchport access vlan 500
Congo(config-if)# cts manual
```

```
Congo(config-if)# sap pmk deadbeef modelist gcm-encrypt
Congo(config-if)# mtu 9216
Congo(config-if)# no shutdown
Congo (config# interface Vlan500
Congo (config-if)# no shutdown
Congo (config-if)# ip address 1.1.1.2/24
--------------------------------------------------------------------------------
Egypt# show runn int e1/8

!Command: show running-config interface Ethernet1/8
!Time: Wed Sep 30 18:25:19 2009

version 4.2(2a)

interface Ethernet1/8
  description to Congo
  cts manual
    sap pmk deadbeef00000000000000000000000000000000000000000000000000000000
  switchport
  switchport access vlan 500
  mtu 9216
  no shutdown
```

Example 5-25 demonstrates how to verify the CTS configuration on Egypt.

Example 5-25   *Verifying the CTS Configuration on Egypt*

```
Egypt# show runn cts

!Command: show running-config cts
!Time: Wed Sep 30 18:25:27 2009

version 4.2(2a)
feature cts
cts device-id egypt-cts password 7 FPW_LrpxlVoh123

interface Ethernet1/8
  cts manual
    sap pmk deadbeef00000000000000000000000000000000000000000000000000000000

Egypt# show cts interface e1/8
CTS Information for Interface Ethernet1/8:
    CTS is enabled, mode:   CTS_MODE_MANUAL
```

```
      IFC state:                CTS_IFC_ST_CTS_OPEN_STATE
      Authentication Status:    CTS_AUTHC_SKIPPED_CONFIG
        Peer Identity:
        Peer is:                Unknown in manual mode
        802.1X role:            CTS_ROLE_UNKNOWN
        Last Re-Authentication:
      Authorization Status:     CTS_AUTHZ_SKIPPED_CONFIG
        PEER SGT:               0
        Peer SGT assignment:    Not Trusted
      SAP Status:               CTS_SAP_SUCCESS
        Configured pairwise ciphers: GCM_ENCRYPT
        Replay protection: Enabled
        Replay protection mode: Strict
        Selected cipher: GCM_ENCRYPT
        Current receive SPI: sci:23ac65020c0000 an:2
        Current transmit SPI: sci:23ac6409d80000 an:2
Egypt#
```

Example 5-26 demonstrates verifying the CTS configuration on Congo.

Example 5-26 *Verify the CTS Configuration on Congo*

```
Congo# show runn int e1/8

!Command: show running-config interface Ethernet1/8
!Time: Wed Sep 30 18:24:39 2009


version 4.2(2a)

interface Ethernet1/8
  description to Egypt
  cts manual
    sap pmk deadbeef00000000000000000000000000000000000000000000000000000000
  switchport
  switchport access vlan 500
  mtu 9216
  no shutdown

Congo# show runn cts

!Command: show running-config cts
!Time: Wed Sep 30 18:24:48 2009


version 4.2(2a)
```

```
feature cts
cts device-id congo-cts password 7 FPW_LrpxlVoh123

interface Ethernet1/8
  cts manual
    sap pmk deadbeef00000000000000000000000000000000000000000000000000000000000000
Congo# show cts interface e1/8
CTS Information for Interface Ethernet1/8:
    CTS is enabled, mode:     CTS_MODE_MANUAL
    IFC state:                CTS_IFC_ST_CTS_OPEN_STATE
    Authentication Status:  CTS_AUTHC_SKIPPED_CONFIG
      Peer Identity:
      Peer is:                Unknown in manual mode
      802.1X role:            CTS_ROLE_UNKNOWN
      Last Re-Authentication:
    Authorization Status:   CTS_AUTHZ_SKIPPED_CONFIG
      PEER SGT:               0
      Peer SGT assignment:  Not Trusted
    SAP Status:               CTS_SAP_SUCCESS
      Configured pairwise ciphers: GCM_ENCRYPT
      Replay protection: Enabled
      Replay protection mode: Strict
      Selected cipher: GCM_ENCRYPT
      Current receive SPI: sci:23ac6409d80000 an:1
      Current transmit SPI: sci:23ac65020c0000 an:1

Congo#
```

Example 5-27 confirms the VLAN used for CTS to verify correct configuration.

Example 5-27   *Confirming the VLAN Used for CTS*

```
Congo# show vlan

VLAN Name                       Status    Ports
-------------------------------------------------------------------------
1    default                    active    Po10
5    Congo_Egypt_Transit        active    Po10
10   Secure_Subnet              active    Po10, Po20, Po30
100  Server_Subnet1             active    Po10, Po30
500  CTS_TrustSec               active    Po10, Eth1/8

VLAN Type
---- -----
```

```
1     enet
5     enet
10    enet
100   enet
500   enet
```

Example 5-28 demonstrates a ping test between Congo and Egypt (the two Nexus 7000 switches), showing an encrypted ping frame is captured on the receiving Nexus 7000 through the embedded WireShark application running in NX-OS on Egypt. The ping test verifies that traffic is making it through the encrypted CTS 802.1AE session between Congo and Egypt.

Example 5-28   *Ping Test Between Congo and Egypt*

```
Started ping from Congo:
Congo# ping 1.1.1.1
PING 1.1.1.1 (1.1.1.1): 56 data bytes
64 bytes from 1.1.1.1: icmp_seq=0 ttl=254 time=1.189 ms
64 bytes from 1.1.1.1: icmp_seq=1 ttl=254 time=0.702 ms
64 bytes from 1.1.1.1: icmp_seq=2 ttl=254 time=0.718 ms
64 bytes from 1.1.1.1: icmp_seq=3 ttl=254 time=0.601 ms
64 bytes from 1.1.1.1: icmp_seq=4 ttl=254 time=0.604 ms


Egypt# ethanalyzer local interface inband detail limit-captured-frames 200


Frame 4 (98 bytes on wire, 98 bytes captured)
    Arrival Time: Sep 30, 2009 18:39:12.837070000
    [Time delta from previous captured frame: 0.255613000 seconds]
    [Time delta from previous displayed frame: 0.255613000 seconds]
    [Time since reference or first frame: 0.256374000 seconds]
    Frame Number: 4
    Frame Length: 98 bytes
    Capture Length: 98 bytes
    [Frame is marked: False]
    [Protocols in frame: eth:ip:icmp:data]
Ethernet II, Src: 00:1b:54:c2:76:41 (00:1b:54:c2:76:41), Dst: 00:1b:54:c2:78:c1
(00:1b:54:c2:78:c1)
    Destination: 00:1b:54:c2:78:c1 (00:1b:54:c2:78:c1)
        Address: 00:1b:54:c2:78:c1 (00:1b:54:c2:78:c1)
        .... ...0 .... .... .... .... = IG bit: Individual address (unicast)
        .... ..0. .... .... .... .... = LG bit: Globally unique address (factory
default)
    Source: 00:1b:54:c2:76:41 (00:1b:54:c2:76:41)
```

```
        Address: 00:1b:54:c2:76:41 (00:1b:54:c2:76:41)
        .... ...0 .... .... .... .... = IG bit: Individual address (unicast)
        .... ..0. .... .... .... .... = LG bit: Globally unique address (factory
 default)
      Type: IP (0x0800)
Internet Protocol, Src: 1.1.1.2 (1.1.1.2), Dst: 1.1.1.1 (1.1.1.1)
      Version: 4
      Header length: 20 bytes
      Differentiated Services Field: 0x00 (DSCP 0x00: Default; ECN: 0x00)
          0000 00.. = Differentiated Services Codepoint: Default (0x00)
          .... ..0. = ECN-Capable Transport (ECT): 0
          .... ...0 = ECN-CE: 0
      Total Length: 84
      Identification: 0x43b2 (17330)
      Flags: 0x00
          0... = Reserved bit: Not set
          .0.. = Don't fragment: Not set
          ..0. = More fragments: Not set
      Fragment offset: 0
      Time to live: 255
      Protocol: ICMP (0x01)
      Header checksum: 0x73f2 [correct]
          [Good: True]
          [Bad : False]
      Source: 1.1.1.2 (1.1.1.2)
      Destination: 1.1.1.1 (1.1.1.1)
Internet Control Message Protocol
      Type: 8 (Echo (ping) request)
      Code: 0 ()
      Checksum: 0x5573 [correct]
      Identifier: 0x572d
      Sequence number: 0 (0x0000)
      Data (56 bytes)

0000   e1 a5 c3 4a cd e7 03 00 cd ab 00 00 cd ab 00 00    ...J............
0010   cd ab 00 00 cd ab 00 00 cd ab 00 00 cd ab 00 00    ................
0020   cd ab 00 00 cd ab 00 00 cd ab 00 00 cd ab 00 00    ................
0030   30 31 32 33 34 35 36 37                            01234567
        Data: E1A5C34ACDE70300CDAB0000CDAB0000CDAB0000CDAB0000...
```

Note Ethanalyzer is available only in the default virtual device context (VDC). Ethanalyzer can capture traffic received by the Supervisor from both the out-of-band management port (mgmt0) and the I/O modules.

Layer 2 Solutions Between Data Centers

A top customer request is to have Layer 2 connectivity between data centers to accommodate the clustering and server virtualization applications. With the Layer 2 requirement often follows the need for encryption whether driven by regulatory and compliance regulations or other factors. The Nexus 7000 supports 802.1ae point-to-point Linksec encryption on all interfaces in hardware. Refer to Figure 5-8 if you have a Multiprotocol Label Switching (MPLS) environment; you can front-end the Nexus 7000 switches with an ASR1000 or a Catalyst 6500 running port-mode Ethernet over MPLS (EoMPLS). Port-mode EoMPLS looks like a wire to the Nexus 7000; this is important because you need to make sure that the control-plane SAP messages (Security Association Protocol EAPOL frames) for CTS Encryption are forwarded through the EoMPLS pseudo-wire (PW). Also, Virtual port-channel (vPC) on the Nexus 7000 enables for a loop-free spanning-tree environment and STP isolation so that you can have an STP root in each data center.

As MPLS encryption presents challenges to accomplish; if MPLS is not required, the Nexus 7000 TrustSec can secure data across a remote data center if Layer 2 and BPDU transparency is ensured through dark fiber or dense wavelength division multiplexing (DWDM) transport.

If the Cisco ASR1000 is used for the port-mode EoMPLS connectivity, it provides remote-port shutdown where communication of link status to a CE and traffic from the Customer Edge (CE) can be stopped if MPLS or the pseudowire is down. Remote port shutdown enables subsecond failover and restoration to local/remote links/nodes end-to-end signaled through LDP.

Figure 5-10 illustrates Data Center Interconnect, which provides P2P interconnect with encryption through the MPLS cloud. The Nexus 7000s and ASR1002s are configured with Cisco TrustSec and port-mode EoMPLS PW, respectively.

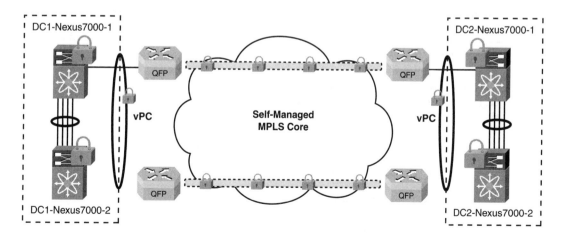

Figure 5-10 *Data Center Interconnects Across an MPLS Cloud Leveraging Cisco TrustSec on the Nexus 7000*

Configuring IP ACLs

Access control lists (ACLs) are ordered sets of rules that you can use to filter traffic; each rule specifies a set of conditions that a packet must satisfy to match the rule. The first matching rule determines whether the packet is permitted or denied. ACLs protect networks and specific hosts from unnecessary or unwanted traffic. NX-OS supports IPv4 and IPv6 IP ACLs to be created and applied to interfaces, VLAN interfaces, and port-channels.

To improve the scalability of ACL management, using Session Manager is recommended to perform ACL configuration, verify ACL configuration, and confirm that the resources required by the configuration are available prior to committing them to the running configuration. Session Manager supports the following benefits for ACL management:

- **Configuration session:** Creates a list of commands that you want to implement in Session Manager mode.

- **Validation:** Provides a basic semantic check on your configuration.

- **Verification:** Verifies the configuration as a whole, based on the existing hardware and software configuration and resources.

- **Commit:** Cisco NX-OS verifies the complete configuration and applies the changes to the device.

- **Session termination:** Session Manager enables termination of a configuration session without committing the changes. Session Manager enables session configuration to be saved. Session configurations can be saved to bootflash:, slot0:, or volatile:.

Example 5-29 shows how to create a configuration session and enter session configuration mode.

Example 5-29 *Creating a Configuration Session and Entering Session Configuration Mode*

```
Congo# conf t
Enter configuration commands, one per line. End with CNTL/Z.
Congo(config)# configure session ACL-TCP-IN
Config Session started, Session ID is 3
```

Example 5-30 shows how to create an ACL to enable TCP.

Example 5-30 *Creating an ACL*

```
Congo(config-s)# ip access-list TCP1
Congo(config-s-acl)# permit tcp any any
Congo(config-s-acl)# exit
Congo(config-s)# save bootflash:SessionMgrTCPIn
Congo(config-s)# interface ethernet 1/1
```

Example 5-31 shows how to apply the ACL to the interface and specify the direction to apply the access group.

Example 5-31 *Applying the ACL to the Interface and Specifying the Direction to Apply the Access Group*

```
Congo(config-s-if)# ip access-group TCP1 in
```

Example 5-32 shows how to verify the configuration as a whole, based on the existing hardware and software configuration and resources. The NX-OS device returns errors if the configuration does not pass this verification.

Example 5-32 *Verifying the Configuration as a Whole, Based on the Existing Hardware and Software Configuration and Resources*

```
Congo(config-s-if)# verify
Verification Successful
```

Example 5-33 validates the configuration changes made in the current session and applies the changes to the device. If the validation fails, the NX-OS device reverts to the original configuration.

Example 5-33 *Validating the Configuration Changes Made in the Current Session and Applying the Changes to the Device*

```
Congo(config-s)# commit
Commit Successful
```

Example 5-34 shows how to verify the Session Manager and the ACL.

Example 5-34 *Verifying the Session Manager and the ACL*

```
Congo# conf t
Congo(config)# configure session ACL-TCP-IN
Config Session started, Session ID is 3
Congo(config-s)# ip access-list TCP1
Congo(config-s-acl)# permit tcp any any
Congo(config-s-acl)# interface e1/1
Congo(config-s-if)# ip access-group TCP1 in
Congo(config-s-if)# show configuration session
config session IP-ACL1

config session ACL-TCP-IN
0001  ip access-list TCP1
```

```
0002  permit tcp any any
0003  interface Ethernet1/1
0004  ip access-group TCP1 in

Number of active configuration sessions = 3
Congo(config-s-if)# save  bootflash:SessionMgrTCPIn
Congo(config-s)# verify
Verification Successful
Congo(config-s)# commit
Commit Successful

Congo# show access-lists TCP1

IP access list TCP1
        10 permit tcp any any
Congo# show running-config interface e1/1

!Command: show running-config interface Ethernet1/1
!Time: Sat Oct 10 12:10:55 2009

version 4.2(2a)

interface Ethernet1/1
  description to Egypt
  ip access-group TCP1 in
  switchport
  switchport access vlan 500
  mtu 9216
  no shutdown

Congo#
```

Configuring MAC ACLs

MAC ACLs match traffic information in the Layer 2 header of packets to filter traffic. MAC packet classification enables you to control whether a MAC ACL on a Layer 2 interface applies to all traffic entering the interface, including IP traffic, or to non-IP traffic only.

Note   MAC ACLs can be applied to ingress traffic only.

Example 5-35 shows how to create a MAC ACL and enter ACL configuration.

Example 5-35   *Creating a MAC ACL and Entering ACL Configuration*

```
Egypt# conf t
Enter configuration commands, one per line. End with CNTL/Z.
Egypt(config)# mac access-list mac-acl
Egypt(config-mac-acl)# permit 0050.561f.73d3 0050.56bc.48dd any
```

Example 5-36 shows how to maintain global statistics and a counter for packets that match the ACL rules. The switch maintains global statistics for packets that match the rules in the ACL.

Example 5-36   *Maintaining Global Statistics and Counter for Packets That Match the ACL Rules*

```
Egypt(config-mac-acl)# statistics per-entry
```

Example 5-37 shows how to verify the MAC ACL configuration.

Example 5-37   *Verifying the MAC ACL Configuration*

```
Egypt(config-mac-acl)# show mac access-lists mac-acl

MAC access list mac-acl
        statistics per-entry
        10 permit 0050.561f.73d3 0050.56bc.48dd any
Egypt(config-mac-acl)# exit
Egypt(config)# exit

Egypt(config)# mac access-list mac-acl
Egypt(config-mac-acl)# 100 permit  0050.561f.73d3 0000.00ff.ffff any
Egypt# show mac access-lists mac-acl

MAC access list mac-acl
        statistics per-entry
        10 permit 0050.561f.73d3 0050.56bc.48dd any
        100 permit 0050.561f.73d3 0000.00ff.ffff any
```

Example 5-38 shows how to change the ACL sequence numbers assigned to rules in a MAC ACL. Resequencing is useful when you need to insert rules into an ACL. The first rule receives the number specified, and each subsequent rule receives a number larger than the preceding rule. The difference in numbers is determined by the increment number that you specify.

Example 5-38 *Changing the ACL Sequence Numbers Assigned to Rules in a MAC ACL*

```
Egypt(config)# resequence mac access-list mac-acl 200 10
Egypt(config)# exit
Egypt# show mac access-lists mac-acl

MAC access list mac-acl
        statistics per-entry
        200 permit 0050.561f.73d3 0050.56bc.48dd any
        210 permit 0050.561f.73d3 0000.00ff.ffff any
Egypt#
```

Configuring VLAN ACLs

A VLAN ACL (VACL) is an application of a MAC ACL or IP ACL. You can configure VACLs to apply to all packets routed into or out of a VLAN or bridged within a VLAN. VACLs are deployed for security packet filtering and redirecting traffic to specific physical interfaces.

Note VACLs are not defined by direction (ingress or egress).

Example 5-39 shows how to configure a VACL to forward traffic permitted by a MAC ACL named acl-mac-map.

Example 5-39 *Creating an VACL or Adding an VACL Entry*

```
Egypt# conf t
Enter configuration commands, one per line. End with CNTL/Z.
Egypt(config)# vlan access-map acl-mac-map
Egypt(config-access-map)# match mac address mac-acl
Egypt(config-access-map)# action forward
Egypt(config-access-map)# statistics per-entry
Egypt(config-access-map)# exit
Egypt(config)# exit
Egypt# show runn aclmgr

!Command: show running-config aclmgr
!Time: Thu Oct  1 17:19:24 2009

version 4.2(2a)
mac access-list mac-acl
  statistics per-entry
  200 permit 0050.561f.73d3 0050.56bc.48dd any
```

```
   210 permit 0050.561f.73d3 0000.00ff.ffff any
vlan access-map acl-mac-map 10
        match mac address mac-acl
        action forward
        statistics per-entry
Egypt#
```

Example 5-40 shows how to apply the VACL to the VLAN list.

Example 5-40   *Applying the VACL to the VLAN List*

```
Egypt(config)# vlan filter acl-mac-map vlan-list 10
Egypt(config)# show running-config aclmgr

!Command: show running-config aclmgr
!Time: Thu Oct  1 17:24:17 2009
version 4.2(2a)
mac access-list mac-acl
  statistics per-entry

  200 permit 0050.561f.73d3 0050.56bc.48dd any
  210 permit 0050.561f.73d3 0000.00ff.ffff any
vlan access-map acl-mac-map 10
        match mac address mac-acl
        action forward
        statistics per-entry
vlan filter acl-mac-map vlan-list 10
Egypt(config)#
```

Configuring Port Security

Port security enables you to configure Layer 2 physical interfaces and Layer 2 port-channel interfaces that enable inbound traffic from only a restricted set of MAC addresses. The MAC addresses in the restricted set are called *secure MAC addresses*. In addition, the device does not enable traffic from these MAC addresses on another interface within the same VLAN. The number of MAC addresses that the device can secure is configurable per interface.

Example 5-41 shows how to verify the port security feature and enable it if it currently disabled.

Example 5-41   *Verifying and Enabling the Port Security Feature Is Enabled Globally*

```
Egypt(config)# show feature | i port
eth_port_sec            1           disabled
Egypt(config)# feature port-security
Egypt(config)# show feature | i port
eth_port_sec            1           enabled
Egypt(config)#
```

Example 5-42 shows how to enable port security on Layer 2 interfaces.

Example 5-42   *Enabling Port Security on Layer 2 Interfaces*

```
Egypt# conf t
Enter configuration commands, one per line. End with CNTL/Z.
Egypt(config)# int e1/1
Egypt(config-if)# switchport port-security
Egypt(config-if)#
Egypt# show running-config port-security
!Command: show running-config port-security
!Time: Thu Oct  1 17:41:20 2009
version 4.2(2a)

feature port-security

interface Ethernet1/1
  switchport port-security

Egypt#
```

Note   When port security is disabled on an interface, all port security configuration for the interface is lost, including any secure MAC addresses learned on the interface.

Example 5-43 shows how to enable sticky MAC address learning. When you enable sticky learning on an interface, the switch does not perform dynamic learning and performs sticky learning instead; the switch does not age sticky secure MAC addresses.

Example 5-43 *Enabling Sticky MAC Address Learning*

```
Egypt# conf t
Enter configuration commands, one per line. End with CNTL/Z.
Egypt(config)# int e1/1
Egypt(config-if)# switchport port-security mac-address sticky
Egypt(config-if)# exit
Egypt# show running-config port-security

!Command: show running-config port-security
!Time: Thu Oct  1 17:43:06 2009

version 4.2(2a)
feature port-security

interface Ethernet1/1
  switchport port-security
  switchport port-security mac-address sticky

Egypt#
```

Note   If sticky learning is disabled on an interface; the interface reverts back to the default state of dynamic MAC address learning.

Example 5-44 shows how to add a static secure MAC address to Interface Ethernet 1/1. The static MAC is useful for "misbehaving" applications with MAC addresses (for example, cluster servers and load balancers).

Example 5-44 *Add a Static Secure MAC Address to an Interface*

```
Egypt# conf t
Enter configuration commands, one per line. End with CNTL/Z.
Egypt(config)# int e1/1
Egypt(config-if)# switchport port-security mac-address 0050.561f.73d3
Egypt(config-if)# exit
Egypt# show running-config port-security

!Command: show running-config port-security
!Time: Thu Oct  1 17:46:20 2009

version 4.2(2a)
feature port-security
```

```
interface Ethernet1/1
  switchport port-security
  switchport port-security mac-address 0050.561F.73D3

Egypt# show port-security

Total Secured Mac Addresses in System (excluding one mac per port)     : 0
Max Addresses limit in System (excluding one mac per port) : 8192
-------------------------------------------------------------------------------
-----

Secure Port  MaxSecureAddr  CurrentAddr  SecurityViolation  Security Action
             (Count)        (Count)      (Count)
-------------------------------------------------------------------------------
Ethernet1/1         1              1            0            Shutdown
===============================================================================
Egypt#
```

Security Violations and Actions

When a security violation occurs, a violation action is configurable on each interface enabled with port security. The configurable violation actions are as follows:

- **shutdown:** Shuts down the interface that received the packet that triggered the violation; the interface is error disabled. Reenabling the interface, it retains its port security configuration, including its secure MAC addresses.

- **errdisable:** Global configuration command to configure the device to reenable the interface automatically if a shutdown occurs, or you can manually reenable the interface by entering the **shutdown** and **no shutdown** interface configuration commands.

- **restrict:** After 100 security violations occur, the device disables learning on the interface and drops all ingress traffic from nonsecure MAC addresses. In addition, the device generates an SNMP notification for each security violation. The address that triggered the security violation is learned, but any traffic from the address is dropped.

- **protect:** Prevents further violations from occurring. The address that triggered the security violation is learned, but any traffic from the address is dropped.

Note   The default security action is to shut down the port on which the security violation occurs.

Example 5-45 shows how to configure the specific port security violations on interface Ethernet 1/1.

Example 5-45 *Configuring the Specific Port Security Violations on Interface Ethernet 1/1*

```
Egypt# conf t
Enter configuration commands, one per line. End with CNTL/Z.
Egypt(config)# interface ethernet 1/1
Egypt(config-if)# switchport port-security violation ?
  protect   Security violation protect mode
  restrict  Security violation restrict mode
  shutdown  Security violation shtudown mode

Egypt(config-if)# switchport port-security violation
```

Example 5-46 shows how to configure a maximum number of MAC addresses on
Interface Ethernet 1/1. Depending on what connects to the interface, such as a virtualized
server, you need to increase the number of MAC addresses, based on the number of virtual
machines and virtual interfaces.

Note A maximum number of MAC addresses can be learned or statically configured on
a Layer 2 interface. By default, an interface has a maximum of one secure MAC address;
VLANs have no default maximum.

Example 5-46 *Configuring a Maximum Number of MAC Addresses on Interface
Ethernet 1/1*

```
Egypt(config)# int e1/1
Egypt(config-if)# switchport port-security maximum 51
Egypt(config-if)# show port-security

Total Secured Mac Addresses in System (excluding one mac per port)    : 0
Max Addresses limit in System (excluding one mac per port) : 8192
------------------------------------------------------------------------------

Secure Port   MaxSecureAddr  CurrentAddr  SecurityViolation  Security Action
              (Count)        (Count)      (Count)
------------------------------------------------------------------------------
Ethernet1/1       51            0             0              Shutdown
==============================================================================
Egypt(config-if)#

Egypt# show port-security int e1/1
Port Security          : Enabled
Port Status            : Secure UP
Violation Mode         : Shutdown
```

```
Aging Time               : 0 mins
Aging Type               : Absolute
Maximum MAC Addresses    : 51
Total MAC Addresses      : 0
Configured MAC Addresses : 0
Sticky MAC Addresses     : 0
Security violation count : 0
Egypt#
```

Configuring DHCP Snooping

DHCP snooping is the traffic cop between untrusted hosts and trusted DHCP servers. DHCP snooping performs the following responsibilities:

- Validates DHCP messages received from untrusted sources and filters out invalid messages

- Builds and maintains the DHCP snooping binding database, which contains information about untrusted hosts with leased IP addresses

- Uses the DHCP snooping binding database to validate subsequent requests from untrusted hosts

Note By default, the feature is inactive on all VLANs; DHCP snooping is enabled on a per-VLAN basis.

Refer to Figure 5-11 for the configurations in this section.

Example 5-47 shows how to enable and verify the DHCP snooping process/feature.

Example 5-47 *Enabling the DHCP Snooping Process/Feature*

```
Egypt# show feature | i dhcp-snooping
dhcp-snooping          1           disabled
Egypt# conf t
Enter configuration commands, one per line. End with CNTL/Z.
Egypt(config)# feature dhcp
Egypt(config)# show feature | i dhcp-snooping
dhcp-snooping          1           enabled
Egypt(config)#
```

```
Egypt(config)# show running-config dhcp

!Command: show running-config dhcp
!Time: Thu Oct  1 18:08:40 2009

version 4.2(2a)
feature dhcp

service dhcp
ip dhcp relay

Egypt(config)#
```

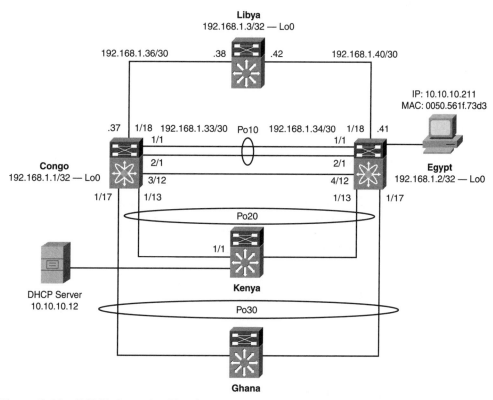

Figure 5-11   *DHCP Snooping Topology*

> **Note** Enable DHCP snooping globally on the switch. Globally disabling DHCP snooping stops the device from performing any DHCP snooping or relaying DHCP messages.

Example 5-48 shows how to enable DHCP snooping globally.

Example 5-48 *Enabling DHCP snooping Globally*

```
Egypt# conf t
Enter configuration commands, one per line. End with CNTL/Z.
Egypt(config)# ip dhcp snooping
Egypt(config)# show running-config dhcp

!Command: show running-config dhcp
!Time: Thu Oct  1 18:11:05 2009

version 4.2(2a)
feature dhcp

ip dhcp snooping
service dhcp
ip dhcp relay

Egypt(config)#
```

Example 5-49 shows how to enable DHCP snooping on a per VLAN basis, allowing granularity of configuration.

Example 5-49 *Enabling DHCP Snooping on a Per VLAN Basis*

```
Egypt(config)# ip dhcp snooping vlan 5,10,100,500
Egypt(config)# show runn dhcp

!Command: show running-config dhcp
!Time: Thu Oct  1 18:12:28 2009

version 4.2(2a)
feature dhcp

ip dhcp snooping
ip dhcp snooping vlan 5,10,100,500
service dhcp
ip dhcp relay

Egypt(config)#
```

If the device receives a packet on an untrusted interface and the source MAC address and the DHCP client hardware address do not match, address verification causes the device to drop the packet.

Example 5-50 shows how to enable DHCP Snooping MAC Address verification.

Example 5-50   *Enabling DHCP Snooping MAC Address Verification*

```
Egypt(config)# ip dhcp snooping verify mac-address
```

Example 5-51 shows how to configure interface Ethernet 1/1 trusted source of DHCP messages. The trusted interface is an interface configured to receive only messages from within the network.

Example 5-51   *Configuring Interface Ethernet 1/1 Trusted Source of DHCP Messages*

```
Egypt# conf t
Enter configuration commands, one per line. End with CNTL/Z.
Egypt(config)# int e1/1
Egypt(config-if)# ip dhcp snooping trust
Egypt(config-if)# exit
Egypt# show running-config dhcp

!Command: show running-config dhcp
!Time: Thu Oct  1 18:16:13 2009

version 4.2(2a)
feature dhcp

interface Ethernet1/1
  ip dhcp snooping trust
ip dhcp snooping
ip dhcp snooping vlan 5,10,100,500
service dhcp
ip dhcp relay

Egypt#
```

Example 5-52 shows how to verify the DHCP Snooping configuration.

Example 5-52   *Verifying the DHCP Snooping Configuration*

```
Egypt# show ip dhcp snooping
DHCP snooping service is enabled
Switch DHCP snooping is enabled
```

```
DHCP snooping is configured on the following VLANs:
5,10,100,500
DHCP snooping is operational on the following VLANs:
5,10,100,500
Insertion of Option 82 is disabled
Verification of MAC address is enabled
DHCP snooping trust is configured on the following interfaces:
Interface            Trusted
------------         -------
Ethernet1/1          Yes
Egypt#

Egypt# show ip dhcp snooping binding
MacAddress        IpAddress        LeaseSec  Type       VLAN  Interface
0050.561f.73d3    10.10.10.211     1600      dynamic    100   ethernet4/1
----------------  ---------------  --------  ---------- ----  -------------
Egypt#
```

The DHCP binding table shows the client MAC address; client IP address assigned from the DHCP server; IP address lease time; binding type, statically configured from CLI or dynamically learned; VLAN number of the client interface; and the interface that connects to the DHCP client host.

Configuring Dynamic ARP Inspection

Address Resolution Protocol (ARP) provides IP communication within a Layer 2 broadcast domain by mapping an IP address to a MAC address. There are known security issues with ARP, such as ARP spoofing attacks. ARP spoofing attacks affect hosts, switches, and routers connected to your Layer 2 network by sending false information to the ARP caches of the devices connected to the subnet.

Dynamic ARP Inspection (DAI) ensures that only valid ARP requests and responses are relayed. When DAI is enabled and properly configured, an NX-OS device performs the following activities:

- Intercepts all ARP requests and responses on untrusted ports

- Verifies that each of these intercepted packets has a valid IP-to-MAC address binding before updating the local ARP cache or before forwarding the packet to the appropriate destination

- Drops invalid ARP packets

DAI can determine the validity of an ARP packet based on valid IP-to-MAC address bindings stored in a DHCP snooping binding database. This database is built by DHCP snooping if DHCP snooping is enabled on the VLANs and on the device. It can also contain static entries that you create. If the ARP packet is received on a trusted interface, the device forwards the packet without any checks. On untrusted interfaces, the device forwards the packet only if it is valid.

Example 5-53 shows how to enable DAI for VLAN 10.

Example 5-53   *Enabling DAI for a VLAN 10*

```
Egypt# conf t
Enter configuration commands, one per line. End with CNTL/Z.
Egypt(config)# ip arp inspection vlan 10
Egypt(config)# show ip arp inspection vlan 10


Source Mac Validation     : Disabled
Destination Mac Validation : Disabled
IP Address Validation     : Disabled


Vlan : 10
- - - - - - - - - - -
Configuration    : Enabled
Operation State  : Active
Egypt(config)#
```

Dynamic ARP Inspection Trust State

A device forwards ARP packets that it receives on a trusted Layer 2 interface but does not check them. On untrusted interfaces, the device intercepts all ARP requests and responses and verifies that the intercepted packets have valid IP-MAC address bindings before updating the local cache and forwarding the packet to the appropriate destination.

Example 5-54 shows how to configure DAI trust state of a Layer 2 interface.

Note   By default, all interfaces are untrusted.

Example 5-54   *Configuring DAI Trust State of a Layer 2 Interface*

```
Egypt(config)# int e1/1
Egypt(config-if)# ip arp inspection trust
Egypt(config-if)# show ip arp inspection int e1/1


 Interface        Trust State
 - - - - - - - - -     - - - - - - - - -
 Ethernet1/1        Trusted


Egypt(config-if)#
```

Example 5-55 shows how to apply ACLs to VLANs for DAI filtering. The NX-OS device permits only packets that the ACL permits. In this case, the ACL creates a rule that permits any ARP message with IP address 10.10.10.12 and MAC address of 0050.561f.73d3.

Example 5-55   *Applying ACLs to VLANs for DAI Filtering*

```
Egypt(config)# arp access-list arp-list
Egypt(config-arp-acl)# 10 permit request ip 10.10.10.12 0.0.0.0 mac 0050.561f.73d3
EEEE.EEEE.EEEE
Egypt(config-arp-acl)# exit
Egypt(config)# ip arp inspection filter arp-list vlan 10
Egypt(config)# show ip arp inspection vlan 10


Source Mac Validation      : Disabled
Destination Mac Validation : Disabled
IP Address Validation      : Disabled


Vlan : 10
- - - - - - - - - - -
Configuration    : Enabled
Operation State  : Active
ACL Match        : arp-list
Egypt(config)#
```

Example 5-56 shows how to enable additional DAI validation including DAI intercepts, logs, and the discard of ARP packets with invalid IP-to-MAC address bindings. You can enable additional validation on the destination MAC address, the sender and target IP addresses, and the source MAC address.

Example 5-56   *Enabling Additional DAI Validation*

```
Egypt(config)# ip arp inspection validate src-mac dst-mac ip
Egypt(config)# show running-config dhcp

!Command: show running-config dhcp
!Time: Thu Oct  1 18:42:12 2009


version 4.2(2a)
feature dhcp



interface Ethernet1/1
```

```
   ip dhcp snooping trust
   ip arp inspection trust
 ip dhcp snooping
 ip dhcp snooping vlan 5,10,100,500
 service dhcp
 ip dhcp relay
 ip arp inspection validate src-mac dst-mac ip
 ip arp inspection vlan 10
 ip arp inspection filter arp-list vlan 10

 Egypt(config)#
```

Example 5-57 shows how to verify the DAI configuration.

Example 5-57   *Verifying the DAI Configuration on Egypt*

```
Egypt# show ip arp inspection

Source Mac Validation      : Enabled
Destination Mac Validation : Enabled
IP Address Validation      : Enabled


Vlan : 1
-----------
Configuration    : Disabled
Operation State  : Inactive


Vlan : 5
-----------
Configuration    : Disabled
Operation State  : Inactive
Vlan : 10
-----------
Configuration    : Enabled
Operation State  : Active
ACL Match        : arp-list

ARP Req Forwarded  = 0
ARP Res Forwarded  = 0
ARP Req Dropped    = 2
ARP Res Dropped    = 6
DHCP Drops         = 8
DHCP Permits       = 0
SMAC Fails-ARP Req = 0
```

```
SMAC Fails-ARP Res = 0
DMAC Fails-ARP Res = 0
IP Fails-ARP Req  = 0
IP Fails-ARP Res  = 0


Vlan : 100
- - - - - - - - - - -
Configuration   : Disabled
Operation State : Inactive


Vlan : 500
- - - - - - - - - - -
Configuration   : Disabled
Operation State : Inactive
Egypt# show ip arp inspection interface ethernet 1/1

 Interface       Trust State
 - - - - - - - - - - - -   - - - - - - - - - - -
 Ethernet1/1       Trusted
Egypt# show ip arp inspection vlan 10
Source Mac Validation      : Enabled
Destination Mac Validation : Enabled
IP Address Validation      : Enabled


Vlan : 10
- - - - - - - - - - -
Configuration   : Enabled
Operation State : Active
ACL Match       : arp-list
Egypt# show arp access-lists
ARP access list arp-list
10 permit request ip 10.10.10.12 255.255.255.0 mac 0050.561f.73d3 eeee.eeee
Egypt#
```

Configuring IP Source Guard

IP Source Guard is configured on a per-interface traffic filter that permits IP traffic only when the IP address and MAC address of each packet matches one of two sources of IP and MAC address bindings:

■   Entries in the DHCP snooping binding table

■   Static IP source entries

Filtering on trusted IP and MAC address bindings helps prevent spoofing attacks, in which an attacker uses the IP address of a valid host to gain unauthorized network access. To circumvent IP Source Guard, an attacker would have to spoof both the IP address and the MAC address of a valid host.

You can enable IP Source Guard on Layer 2 interfaces that are not trusted by DHCP snooping. IP Source Guard supports interfaces that are configured to operate in access mode and trunk mode. When you initially enable IP Source Guard, all inbound IP traffic on the interface is blocked except for the following:

- DHCP packets, which DHCP snooping inspects and then forwards or drops, depending upon the results of inspecting the packet

- IP traffic from static IP source entries that you have configured in the Cisco NX-OS device

Example 5-58 demonstrates how to enable IP Source Guard on Layer 2 interface Ethernet 1/1.

Example 5-58   *Enabling IP Source Guard on a Layer 2 Interface*

```
Egypt# conf t
Enter configuration commands, one per line. End with CNTL/Z.
Egypt(config)# interface ethernet 1/1
Egypt(config-if)# ip verify source dhcp-snooping-vlan
Egypt(config-if)# show running-config dhcp

!Command: show running-config dhcp
!Time: Thu Oct  1 18:47:28 2009

version 4.2(2a)
feature dhcp
interface Ethernet1/1
  ip dhcp snooping trust
  ip arp inspection trust
  ip verify source dhcp-snooping-vlan
ip dhcp snooping
ip dhcp snooping vlan 5,10,100,500

service dhcp
ip dhcp relay
ip arp inspection validate src-mac dst-mac ip
ip arp inspection vlan 10
ip arp inspection filter arp-list vlan 10

Egypt(config-if)#
```

Example 5-59 demonstrates how to add a static IP source entry on interface Ethernet 1/1.

Example 5-59   *Adding a Static IP Source Entry on Interface Ethernet 1/1*

```
Egypt(config)# ip source binding 10.10.10.12 0050.561f.73d3 vlan 10 interface e1
Egypt(config)# show ip dhcp snooping binding
MacAddress          IpAddress        LeaseSec  Type        VLAN  Interface
-------------------------------------------------------------------------------
00:50:56:1f:73:d3   10.10.10.12      infinite  static      10    Ethernet1/1
Egypt(config)#
```

Configuring Keychain Management

Keychain management includes the creation and maintenance of keychains, which are sequences of keys or shared secrets. Keychains can be used with features such as routing protocols for secure, authenticated communication with other devices.

Example 5-60 demonstrates how to configure keychain management and create a keychain.

Example 5-60   *Configuring Keychain Management and Creating a Keychain*

```
Egypt(config)# key chain nexus
Egypt(config-keychain)#
```

Example 5-61 demonstrates how to configure the key for the keychain, the default accept and send lifetime for a new key are infinite.

Example 5-61   *Configuring the Key for the Keychain*

```
Egypt(config-keychain)# key 7010
Egypt(config-keychain)#
```

Example 5-62 demonstrates how to associate the keychain. This example shows associating the keychain nexus with OSPF authentication.

Example 5-62   *Associating the Keychain*

```
ip ospf authentication key-chain nexus
```

Example 5-63 verifies the keychain association and management.

Example 5-63   *Verifying the Keychain Association and Management*

```
Egypt# show key chain nexus
Key-Chain nexus
  Key 1 -- text 7 070124545b1a12000e
```

```
      accept lifetime (always valid) [active]
      send lifetime (always valid) [active]
Egypt# show ip ospf
Area BACKBONE(0.0.0.0)
      Area has existed for 1d00h
      Interfaces in this area: 3 Active interfaces: 3
      Passive interfaces: 0  Loopback interfaces: 1
      Message-digest authentication
      SPF calculation has run 15 times
        Last SPF ran for 0.000527s
      Area ranges are
      Number of LSAs: 8, checksum sum 0x3c6ce
```

Configuring Traffic Storm Control

Traffic storms occur when packets flood the LAN, creating excessive traffic and degrading network performance. The traffic storm control feature in NX-OS prevents disruptions on Layer 2 ports by a broadcast, multicast, or unknown unicast traffic storm on physical interfaces. Within NX-OS, the administrator is allowed to monitor the levels of the incoming broadcast, multicast, and unicast traffic over a 1-second interval. During the 1-second interval, the traffic level is compared with the traffic storm control level configured. The storm control levels are configured as a percentage of the total available bandwidth of the port. If the ingress traffic reaches the traffic storm control level configured as a percentage of bandwidth of the port, storm control drops the traffic until the interval ends.

Example 5-64 shows how to configure broadcast traffic storm control on interface Ethernet 1/1.

Example 5-64   *Configuring Broadcast Traffic Storm Control*

```
Egypt(config)# interface ethernet 1/1
Egypt(config-if)# storm-control broadcast level 20
```

Example 5-65 verifies broadcast storm control percentage of bandwidth on interface Ethernet 1/1.

Example 5-65   *Verifying Broadcast Storm Control Percentage of Bandwidth*

```
Egypt# show interface ethernet 1/1 counters storm-control

Port       UcastSupp %     McastSupp %     BcastSupp %     TotalSuppDiscards
- - - - - - - - - - - - - - - - - - - - - - - - - - - - - - - - - - - - - - - - - - - - -
Eth1/1        100.00          100.00          20.00                        0
Egypt#
```

```
Egypt# show interface ethernet 1/1 counters storm-control
--------------------------------------------------------------------------------

Port        UcastSupp %    McastSupp %    BcastSupp %    TotalSuppDiscards
--------------------------------------------------------------------------------
Eth1/1        100.00         100.00         20.00                      0
Egypt#
```

Example 5-66 shows how to configure multicast traffic storm control on interface Ethernet 1/1.

Example 5-66 *Configuring Multicast Traffic Storm Control on an Interface*

```
Egypt# conf t
Enter configuration commands, one per line. End with CNTL/Z.
Egypt(config)# interface ethernet 1/1
Egypt(config-if)# storm-control multicast level 20
```

Example 5-67 verifies the multicast storm control percentage of bandwidth on interface Ethernet 1/1.

Example 5-67 *Verifying the Multicast Storm Control Percentage of Bandwidth on Interface Ethernet 1/1*

```
Egypt# show interface ethernet 1/1 counters storm-control
--------------------------------------------------------------------------------
-----

Port        UcastSupp %    McastSupp %    BcastSupp %    TotalSuppDiscar
--------------------------------------------------------------------------------
Eth1/1        100.00         20.00          20.00
Egypt#
```

Example 5-68 shows how to configure unicast traffic storm control on interface Ethernet 1/1.

Example 5-68 *Configuring Unicast Traffic Storm Control on Interface Ethernet 1/1*

```
Egypt# conf t
Enter configuration commands, one per line. End with CNTL/Z.
Egypt(config)# interface ethernet 1/1
Egypt(config-if)# storm-control unicast level 20
Egypt(config-if)#
```

Example 5-69 verifies the unicast storm control percentage of bandwidth on interface Ethernet 1/1

Example 5-69 *Verifying the Unicast Storm Control Percentage of Bandwidth on Interface Ethernet 1/1*

```
Egypt# show interface ethernet 1/1 counters storm-control
- - - - - - - - - - - - - - - - - - - - - - - - - - - - - - - - - - - - - - - - - - - - - - - - - - - - - - - - - -

Port      UcastSupp %     McastSupp %     BcastSupp %    TotalSuppDiscar
- - - - - - - - - - - - - - - - - - - - - - - - - - - - - - - - - - - - - - - - - - - - - - - - - - - - - - - - - -

Eth1/1         20.00           20.00           20.00
Egypt#
```

Configuring Unicast RPF

Unicast Reverse Path Forwarding (RPF) reduces the chances of malformed or forged (spoofed) IPv4 or IPv6 source addresses into a network by discarding IPv4 or IPv6 packets that are not valid IP source addresses. Several security threats or types of attacks such as Denial-of-Service (DoS) attacks, Smurf attacks, and Tribal Flood Network (TFN) attacks take advantage of forged or rapidly changing source IPv4 or IPv6 addresses. Unicast RPF deflects attacks by forwarding only the packets that have source addresses that are valid and consistent with the IP routing table. When Unicast RPF is enabled on an interface, the NX-OS device examines all ingress packets received on that interface to ensure that the source address and source interface appear in the routing table and match the interface on which the packet was received.

Unicast RFP can be configured in two different modes on the ingress interface:

■ **Strict Unicast RPF mode:** Strict mode check is successful when Unicast RFP finds a match in the Forwarding Information Base (FIB) for the packet source address and the ingress interface through which the packet is received matches one of the Unicast RPF interfaces in the FIB match. If this check fails, the packet is discarded. You can use this type of Unicast RPF check where packet flows are expected to be symmetrical.

■ **Loose Unicast RPF mode:** Loose mode check is successful when a lookup of a packet source address in the FIB returns a match and the FIB result indicates that the source is reachable through at least one real interface. The ingress interface through which the packet is received is not required to match any of the interfaces in the FIB result.

Note   Unicast RFP is applied only on the ingress interface of a device. The **any** keyword specifies loose Unicast RPF; the **rx** keyword specifies strict Unicast RPF.

Example 5-70 shows how to configure Unicast RPF on interface Ethernet1/1 for IPv4.

Example 5-70   *Configuring Unicast RPF on Interface Ethernet1/1 for IPv4*

```
Egypt(config)# interface ethernet 1/1
Egypt(config-if)# ip address 20.20.20.20 255.0.0.0
Egypt(config-if)# ip verify unicast source reachable-via any
Egypt(config-if)# exit
```

Example 5-71 verifies the Unicast RPF on interface ethernet1/1 for IPv4.

Example 5-71   *Verifying the Unicast RPF on Interface Ethernet1/1 for IPv4*

```
Egypt(config)# show ip interface ethernet 1/1
IP Interface Status for VRF "default"(1)
Ethernet1/1, Interface status: protocol-up/link-up/admin-up, iod: 99,
  IP address: 20.20.20.20, IP subnet: 20.0.0.0/8
  IP broadcast address: 255.255.255.255
  IP multicast groups locally joined: none
  IP MTU: 9216 bytes (using link MTU)
  IP primary address route-preference: 0, tag: 0
  IP proxy ARP : disabled
  IP Local Proxy ARP : disabled
  IP multicast routing: disabled
  IP icmp redirects: enabled
  IP directed-broadcast: disabled
  IP icmp unreachables (except port): disabled
  IP icmp port-unreachable: enabled
  IP unicast reverse path forwarding: loose
  IP interface statistics last reset: never
  IP interface software stats: (sent/received/forwarded/originated/consume
    Unicast packets    : 0/0/0/0/0
    Unicast bytes      : 0/0/0/0/0
    Multicast packets  : 0/0/0/0/0
    Multicast bytes    : 0/0/0/0/0
    Broadcast packets  : 0/0/0/0/0
    Broadcast bytes    : 0/0/0/0/0
    Labeled packets    : 0/0/0/0/0
    Labeled bytes      : 0/0/0/0/0
Egypt(config)# exit

Egypt # show running-config interface ethernet 1/1
!Command: show running-config interface Ethernet1/1
!Time: Thu Oct  1 20:06:53 2009


version 4.2(2a)
```

```
interface Ethernet1/1
  description to Congo
  mtu 9216
  ip address 20.20.20.20/8
  ip verify unicast source reachable-via any
  no shutdown
```

Configuring Control Plane Policing

The Cisco NX-OS device provides control plane policing to prevent DoS attacks from impacting performance.

The supervisor module divides the traffic that it manages into three functional planes:

- **Data plane:** Forwards packets from one interface to another; the packets are not destined to the switch.

- **Control plane:** Controls packets between devices, the packets are destined to router addresses.

- **Management plane:** Supervisor module has both the management plane and control plane and is critical to the operation of the network.

By default, when booting up the Cisco NX-OS device for the first time, the Cisco NX-OS Software installs the default copp-system-policy policy to protect the Supervisor module from DoS attacks. You can set the level of protection by choosing one of the following Control Plane Policing (CoPP) policy options from the initial setup utility:

- Strict

- Moderate

- Lenient

- None

If the setup script is run at initial setup, the CoPP policy can be selected; the default CoPP policy is strict policing. If the administrator would like to change the default CoPP policy, this can also be done at the CLI.

Note   You can find additional information about the default CoPP policies at http://tinyurl.com/ykdlejl.

To change the default CoPP policy through the initial setup script, enter the following:

```
Configure best practices CoPP profile
(strict/moderate/lenient/none) [strict]:
```

Example 5-72 shows the default, strict, copp-system-policy, which can be changed based on specific requirements.

Example 5-72   *Default, Strict, Copp-System-Policy*

```
Congo(config)# ip access-list copp-system-acl-bgp
Congo(config-acl)# 10 permit tcp any gt 1024 any eq bgp
Congo(config-acl)# 20 permit tcp any eq bgp any gt 1024
Congo(config-acl)# ipv6 access-list copp-system-acl-bgp6
Congo(config-acl)# 10 permit tcp any gt 1024 any eq bgp
Congo(config-acl)# 20 permit tcp any eq bgp any gt 1024
Congo(config-acl)# ip access-list copp-system-acl-cts
Congo(config-acl)# 10 permit tcp any any eq 64999
Congo(config-acl)# 20 permit tcp any eq 64999 any
Congo(config-acl)# ip access-list copp-system-acl-dhcp
Congo(config-acl)# 10 permit udp any eq bootpc any
Congo(config-acl)# 20 permit udp any eq bootps any
Congo(config-acl)# 30 permit udp any any eq bootpc
Congo(config-acl)# 40 permit udp any any eq bootps
Congo(config-acl)# ip access-list copp-system-acl-eigrp
Congo(config-acl)# 10 permit eigrp any any
Congo(config-acl)# ip access-list copp-system-acl-ftp
Congo(config-acl)# 10 permit tcp any any eq ftp-data
Congo(config-acl)# 20 permit tcp any any eq ftp
Congo(config-acl)# 30 permit tcp any eq ftp-data any
Congo(config-acl)# 40 permit tcp any eq ftp any
Congo(config-acl)# ip access-list copp-system-acl-glbp
Congo(config-acl)# 10 permit udp any eq 3222 224.0.0.0/24 eq 3222
Congo(config-acl)# ip access-list copp-system-acl-hsrp
Congo(config-acl)# 10 permit udp any 224.0.0.0/24 eq 1985
Congo(config-acl)# ip access-list copp-system-acl-icmp
Congo(config-acl)# 10 permit icmp any any echo
Congo(config-acl)# 20 permit icmp any any echo-reply
Congo(config-acl)# ipv6 access-list copp-system-acl-icmp6
Congo(config-acl)# 10 permit icmp any any echo-request
Congo(config-acl)# 20 permit icmp any any echo-reply
Congo(config-acl)# ipv6 access-list copp-system-acl-icmp6-msgs
Congo(config-acl)# 10 permit icmp any any router-advertisement
Congo(config-acl)# 20 permit icmp any any router-solicitation
Congo(config-acl)# 30 permit icmp any any nd-na
Congo(config-acl)# 40 permit icmp any any nd-ns
Congo(config-acl)# 50 permit icmp any any mld-query
Congo(config-acl)# 60 permit icmp any any mld-report
Congo(config-acl)# 70 permit icmp any any mld-reduction
```

```
Congo(config-acl)# ip access-list copp-system-acl-igmp
Congo(config-acl)# 10 permit igmp any 224.0.0.0/3
Congo(config-acl)# ip access-list copp-system-acl-msdp
Congo(config-acl)# 10 permit tcp any gt 1024 any eq 639
Congo(config-acl)# 20 permit tcp any eq 639 any gt 1024
Congo(config-acl)# ip access-list copp-system-acl-ntp
Congo(config-acl)# 10 permit udp any any eq ntp
Congo(config-acl)# 20 permit udp any eq ntp any
Congo(config-acl)# ipv6 access-list copp-system-acl-ntp6
Congo(config-acl)# 10 permit udp any any eq ntp
Congo(config-acl)# 20 permit udp any eq ntp any
Congo(config-acl)# 20 permit tcp any eq bgp any gt 1024
Congo(config-acl)# ip access-list copp-system-acl-cts
Congo(config-acl)# 10 permit tcp any any eq 64999
Congo(config-acl)# 20 permit tcp any eq 64999 any
Congo(config-acl)# ip access-list copp-system-acl-dhcp
Congo(config-acl)# 10 permit udp any eq bootpc any
Congo(config-acl)# 20 permit udp any eq bootps any
Congo(config-acl)# 30 permit udp any any eq bootpc
Congo(config-acl)# 40 permit udp any any eq bootps
Congo(config-acl)# ip access-list copp-system-acl-eigrp
Congo(config-acl)# 10 permit eigrp any any
Congo(config-acl)# ip access-list copp-system-acl-ftp
Congo(config-acl)# 10 permit tcp any any eq ftp-data
Congo(config-acl)# 20 permit tcp any any eq ftp
Congo(config-acl)# 30 permit tcp any eq ftp-data any
Congo(config-acl)# 40 permit tcp any eq ftp any
Congo(config-acl)# ip access-list copp-system-acl-glbp
Congo(config-acl)# 10 permit udp any eq 3222 224.0.0.0/24 eq 3222
Congo(config-acl)# ip access-list copp-system-acl-hsrp
Congo(config-acl)# 10 permit udp any 224.0.0.0/24 eq 1985
Congo(config-acl)# ip access-list copp-system-acl-icmp
Congo(config-acl)# 10 permit icmp any any echo
Congo(config-acl)# 20 permit icmp any any echo-reply
Congo(config-acl)# ipv6 access-list copp-system-acl-icmp6
Congo(config-acl)# 10 permit icmp any any echo-request
Congo(config-acl)# 20 permit icmp any any echo-reply
Congo(config-acl)# ipv6 access-list copp-system-acl-icmp6-msgs
Congo(config-acl)# 10 permit icmp any any router-advertisement
Congo(config-acl)# 20 permit icmp any any router-solicitation
Congo(config-acl)# 30 permit icmp any any nd-na
Congo(config-acl)# 40 permit icmp any any nd-ns
Congo(config-acl)# 50 permit icmp any any mld-query
Congo(config-acl)# 60 permit icmp any any mld-report
```

```
Congo(config-acl)# 70 permit icmp any any mld-reduction
Congo(config-acl)# ip access-list copp-system-acl-igmp
Congo(config-acl)# 10 permit igmp any 224.0.0.0/3
Congo(config-acl)# ip access-list copp-system-acl-msdp
Congo(config-acl)# 10 permit tcp any gt 1024 any eq 639
Congo(config-acl)# 20 permit tcp any eq 639 any gt 1024
Congo(config-acl)# ip access-list copp-system-acl-ntp
Congo(config-acl)# 10 permit udp any any eq ntp
Congo(config-acl)# 20 permit udp any eq ntp any
Congo(config-acl)# ipv6 access-list copp-system-acl-ntp6
Congo(config-acl)# 10 permit udp any any eq ntp
Congo(config-acl)# 20 permit udp any eq ntp any
Congo(config-acl)# 10 permit tcp any any eq tacacs
Congo(config-acl)# 20 permit tcp any eq tacacs any
Congo(config-acl)# ipv6 access-list copp-system-acl-tacacs6
Congo(config-acl)# 10 permit tcp any any eq tacacs
Congo(config-acl)# 20 permit tcp any eq tacacs any
Congo(config-acl)# ip access-list copp-system-acl-telnet
Congo(config-acl)# 10 permit tcp any any eq telnet
Congo(config-acl)# 20 permit tcp any any eq 107
Congo(config-acl)# 30 permit tcp any eq telnet any
Congo(config-acl)# 40 permit tcp any eq 107 any
Congo(config-acl)# ipv6 access-list copp-system-acl-telnet6
Congo(config-acl)# 10 permit tcp any any eq telnet
Congo(config-acl)# 20 permit tcp any any eq 107
Congo(config-acl)# 30 permit tcp any eq telnet any
Congo(config-acl)# 40 permit tcp any eq 107 any
Congo(config-acl)# ip access-list copp-system-acl-tftp
Congo(config-acl)# 10 permit udp any any eq tftp
Congo(config-acl)# 20 permit udp any any eq 1758
Congo(config-acl)# 30 permit udp any eq tftp any
Congo(config-acl)# 40 permit udp any eq 1758 any
Congo(config-acl)# ipv6 access-list copp-system-acl-tftp6
Congo(config-acl)# 10 permit udp any any eq tftp
Congo(config-acl)# 20 permit udp any any eq 1758
Congo(config-acl)# 30 permit udp any eq tftp any
Congo(config-acl)# 40 permit udp any eq 1758 any
Congo(config-acl)# ip access-list copp-system-acl-traceroute
Congo(config-acl)# 10 permit icmp any any ttl-exceeded
Congo(config-acl)# 20 permit icmp any any port-unreachable
Congo(config-acl)# ip access-list copp-system-acl-undesirable
Congo(config-acl)# 10 permit udp any any eq 1434
Congo(config-acl)# ip access-list copp-system-acl-vpc
Congo(config-acl)# 10 permit udp any any eq 3200
```

```
Congo(config-acl)# ip access-list copp-system-acl-vrrp
Congo(config-acl)# 10 permit 112 any 224.0.0.0/24
Congo(config-acl)# ip access-list copp-system-acl-wccp
Congo(config-acl)# 10 permit udp any eq 2048 any eq 2048
Congo(config-acl)# mac access-list mac-acl
 Congo(config-acl)# statistics per-entry
Congo(config-acl)# 200 permit 0050.561f.73d3 0050.56bc.48dd any
Congo(config-acl)# 210 permit 0050.561f.73d3 0000.00ff.ffff any
Congo(config-cmap-qos)# class-map type control-plane match-any copp-system-class-
critical
Congo(config-cmap-qos)# match access-group name copp-system-acl-bgp
Congo(config-cmap-qos)# match access-group name copp-system-acl-bgp6
Congo(config-cmap-qos)# match access-group name copp-system-acl-eigrp
Congo(config-cmap-qos)# match access-group name copp-system-acl-igmp
Congo(config-cmap-qos)# match access-group name copp-system-acl-msdp
Congo(config-cmap-qos)# match access-group name copp-system-acl-ospf
Congo(config-cmap-qos)# match access-group name copp-system-acl-ospf6
Congo(config-cmap-qos)# match access-group name copp-system-acl-pim
Congo(config-cmap-qos)# match access-group name copp-system-acl-pim6
Congo(config-cmap-qos)# match access-group name copp-system-acl-rip
Congo(config-cmap-qos)# match access-group name copp-system-acl-vpc
Congo(config-cmap-qos)# class-map type control-plane match-any copp-system-class-
exception
Congo(config-cmap-qos)# match exception ip option
Congo(config-cmap-qos)# match exception ip icmp unreachable
Congo(config-cmap-qos)# match exception ipv6 option
Congo(config-cmap-qos)# match exception ipv6 icmp unreachable
Congo(config-cmap-qos)# class-map type control-plane match-any copp-system-class-
important
Congo(config-cmap-qos)# match access-group name copp-system-acl-cts
Congo(config-cmap-qos)# match access-group name copp-system-acl-glbp
Congo(config-cmap-qos)# match access-group name copp-system-acl-hsrp
Congo(config-cmap-qos)# match access-group name copp-system-acl-vrrp
Congo(config-cmap-qos)# match access-group name copp-system-acl-wccp
Congo(config-cmap-qos)# match access-group name copp-system-acl-icmp6-msgs
Congo(config-cmap-qos)# match access-group name copp-system-acl-pim-reg
Congo(config-cmap-qos)# class-map type control-plane match-any copp-system-class-
management
Congo(config-cmap-qos)# match access-group name copp-system-acl-ftp
Congo(config-cmap-qos)# match access-group name copp-system-acl-ntp
Congo(config-cmap-qos)# match access-group name copp-system-acl-ntp6
Congo(config-cmap-qos)# match access-group name copp-system-acl-radius
Congo(config-cmap-qos)# match access-group name copp-system-acl-sftp
Congo(config-cmap-qos)# match access-group name copp-system-acl-snmp
Congo(config-cmap-qos)# match access-group name copp-system-acl-ssh
```

```
Congo(config-cmap-qos)# match access-group name copp-system-acl-ssh6
Congo(config-cmap-qos)# match access-group name copp-system-acl-tacacs
Congo(config-cmap-qos)# match access-group name copp-system-acl-telnet
Congo(config-cmap-qos)# match access-group name copp-system-acl-tftp
Congo(config-cmap-qos)# match access-group name copp-system-acl-tftp6
Congo(config-cmap-qos)# match access-group name copp-system-acl-radius6
Congo(config-cmap-qos)# match access-group name copp-system-acl-tacacs6
Congo(config-cmap-qos)# match access-group name copp-system-acl-telnet6
Congo(config-cmap-qos)# class-map type control-plane match-any copp-system-class-
monitoring
Congo(config-cmap-qos)# match access-group name copp-system-acl-icmp
Congo(config-cmap-qos)# match access-group name copp-system-acl-icmp6
Congo(config-cmap-qos)# match access-group name copp-system-acl-traceroute
Congo(config-cmap-qos)# class-map type control-plane match-any copp-system-class-
normal
Congo(config-cmap-qos)# match access-group name copp-system-acl-dhcp
Congo(config-cmap-qos)# match redirect dhcp-snoop
Congo(config-cmap-qos)# match protocol arp
Congo(config-cmap-qos)# class-map type control-plane match-any copp-system-class-
redirect
Congo(config-cmap-qos)# match redirect arp-inspect
Congo(config-cmap-qos)# class-map type control-plane match-any copp-system-class-
undesirable
Congo(config-cmap-qos)# match access-group name copp-system-acl-undesirable
Congo(config-cmap-qos)# policy-map type control-plane copp-system-policy
Congo(config-cmap-qos)# class copp-system-class-critical
Congo(config-cmap-qos)# police cir 39600 kbps bc 250 ms conform transmit violate
drop
Congo(config-cmap-qos)# class copp-system-class-important
Congo(config-cmap-qos)# police cir 1060 kbps bc 1000 ms conform transmit violate
drop
Congo(config-cmap-qos)# class copp-system-class-management
Congo(config-cmap-qos)# police cir 10000 kbps bc 250 ms conform transmit violate
drop
Congo(config-cmap-qos)# class copp-system-class-normal
Congo(config-cmap-qos)# police cir 680 kbps bc 250 ms conform transmit violate drop
Congo(config-cmap-qos)# class copp-system-class-redirect
Congo(config-cmap-qos)# police cir 280 kbps bc 250 ms conform transmit violate drop
Congo(config-cmap-qos)# class copp-system-class-monitoring
Congo(config-cmap-qos)# police cir 130 kbps bc 1000 ms conform transmit violate drop
Congo(config-cmap-qos)# class copp-system-class-exception
Congo(config-cmap-qos)# police cir 360 kbps bc 250 ms conform transmit violate drop
Congo(config-cmap-qos)# class copp-system-class-undesirable
Congo(config-cmap-qos)# police cir 32 kbps bc 250 ms conform drop violate drop
Congo(config-cmap-qos)# class class-default
Congo(config-cmap-qos)# police cir 100 kbps bc 250 ms conform transmit violate drop
```

```
Congo(config-cmap-qos)# control-plane
Congo(config-cmap-qos)# service-policy input copp-system-policy

Congo(config-cmap-qos)# class-map type control-plane match-any copp-system-class-
critical
Congo(config-cmap-qos)# match access-group name copp-system-acl-bgp
Congo(config-cmap-qos)# match access-group name copp-system-acl-bgp6
Congo(config-cmap-qos)# match access-group name copp-system-acl-eigrp
Congo(config-cmap-qos)# match access-group name copp-system-acl-igmp
Congo(config-cmap-qos)# match access-group name copp-system-acl-msdp
Congo(config-cmap-qos)# match access-group name copp-system-acl-ospf
Congo(config-cmap-qos)# match access-group name copp-system-acl-ospf6
Congo(config-cmap-qos)# match access-group name copp-system-acl-pim
Congo(config-cmap-qos)# match access-group name copp-system-acl-pim6
Congo(config-cmap-qos)# match access-group name copp-system-acl-rip
Congo(config-cmap-qos)# match access-group name copp-system-acl-vpc
Congo(config-cmap-qos)# class-map type control-plane match-any copp-system-class-
exception
Congo(config-cmap-qos)# match exception ip option
Congo(config-cmap-qos)# match exception ip icmp unreachable
Congo(config-cmap-qos)# match exception ipv6 option
Congo(config-cmap-qos)# match exception ipv6 icmp unreachable
Congo(config-cmap-qos)# class-map type control-plane match-any copp-system-class-
important
Congo(config-cmap-qos)# match access-group name copp-system-acl-cts
Congo(config-cmap-qos)# match access-group name copp-system-acl-glbp
Congo(config-cmap-qos)# match access-group name copp-system-acl-hsrp
Congo(config-cmap-qos)# match access-group name copp-system-acl-vrrp
Congo(config-cmap-qos)# match access-group name copp-system-acl-wccp
Congo(config-cmap-qos)# match access-group name copp-system-acl-icmp6-msgs
Congo(config-cmap-qos)# match access-group name copp-system-acl-pim-reg
Congo(config-cmap-qos)# class-map type control-plane match-any copp-system-class-
management
Congo(config-cmap-qos)# match access-group name copp-system-acl-ftp
Congo(config-cmap-qos)# match access-group name copp-system-acl-ntp
Congo(config-cmap-qos)# match access-group name copp-system-acl-ntp6
Congo(config-cmap-qos)# match access-group name copp-system-acl-radius
Congo(config-cmap-qos)# match access-group name copp-system-acl-sftp
Congo(config-cmap-qos)# match access-group name copp-system-acl-snmp
Congo(config-cmap-qos)# match access-group name copp-system-acl-ssh
Congo(config-cmap-qos)# match access-group name copp-system-acl-ssh6
Congo(config-cmap-qos)# match access-group name copp-system-acl-tacacs
Congo(config-cmap-qos)# match access-group name copp-system-acl-telnet
Congo(config-cmap-qos)# match access-group name copp-system-acl-tftp
Congo(config-cmap-qos)# match access-group name copp-system-acl-tftp6
```

```
Congo(config-cmap-qos)# match access-group name copp-system-acl-radius6
Congo(config-cmap-qos)# match access-group name copp-system-acl-tacacs6
Congo(config-cmap-qos)# match access-group name copp-system-acl-telnet6
Congo(config-cmap-qos)# class-map type control-plane match-any copp-system-class-
monitoring
Congo(config-cmap-qos)# match access-group name copp-system-acl-icmp
Congo(config-cmap-qos)# match access-group name copp-system-acl-icmp6
Congo(config-cmap-qos)# match access-group name copp-system-acl-traceroute
Congo(config-cmap-qos)# class-map type control-plane match-any copp-system-class-
normal
Congo(config-cmap-qos)# match access-group name copp-system-acl-dhcp
Congo(config-cmap-qos)# match redirect dhcp-snoop
Congo(config-cmap-qos)# match protocol arp
Congo(config-cmap-qos)# class-map type control-plane match-any copp-system-class-
redirect
Congo(config-cmap-qos)# match redirect arp-inspect
Congo(config-cmap-qos)# class-map type control-plane match-any copp-system-class-
undesirable
Congo(config-cmap-qos)# match access-group name copp-system-acl-undesirable
Congo(config-cmap-qos)# policy-map type control-plane copp-system-policy
Congo(config-cmap-qos)# class copp-system-class-critical
Congo(config-cmap-qos)# police cir 39600 kbps bc 250 ms conform transmit violate
drop
Congo(config-cmap-qos)# class copp-system-class-important
Congo(config-cmap-qos)# police cir 1060 kbps bc 1000 ms conform transmit violate
drop
Congo(config-cmap-qos)# class copp-system-class-management
Congo(config-cmap-qos)# police cir 10000 kbps bc 250 ms conform transmit violate
drop
Congo(config-cmap-qos)# class copp-system-class-normal
Congo(config-cmap-qos)# police cir 680 kbps bc 250 ms conform transmit violate drop
Congo(config-cmap-qos)# class copp-system-class-redirect
Congo(config-cmap-qos)# police cir 280 kbps bc 250 ms conform transmit violate drop
Congo(config-cmap-qos)# class copp-system-class-monitoring
Congo(config-cmap-qos)# police cir 130 kbps bc 1000 ms conform transmit violate drop
Congo(config-cmap-qos)# class copp-system-class-exception
Congo(config-cmap-qos)# police cir 360 kbps bc 250 ms conform transmit violate drop
Congo(config-cmap-qos)# class copp-system-class-undesirable
Congo(config-cmap-qos)# police cir 32 kbps bc 250 ms conform drop violate drop
Congo(config-cmap-qos)# class class-default
Congo(config-cmap-qos)# police cir 100 kbps bc 250 ms conform transmit violate drop
Congo(config-cmap-qos)# control-plane
Congo(config-cmap-qos)# service-policy input copp-system-policy
Congo(config-cmap-qos)# class-map type control-plane match-any copp-system-class-
critical
Congo(config-cmap-qos)# match access-group name copp-system-acl-bgp
```

```
Congo(config-cmap-qos)# match access-group name copp-system-acl-bgp6
Congo(config-cmap-qos)# match access-group name copp-system-acl-eigrp
Congo(config-cmap-qos)# match access-group name copp-system-acl-igmp
Congo(config-cmap-qos)# match access-group name copp-system-acl-msdp
Congo(config-cmap-qos)# match access-group name copp-system-acl-ospf
Congo(config-cmap-qos)# match access-group name copp-system-acl-ospf6
Congo(config-cmap-qos)# match access-group name copp-system-acl-pim
Congo(config-cmap-qos)# match access-group name copp-system-acl-pim6
Congo(config-cmap-qos)# match access-group name copp-system-acl-rip
Congo(config-cmap-qos)# match access-group name copp-system-acl-vpc
Congo(config-cmap-qos)# class-map type control-plane match-any copp-system-class-
exception
Congo(config-cmap-qos)# match exception ip option
Congo(config-cmap-qos)# match exception ip icmp unreachable
Congo(config-cmap-qos)# match exception ipv6 option
Congo(config-cmap-qos)# match exception ipv6 icmp unreachable
Congo(config-cmap-qos)# class-map type control-plane match-any copp-system-class-
important
Congo(config-cmap-qos)# match access-group name copp-system-acl-cts
Congo(config-cmap-qos)# match access-group name copp-system-acl-glbp
Congo(config-cmap-qos)# match access-group name copp-system-acl-hsrp
Congo(config-cmap-qos)# match access-group name copp-system-acl-vrrp
Congo(config-cmap-qos)# match access-group name copp-system-acl-wccp
Congo(config-cmap-qos)# match access-group name copp-system-acl-icmp6-msgs
Congo(config-cmap-qos)# match access-group name copp-system-acl-pim-reg
Congo(config-cmap-qos)# class-map type control-plane match-any copp-system-class-
management
Congo(config-cmap-qos)# match access-group name copp-system-acl-ftp
Congo(config-cmap-qos)# match access-group name copp-system-acl-ntp
Congo(config-cmap-qos)# match access-group name copp-system-acl-ntp6
Congo(config-cmap-qos)# match access-group name copp-system-acl-radius
Congo(config-cmap-qos)# match access-group name copp-system-acl-sftp
Congo(config-cmap-qos)# match access-group name copp-system-acl-snmp
Congo(config-cmap-qos)# match access-group name copp-system-acl-ssh
Congo(config-cmap-qos)# match access-group name copp-system-acl-ssh6
Congo(config-cmap-qos)# match access-group name copp-system-acl-tacacs
Congo(config-cmap-qos)# match access-group name copp-system-acl-telnet
Congo(config-cmap-qos)# match access-group name copp-system-acl-tftp
Congo(config-cmap-qos)# match access-group name copp-system-acl-tftp6
Congo(config-cmap-qos)# match access-group name copp-system-acl-radius6
 Congo(config-cmap-qos)# match access-group name copp-system-acl-tacacs6
Congo(config-cmap-qos)# match access-group name copp-system-acl-telnet6
Congo(config-cmap-qos)# class-map type control-plane match-any copp-system-class-
monitoring
Congo(config-cmap-qos)# match access-group name copp-system-acl-icmp
```

```
Congo(config-cmap-qos)# match access-group name copp-system-acl-icmp6
Congo(config-cmap-qos)# match access-group name copp-system-acl-traceroute
Congo(config-cmap-qos)# class-map type control-plane match-any copp-system-class-
normal
Congo(config-cmap-qos)# match access-group name copp-system-acl-dhcp
Congo(config-cmap-qos)# match redirect dhcp-snoop
Congo(config-cmap-qos)# match protocol arp
Congo(config-cmap-qos)# class-map type control-plane match-any copp-system-class-
redirect
Congo(config-cmap-qos)# match redirect arp-inspect
Congo(config-cmap-qos)# class-map type control-plane match-any copp-system-class-
undesirable
Congo(config-cmap-qos)# match access-group name copp-system-acl-undesirable
Congo(config-cmap-qos)# policy-map type control-plane copp-system-policy
Congo(config-cmap-qos)# class copp-system-class-critical
Congo(config-cmap-qos)# police cir 39600 kbps bc 250 ms conform transmit violate
drop
Congo(config-cmap-qos)# class copp-system-class-important
Congo(config-cmap-qos)# police cir 1060 kbps bc 1000 ms conform transmit violate
drop
Congo(config-cmap-qos)# class copp-system-class-management
Congo(config-cmap-qos)# police cir 10000 kbps bc 250 ms conform transmit violate
drop
Congo(config-cmap-qos)# class copp-system-class-normal
Congo(config-cmap-qos)# police cir 680 kbps bc 250 ms conform transmit violate drop
Congo(config-cmap-qos)# class copp-system-class-redirect
Congo(config-cmap-qos)# police cir 280 kbps bc 250 ms conform transmit violate drop
Congo(config-cmap-qos)# class copp-system-class-monitoring
Congo(config-cmap-qos)# police cir 130 kbps bc 1000 ms conform transmit violate drop
Congo(config-cmap-qos)# class copp-system-class-exception
Congo(config-cmap-qos)# police cir 360 kbps bc 250 ms conform transmit violate drop
Congo(config-cmap-qos)# class copp-system-class-undesirable
Congo(config-cmap-qos)# police cir 32 kbps bc 250 ms conform drop violate drop
Congo(config-cmap-qos)# class class-default
Congo(config-cmap-qos)# police cir 100 kbps bc 250 ms conform transmit violate drop
Congo(config-cmap-qos)# control-plane
Congo(config-cmap-qos)# service-policy input copp-system-policy
```

Configuring Rate Limits

Rate limits can prevent redirected packets for egress exceptions from overwhelming the supervisor module on a Cisco NX-OS device. Rate limits are configured in packets per second for the following types of redirected packets:

■   Access list logging packets

- Data and control packets copied to the Supervisor module

- Layer 2 storm control packets

- Layer 2 port security packets

- Layer 3 glean packets

- Layer 3 maximum transmission unit (MTU) check failure packets

- Layer 3 multicast directly connected packets

- Layer 3 multicast local group packets

- Layer 3 multicast Reverse Path Forwarding (RPF) leak packets

- Layer 3 Time-to-Live (TTL) check failure packets

- Layer 3 control packets

- Receive packets

The general command syntax for configuring rate limiting is as follows:

```
Switch(config)# hardware rate-limit {access-list-log | copy | layer-2 {port-secu-
rity | storm-control} | layer-3 {control | glean | mtu |multicast {directly-connect |
local-groups | rpf-leak} | ttl} | receive} packets
```

Note Rate limits are applied only to egress traffic. If you need to apply ingress rate limits, use CoPP.

Example 5-73 verifies the default rate limit settings.

Example 5-73 *Verifying the Default Rate-Limit Settings*

```
Egypt# show hardware rate-limiter

Units for Config: packets per second
Allowed, Dropped & Total: aggregated since last clear counters


Rate Limiter Class                      Parameters
-----------------------------------------------------------------------

layer-3 mtu                             Config  : 500
                                        Allowed : 0
                                        Dropped : 0


layer-3 multicast directly-connected    Config  : 3000
                                        Allowed : 0
                                        Dropped : 0
                                        Total   : 0
```

```
layer-3 multicast local-groups      Config   : 3000
                                    Allowed  : 0
                                    Dropped  : 0
                                    Total    : 0

layer-3 multicast rpf-leak          Config   : 500
                                    Allowed  : 0
                                    Dropped  : 0
                                    Total    : 0

layer-2 storm-control               Config   : Disabled
access-list-log                     Config   : 100
                                    Allowed  : 0
                                    Dropped  : 0
                                    Total    : 0

copy                                Config   : 30000
                                    Allowed  : 197080
                                    Dropped  : 0
                                    Total    : 197080

receive                             Config   : 30000
                                    Allowed  : 905484
                                    Dropped  : 0
                                    Total    : 905484

layer-2 port-security               Config   : Disabled

layer-2 mcast-snooping              Config   : 10000
                                    Allowed  : 21
                                    Dropped  : 0
                                    Total    : 21

Egypt#
```

Example 5-74 shows how to configure rate limits on Layer 3 control packets. Rate limits are in packets per second for Layer 3 control packets.

Example 5-74   *Configuring Rate-Limits on Layer 3 Control Packets*

```
Congo(config)# hardware rate-limiter layer-3 control 50000
```

Example 5-75 shows how to configure rate limits for Layer 3 glean packets. Rate limits are in packets per second for Layer 3 control packets.

Example 5-75   *Configuring Rate-Limits for Layer 3 Glean Packets*

```
Congo(config)# hardware rate-limiter layer-3 glean 500
```

Example 5-76 shows how to configure rate limits for Layer 2 storm control limits (in packets per seconds).

Example 5-76   *Configuring Rate-Limits for Layer 2 Storm Control Limits in Packets per Second*

```
Congo(config)# hardware rate-limiter layer-2 storm-control 60000
```

Example 5-77 shows how to verify rate limit configuration changes and settings.

Example 5-77   *Verifying Rate Limit Configuration Changes and Settings*

```
                                     Dropped   : 0
                                     Total     : 3
Congo# show hardware rate-limiter layer-2 storm-control

Units for Config: packets per second
Allowed, Dropped & Total: aggregated since last clear counters

Rate Limiter Class                   Parameters
-----------------------------------------------------------------------
layer-2 storm-control                Config    : 60000
                                     Allowed   : 113
                                     Dropped   : 1
                                     Total     : 114
Congo# show hardware rate-limiter

Units for Config: packets per second
Allowed, Dropped & Total: aggregated since last clear counters

Rate Limiter Class                   Parameters
-----------------------------------------------------------------------
layer-3 mtu                          Config    : 500
                                     Allowed   : 0
                                     Dropped   : 0
                                     Total     : 0

layer-3 ttl                          Config    : 500
```

```
                                       Allowed   : 7771
                                       Dropped   : 0
                                       Total     : 7771

layer-3 control                        Config    : 50000
                                       Allowed   : 1042557
                                       Dropped   : 0
                                       Total     : 1042557

layer-3 glean                          Config    : 500
                                       Allowed   : 3
                                       Dropped   : 0
                                       Total     : 3

layer-3 multicast directly-connected   Config    : 3000
                                       Allowed   : 0
                                       Dropped   : 0
                                       Total     : 0

layer-3 multicast local-groups         Config    : 3000
                                       Allowed   : 0
                                       Dropped   : 0
                                       Total     : 0

layer-3 multicast rpf-leak             Config    : 500
                                       Allowed   : 0
                                       Dropped   : 0
                                       Total     : 0

layer-2 storm-control                  Config    : 60000
                                       Allowed   : 126
                                       Dropped   : 1
                                       Total     : 127

access-list-log                        Config    : 100
                                       Allowed   : 0
                                       Dropped   : 0
                                       Total     : 0

copy                                   Config    : 30000
                                       Allowed   : 2634651
                                       Dropped   : 0
                                       Total     : 2634651
receive                                Config    : 30000
```

```
                                 Allowed     : 8275085
                                 Dropped     : 0
                                 Total       : 8275085

layer-2 port-security            Config      : Disabled

layer-2 mcast-snooping           Config      : 10000
                                 Allowed     : 0
                                 Dropped     : 0
                                 Total       : 0
Congo#
```

SNMPv3

The section covers SNMPv3 only. SNMPv3 provides secure access to devices by a combination of authenticating and encrypting frames over the network. The security features provided in SNMPv3 are as follows:

- **Message integrity:** Ensures that a packet has not been tampered.

- **Authentication:** Message is from a valid source.

- **Encryption:** Prevent from being seen by unauthorized sources.

SNMPv3 provides for both security models and security levels. A security model is an authentication strategy set up for a user and the role in which the user resides. A security level is the permitted level of security within a security model. A combination of a security model and a security level determines which security mechanism is employed when handling an SNMP packet.

Example 5-78 shows how to configure SNMP users with authentication and privacy configuration.

Example 5-78   *Configuring SNMP Users with Authentication and Privacy Configuration*

```
Egypt(config)# snmp-server user manager auth sha MGTUser123 priv MGTUser
Egypt(config)# show snmp user
                SNMP USERS

User                       Auth  Priv(enforce)  Groups

____                       ____  _____  _____
admin                      md5   des(no)        network-admin
manager                    sha   des(no)        network-operator


NOTIFICATION TARGET USERS (configured  for sending V3 Inform)
```

```
_____

User                          Auth  Priv

____                          ____  ____

Egypt(config)#
```

Example 5-79 shows how to enforce SNMP message encryption on a per user basis.

Example 5-79   *Enforcing SNMP Message Encryption on a Per User Basis*

```
Egypt(config)# snmp-server user manager enforcePriv
Egypt(config)# show snmp user
                  SNMP USERS
- - - - - - - - - - - - - - - - - - - - - - - - - - - - - - - - - - - - - - - - -

User                      Auth  Priv(enforce) Groups

____                      ____  _____  _____

admin                     md5   des(no)       network-admin

manager                   sha   des(no)       network-operator
                                              enforcePriv

- - - - - - - - - - - - - - - - - - - - - - - - - - - - - - - - - - - - - - - - -


NOTIFICATION TARGET USERS (configured  for sending V3 Inform)

User                      Auth  Priv

____                      ____  ____
```

Example 5-80 shows how to enforce message encryption for all users.

Example 5-80   *Enforcing Message Encryption for All Users*

```
Egypt(config)# snmp-server globalEnforcePriv
Egypt(config)# show snmp user
                  SNMP USERS [global privacy flag enabled]
- - - - - - - - - - - - - - - - - - - - - - - - - - - - - - - - - - - - - - - - -


User                      Auth  Priv(enforce) Groups

____                      ____  _____  _____

admin                     md5   des(no)       network-admin

manager                   sha   des(no)       network-operator
                                              enforcePriv

- - - - - - - - - - - - - - - - - - - - - - - - - - - - - - - - - - - - - - - - -
```

```
NOTIFICATION TARGET USERS (configured  for sending V3 Inform)


User                             Auth  Priv

____                             ____  ____
Egypt(config)#
```

Example 5-81 shows how to assign SNMPv3 users to multiple roles.

Example 5-81 *Assigning SNMPv3 Users to Multiple Roles*

```
Egypt(config)# snmp-server user manager network-admin
Egypt(config)# show snmp user
                    SNMP USERS [global privacy flag enabled]
---------------------------------------------------------------------------


User                         Auth  Priv(enforce) Groups

____                         ____  _____  _____
admin                        md5   des(no)       network-admin

manager                      sha   des(no)       network-operator
                                                 enforcePriv
                                                 network-admin
      ---------------------------------------------------------------------


NOTIFICATION TARGET USERS (configured  for sending V3 Inform)


User                         Auth  Priv

____                         ____  ____
Egypt(config)# show role


Role: network-admin
  Description: Predefined network admin role has access to all commands
  on the switch
  Rule   Perm   Type    Scope           Entity
---------------------------------------------------------------------------
  1      permit read-write

Role: network-operator
  Description: Predefined network operator role has access to all read
  commands on the switch
  Rule   Perm   Type    Scope           Entity
  1      permit read
```

```
Role: vdc-admin
  Description: Predefined vdc admin role has access to all commands with
  a VDC instance
  Rule   Perm   Type      Scope            Entity
  ----------------------------------------------------------------------
   1      permit read-write

Role: vdc-operator
  Description: Predefined vdc operator role has access to all read comm
  within a VDC instance
  Rule   Perm   Type      Scope            Entity
  ----------------------------------------------------------------------
   1      permit read

Role: enforcePriv
  Description: new role
  Vlan policy: permit (default)
  Interface policy: permit (default)
  Vrf policy: permit (default)
Egypt(config)#
```

Example 5-82 shows how to create SNMP communities. The SNMP community is a collection of hosts grouped together for administrative purposes.

Example 5-82 *Creating SNMP Communities*

```
Egypt(config)# snmp-server community public ro
Egypt(config)# snmp-server community private rw
Egypt(config)# show snmp community
Community          Group / Access      context   acl_filter
---------          --------------      -------   ----------
public             network-operator
private            network-admin
Egypt(config)#
```

Example 5-83 shows how to configure notification receivers. For example, the notification receiver can determine whether a syslog message notification contained the structured data elements of a SYSLOG message.

Example 5-83 *Configuring Notification Receivers*

```
Egypt(config)# snmp-server host 10.10.10.12 informs version 3 priv private
Egypt(config)# show snmp host
----------------------------------------------------------------------
```

```
Host                           Port Version  Level  Type   SecName
--------------------------------------------------------------------
10.10.10.12                    162  v3        priv   inform private
Egypt(config)#


Configuring a Source Interface for SNMP Notifications


Egypt(config)# show snmp source-interface
Notification                   source-interface
--------------------------------------------------------------------
trap                           -
inform                         -
```

Example 5-84 shows how to configure the SNMP source interface. The source interface specifies the source IP address of the SMTP messages, trap messages for example.

Example 5-84 *Configuring the SNMP Source Interface*

```
Egypt(config)# snmp-server source-interface traps loopback 0
Egypt(config)# show snmp source-interface
Notification                   source-interface
-------------------------------------------------------------------------------
trap                           loopback0
inform                         -
-------------------------------------------------------------------------------
---------------
Egypt(config)# snmp-server source-interface informs loopback 0
Egypt(config)# show snmp source-interface
Notification                   source-interface
-------------------------------------------------------------------------------
trap                           loopback0
inform                         loopback0
-------------------------------------------------------------------------------
Egypt(config)#
```

Example 5-85 shows how to disable LinkUp/LinkDown SNMP notifications globally.

Example 5-85 *Disabling LinkUp/LinkDown SNMP Notifications Globally*

```
Egypt# show snmp trap
Trap type                                                   Enabled
-------------------------------------------------------------------------------
entity          : entity_mib_change                         Yes
entity          : entity_module_status_change               Yes
```

```
entity                : entity_power_status_change          Yes
entity                : entity_module_inserted              Yes
entity                : entity_module_removed               Yes
entity                : entity_unrecognised_module          Yes
entity                : entity_fan_status_change            Yes
entity                : entity_power_out_change             Yes
link                  : linkDown                            Yes
link                  : linkUp                              Yes
link                  : extended-linkDown                   Yes
link                  : extended-linkUp                     Yes
link                  : cieLinkDown                         Yes
link                  : cieLinkUp                           Yes
callhome              : event-notify                        No
callhome              : smtp-send-fail                      No
cfs                   : state-change-notif                  No
cfs                   : merge-failure                       No
rf                    : redundancy_framework                Yes
port-security         : access-secure-mac-violation         No
port-security         : trunk-secure-mac-violation          No
aaa                   : server-state-change                 No
license               : notify-license-expiry               Yes
license               : notify-no-license-for-feature       Yes
license               : notify-licensefile-missing          Yes
license               : notify-license-expiry-warning       Yes
hsrp                  : state-change                        No
upgrade               : UpgradeOpNotifyOnCompletion          No
upgrade               : UpgradeJobStatusNotify               No
feature-control       : FeatureOpStatusChange                No
snmp                  : authentication                      No
Egypt# conf t
Enter configuration commands, one per line. End with CNTL/Z.
Egypt(config)# no snmp-server enable traps link linkup
Egypt(config)# no snmp-server enable traps link linkdown
Egypt(config)# show snmp trap
Trap type                                               Enabled
-----------------------------------------------------------------------------
entity                : entity_mib_change                   Yes
entity                : entity_module_status_change          Yes
entity                : entity_power_status_change           Yes
entity                : entity_module_inserted               Yes
entity                : entity_module_removed                Yes
entity                : entity_unrecognised_module           Yes
entity                : entity_fan_status_change             Yes
entity                : entity_power_out_change              Yes
```

```
link                 : linkDown                              No
link                 : linkUp                                No
link                 : extended-linkDown                     Yes
link                 : extended-linkUp                       Yes
link                 : cieLinkDown                           Yes
link                 : cieLinkUp                             Yes
callhome             : event-notify                          No
callhome             : smtp-send-fail                        No
cfs                  : state-change-notif                    No
cfs                  : merge-failure                         No
rf                   : redundancy_framework                  Yes
port-security        : access-secure-mac-violation           No
port-security        : trunk-secure-mac-violation            No
aaa                  : server-state-change                   No
license              : notify-license-expiry                 Yes
license              : notify-no-license-for-feature         Yes
license              : notify-licensefile-missing            Yes
license              : notify-license-expiry-warning         Yes
hsrp                 : state-change                          No
upgrade              : UpgradeOpNotifyOnCompletion           No
upgrade              : UpgradeJobStatusNotify                No
feature-control      : FeatureOpStatusChange                 No
snmp                 : authentication                        No
Egypt(config)#
```

Example 5-86 shows how to disable LinkUp/LinkDown SNMP notifications on a specific interface.

Example 5-86 *Disabling LinkUp/LinkDown SNMP Notifications on Interface Ethernet 1/1*

```
Egypt(config)# int e1/1
Egypt(config-if)# no snmp trap link-status
```

Example 5-87 shows how to enable SNMP notifications.

Example 5-87 *Enabling SNMP Notifications*

```
Egypt# conf t
Enter configuration commands, one per line. End with CNTL/Z.
Egypt(config)# snmp-server enable traps
Egypt(config)# show snmp trap
Trap type                                                    Enabled
-------------------------------------------------------------------------------
```

```
entity            : entity_mib_change                    Yes
entity            : entity_module_status_change          Yes
entity            : entity_power_status_change           Yes
entity            : entity_module_inserted               Yes
entity            : entity_module_removed                Yes
entity            : entity_unrecognised_module           Yes
entity            : entity_fan_status_change             Yes
entity            : entity_power_out_change              Yes
link              : linkDown                             Yes
link              : linkUp                               Yes
link              : extended-linkDown                    Yes
link              : extended-linkUp                      Yes
link              : cieLinkDown                          Yes
link              : cieLinkUp                            Yes
callhome          : event-notify                         Yes
callhome          : smtp-send-fail                       Yes
cfs               : state-change-notif                   Yes
cfs               : merge-failure                        Yes
rf                : redundancy_framework                 Yes
port-security     : access-secure-mac-violation          Yes
port-security     : trunk-secure-mac-violation           Yes
aaa               : server-state-change                  Yes
license           : notify-license-expiry                Yes
license           : notify-no-license-for-feature        Yes
license           : notify-licensefile-missing           Yes
license           : notify-license-expiry-warning        Yes
hsrp              : state-change                          Yes
upgrade           : UpgradeOpNotifyOnCompletion          Yes
upgrade           : UpgradeJobStatusNotify               Yes
feature-control   : FeatureOpStatusChange                Yes
snmp              : authentication                       Yes
Egypt(config)#
```

Summary

NX-OS security capabilities are scalable, flexible, and support a wide range of solutions and protocols. Combining an underlying architecture focused on high availability with years of security features experience makes for a secure and robust platform. VRF-aware features enable the network administrator to develop and deploy flexible, scalable, and resilient secure data center architectures.

Chapter 6

High Availability

This chapter covers the following topics focused on high availability:

- Physical Redundancy

- Generic Online Diagnostics

- NX-OS High Availability Architecture

- Process Modularity

- Process Restart

- Stateful Switchover

- Nonstop Forwarding

- In-Service Software Upgrades (ISSU)

Requirements in the data center are rapidly changing—where there were once generous maintenance windows, now there are none. Best effort delivery of service has been replaced with strict Service Level Agreements (SLA), sometimes with financial penalties incurred to lines of business or customers. This chapter introduces various hardware and software components that make the Nexus 7000 a highly available platform to meet these changing data center requirements.

Physical Redundancy

Redundancy within the Nexus 7000 begins at the physical chassis and extends into the software and operational characteristics of the system. To provide a redundant hardware platform from which to build on, the Nexus 7000 provides the following hardware components:

- Redundant power supplies

- Cooling system

- Redundant Supervisors

- Redundant Ethernet Out-of-Band (EOBC)

- Redundant Fabric Modules

The following sections describe these components in greater detail.

Redundant Power Supplies

The Nexus 7010 provides the ability to install up to three power supplies. To account for the additional line cards in the system, the Nexus 7018 provides the ability to install up to four power supplies. Each power supply has redundant inputs that feed completely independent power units that feed two redundant power buses within the chassis. The mode in which redundancy is achieved is user configurable to one of four modes; these power redundancy schemes are consistent between the 10 slot and 18 slot versions of the Nexus 7000:

- **Non-redundant (combined):** All available power from all available power supplies and inputs is made available for the system to draw from. This mode is available but not recommended unless extraordinary circumstances exist.

- **N+1 (ps-redundant):** The default mode that protects against the failure of one power supply. When operating in this mode, the power made available to the system is the sum of all the power supplies minus the largest.

- **Grid redundancy (insrc-redundant):** Also called input source redundancy. Most data centers today are equipped with redundant power feeds to the data center and redundant distribution systems within the data center. In grid redundancy, each input of the installed power supplies connects to different power grids. If a total loss of power occurs on either side, the system remains powered on. In this mode, the power made available to the system is the sum of all the power supplies installed in the system. This number is then cut in half to create the power budget for modules.

- **Full redundancy (redundant):** The combination of input source redundancy and power supply redundancy. This provides the least amount of power available for line cards and crossbars but ensures that no failure, whether internal or external, compromises the availability of the system.

Example 6-1 shows how to configure the power redundancy mode and verify the operating mode.

Example 6-1 *Configuring and Verifying Power Redundancy*

```
Congo(config)# power redundancy-mode ?
  combined         Configure power supply redundancy mode as combined
  insrc-redundant  Configure power supply redundancy mode as grid/AC input
                   source redundant
```

```
     ps-redundant      Configure power supply redundancy mode as PS redundant
     redundant         Configure power supply redundancy mode as InSrc and PS
                       redundant


Congo(config)# power redundancy-mode redundant

Congo(config)# show environment power
Power Supply:
Voltage: 50 Volts
Power                       Actual       Total
Supply    Model             Output      Capacity    Status
                            (Watts )    (Watts )
------------------------------------------------------------------------------
1         N7K-AC-6.0KW       668 W       3000 W      Ok
2         N7K-AC-6.0KW       663 W       3000 W      Ok
3         -----------          0 W          0 W      Absent


                            Actual       Power
Module    Model             Draw        Allocated   Status
                            (Watts )    (Watts )
------------------------------------------------------------------------------
1         N7K-M132XP-12      N/A          750 W      Powered-Up
2         N7K-M148GT-11      N/A          400 W      Powered-Up
5         N7K-SUP1           N/A          210 W      Powered-Up
6         N7K-SUP1           N/A          210 W      Powered-Up
Xb1       N7K-C7010-FAB-1    N/A           60 W      Powered-Up
Xb2       N7K-C7010-FAB-1    N/A           60 W      Powered-Up
Xb3       N7K-C7010-FAB-1    N/A           60 W      Powered-Up
Xb4       xbar               N/A           60 W      Absent
Xb5       xbar               N/A           60 W      Absent
fan1      N7K-C7010-FAN-S    N/A          720 W      Powered-Up
fan2      N7K-C7010-FAN-S    N/A          720 W      Powered-Up
fan3      N7K-C7010-FAN-F    N/A          120 W      Powered-Up
fan4      N7K-C7010-FAN-F    N/A          120 W      Powered-Up


N/A - Per module power not available



Power Usage Summary:
------------------------------------------------------------------------------
Power Supply redundancy mode (configured)        PS-Redundant
Power Supply redundancy mode (operational)       Non-Redundant


Total Power Capacity (based on configured mode)       6000 W
```

Total Power of all Inputs (cumulative)	6000 W
Total Power Output (actual draw)	1331 W
Total Power Allocated (budget)	3550 W
Total Power Available for additional modules	2450 W

Redundant Cooling System

The Nexus 7010 has two redundant fans for line cards and two redundant fans for fabric modules located in the rear of the chassis. For the Nexus 7018, the system I/O and fabric fans are located within the same field replaceable unit (FRU). Placing the fan trays in the rear of the chassis makes the system extremely serviceable and ensures that cabling does not get in the way of removal or replacement of the fan tray. All the fans in the system are hot-swappable. If one of these fans fails, the redundant module increases rotation speed to continue to cool the entire system. Although a single fan can cool the entire system in the event of a failure, it is critical that all fans be physically present in the system at all times. This keeps the airflow characteristics of the system intact. If one of the fans is physically removed and not replaced, the system shuts down after several warnings and a 3-minute timer has expired.

Example 6-2 shows how to verify the status of the fans installed in the system.

Example 6-2   *Verifying System and I/O Fans*

```
Congo# show environment fan
Fan:
Fan             Model            Hw       Status
-------------------------------------------------------------------------
Fan1(sys_fan1)  N7K-C7010-FAN-S  1.1      Ok
Fan2(sys_fan2)  N7K-C7010-FAN-S  1.1      Ok
Fan3(fab_fan1)  N7K-C7010-FAN-F  1.1      Ok
Fan4(fab_fan2)  N7K-C7010-FAN-F  1.1      Ok
Fan_in_PS1      --               --       Ok
Fan_in_PS2      --               --       Ok
Fan_in_PS3      --               --       Absent
Fan Air Filter : Absent
Congo#
```

A status of **Ok** should be in all installed fans; anything other than this status would require attention from the administrator, ensuring that the appropriate fan tray is properly seated, which is a good first step. If one or more fans fail within a tray, the Nexus 7000 switch can adjust the speed of the remaining fans to compensate for the failed fans. A fan failure could also lead to temperature alarms if not corrected in a timely manner.

Temperature sensors are located throughout the system to monitor temperature and adjust fan speeds as necessary to ensure all components are within their appropriate operational range. Each module is equipped with intake, outlet, and on-board sensors. Two temperature thresholds are tracked for each sensor:

■ **Minor temperature threshold:** When a minor threshold is exceeded, a system message will be logged; call home and SNMP notifications are sent if configured.

■ **Major temperature threshold:** A major temperature threshold being exceeded would cause the same actions as a minor threshold, unless the intake sensor experiences a major threshold violation. In this scenario, the module is powered down. If the intake module of the active Supervisor experiences a major threshold violation and a HA-standby Supervisor is present, the module shuts down. If no standby Supervisor is present, the system monitors the temperature every 5 seconds for 2 minutes and then shuts down the module.

Example 6-3 shows how to monitor the temperature at various points within the system.

Example 6-3 *Verifying System Temperature*

```
Congo# show environment temperature
Temperature:
- - - - - - - - - - - - - - - - - - - - - - - - - - - - - - - - - - - - - - - - - - -
Module    Sensor          MajorThresh    MinorThres    CurTemp    Status
                          (Celsius)      (Celsius)     (Celsius)
- - - - - - - - - - - - - - - - - - - - - - - - - - - - - - - - - - - - - - - - - - -
1         Crossbar(s5)    105            95            49         Ok
1         QEng1Sn1(s12)   115            110           62         Ok
1         QEng1Sn2(s13)   115            110           61         Ok
1         QEng1Sn3(s14)   115            110           58         Ok
1         QEng1Sn4(s15)   115            110           59         Ok
1         QEng2Sn1(s16)   115            110           62         Ok
1         QEng2Sn2(s17)   115            110           60         Ok
1         QEng2Sn3(s18)   115            110           59         Ok
1         QEng2Sn4(s19)   115            110           60         Ok
1         L2Lookup(s27)   115            105           44         Ok
1         L3Lookup(s28)   120            110           55         Ok
2         Crossbar(s5)    105            95            36         Ok
2         CTSdev4 (s9)    115            105           52         Ok
2         CTSdev5 (s10)   115            105           50         Ok
2         CTSdev7 (s12)   115            105           51         Ok
2         CTSdev9 (s14)   115            105           48         Ok
2         CTSdev10(s15)   115            105           47         Ok
2         CTSdev11(s16)   115            105           46         Ok
2         CTSdev12(s17)   115            105           44         Ok
```

```
2          QEng1Sn1(s18)   115        105        44        Ok
2          QEng1Sn2(s19)   115        105        43        Ok
2          QEng1Sn3(s20)   115        105        40        Ok
2          QEng1Sn4(s21)   115        105        42        Ok
2          L2Lookup(s22)   115        105        40        Ok
2          L3Lookup(s23)   120        110        48        Ok
5          Intake  (s3)    60         42         17        Ok
5          EOBC_MAC(s4)    105        95         35        Ok
5          CPU     (s5)    105        95         29        Ok
5          Crossbar(s6)    105        95         40        Ok
5          Arbiter (s7)    110        100        48        Ok
5          CTSdev1 (s8)    115        105        39        Ok
5          InbFPGA (s9)    105        95         36        Ok
5          QEng1Sn1(s10)   115        105        40        Ok
5          QEng1Sn2(s11)   115        105        40        Ok
5          QEng1Sn3(s12)   115        105        36        Ok
5          QEng1Sn4(s13)   115        105        39        Ok
6          Intake  (s3)    60         42         18        Ok
6          EOBC_MAC(s4)    105        95         36        Ok
6          CPU     (s5)    105        95         28        Ok
6          Crossbar(s6)    105        95         39        Ok
6          Arbiter (s7)    110        100        46        Ok
6          CTSdev1 (s8)    115        105        39        Ok
6          InbFPGA (s9)    105        95         34        Ok
6          QEng1Sn1(s10)   115        105        39        Ok
6          QEng1Sn2(s11)   115        105        38        Ok
6          QEng1Sn3(s12)   115        105        35        Ok
6          QEng1Sn4(s13)   115        105        36        Ok
xbar-1     Intake  (s2)    60         42         19        Ok
xbar-1     Crossbar(s3)    105        95         47        Ok
xbar-2     Intake  (s2)    60         42         19        Ok
xbar-2     Crossbar(s3)    105        95         42        Ok
xbar-3     Intake  (s2)    60         42         18        Ok
xbar-3     Crossbar(s3)    105        95         45        Ok
Congo#
xbar-1     Intake  (s2)    60         42         19        Ok
xbar-1     Crossbar(s3)    105        95         47        Ok
xbar-2     Intake  (s2)    60         42         19        Ok
xbar-2     Crossbar(s3)    105        95         42        Ok
xbar-3     Intake  (s2)    60         42         18        Ok
xbar-3     Crossbar(s3)    105        95         45        Ok
Congo#
```

In this example, all current temperature values are well below any threshold violation. Each environment might be slightly different; therefore, it is considered good practice to baseline these temperatures in your environment and trend these over time.

Redundant Supervisors

Supervisor modules provide the control plane operations for the system. These functions include building forwarding tables, maintaining protocol adjacencies, and providing management interfaces to the system. In the Nexus 7010, slots 5 and 6 are reserved for Supervisor modules. In the Nexus 7018, slots 9 and 10 are reserved for Supervisor modules. Supervisor modules have a slightly different form factor, so I/O modules *cannot* be installed in these slots. Redundant Supervisor modules provide a completely redundant control plane and redundant management interfaces for the platform. Redundant Supervisors behave in an active/standby configuration where only one Supervisor is active at any time. This level of control plane redundancy provides protection against hardware failure and provides a foundation for advanced features such as Stateful Switchover (SSO) and In-Service Software Upgrades (ISSU) that are covered later in this chapter. From a management standpoint, each Supervisor provides an out-of-band Connectivity Management Processor (CMP) and an in-band management (mgmt0)interface. These interfaces were covered in detail in the previous chapter.

The CMP provides a standalone network stack that is always available as long as power is applied to the system. This type of technology is analogous to the "lights out" capabilities of most modern server offerings. When comparing this to legacy networking applications, the CMP functionality can be used to replace terminal servers that provide console connectivity if the system has experienced major issues causing normal connectivity to be lost. From the CMP, a network operator can monitor log files and console ports and power cycle the entire system. The CMP is completely independent of NX-OS and guarantees that any outages will not be prolonged due to the inability to access the device remotely. The management interfaces operate in an active/standby just as the Supervisors do. Whichever Supervisor is active is where connectivity for the mgmt0 interface is derived.

Note   Due to the active/standby nature of the mgmt0 interface, it is recommended that the management interfaces of both supervisors are physically connected to an external switching infrastructure at all times.

Example 6-4 shows how to verify Supervisor redundancy.

Example 6-4   *Verifying Supervisor Redundancy*

```
Congo# show system redundancy status
Redundancy mode
---------------------------------------------------------------------------
      administrative:    HA
```

```
         operational:    HA

This supervisor (sup-1)
- - - - - - - - - - - - - - - - - - - - - - - - - - - - - - - - - - - - - - - - - - - - - - - - - - -
    Redundancy state:    Active
    Supervisor state:    Active
      Internal state:    Active with HA standby


Other supervisor (sup-2)
- - - - - - - - - - - - - - - - - - - - - - - - - - - - - - - - - - - - - - - - - - - - - - - - - - -
    Redundancy state:    Standby
    Supervisor state:    HA standby
      Internal state:    HA standby
```

Redundant Ethernet Out-of-Band (EOBC)

Various forms of communication between line cards, fabric modules, and Supervisors are required within a normal system operation. This communication occurs over an internal switching infrastructure called the Ethernet Out-of-Band Channel (EOBC). Each Supervisor contains a 24-port Gigabit switch that connects to line cards and fabric modules within the system. Additionally, each line card contains a small switch with ports connecting to both Supervisors and the local processor. The components that make up the EOBC bus provide a redundant infrastructure for management and control traffic local to the system.

Redundant Fabric Modules

The Nexus 7000 series of switches provides the ability to install up to five fabric modules per system. The fabric modules are installed to meet the capacity and redundancy requirements of the system. Each line card load balances data plane traffic across all the available fabric modules within the system. If one of the fabric modules should fail, traffic rebalances across the remaining fabrics. When the failed fabric is replaced, traffic is automatically redistributed again. You can monitor fabric module status and utilization, as demonstrated in Example 6-5.

Example 6-5 *Verifying Fabric Module Status and Utilization*

```
Congo# show module xbar
Xbar Ports  Module-Type              Model            Status
- - - - - - - - - - - - - - - - - - - - - - - - - - - - - - - - - - - - - - - - - - - - - - - -
1    0      Fabric Module 1          N7K-C7010-FAB-1  ok
2    0      Fabric Module 1          N7K-C7010-FAB-1  ok
```

```
3    0        Fabric Module 1           N7K-C7010-FAB-1    ok
4    0        Fabric Module 1           N7K-C7010-FAB-1    ok


Xbar Sw                Hw
----------------------------------------------------------------------------
1    NA                1.0
2    NA                1.0
3    NA                1.0
4    NA                1.0



Xbar MAC-Address(es)                    Serial-Num
----------------------------------------------------------------------------
1    NA                                 JAB1211019U
2    NA                                 JAB121101AQ
3    NA                                 JAB121101A9
4    NA                                 JAB1211018G


* this terminal session
Congo#


Congo# show hardware fabric-utilization
Slot  Direction   Utilization
----------------------------------------------------------------------------
  1   ingress     0.0%
  1   egress      0.0%
  2   ingress     0.0%
  2   egress      0.0%
  3   ingress     0.0%
  3   egress      0.0%
  5   ingress     0.0%
  5   egress      0.0%
  6   ingress     0.0%
  6   egress      0.0%
```

Generic Online Diagnostics

There is a strong interest within data centers today to move operations from reactive to proactive. As part of this operational shift, it becomes necessary to identify hardware failures before they happen and to take preventative action prior to their failure. NX-OS follows the tradition of the widely deployed Catalyst line of switches with its implementation of Generic Online Diagnostics (GOLD), which provides the mechanisms necessary to test and verify the functionality of a particular component at various times during the operation of the component. As the name implies, GOLD provides these mechanisms in a fashion that can usually be done on a device that is connected to the network with minimal or no disruption to the operation of the device. In this section, we provide an overview of the capabilities, operation, and configuration of GOLD.

Note   GOLD provides a robust suite of diagnostic tests, many of them are executed in the background with no disruption to the system. Some of the tests, however, are disruptive and should be utilized with caution within a production environment.

GOLD verifies functionality using a variety of techniques; the full suite of diagnostic utilities is broken down into the following categories:

- Bootup diagnostics
- Runtime diagnostics
- On-demand diagnostics

Within each of these categories, specific tests are also classified as disruptive or nondisruptive.

Bootup Diagnostics

Prior to a module coming online within NX-OS, several checks are run on the hardware depending on the type. By default, a complete set of tests are run prior to placing the module in service. It is not recommended to alter this behavior, but if necessary to decrease boot time, these tests can be bypassed, as shown in Example 6-6.

Example 6-6   *Bypassing Bootup Diagnostics*

```
Congo# show diagnostic bootup level

        Current bootup diagnostic level: complete

Congo# conf t
Enter configuration commands, one per line. End with CNTL/Z.
Congo(config)# diagnostic bootup level bypass
Congo(config)# sho diagnostic bootup level

        Current bootup diagnostic level: bypass

Congo(config)#
```

Runtime Diagnostics

Although bootup diagnostics prevent a module from coming online without exhaustively testing the hardware functionality, it is not uncommon for modules or entire systems to run for months or years without rebooting. It is therefore necessary to run periodic checks on the hardware during the normal operation of the device. These checks are referred to as runtime diagnostics and can be viewed from the command-line interface (CLI).

Example 6-7 shows the runtime diagnostics performed on a Supervisor module.

Example 6-7   *Supervisor Runtime Diagnostics*

```
Congo# show diagnostic description module 5 test all
ManagementPortLoopback :
        A bootup test that tests loopback on the management port of
        the module

EOBCPortLoopback :
        A bootup test that tests loopback on the EOBC

ASICRegisterCheck :
        A health monitoring test,enabled by default that checks read/write
        access to scratch registers on ASICs on the module.

USB :
        A bootup test that checks the USB controller initialization
        on the module.

CryptoDevice :
        A bootup test that checks the CTS device initialization on
        the module.

NVRAM :
        A health monitoring test, enabled by default that checks the
        sanity of the NVRAM device on the module.

RealTimeClock :
        A health monitoring test, enabled by default that verifies
        the real time clock on the module.

PrimaryBootROM :
        A health monitoring  test that verifies the primary BootROM
        on the module.

SecondaryBootROM :
        A health monitoring  test that verifies the secondary BootROM
```

```
          on the module.

CompactFlash :
          A Health monitoring test, enabled by default, that verifies
          access to the internal compactflash devices.

ExternalCompactFlash :
          A Health monitoring test, enabled by default, that verifies
          access to the external compactflash devices.

PwrMgmtBus :
          A Health monitoring test, enabled by default, that verifies
          the standby Power Management Control Bus.

SpineControlBus :
          A Health monitoring, enabled by default, test that verifies
          the standby Spine Card Control Bus.

SystemMgmtBus :
          A Health monitoring test, enabled by default, that verifies
          the standby System Bus.

StatusBus :
          A Health monitoring test, enabled by default, that verifies
          status transmitted along Status Bus.

StandbyFabricLoopback :
          A Health monitoring test, enabled by default, that verifies
          packet path from the Standby supervisor to the Fabric
```

Example 6-8 shows the runtime diagnostics performed on a line card.

Example 6-8   *Line Card Runtime Diagnostics*

```
Congo# show diagnostic description module 2 test all
EOBCPortLoopback :
          A bootup test that tests loopback on the EOBC

ASICRegisterCheck :
          A health monitoring test,enabled by default that checks read/write
          access to scratch registers on ASICs on the module.

PrimaryBootROM :
          A health monitoring test that verifies the primary BootROM
```

```
           state.

SecondaryBootROM :

           A health monitoring test that verifies the secondary BootROM
           state.

PortLoopback :

           A health monitoring test that will test the packet path from
           the Supervisor card to the physical port in ADMIN DOWN state
           on Line cards.

RewriteEngineLoopback :

           A health monitoring test, enabled by default, that does non
           disruptive loopback for all LC ports upto the Rewrite Engine
           ASIC (i.e. Metro) device.
```

Each of these tests has a default run interval that can be verified, as shown in Example 6-9.

Example 6-9   *Default Runtime Diagnostics Schedule*

```
Congo# show diagnostic content module 2


Module 2: 10/100/1000 Mbps Ethernet Module


Diagnostics test suite attributes:
B/C/* - Bypass bootup level test / Complete bootup level test / NA
P/*   - Per port test / NA
M/S/* - Only applicable to active / standby unit / NA
D/N/* - Disruptive test / Non-disruptive test / NA
H/*   - Always enabled monitoring test / NA
F/*   - Fixed monitoring interval test / NA
X/*   - Not a health monitoring test / NA
E/*   - Sup to line card test / NA
L/*   - Exclusively run this test / NA
T/*   - Not an ondemand test / NA
A/I/* - Monitoring is active / Monitoring is inactive / NA


                                           Testing Interval
ID     Name                     Attributes  (hh:mm:ss)
--------------------------------------------------------------------
  1)   EOBCPortLoopback-------------->   C**N**X**T*   -NA-
  2)   ASICRegisterCheck------------->   ***N******A   00:01:00
  3)   PrimaryBootROM--------------->    ***N******A   00:30:00
  4)   SecondaryBootROM------------->    ***N******A   00:30:00
```

```
   5)    PortLoopback------------------>    CP*N***E**A    00:15:00
   6)    RewriteEngineLoopback--------->    *P*N***E**A    00:01:00


Congo# show diagnostic content module 5

Module 5: Supervisor module-1X (Active)

Diagnostics test suite attributes:
B/C/* - Bypass bootup level test / Complete bootup level test / NA
P/*   - Per port test / NA
M/S/* - Only applicable to active / standby unit / NA
D/N/* - Disruptive test / Non-disruptive test / NA
H/*   - Always enabled monitoring test / NA
F/*   - Fixed monitoring interval test / NA
X/*   - Not a health monitoring test / NA
E/*   - Sup to line card test / NA
L/*   - Exclusively run this test / NA
T/*   - Not an ondemand test / NA
A/I/* - Monitoring is active / Monitoring is inactive / NA


                                              Testing Interval
   ID    Name                    Attributes   (hh:mm:ss)
   -------------------------------------------------------------------
    1)   ManagementPortLoopback-------->    C**D**X**T*    -NA-
    2)   EOBCPortLoopback------------->     C**D**X**T*    -NA-
    3)   ASICRegisterCheck------------>     ***N******A    00:00:20
    4)   USB------------------------->      C**N**X**T*    -NA-
    5)   CryptoDevice----------------->     C**N**X**T*    -NA-
    6)   NVRAM----------------------->      ***N******A    00:00:30
    7)   RealTimeClock--------------->      ***N******A    00:05:00
    8)   PrimaryBootROM-------------->      ***N******A    00:30:00
    9)   SecondaryBootROM------------>      ***N******A    00:30:00
   10)   CompactFlash---------------->      ***N******A    00:30:00
   11)   ExternalCompactFlash-------->      ***N******A    00:30:00
   12)   PwrMgmtBus------------------>      **MN******A    00:00:30
   13)   SpineControlBus------------->      **MN******A    00:00:30
   14)   SystemMgmtBus--------------->      **MN******A    00:00:30
   15)   StatusBus------------------->      **MN******A    00:00:30
   16)   StandbyFabricLoopback------->      **SN******A    00:00:30
```

In certain configurations, these tests might not be applicable and can be disabled. If performance issues are experienced and a hardware failure is suspected, it might be preferable to change the runtime interval. Example 6-10 shows how to disable or change the runtime interval of these tests.

Example 6-10 *Manipulating Runtime Diagnostic Parameters*

```
Congo(config)# no diagnostic monitor module 5 test 9
Congo(config)# diagnostic monitor interval module 5 test 3 hour 00 min 00 second 45
Congo(config)# show diagnostic content module 5

Module 5: Supervisor module-1X (Active)

Diagnostics test suite attributes:
B/C/* - Bypass bootup level test / Complete bootup level test / NA
P/*   - Per port test / NA
M/S/* - Only applicable to active / standby unit / NA
D/N/* - Disruptive test / Non-disruptive test / NA
H/*   - Always enabled monitoring test / NA
F/*   - Fixed monitoring interval test / NA
X/*   - Not a health monitoring test / NA
E/*   - Sup to line card test / NA
L/*   - Exclusively run this test / NA
T/*   - Not an ondemand test / NA
A/I/* - Monitoring is active / Monitoring is inactive / NA


                                              Testing Interval
    ID    Name                       Attributes   (hh:mm:ss)
    1)    ManagementPortLoopback------->    C**D**X**T*    -NA-
    2)    EOBCPortLoopback------------->    C**D**X**T*    -NA-
    3)    ASICRegisterCheck------------>    ***N******A    00:00:45
    4)    USB------------------------->    C**N**X**T*    -NA-
    5)    CryptoDevice----------------->    C**N**X**T*    -NA-
    6)    NVRAM------------------------>    ***N******A    00:00:30
    7)    RealTimeClock---------------->    ***N******A    00:05:00
    8)    PrimaryBootROM--------------->    ***N******A    00:30:00
    9)    SecondaryBootROM------------->    ***N******I    00:30:00
   10)    CompactFlash----------------->    ***N******A    00:30:00
   11)    ExternalCompactFlash--------->    ***N******A    00:30:00
   12)    PwrMgmtBus------------------->    **MN******A    00:00:30
   13)    SpineControlBus-------------->    **MN******A    00:00:30
   14)    SystemMgmtBus---------------->    **MN******A    00:00:30
   15)    StatusBus-------------------->    **MN******A    00:00:30
   16)    StandbyFabricLoopback-------->    **SN******A    00:00:30


Congo(config)#
```

On-Demand Diagnostics

Problems that are intermittent are sometimes attributed to failing hardware. As a troubleshooting step, you should test a particular component to verify that the hardware is operating properly and thus eliminate hardware as a potential cause. In NX-OS, you can do this by using *on-demand tests*.

Example 6-11 shows how to manually initiate a diagnostic test and view the results.

Example 6-11   *On-Demand Diagnostics*

```
Congo# diagnostic start module 5 test non-disruptive
Congo# show diagnostic result module 5

Current bootup diagnostic level: complete
Module 5: Supervisor module-1X  (Active)

        Test results: (. = Pass, F = Fail, I = Incomplete,
        U = Untested, A = Abort, E = Error disabled)

        1)  ManagementPortLoopback-------->  .
        2)  EOBCPortLoopback-------------->  .
        3)  ASICRegisterCheck------------->  .
        4)  USB-------------------------->  .
        5)  CryptoDevice----------------->  .
        6)  NVRAM------------------------>  .
        7)  RealTimeClock---------------->  .
        8)  PrimaryBootROM--------------->  .
        9)  SecondaryBootROM------------->  .
       10)  CompactFlash----------------->  .
       11)  ExternalCompactFlash--------->  .
       12)  PwrMgmtBus------------------->  .
       13)  SpineControlBus-------------->  .
       14)  SystemMgmtBus---------------->  .
       15)  StatusBus-------------------->  .
       16)  StandbyFabricLoopback--------> U

Congo#
```

In the output of Example 6-11, all tests that were run against the module in question passed diagnostics as denoted with a period. Should a particular test fail, further investigation might be required. The Cisco Technical Assistance Center (TAC) can use this information to replace modules that are covered under support agreements.

NX-OS High-Availability Architecture

The high-availability features of NX-OS are managed by several system-level processes:

- **System Manager:** At the highest level, the System Manager is responsible for the overall state of the system. The System Manager monitors the health of the system and the various services that are running based on the configured high availability policies. The System Manager manages the starting, stopping, monitoring, and restarting of services. Along with these high-level tasks, the System Manager also ensures that state is synchronized between Supervisors and coordinates the switchover of Supervisors if necessary. To verify the health of the System Manager process, there is a hardware watchdog timer located on the Supervisor. Periodically, the System Manager resets the watchdog timer with a keepalive indicator. If the hardware watchdog timer expires, with no keepalives from the System Manager, a Supervisor switchover occurs.

- **Persistent Storage Service (PSS):** Where state information for the various services are stored. PSS provides a database of state and runtime information. Services within NX-OS dump information to the PSS at various intervals and after restart glean this information from the PSS to restore the service to prefailure state.

- **Message and transaction services (MTS):** An interprocess communication (IPC) broker that handles message routing and queuing between services and hardware within the system. The function of the MTS ensures that processes can be restarted independently and that messages from the other processes are received after a restart has occurred.

These software features combine to create operational benefits, which as discussed throughout the remainder of this chapter.

Process Modularity

To achieve the highest levels of redundancy, NX-OS represents a complete modular software architecture. Each modular component within NX-OS must be enabled by the network administrator prior to the feature being configured, or even loaded into memory. Most services within NX-OS are represented as loadable modules or features that must be enabled. If one of these processes experiences errors, the service can be restarted independent of other features or services. This level of modularity exists primarily where HA cannot be achieved by mechanisms within the protocol itself—for example, Graceful Restart for Border Gateway Protocol (BGP). Processes can be enabled using the **feature** command or disabled using the **no feature** command.

Example 6-12 shows the modular processes that can be enabled.

Example 6-12 *Modular Features*

```
Congo(config)# feature ?
  bgp             Enable/Disable Border Gateway Protocol (BGP)
  cts             Enable/Disable CTS
  dhcp            Enable/Disable DHCP Snooping
  dot1x           Enable/Disable dot1x
  eigrp           Enable/Disable Enhanced Interior Gateway Routing Protocol (EIGRP)
  eou             Enable/Disable eou(l2nac)
  glbp            Enable/Disable Gateway Load Balancing Protocol (GLBP)
  hsrp            Enable/Disable Hot Standby Router Protocol (HSRP)
  interface-vlan  Enable/Disable interface vlan
  isis            Enable/Disable IS-IS Unicast Routing Protocol (IS-IS)
  lacp            Enable/Disable LACP
  msdp            Enable/Disable Multicast Source Discovery Protocol (MSDP)
  netflow         Enable/Disable NetFlow
  ospf            Enable/Disable Open Shortest Path First Protocol (OSPF)
  ospfv3          Enable/Disable Open Shortest Path First Version 3 Protocol (OSPFv3)
  pbr             Enable/Disable Policy Based Routing(PBR)
  pim             Enable/Disable Protocol Independent Multicast (PIM)
  pim6            Enable/Disable Protocol Independent Multicast (PIM) for IPv6
  port-security   Enable/Disable port-security
  private-vlan    Enable/Disable private-vlan
  rip             Enable/Disable Routing Information Protocol (RIP)
  scheduler       Enable/Disable scheduler
  ssh             Enable/Disable ssh
  tacacs+         Enable/Disable tacacs+
  telnet          Enable/Disable telnet
  tunnel          Enable/Disable Tunnel Manager
  udld            Enable/Disable UDLD
  vpc             Enable/Disable VPC (Virtual Port Channel)
  vrrp            Enable/Disable Virtual Router Redundancy Protocol (VRRP)
  vtp             Enable/Disable VTP
  wccp            Enable/Disable Web Cache Communication Protocol (WCCP)
```

In addition to selectively enabling or disabling particular features, software modularity provides a mechanism in which software can be patched to address security vulnerabilities or apply hot fixes without requiring a complete upgrade of the system.

Process Restart

Services within NX-OS can be restarted if they experience errors or failures. These restarts can be initiated by a network operator or by the System Manager upon detecting an error condition. Each NX-OS service has an associated set of high availability (HA) policies.

HA policies define how the system reacts to a failed service. Following are actions performed by the System Manager:

- **Stateful process restart:** While in a running state, restartable processes checkpoint their runtime state information to the PSS. If a service fails to respond to heartbeats from the System Manager, that process is restarted. When the process has been restarted, all the state information is gleaned from the PSS.

- **Stateless process restart:** The service is restarted, and all runtime information is rebuilt from the configuration or by reestablishing adjacencies.

- **Supervisor switchover:** In a dual Supervisor configuration, the active Supervisor is rebooted and the standby immediately takes over as the active Supervisor.

Following are a few variables associated with the progression of possible System Manager actions:

- **Maximum retries:** Specifies the number of times the System Manager attempts to perform a specific action before declaring the attempt failed. For example, the system might try to perform a stateful restart three times before attempting a stateless restart three times, and finally initiating a Supervisor switchover.

- **Minimum lifetime:** Specifies the time that a service must run after a restart before declaring the restart a success. This value is configurable but must be greater than 4 minutes.

Stateful Switchover

The combination of the NX-OS Software architecture and redundant Supervisors provides the capability to seamlessly switchover to the redundant Supervisor. This switchover can occur for a number of reasons, the most common of which are user-initiated, System Manager-initiated, or as part of an ISSU.

Example 6-13 shows how to verify the Supervisor status of the system and initiate a manual switchover from the active to the standby Supervisor.

Example 6-13 *Supervisor Redundancy*

```
Congo# show redundancy status
Redundancy mode
- - - - - - - - - - - - - -
```

```
        administrative:   HA
          operational:   HA

This supervisor (sup-6)
-----------------------
    Redundancy state:   Active
    Supervisor state:   Active
      Internal state:   Active with HA standby


Other supervisor (sup-5)
-----------------------
    Redundancy state:   Standby

    Supervisor state:   HA standby
      Internal state:   HA standby


System start time:        Mon Nov  2 08:11:50 2009


System uptime:            0 days, 0 hours, 42 minutes, 11 seconds
Kernel uptime:            0 days, 0 hours, 25 minutes, 1 seconds
Active supervisor uptime: 0 days, 0 hours, 20 minutes, 0 seconds
Congo#
Congo# system switchover
Congo#


Congo# sho system redundancy status
Redundancy mode
---------------
        administrative:   HA
          operational:   HA


This supervisor (sup-1)
-----------------------
    Redundancy state:   Active
    Supervisor state:   Active
      Internal state:   Active with HA standby


Other supervisor (sup-2)
-----------------------
    Redundancy state:   Standby
    Supervisor state:   HA standby
      Internal state:   HA standby
Congo#
```

Nonstop Forwarding

Most modern protocols understand that while a control plane switchover might be occurring on an adjacent node, the data plane can still forward traffic. The most common implementations of this functionality are with OSPF, EIGRP, and BGP. These mechanisms are sometimes referred to as a graceful restart. This should not be confused with stateless restart; stateful restart requires no interaction with peers, whereas a graceful restart involves notification of peers.

If a stateful restart of the routing process fails, or is not possible, nonstop forwarding (NSF) specifies a mechanism to notify neighbors that the control plane is undergoing a restart, but the data plane can still forward traffic. All routing updates from this neighbor are held in their current state until the adjacency is restored or a hold timer expires. When the adjacency is reestablished, updates to the routing topology are then updated in the hardware forwarding tables. For NSF to work properly, the adjacent network devices must process the notification, in which case they are said to be *NSF-Aware*. Most modern networking devices, including IOS and NX-OS, are NSF-Aware.

In-Service Software Upgrades

With the combination of the distributing forwarding nature of the Nexus platform and the high-availability features described within this chapter, one of the most immediate and practical benefits of the approach is the ability to upgrade software without requiring a reload of the system or disruption to traffic flows through the system. This capability is referred to as In-Service Software Upgrades (ISSU). ISSU is supported across all NX-OS versions and enables customers to quickly take advantage of new features, protect their infrastructure against security vulnerabilities, and provide a more proactive software upgrade cycle, all while not having to wait for extended maintenance windows or costly downtime. Prior to initiating a software upgrade, an administrator should verify that the features and functionality configured on the system are compatible with the new image and determine whether the upgrade process will have any impact on traffic flows.

Example 6-14 shows how to check for image compatibility based on the running-configuration and any impact associated with the upgrade.

Example 6-14   *Verify System Image Compatibility and Impact*

```
! The following image is an older version of NX-OS which doesn't support vPC and
therefore would be incompatible with the running configuration.
Congo# sho incompatibility system bootflash:///n7000-s1-dk9.4.1.2.bin
The following configurations on active are incompatible with the system image
1) Service : vpc , Capability : CAP_FEATURE_VPC_ENABLED
Description : vPC feature is enabled
Capability requirement : STRICT
Disable command : Disable vPC using "no feature vpc"
```

```
2) Service : ascii-cfg , Capability : CAP_FEATURE_ASCII_CFG_SYSTEM_CHECKPOINT
Description : System checkpoints were created
Capability requirement : STRICT
Disable command : Remove all the system checkpoints


! The following shows an upgrade to a compatible software image

Congo# show incompatibility system bootflash:///n7000-s1-dk9.4.2.2a.bin
No incompatible configurations


! The impact of the software upgrade can also be assessed as shown below

Congo# show install all impact kickstart bootflash:///n7000-s1-kickstart.4.2.2a.bin
system bootflash:///n7000-s1-dk9.4.2.2a.bin

Verifying image bootflash:/n7000-s1-kickstart.4.2.2a.bin for boot variable
"kickstart".
[###################] 100% -- SUCCESS


Verifying image bootflash:/n7000-s1-dk9.4.2.2a.bin for boot variable "system".
[###################] 100% -- SUCCESS


Verifying image type.
[###################] 100% -- SUCCESS


Extracting "lc1n7k" version from image bootflash:/n7000-s1-dk9.4.2.2a.bin.
[###################] 100% -- SUCCESS


Extracting "bios" version from image bootflash:/n7000-s1-dk9.4.2.2a.bin.
[###################] 100% -- SUCCESS


Extracting "system" version from image bootflash:/n7000-s1-dk9.4.2.2a.bin.
[###################] 100% -- SUCCESS


Extracting "kickstart" version from image bootflash:/n7000-s1-kickstart.4.2.2a.bin.
[###################] 100% -- SUCCESS


Extracting "cmp" version from image bootflash:/n7000-s1-dk9.4.2.2a.bin.
[###################] 100% -- SUCCESS


Extracting "cmp-bios" version from image bootflash:/n7000-s1-dk9.4.2.2a.bin.
[###################] 100% -- SUCCESS
```

```
Compatibility check is done:
Module  bootable          Impact  Install-type  Reason

-----------------------------------------------------------------------
     1       yes  non-disruptive      rolling
     2       yes  non-disruptive      rolling
     5       yes  non-disruptive       reset
     6       yes  non-disruptive       reset




Images will be upgraded according to following table:
Module          Image                  Running-Version(pri:alt)          New-Version
Upg-Required
-----------------------------------------------------------------------
     1      lc1n7k                                     4.0(2)
4.2(2a)          yes
     1         bios   v1.10.6(11/04/08):  v1.10.6(11/04/08)
v1.10.6(11/04/08)         no
     2      lc1n7k                                     4.0(2)
4.2(2a)          yes
     2         bios   v1.10.6(11/04/08):  v1.10.6(11/04/08)
v1.10.6(11/04/08)         no
     5      system                                     4.0(2)
4.2(2a)          yes
     5    kickstart                                     4.0(2)
4.2(2a)          yes
     5         bios   v3.19.0(03/31/09):  v3.19.0(03/31/09)
v3.19.0(03/31/09)         no
     5          cmp                                     4.0(2)
4.2(1)          yes
     5    cmp-bios                                     02.01.05
02.01.05          no
     6      system                                     4.0(2)
4.2(2a)          yes
     6    kickstart                                     4.0(2)
4.2(2a)          yes
     6         bios   v3.19.0(03/31/09):  v3.19.0(03/31/09)
v3.19.0(03/31/09)         no
     6          cmp                                     4.0(2)
4.2(1)          yes
     6    cmp-bios                                     02.01.05
02.01.05          no


Congo#
```

When an upgrade is initiated, the system goes through the following process to achieve a nondisruptive upgrade:

Step 1.   BIOS software is upgraded on the active and standby Supervisors and all line cards.

Step 2.   The standby Supervisor is upgraded and rebooted.

Step 3.   When the standby Supervisor is online with the new version of NX-OS, a stateful switchover is initiated. At this point, the control plane is now operating on the new version.

Step 4.   The standby Supervisor (previously Active) is then upgraded to the new version.

Step 5.   Line cards are upgraded one at a time and reloaded. (This reload is only of the CPU, not any of the data plane components and is nondisruptive to traffic flows.)

Step 6.   The CMP on both Supervisors are upgraded.

Example 6-15 demonstrates the entire ISSU process.

Example 6-15   *ISSU Procedure*

```
! Verify the current image
Congo# sho ver
Cisco Nexus Operating System (NX-OS) Software
TAC support: http://www.cisco.com/tac
Copyright (c) 2002-2008, Cisco Systems, Inc. All rights reserved.
The copyrights to certain works contained in this software are
owned by other third parties and used and distributed under
license. Certain components of this software are licensed under
the GNU General Public License (GPL) version 2.0 or the GNU
Lesser General Public License (LGPL) Version 2.1. A copy of each
such license is available at
http://www.opensource.org/licenses/gpl-2.0.php and
http://www.opensource.org/licenses/lgpl-2.1.php


Software
  BIOS:      version 3.19.0
  loader:    version N/A
  kickstart: version 4.0(2)
  system:    version 4.0(2)
  BIOS compile time:       03/31/09
  kickstart image file is: bootflash:/n7000-s1-kickstart.4.0.2.bin
  kickstart compile time:  5/8/2008 13:00:00 [06/12/2008 10:59:41]
  system image file is:    bootflash:/n7000-s1-dk9.4.0.2.bin
  system compile time:     5/8/2008 13:00:00 [06/12/2008 11:37:08]
```

```
Hardware
  cisco Nexus7000 C7010 (10 Slot) Chassis ("Supervisor module-1X")
  Intel(R) Xeon(R) CPU        with 4129620 kB of memory.
  Processor Board ID JAB122100XH


  Device name: Congo
  bootflash:    2000880 kB
  slot0:               0 kB (expansion flash)


Kernel uptime is 0 day(s), 0 hour(s), 13 minute(s), 10 second(s)


Last reset at 628785 usecs after  Mon Nov  2 08:08:30 2009


  Reason: Reset due to upgrade
  System version: 4.2(2a)
  Service:


plugin
  Core Plugin, Ethernet Plugin


CMP (Module 5) ok
 Software
  System image version: 4.0(2) [build 4.0(2)]
  BIOS image version:   02.01.05
  System compile time:  5/8/2008 13:00:00
  BIOS compile time:    7/13/2008 19:44:27


CMP (Module 6) ok
 Software
  System image version: 4.0(2) [build 4.0(2)]
  BIOS image version:   02.01.05
  System compile time:  5/8/2008 13:00:00
  BIOS compile time:    7/13/2008 19:44:27


Congo#
! Initiate the install process
Congo# install all kickstart bootflash:///n7000-s1-kickstart.4.2.2a.bin system
bootflash:///n7000-s1-dk9.4.2.2a.bin


Verifying image bootflash:/n7000-s1-kickstart.4.2.2a.bin for boot variable
"kickstart".
[####################] 100% -- SUCCESS


Verifying image bootflash:/n7000-s1-dk9.4.2.2a.bin for boot variable "system".
[####################] 100% -- SUCCESS
```

```
Verifying image type.
[####################] 100% -- SUCCESS

Extracting "lc1n7k" version from image bootflash:/n7000-s1-dk9.4.2.2a.bin.
[####################] 100% -- SUCCESS

Extracting "bios" version from image bootflash:/n7000-s1-dk9.4.2.2a.bin.
[####################] 100% -- SUCCESS

Extracting "system" version from image bootflash:/n7000-s1-dk9.4.2.2a.bin.
[####################] 100% -- SUCCESS

Extracting "kickstart" version from image bootflash:/n7000-s1-kickstart.4.2.2a.bin.
[####################] 100% -- SUCCESS

Extracting "cmp" version from image bootflash:/n7000-s1-dk9.4.2.2a.bin.
[####################] 100% -- SUCCESS

Extracting "cmp-bios" version from image bootflash:/n7000-s1-dk9.4.2.2a.bin.
[####################] 100% -- SUCCESS




Compatibility check is done:
Module  bootable        Impact  Install-type  Reason
-------------------------------------------------------------------------------
     1         yes  non-disruptive       rolling
     2         yes  non-disruptive       rolling
     5         yes  non-disruptive         reset
     6         yes  non-disruptive         reset




Images will be upgraded according to following table:
Module      Image            Running-Version(pri:alt)       New-Version
Upg-Required
-------------------------------------------------------------------------------
     1      lc1n7k                                      4.0(2)
4.2(2a)          yes
     1      bios    v1.10.6(11/04/08):  v1.10.6(11/04/08)
v1.10.6(11/04/08)          no
     2      lc1n7k                                      4.0(2)
4.2(2a)          yes
     2      bios    v1.10.6(11/04/08):  v1.10.6(11/04/08)
v1.10.6(11/04/08)          no
```

```
    5       system                              4.0(2)
4.2(2a)         yes
    5     kickstart                             4.0(2)
4.2(2a)         yes
    5        bios     v3.19.0(03/31/09):  v3.19.0(03/31/09)
v3.19.0(03/31/09)          no
    5        cmp                                4.0(2)
4.2(1)          yes
    5     cmp-bios                              02.01.05
02.01.05          no
    6       system                              4.0(2)
4.2(2a)         yes
    6     kickstart                             4.0(2)
4.2(2a)         yes
    6        bios     v3.19.0(03/31/09):  v3.19.0(03/31/09)
v3.19.0(03/31/09)          no
    6        cmp                                4.0(2)
4.2(1)          yes
    6     cmp-bios                              02.01.05
02.01.05          no


Do you want to continue with the installation (y/n)?  [n] y
! In this example, no BIOS upgrades are required, therefore Step 1 is skipped
Install is in progress, please wait.
! Step 2: The standby supervisor is upgraded and rebooted
Syncing image bootflash:/n7000-s1-kickstart.4.2.2a.bin to standby.
[####################] 100% -- SUCCESS


Syncing image bootflash:/n7000-s1-dk9.4.2.2a.bin to standby.
[####################] 100% -- SUCCESS


Setting boot variables.
[####################] 100% -- SUCCESS


Performing configuration copy.
[####################] 100% -- SUCCESS
2009 Nov  2 08:28:19 Congo %PLATFORM-2-MOD_REMOVE: Module 6 removed (Serial number
JAB122400VH)
2009 Nov  2 08:31:36 Congo %IDEHSD-STANDBY-2-MOUNT: logflash: online
2009 Nov  2 08:31:47 Congo %CMPPROXY-STANDBY-2-LOG_CMP_UP: Connectivity Management
processor(on module 6) is now UP


Module 6: Waiting for module online.
 -- SUCCESS


Notifying services about the switchover.
[####################] 100% -- SUCCESS
```

```
! Step 3: The standby supervisor is online with the new version of NX-OS, and a
stateful switchover is initiated. "Switching over onto standby".
Connection closed by foreign host.



! At this point the telnet session to the box is lost, as a result of the
  supervisor switchover. The device is immediately available to service sessions
  from the newly active supervisor which is now running the updated software.


User Access Verification
login: admin
Password:
Cisco Nexus Operating System (NX-OS) Software
TAC support: http://www.cisco.com/tac
Copyright (c) 2002-2009, Cisco Systems, Inc. All rights reserved.
The copyrights to certain works contained in this software are
owned by other third parties and used and distributed under
license. Certain components of this software are licensed under
the GNU General Public License (GPL) version 2.0 or the GNU
Lesser General Public License (LGPL) Version 2.1. A copy of each
such license is available at
http://www.opensource.org/licenses/gpl-2.0.php and
http://www.opensource.org/licenses/lgpl-2.1.php
Congo# sho ver
Cisco Nexus Operating System (NX-OS) Software
TAC support: http://www.cisco.com/tac
Copyright (c) 2002-2009, Cisco Systems, Inc. All rights reserved.
The copyrights to certain works contained in this software are
owned by other third parties and used and distributed under
license. Certain components of this software are licensed under
the GNU General Public License (GPL) version 2.0 or the GNU
Lesser General Public License (LGPL) Version 2.1. A copy of each
such license is available at
http://www.opensource.org/licenses/gpl-2.0.php and
http://www.opensource.org/licenses/lgpl-2.1.php

Software
  BIOS:      version 3.19.0
  loader:    version N/A
  kickstart: version 4.2(2a)
  system:    version 4.2(2a)
```

```
   BIOS compile time:       03/31/09
   kickstart image file is: bootflash:/n7000-s1-kickstart.4.2.2a.bin
   kickstart compile time:  9/25/2009 9:00:00 [09/27/2009 12:06:24]
   system image file is:    bootflash:/n7000-s1-dk9.4.2.2a.bin
   system compile time:     9/25/2009 9:00:00 [09/27/2009 12:35:38]


Hardware
  cisco Nexus7000 C7010 (10 Slot) Chassis ("Supervisor module-1X")
  Intel(R) Xeon(R) CPU         with 4129600 kB of memory.
  Processor Board ID JAB122400VH

  Device name: Congo
  bootflash:    2000880 kB
  slot0:             0 kB (expansion flash)

Kernel uptime is 0 day(s), 0 hour(s), 7 minute(s), 0 second(s)

Last reset
  Reason: Unknown
  System version: 4.0(2)
  Service:

plugin
  Core Plugin, Ethernet Plugin

CMP (Module 6) ok
 CMP Software
  CMP BIOS version:       02.01.05
  CMP Image version:      4.0(2) [build 4.0(2)]
  CMP BIOS compile time:  7/13/2008 19:44:27
  CMP Image compile time: 5/8/2008 13:00:00

Congo#
! The interactive installer session can be resumed
Congo# sho install all status
There is an on-going installation...
Enter Ctrl-C to go back to the prompt.


Continuing with installation, please wait
Trying to start the installer...
! Step 4: The standby supervisor (previously active) is now being upgraded and
rebooted
```

```
Module 6: Waiting for module online.
 -- SUCCESS
2009 Nov  2 08:37:14 Congo %IDEHSD-STANDBY-2-MOUNT: logflash: online
2009 Nov  2 08:37:25 Congo %CMPPROXY-STANDBY-2-LOG_CMP_UP: Connectivity Management
processor(on module 5) is now UP
! Step 5: Line cards are upgraded, one at a timeModule 1: Non-disruptive upgrading.
 -- SUCCESS


Module 2: Non-disruptive upgrading.
 -- SUCCESS

! Step 6: Upgrade the CMP on both supervisors



Module 6: Upgrading CMP image.
Warning: please do not reload or power cycle CMP module at this time.
 -- SUCCESS

Module 5: Upgrading CMP image.
Warning: please do not reload or power cycle CMP module at this time.
 -- SUCCESS

Recommended action:
"Please reload CMP(s) manually to have it run in the newer version."

Install has been successful.
Congo#
```

In addition to the NX-OS operating system, the Nexus 7000 switches include electronic programmable logical devices (EPLD) that enable for additional hardware functionality or fixes without having to upgrade or replace the module. If new features or fixes are released that can be implemented in hardware though the use of EPLDs, this process must be done outside of the ISSU and might be disruptive to flowing traffic. The EPLD process is done on one module at a time, and therefore configurations that have module redundancy for port-channels or Layer 3 peering on multiple modules can make this process less disruptive. NX-OS release notes should be reviewed to determine if an EPLD upgrade is required.

Summary

NX-OS was built for the high-availability requirements in the data center. High availability is achieved through the combination of resilient hardware and software architectures within the Nexus 7000. The Nexus 7000 hardware platform represents the highest levels of system redundancy within the control plane, fabric forwarding, power, and cooling systems. Building upon this foundation, NX-OS represents a modular software architecture with features such as stateful process restart, Nonstop Forwarding, and In-Service software upgrades. This combination of hardware and software can provide administrators peace of mind in knowing that they have a system built to achieve the highest levels of availability for mission-critical data center environments.

Chapter 7

Embedded Serviceability Features

The Nexus line of switches provides a robust embedded serviceability feature set. This chapter covers:

- **SPAN:** Describes the configuration and operations of SPAN on Nexus 7000, 5000, and 1000V series switches

- **ERSPAN:** Describes the configuration and operations of ERSPAN on Nexus 1000V series switches

- **Embedded Analyzer:** Describes the configuration and operations of Embedded Analyzer on Nexus 7000

- **Smart Call Home:** Describes the configuration and operations of Smart Call Home on Nexus 7000 series switches

- **Configuration Checkpoint and Rollback:** Describes the configuration and operations of Configuration Checkpoint and Rollback on Nexus 7000 series switches

- **Netflow:** Describes the configuration and operations of Netflow on Nexus 7000 and 1000V series switches

SPAN

Cisco NX-OS was designed from the beginning to be a data center class operating system. A component of such an operating system includes support for a rich set of embedded serviceability features. These features should enable the network administrator and operator to have unprecedented access to tools to support and troubleshoot the network. This chapter covers many of the key features such as Switched Port Analyzer (SPAN), Encapsulated Remote Switch Port Analyzer (ERSPAN), Smart Call Home, Configuration Rollback, and NetFlow.

The SPAN feature is one of the most frequently used troubleshooting components in a network. It is not uncommon for the network team to be approached to provide packet level analysis of the traffic on the network as part of routine analysis, security compliance, or break/fix troubleshooting. SPAN creates a copy or mirror of the source traffic and delivers it to the destination. SPANning traffic does not have an impact on the delivery of the original traffic providing a nonintrusive method to perform high-speed traffic analysis. NX-OS provides the ability to configure SPAN across all three currently available platforms: Nexus 7000, Nexus 5000, and Nexus 1000V series switches. Additionally, the Nexus 1000V supports ERSPAN to provide additional flexibility for network administrators. The following sections cover the various aspects of SPAN for all three platforms.

SPAN on Nexus 7000

The Nexus 7000 series switches have the capability to configure traditional SPAN sessions in addition to Virtual SPAN. SPAN enables the network administrator flexible configuration options using the concepts of source ports and destination ports. Source ports, as their name implies, are the source of the traffic to be sent via SPAN to the destination ports. Source ports have the following requirements:

■ Can be a physical Ethernet Port.

■ Can be a VLAN; when a VLAN is used as a SPAN source, all ports that belong to the VLAN are considered as part of the SPAN source.

■ Can be a Remote SPAN (RSPAN) VLAN.

■ Can be configured with a direction (ingress, egress, or both) to monitor.

■ Can be the inband interface to the switch's supervisor engine control plane.

Note   Note that if you are using Virtual Device Contexts (VDC), only the default VDC can SPAN the inband interface, and all control plane traffic from each VDC will be monitored from the default VDC.

■ A source port cannot be a SPAN destination port.

SPAN destinations, as their name implies, define where traffic copied from the SPAN source will be sent. Destination ports have the following requirements:

■ Can include Ethernet or port channel interfaces in either access or trunk mode.

■ Can be configured in only one SPAN session at a time.

■ Do not participate in a spanning-tree instance; however, SPAN output includes STP hello packets.

■ Can be configured to support Intrusion Detection Systems/Intrusion Prevention Systems (IDS/IPS) applications where the need to have the forwarding engine learn the MAC address of the IDS/IPS is required.

■ Can be configured to inject packets enabling IDS/IPS to disrupt traffic.

Additionally, SPAN destinations have the following restrictions:

- SPAN destinations cannot be SPAN sources.

- SPAN destinations cannot be an RSPAN VLAN.

SPAN on the Nexus 7000 supports the capability to configure up to 18 SPAN sessions with any two active simultaneously. The Nexus 7000 provides support for a feature called Virtual SPAN. Virtual SPAN enables the network administrator to SPAN multiple VLAN sources and selectively determine where the SPAN traffic is sent on multiple destination VLAN ports. This provides the ability to monitor a trunk, for example, and have the output from different VLANs sent to specific destinations or network analyzers without the need for multiple SPAN sessions. Table 7-1 lists the SPAN session limits on the Nexus 7000.

Table 7-1   *Nexus 7000 SPAN Session Limits*

Session Characteristic	Limit
Configured SPAN sessions	18
Simultaneously running SPAN sessions	2
Source interfaces per session	128
Source VLANs per session	32
Destination interfaces per session	32

Configuring SPAN on Nexus 7000

Configuration of SPAN on Nexus 7000 is a multistep process in which the SPAN source, destination, and monitoring ports are defined. The first step is to define the monitor port connection where the network analysis, IDS/IPS, or other device collects the SPAN traffic, as demonstrated in Example 7-1. Figure 7-1 illustrates the topology used in this example.

Figure 7-1   *Network Topology for Configuring a SPAN Session*

Note   Note that the monitor port must be in *switchport* mode: either in access or trunk mode. SPAN monitor ports cannot be routed ports.

Example 7-1   *Configuring a SPAN Monitor Port*

```
Jealousy# confi t
Enter configuration commands, one per line.  End with CNTL/Z.
Jealousy(config)# int e1/26
Jealousy(config-if)# switchport
Jealousy(config-if)# switchport monitor
Jealousy(config-if)# end
Jealousy#
```

If the device is an IDS/IPS, it might be required to have it participate in the network where the switch must learn the MAC address of the device and where the IDS/IPS might need to inject traffic, as demonstrated in Example 7-2. Typically, IPS actively participate in the network to inject traffic to thwart an attack. In these cases, the ingress and the learning configuration parameters will be desired.

Example 7-2   *Configuring a SPAN Monitor Port for IDS/IPS*

```
Jealousy# confi t
Enter configuration commands, one per line.  End with CNTL/Z.
Jealousy(config)# int e1/26
Jealousy(config-if)# switchport
Jealousy(config-if)# switchport monitor ingress learning
Jealousy(config-if)# end
Jealousy#
```

After the monitor port is configured, the next step is to configure the SPAN monitor session. Source and destination interfaces are configured under the SPAN monitor session in addition to VLAN filters. Finally the state of the SPAN session, shut or no shut, is configured in SPAN monitor session mode as well. In Example 7-3, a monitor session is configured that will SPAN traffic from VLANs 100, 101, and 102 to destination port e1/26. This SPAN monitors traffic that ingresses (rx) VLAN 100, traffic that egresses (tx) VLAN 101, and both on VLAN 102.

Note   The default direction for SPAN monitoring is both. Use of tx or rx direction narrows the traffic monitored.

Example 7-3   *Configuring a SPAN Monitor Session*

```
Jealousy# confi t

Enter configuration commands, one per line.  End with CNTL/Z.
Jealousy(config)# monitor session 1
Jealousy(config-monitor)# source vlan 100 rx
Jealousy(config-monitor)# source vlan 101 tx
```

```
Jealousy(config-monitor)# source vlan 102
Jealousy(config-monitor)# description SPAN Session 1
Jealousy(config-monitor)# destination interface e1/26
Jealousy(config-monitor)# no shut
Jealousy(config-monitor)# end
```

Tip Don't forget to **no shut** the monitor session!

The monitor session's status can be reviewed through the use of the **show monitor** command, as demonstrated in Example 7-4. This information is helpful when verifying the SPAN session's configuration and status.

Example 7-4 *Displaying a Monitor Session's Configuration*

```
Jealousy# show monitor session 1
   session 1
---------------
description       : SPAN Session 1
type              : local
state             : down (No operational src/dst)
source intf       :
   rx             :
   tx             :
   both           :
source VLANs      :
   rx             : 100,102
   tx             : 101-102
   both           : 102
filter VLANs      : filter not specified
destination ports : Eth1/26

Legend: f = forwarding enabled, l = learning enabled
```

When the **ingress** and **learning** keywords are present on the monitor port configuration—for example, to support an IDS/IPS—the destination port's status reflects, this as demonstrated in Example 7-5.

Example 7-5 *Displaying a Monitor Session Configuration with Ingress and Learning*

```
Jealousy# conf t
Enter configuration commands, one per line.  End with CNTL/Z.
Jealousy(config)# int e1/26
Jealousy(config-if)# switchport monitor ingress learning
```

```
Jealousy(config-if)# end
Jealousy# show monitor session 1
   session 1
---------------
description      : SPAN Session 1
type             : local
state            : down (No operational src/dst)
source intf      :
   rx            :
   tx            :
   both          :
source VLANs     :
   rx            : 100,102
   tx            : 101-102
   both          : 102
filter VLANs     : filter not specified
destination ports : Eth1/26 (f+l)


Legend: f = forwarding enabled, l = learning enabled
```

Configuration of a virtual SPAN session is the same as a normal SPAN session with the difference residing in the configuration of the destination ports. A virtual SPAN session enables the network administrator to use a single SPAN session on an 802.1Q trunk and direct traffic from specific VLANs to the appropriate network analyzers, as demonstrated in Example 7-6 for the network in Figure 7-2.

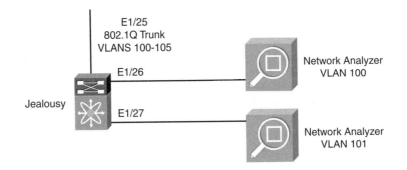

Figure 7-2   *Network Topology for Configuring a Virtual SPAN Session*

Example 7-6   *Configuring a Virtual SPAN Session*

```
Jealousy# confi t
Enter configuration commands, one per line.  End with CNTL/Z.
```

```
Jealousy(config)# int e1/25
Jealousy(config-if)# switchport
Jealousy(config-if)# switch mode trunk
Jealousy(config-if)# switchport trunk allowed vlan 100-105
Jealousy(config-if)# no shut
Jealousy(config-if)# int e1/26
Jealousy(config-if)# desc Connection to Network Analyzer for VLAN 100
Jealousy(config-if)# switchport
Jealousy(config-if)# switchport monitor
Jealousy(config-if)# switchport mode trunk
Jealousy(config-if)# switchport trunk allowed vlan 100
Jealousy(config-if)# int e1/27
Jealousy(config-if)# desc Connection to Network Analyzer for VLAN 101
Jealousy(config-if)# switchport
Jealousy(config-if)# switchport monitor
Jealousy(config-if)# switchport mode trunk
Jealousy(config-if)# switchport trunk allowed vlan 101
Jealousy(config-if)# monitor session 2
Jealousy(config-monitor)# desc Virtual SPAN Session
Jealousy(config-monitor)# source int e1/25
Jealousy(config-monitor)# destination in e1/26,e1/27
Jealousy(config-monitor)# no shut
Jealousy(config-monitor)# end
```

Note   It is necessary for a virtual SPAN session destination port to be a trunk. VLAN member ports can be used for traditional SPAN destinations.

The virtual SPAN session is verified using the same syntax as a normal SPAN session, as demonstrated in Example 7-7.

Example 7-7   *Displaying a Virtual SPAN Session*

```
Jealousy# show monitor session 2
   session 2
---------------
description      : Virtual SPAN Session
type            : local
state           : down (No operational src/dst)
source intf     :
   rx           : Eth1/25
   tx           : Eth1/25
   both         : Eth1/25
```

```
source VLANs      :
    rx            :
    tx            :
    both          :
filter VLANs      : filter not specified
destination ports : Eth1/26       Eth1/27


Legend: f = forwarding enabled, l = learning enabled
```

SPAN on Nexus 5000

The Nexus 5000 series switches have the capability to configure traditional SPAN sessions for Ethernet traffic in addition to Fibre Channel and Fibre Channel over Ethernet (FCoE) traffic. SPAN enables the network administrator to configure SPAN using the concepts of source ports and destination ports. Source ports, as their name implies, are the source of the traffic to be sent via SPAN to the destination ports. Source ports have the following requirements:

■   Can be any port type including Ethernet, Fibre Channel, port channel, SAN port channel, VLAN, and virtual storage area network (VSAN).

■   Can be a VLAN or VSAN. When a VLAN or VSAN is used as the SPAN source, all ports that belong to the VLAN or VSAN are considered as part of the SPAN source.

■   Can be configured with a direction (ingress, egress, or both) to monitor on Ethernet and Fibre Channel ports. In the case of VLAN, VSAN, Ethernet port channel, and SAN port channel sources, the monitored direction can only be ingress.

■   Cannot be a SPAN destination port.

SPAN destinations, as their name implies, define where traffic copied from the SPAN source will be sent. Destination ports have the following requirements:

■   Can include any physical port including Ethernet or Fibre Channel

Note   Logical interfaces such as virtual Fibre Channel, Ethernet port channel, and SAN port channel interfaces cannot be SPAN destinations.

■   Can be configured in only one SPAN session at a time

■   Do not participate in a spanning-tree instance

■   Can be configured to support IDS/IPS applications where the need to have the forwarding engine learn the MAC address of the IDS/IPS is required

■   Can be configured to inject packets enabling IDS/IPS to disrupt traffic

Additionally, SPAN destinations have the following restrictions:

- Cannot be SPAN sources

- Cannot be Virtual Fibre Channel, Ethernet port channel, and SAN port channel interfaces

SPAN on the Nexus 5000 supports the capability to configure up to 18 SPAN sessions with any two active simultaneously. Table 7-2 lists the SPAN session limits for the Nexus 5000.

Table 7-2 *Nexus 5000 SPAN Session Limits*

Session Characteristic	Limit
Configured SPAN sessions	18
Simultaneously running SPAN sessions	2
Source interfaces per session	128
Source VLANs per session	32
Destination interfaces per session	32

Configuring SPAN on Nexus 5000

Configuring SPAN on a Nexus 5000 is a multistep process in which the SPAN source, SPAN destination, and monitoring ports are defined. The first step is to define the monitor port connection where the network analysis, IDS/IPS, or other device collects the SPAN traffic, as demonstrated in Example 7-8. Figure 7-3 illustrates the topology used in Examples 7-8 through 7-14.

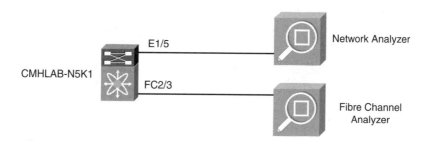

Figure 7-3 *Nexus 5000 SPAN Topology*

Example 7-8 *Configuring a SPAN Monitor Port*

```
CMHLAB-N5K1# confi t
Enter configuration commands, one per line.  End with CNTL/Z.
CMHLAB-N5K1(config)# int e1/5
```

```
CMHLAB-N5K1(config-if)# desc Connection to Network Analyzer
CMHLAB-N5K1(config-if)# switchport
CMHLAB-N5K1(config-if)# switchport monitor
CMHLAB-N5K1(config-if)# no shut
CMHLAB-N5K1(config-if)# end
CMHLAB-N5K1#
```

If the device is an IDS/IPS, it might be required to have it participate in the network where the switch must learn the MAC address of the device and where the IDS/IPS might need to inject traffic, as demonstrated in the configuration in Example 7-9. Typically, IPS actively participate in the network to inject traffic to thwart an attack. In these cases, the ingress and the learning configuration parameters will be wanted.

Example 7-9   *Configuring a SPAN Monitor Port for IDS/IPS*

```
CMHLAB-N5K1# confi t
Enter configuration commands, one per line.  End with CNTL/Z.
CMHLAB-N5K1(config)# int e1/5
CMHLAB-N5K1(config-if)# desc Connection to Network Analyzer
CMHLAB-N5K1(config-if)# switchport
CMHLAB-N5K1(config-if)# switchport monitor ingress learning
CMHLAB-N5K1(config-if)# end
CMHLAB-N5K1#
```

After the monitor port is configured, the next step is to configure the SPAN monitor session. Source and destination interfaces are configured under the SPAN monitor session. Finally, the state of the SPAN session, shut or no shut, is configured in SPAN monitor session mode as well. In Example 7-10, a monitor session is configured that will SPAN traffic from interface e1/28, e1/29, and e1/30 to destination port e1/5. This SPAN monitors traffic that ingresses (rx) e1/28, traffic that egresses (tx) e1/29, and both on e1/30.

Note   The default direction for SPAN monitoring is both. Use of tx or rx direction narrows the traffic monitored.

Example 7-10   *Configuring a SPAN Monitor Session*

```
CMHLAB-N5K1# confi t
Enter configuration commands, one per line.  End with CNTL/Z.
CMHLAB-N5K1(config)# monitor session 1
CMHLAB-N5K1(config-monitor)# source int e1/28 rx
CMHLAB-N5K1(config-monitor)# source int e1/29 tx
```

```
CMHLAB-N5K1(config-monitor)# source int e1/30
CMHLAB-N5K1(config-monitor)# desc SPAN Session 1
CMHLAB-N5K1(config-monitor)# destination interface e1/5
CMHLAB-N5K1(config-monitor)# no shut
CMHLAB-N5K1(config-monitor)# end
CMHLAB-N5K1#
```

Note Don't forget to **no shut** the monitor session!

You can review the monitor session's status through the use of the **show monitor** command, as demonstrated in Example 7-11. This information is helpful when verifying the SPAN session's configuration and status.

Example 7-11 *Displaying a Monitor Session's Configuration*

```
CMHLAB-N5K1# show monitor session 1
   session 1
---------------
description       : SPAN Session 1
type              : local
state             : down (No operational src/dst)
source intf       :
    rx            : Eth1/28        Eth1/30
    tx            : Eth1/29        Eth1/30
    both          : Eth1/30
source VLANs      :
    rx            :
destination ports : Eth1/5


Legend: f = forwarding enabled, l = learning enabled
source VSANs      :
    rx            :       rx           :


Legend: f = forwarding enabled, l = learning enabled
```

When the **ingress** and **learning** keywords are present on the monitor port configuration (for example, to support an IDS/IPS), the destination port's status reflects this, as shown in Example 7-12.

Example 7-12 *Displaying a Monitor Session Configuration with Ingress and Learning*

```
CMHLAB-N5K1(config)# int e1/5
CMHLAB-N5K1(config-if)# switchport
```

```
CMHLAB-N5K1(config-if)# switchport monitor ingress learning
CMHLAB-N5K1# show monitor session 1
  session 1
- - - - - - - - - - - - - -
description       : SPAN Session 1
type              : local
state             : down (No operational src/dst)
source intf       :
   rx             : Eth1/28      Eth1/30
   tx             : Eth1/29      Eth1/30
   both           : Eth1/30
source VLANs      :
   rx             :
destination ports : Eth1/5   (f+l)

Legend: f = forwarding enabled, l = learning enabled
source VSANs      :
   rx             :      rx            :
```

Configuration of Fibre Channel SPAN is similar to a typical Ethernet SPAN configuration. If the destination port is a Fibre Channel interface, it must be configured as a SPAN Destination (SD) port under the interface configuration, as demonstrated in Example 7-13.

Example 7-13 *Configuring a SPAN Session with a Fibre Channel Destination Port*

```
CMHLAB-N5K1# config t
Enter configuration commands, one per line.  End with CNTL/Z.
CMHLAB-N5K1(config)# int fc2/3
CMHLAB-N5K1(config-if)# switchport speed 2000
CMHLAB-N5K1(config-if)# switchport mode sd
CMHLAB-N5K1(config-if)# no shut
CMHLAB-N5K1(config)# monitor session 2
CMHLAB-N5K1(config-monitor)# desc SPAN Session for Fibre Channel
CMHLAB-N5K1(config-monitor)# source interface vfc10
CMHLAB-N5K1(config-monitor)# destination int fc2/3
CMHLAB-N5K1(config-monitor)# no shut
CMHLAB-N5K1(config-monitor)# end
CMHLAB-N5K1#
```

The session's configuration can be verified by using the **show monitor session** command, as demonstrated in Example 7-14.

Example 7-14 *Displaying a Fibre Channel Monitor Session*

```
CMHLAB-N5K1# show mon sess 2
   session 2
--------------
description        : SPAN Session for Fibre Channel
type               : local
state              : up
source intf        :
    rx             : vfc10
    tx             : vfc10
    both           : vfc10
source VLANs       :
    rx             :
destination ports : fc2/3

Legend: f = forwarding enabled, l = learning enabled
source VSANs       :
    rx             :     rx          :
```

SPAN on Nexus 1000V

The Nexus 1000V series switches have the capability to configure traditional SPAN sessions, referred to as local SPAN sessions, for Ethernet traffic in addition to ERSPAN. SPAN enables the network administrator to configure SPAN using the concepts of source ports and destination ports. Source ports, as their name implies, are the source of the traffic to be sent via SPAN to the destination ports. Source ports have the following requirements:

- Can be any port type including Ethernet, virtual Ethernet, port channel, or VLAN.

- Can be a VLAN. When a VLAN is used as a SPAN source, all ports that belong to the VLAN are considered as part of the SPAN source.

- Can be configured with a direction (ingress, egress, or both) to monitor.

- Cannot be a SPAN destination port.

- A local SPAN session must be on the same host Virtual Ethernet Module (VEM) as the destination port.

SPAN destinations, as their name implies, define where traffic copied from the SPAN source will be sent. As the Nexus 1000V supports local SPAN and ERSPAN, the destination ports have distinctly different requirements and configuration.

Local SPAN destination ports have the following requirements:

- Can be any Ethernet or virtual Ethernet port

■ Must be on the same host VEM as the source port

Additionally, SPAN destinations have the following restrictions:

■ Cannot be SPAN sources

ERSPAN destinations have the following characteristics:

■ IP addresses rather than ports or VLANs.

■ Generic Routing Encapsulation (GRE) will be used to encapsulate the ERSPAN traffic enabling it to traverse an IP network.

SPAN on the Nexus 1000V supports the capability to configure up to 64 SPAN and/or 64 ERSPAN sessions. Table 7-3 lists the SPAN and ERSPAN session limits for the Nexus 1000V.

Table 7-3   *Nexus 1000V SPAN and ERSPAN Session Limits*

Session Characteristic	Limit
Configured SPAN and ERSPAN sessions	64
Simultaneously running SPAN and ERSPAN sessions	64
Source interfaces per session	128
Source VLANs per session	32

Configuring SPAN on Nexus 1000V

Configuration of SPAN on Nexus 1000V is a multistep process in which the SPAN source, SPAN destination, and monitoring ports are defined. The first step is to define the monitor port connection where the network analysis, IDS/IPS, or other device will collect the SPAN traffic, as demonstrated in Example 7-15. Figure 7-4 illustrates the topology used in Examples 7-15 through 7-17.

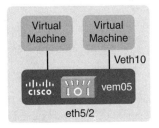

Figure 7-4   *Network Topology for Nexus 1000V SPAN Configuration*

Example 7-15 *Configuring a SPAN Monitor Port*

```
CMHLAB-DC2-VSM1# confi t
CMHLAB-DC2-VSM1(config)# int e5/1
CMHLAB-DC2-VSM1 (config-if)# desc Connection to Network Analyzer
CMHLAB-DC2-VSM1 (config-if)# switchport
CMHLAB-DC2-VSM1(config-if)# switchport monitor
CMHLAB-DC2-VSM1 (config-if)# no shut
CMHLAB-DC2-VSM1 (config-if)# end
CMHLAB-DC2-VSM1#
```

Note   The Nexus 1000V does not support the ingress and learning configuration parameters at this time.

After the monitor port is configured, the next step is to configure the SPAN monitor session. Source and destination interfaces are configured under the SPAN monitor session. Finally, the state of the SPAN session, shut or no shut, is configured in SPAN monitor session mode as well. In Example 7-16, a monitor session is configured that will SPAN traffic from interface vEthernet10 to destination port e5/1.

Note   The default direction for SPAN monitoring is both. Use of tx or rx direction narrows the traffic monitored.

Example 7-16 *Configuring a SPAN Monitor Session*

```
CMHLAB-DC2-VSM1# confi t
CMHLAB-DC2-VSM1(config)# monitor session 1
CMHLAB-DC2-VSM1(config-monitor)# desc Local SPAN Session 1
CMHLAB-DC2-VSM1(config-monitor)# source int vethernet10
CMHLAB-DC2-VSM1(config-monitor)# destination int e5/1
CMHLAB-DC2-VSM1(config-monitor)# no shut
CMHLAB-DC2-VSM1(config-monitor)# end
```

Note   Don't forget to **no shut** the monitor session!

The monitor session's status can be reviewed through the use of the **show monitor** command, as demonstrated in Example 7-17. This information is helpful when verifying the SPAN session's configuration and status.

Example 7-17   *Displaying a Monitor Session's Configuration*

```
CMHLAB-DC2-VSM1# show monitor session 1
   session 1
- - - - - - - - - - - - - - -
description       : Local SPAN Session 1
type              : local
state             : up
source intf       :
    rx            : Veth10
    tx            : Veth10
    both          : Veth10
source VLANs      :
    rx            :
    tx            :
    both          :
filter VLANs      : filter not specified
destination ports : Eth5/1
```

ERSPAN on Nexus 1000V

The Nexus 1000V series switches have the capability to configure traditional SPAN sessions, referred to as local SPAN sessions, for Ethernet traffic in addition to Encapsulated Remote SPAN (ERSPAN). ERSPAN differs from traditional SPAN in that ERSPAN enables the monitored traffic to be encapsulated in a Generic Route Encapsulation (GRE) packet and routed across an IP network. With ERSPAN, network administrators can centralize network analysis tools and route the monitored traffic.

ERSPAN builds on the concepts of source ports and destination ports. Source ports, as their name implies, are the source of the traffic to be sent via ERSPAN to the destination ports. Source ports have the following requirements:

- Can be any port type including Ethernet, virtual Ethernet, port channel, or VLAN.

- Can be a VLAN. When a VLAN is used as SPAN source, all ports that belong to the VLAN are considered as part of the SPAN source.

- Can be configured with a direction (ingress, egress or both) to monitor.

- Cannot be a SPAN destination port.

ERSPAN destinations define where traffic copied from the ERSPAN source will be sent. ERSPAN destination ports are specified by an IP address.

Additionally, ERSPAN destinations have the following restrictions:

- Cannot be ERSPAN sources

SPAN on the Nexus 1000V supports the ability to configure up to 64 SPAN and ERSPAN sessions.

Configuration of ERSPAN on Nexus 1000V is a multistep process where the ERSPAN source and ERSPAN destination are defined. The first step is to configure the ERSPAN port profile. Refer to Chapter 9, "Nexus 1000V," for additional details on port profile configuration. Example 7-18 illustrates a port profile that will be used for ERSPAN.

Example 7-18 *ERSPAN Port Profile Configuration*

```
CMHLAB-DC2-VSM1# confi t
CMHLAB-DC2-VSM1(config-port-prof)# port-profile DC2-N1K-ERSPAN
CMHLAB-DC2-VSM1(config-port-prof)# capability l3control
CMHLAB-DC2-VSM1(config-port-prof)# vmware port-group
CMHLAB-DC2-VSM1(config-port-prof)# switchport mode access
CMHLAB-DC2-VSM1(config-port-prof)# switchport access vlan 702
CMHLAB-DC2-VSM1(config-port-prof)# no shutdown
CMHLAB-DC2-VSM1(config-port-prof)# system vlan 702
CMHLAB-DC2-VSM1(config-port-prof)# state enabled
CMHLAB-DC2-VSM1(config-port-prof)# end
```

The two differences between the ERSPAN port profile and a port profile that would be used directly by a guest machine are the following commands:

```
CMHLAB-DC2-VSM1(config-port-prof)# capability l3control
CMHLAB-DC2-VSM1(config-port-prof)# system vlan 702
```

The **capability l3control** command indicates that the interface created will use Layer 3 (IP) control functions. In this case, ERSPAN will encapsulate traffic in GRE for transport across an IP network.

The **system vlan 702** command indicates a VLAN that will be brought up before communication between the VEM and Virtual Supervisor Module (VSM) is established. Use of the system VLAN is recommended for all VMware Kernel Port (vmk) ports because the vmk ports are used for system functions such as IP-based network attached storage connectivity, VEM to VSM communication, service consoles, and more.

Next, use the ERSPAN port profile to create a new vmk port on the host from which traffic will be sourced. A typical cluster configuration will have a vmk port configured on each cluster member server that uses the ERSPAN port profile. Figure 7-5 demonstrates how to do this. You can find details on adding a vmk port in Chapter 9.

Click **Add** in the upper-left corner. The screen in Figure 7-6 displays.

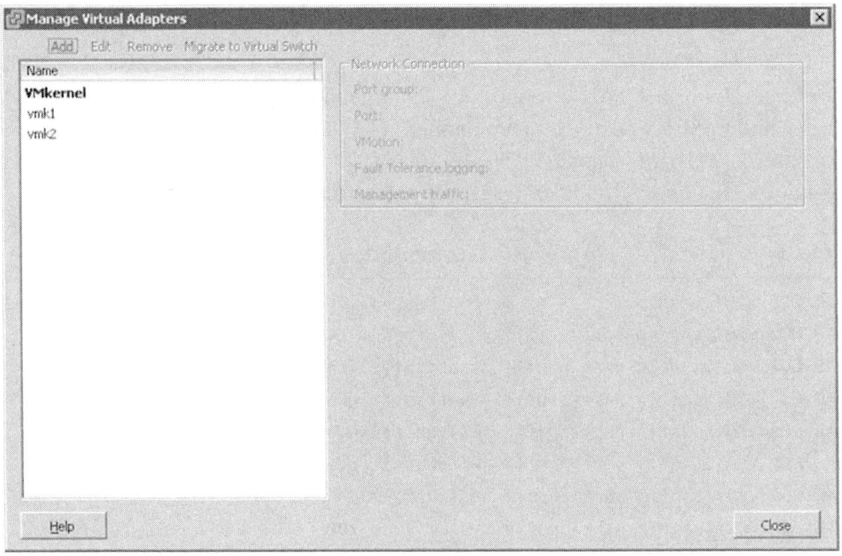

Figure 7-5   *Create a vmk Port Using the ERSPAN Port Profile: Step 1*

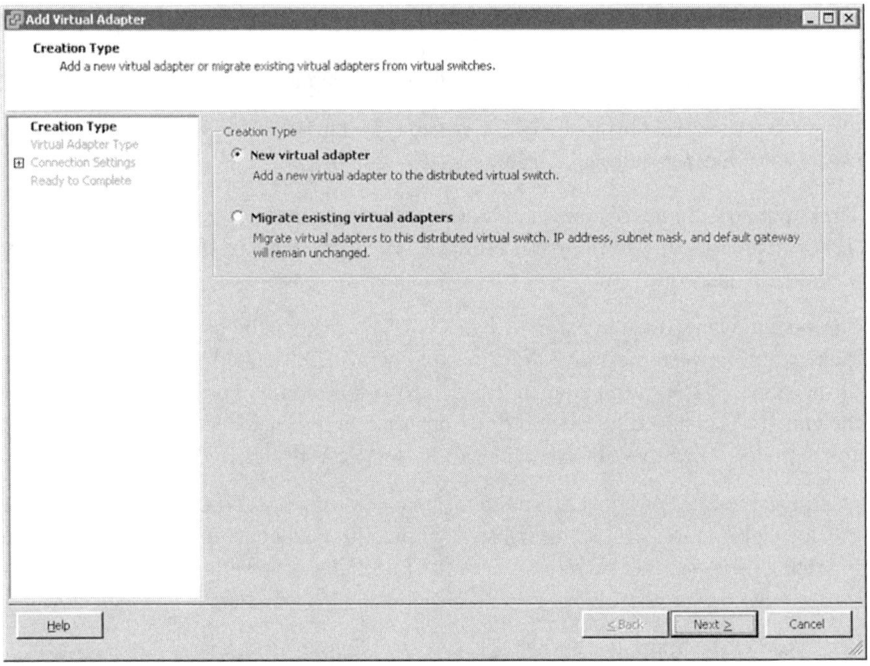

Figure 7-6   *Create a vmk Port Using the ERSPAN Port Profile: Step 2*

Select **New virtual adapter** and then click **Next**. The screen in Figure 7-7 displays.

Select the ERSPAN port group from the drop-down list and click **Next**. The screen in Figure 7-8 displays.

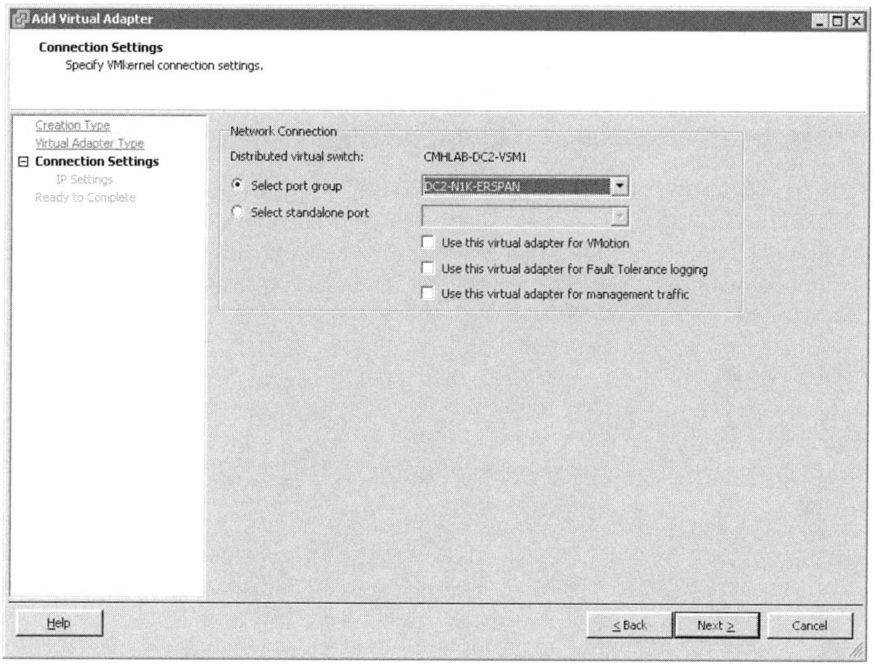

Figure 7-7   *Create a vmk Port Using the ERSPAN Port Profile: Step 3*

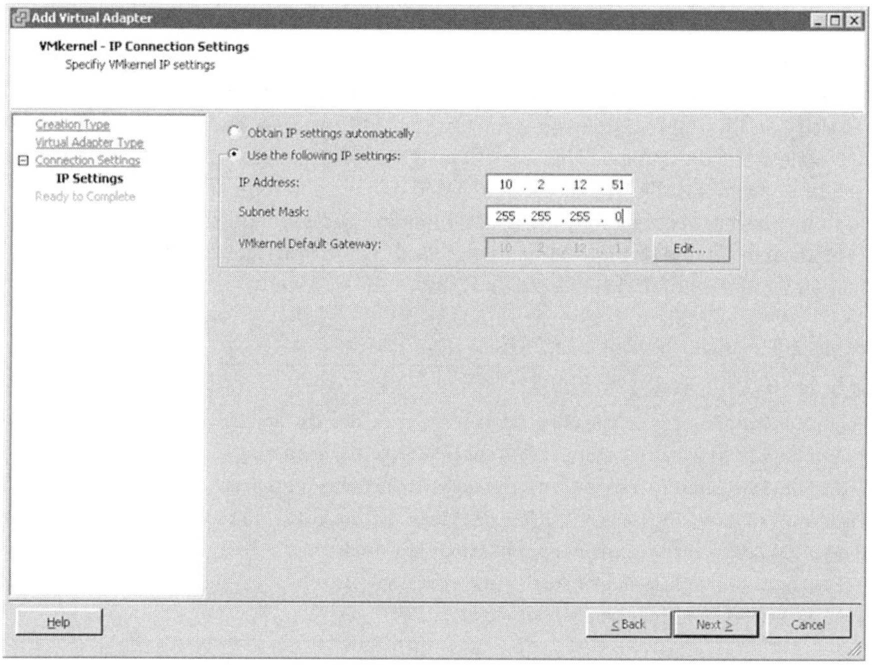

Figure 7-8   *Create a vmk Port Using the ERSPAN Port Profile: Step 4*

Configure a unique IP address for the ERSPAN vmk to use, the subnet mask, and default gateway and then click **Next**. The screen in Figure 7-9 displays.

Review the configuration and click **Finish**.

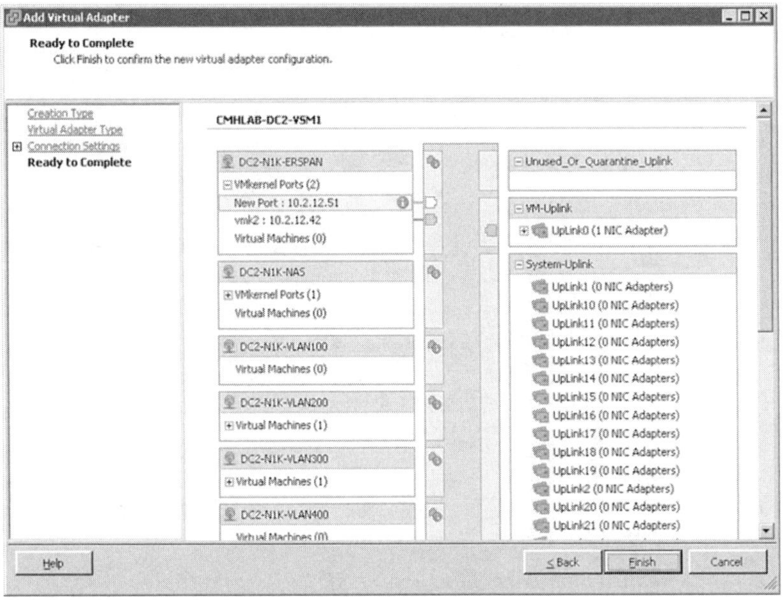

Figure 7-9 *Create a vmk Port Using the ERSPAN Port Profile: Step 5*

Source and destination IP addresses are configured under the ERSPAN monitor session along with the ERSPAN ID. ERSPAN IDs perform an important role in that they uniquely identify an ERSPAN session and can be used to differentiate between multiple ERSPAN sessions at the destination. This is particularly helpful in a centralized model where there might be many ERSPAN sessions aggregated. Finally, the state of the ERSPAN session, shut or no shut, is configured in ERSPAN monitor session mode as well. In Example 7-19, a monitor session is configured that will SPAN traffic from interface vEthernet27 to destination IP address of 10.1.1.100 and an ERSPAN-ID of 1000.

Example 7-19 *Configuring an ERSPAN Monitor Session*

```
CMHLAB-DC2-VSM1# confi t
CMHLAB-DC2-VSM1(config)# monitor session 1 type erspan-source
CMHLAB-DC2-VSM1(config-erspan-src)# desc ERSPAN Session 1
CMHLAB-DC2-VSM1(config-erspan-src)# source interface vethernet27
CMHLAB-DC2-VSM1(config-erspan-src)# destination ip 10.1.1.100
CMHLAB-DC2-VSM1(config-erspan-src)# erspan-id 1000
CMHLAB-DC2-VSM1(config-erspan-src)# no shut
CMHLAB-DC2-VSM1(config-erspan-src)# end
```

Note Don't forget to **no shut** the monitor session!

The monitor session's status can be reviewed through the use of the **show monitor** command, as shown in Example 7-20. This information is helpful when verifying the ERSPAN session's configuration and status.

Example 7-20   *Displaying a Monitor Session's Configuration*

```
CMHLAB-DC2-VSM1(config-erspan-src)# show monitor session 1
   session 1
---------------
description        : ERSPAN Session
type               : erspan-source
state              : up
source intf        :
    rx             : Veth27
    tx             : Veth27
    both           : Veth27
source VLANs       :
    rx             :
    tx             :
    both           :
filter VLANs       : filter not specified
destination IP     : 10.1.1.100
ERSPAN ID          : 1000
ERSPAN TTL         : 64
ERSPAN IP Prec.    : 0
ERSPAN DSCP        : 0
ERSPAN MTU         : 1500
```

Embedded Analyzer

NX-OS on the Nexus 7000 and 5000 series switches has the capability to perform detailed protocol-level analysis of traffic from the network destined for the control plane of the switch. This capability is extremely valuable when troubleshooting issues with control plane protocols such as STP, OSPF, SNMP, CDP, and more. The embedded analyzer is based on Wireshark, which is open source code that provides a multitude of filtering options and a familiar interface. Output from the embedded analyzer is saved in a format readable in many packet analysis tools for easy decoding.

Note   Note that the embedded analyzer feature cannot be used to capture and analyze data plane traffic. Traffic traversing through the switch is not handled by the control plane and therefore cannot be processed by the embedded analyzer. Data plane traffic analysis can be performed by using SPAN or ERSPAN and an external network analyzer.

The embedded analyzer can be configured to filter traffic based on filters defined in TCPdump and Wireshark. The comprehensive list of filters can be found here:

■ **Capture filters:** http://www.tcpdump.org/tcpdump_man.html

■ **Display filters:** http://wiki.wireshark.org/DisplayFilters

Example 7-21 illustrates using the embedded analyzer feature to review IGMP traffic.

Example 7-21 *Using the Embedded Analyzer for IGMP Traffic Analysis*

```
CMHLAB-N5K1# ethanalyzer local interface inbound-lo display-filter "igmp"
Capturing on eth3

Frame 80 (64 bytes on wire, 64 bytes captured)
    Arrival Time: Mar  1, 2010 10:58:37.011710000
    [Time delta from previous captured frame: 0.287940000 seconds]
    [Time delta from previous displayed frame: 0.813212000 seconds]
    [Time since reference or first frame: 1267441117.011710000 seconds]
    Frame Number: 80
    Frame Length: 64 bytes
    Capture Length: 64 bytes
    [Frame is marked: False]
    [Protocols in frame: eth:vlan:ip:igmp]
Ethernet II, Src: 00:50:56:86:09:eb (00:50:56:86:09:eb), Dst: 01:00:5e:00:01:18
(01:00:5e:00:01:18)
    Destination: 01:00:5e:00:01:18 (01:00:5e:00:01:18)
        Address: 01:00:5e:00:01:18 (01:00:5e:00:01:18)
        .... ...1 .... .... .... .... = IG bit: Group address (multicast/broadcast)
        .... ..0. .... .... .... .... = LG bit: Globally unique address (factory
default)
    Source: 00:50:56:86:09:eb (00:50:56:86:09:eb)
        Address: 00:50:56:86:09:eb (00:50:56:86:09:eb)
        .... ...0 .... .... .... .... = IG bit: Individual address (unicast)
        .... ..0. .... .... .... .... = LG bit: Globally unique address (factory
default)
    Type: 802.1Q Virtual LAN (0x8100)
802.1Q Virtual LAN
    000. .... .... .... = Priority: 0
    ...0 .... .... .... = CFI: 0
    .... 0000 0000 1001 = ID: 9
    Type: IP (0x0800)
    Trailer: 1164EE9B00000000000900017CE0
Internet Protocol, Src: 10.2.1.20 (10.2.1.20), Dst: 224.0.1.24 (224.0.1.24)
    Version: 4
    Header length: 24 bytes
```

```
      Differentiated Services Field: 0x00 (DSCP 0x00: Default; ECN: 0x00)
          0000 00.. = Differentiated Services Codepoint: Default (0x00)
          .... ..0. = ECN-Capable Transport (ECT): 0
          .... ...0 = ECN-CE: 0
      Total Length: 32
      Identification: 0x4f70 (20336)
      Flags: 0x00
          0... = Reserved bit: Not set
          .0.. = Don't fragment: Not set
          ..0. = More fragments: Not set
      Fragment offset: 0
      Time to live: 1
      Protocol: IGMP (0x02)
      Header checksum: 0xe939 [correct]
          [Good: True]
          [Bad : False]
      Source: 10.2.1.20 (10.2.1.20)
      Destination: 224.0.1.24 (224.0.1.24)
      Options: (4 bytes)
          Router Alert: Every router examines packet
Internet Group Management Protocol
      IGMP Version: 2
      Type: Membership Report (0x16)
      Max Response Time: 0.0 sec (0x00)
      Header checksum: 0x08e7 [correct]
      Multicast Address: 224.0.1.24 (224.0.1.24)

1 packet captured
CMHLAB-N5K1#
```

The capture was stopped by pressing Ctrl-C.

In the output in Example 7-21, an IGMP frame has been captured, providing you with the ability to see all the information available regarding the Ethernet framing, source and destination IP address, and into the protocol where you see it is an IGMP packet destined for the multicast address of 224.0.1.24, which is used by Windows machines for Windows Internet Naming Services (WINS).

Note   Note that with the Nexus 5000, the hardware architecture of the switch is such that there are two interfaces—inbound-hi and inbound-low—that are used for high- and low-priority traffic. High-priority traffic consists of protocols such as STP, LACP, Fibre Channel, and so on, while low-priority traffic is CDP, Telnet, SSH, and IP ARP for management of the switch.

The embedded analyzer provides the facility to write the captured output to a file that can be stored locally and then transferred to a network analyzer for further decoding. Example 7-22 shows a capture of STP traffic that will be saved to a file.

Example 7-22 *Capturing Traffic to a File*

```
CMHLAB-N5K1# ethanalyzer local interface inbound-hi display-filter "stp" write
bootflash:stp.pcap
Capturing on eth4
Frame 1 (68 bytes on wire, 68 bytes captured)
    Arrival Time: Mar  1, 2010 11:16:21.875330000
    [Time delta from previous captured frame: 1267442181.875330000 seconds]
    [Time delta from previous displayed frame: 1267442181.875330000 seconds]
    [Time since reference or first frame: 1267442181.875330000 seconds]
    Frame Number: 1
    Frame Length: 68 bytes
    Capture Length: 68 bytes
    [Frame is marked: False]
    [Protocols in frame: eth:vlan:llc:stp]
Ethernet II, Src: 00:0d:ec:d3:86:30 (00:0d:ec:d3:86:30), Dst: 01:00:0c:cc:cc:cd
(01:00:0c:cc:cc:cd)
    Destination: 01:00:0c:cc:cc:cd (01:00:0c:cc:cc:cd)
        Address: 01:00:0c:cc:cc:cd (01:00:0c:cc:cc:cd)
            .... ...1 .... .... .... .... = IG bit: Group address (multicast/broadcast)
            .... ..0. .... .... .... .... = LG bit: Globally unique address (factory
default)
    Source: 00:0d:ec:d3:86:30 (00:0d:ec:d3:86:30)
        Address: 00:0d:ec:d3:86:30 (00:0d:ec:d3:86:30)
            .... ...0 .... .... .... .... = IG bit: Individual addres      .... ..0.
.... .... .... .... = LG bit: Globally unique address (factory default)
    Source: 00:50:56:86:09:eb (00:50:56:86:09:eb)
        Address: 00:50:56:86:09:eb (00:50:56:86:09:eb)
            .... ...0 .... .... .... .... = IG bit: Individual address (unicast)
            .... ..0. .... .... .... .... = LG bit: Globally unique address (factory
default)
    Type: 802.1Q Virtual LAN (0x8100)
802.1Q Virtual LAN
    000. .... .... .... = Priority: 0
    ...0 .... .... .... = CFI: 0
    .... 0000 0000 1001 = ID: 9
    Type: IP (0x0800)
    Trailer: 1164EE9B00000000000900017CE0
Internet Protocol, Src: 10.2.1.20 (10.2.1.20), Dst: 224.0.1.24 (224.0.1.24)
    Version: 4
    Header length: 24 bytes
    Differentiated Services Field: 0x00 (DSCP 0x00: Default; ECN: 0x00)
```

```
        0000 00.. = Differentiated Services Codepoint: Default (0x00)
        .... ..0. = ECN-Capable Transport (ECT): 0
        .... ...0 = ECN-CE: 0
    Total Length: 32
    Identification: 0x4f70 (20336)
    Flags: 0x00
        0... = Reserved bit: Not set
        .0.. = Don't fragment: Not set
        ..0. = More fragments: Not set
    Fragment offset: 0
 (unicast)
        .... ..0. .... .... .... .... = LG bit: Globally unique address (factory
default)
    Type: 802.1Q Virtual LAN (0x8100)
802.1Q Virtual LAN
    111. .... .... .... = Priority: 7
    ...0 .... .... .... = CFI: 0
    .... 0010 0000 0001 = ID: 513
    Length: 50
Logical-Link Control
    DSAP: SNAP (0xaa)
    IG Bit: Individual
    SSAP: SNAP (0xaa)
    CR Bit: Command
    Control field: U, func=UI (0x03)
        000. 00.. = Command: Unnumbered Information (0x00)
        .... ..11 = Frame type: Unnumbered frame (0x03)
    Organization Code: Cisco (0x00000c)
    PID: PVSTP+ (0x010b)
Spanning Tree Protocol
    Protocol Identifier: Spanning Tree Protocol (0x0000)
    Protocol Version Identifier: Rapid Spanning Tree (2)
        Address: 00:0d:ec:d3:86:30 (00:0d:ec:d3:86:30)
        .... ...0 .... .... .... .... = IG bit: Individual address (unicast)
        .... ..0. .... .... .... .... = LG bit: Globally unique address (factory
default)
    Type: 802.1Q Virtual LAN (0x8100)
802.1Q Virtual LAN
    111. .... .... .... = Priority: 7
    ...0 .... .... .... = CFI: 0
    .... 0010 0000 0001 = ID: 513
    Length: 50
Logical-Link Control
    DSAP: SNAP (0xaa)
```

```
    IG Bit: Individual
    SSAP: SNAP (0xaa)
    CR Bit: Command
    Control field: U, func=UI (0x03)
        000. 00.. = Command: Unnumbered Information (0x00)
        .... ..11 = Frame type: Unnumbered frame (0x03)
    Organization Code: Cisco (0x00000c)
    PID: PVSTP+ (0x010b)
Spanning Tree Protocol
    Protocol Identifier: Spanning Tree Protoco        Address: 00:0d:ec:d3:86:30
(00:0d:ec:d3:86:30)
        .... ...0 .... .... .... .... = IG bit: Individual address (unicast)
        .... ..0. .... .... .... .... = LG bit: Globally unique address (factory
default)
    Type: 802.1Q Virtual LAN (0x8100)
802.1Q Virtual LAN
    111. .... .... .... = Priority: 7
    ...0 .... .... .... = CFI: 0
    .... 0010 0000 000d Information (0x00)
Spanning Tree Protocol
    Protocol Identifier: Spanning Tree Protocol (0x0000)
    Protocol Version Identifier: Rapid Spanning Tree (2)
    BPDU Type: Rapid/Multiple Spanning Tree (0x02)
    BPDU flags: 0x78 (Agreement, Forwarding, Learning, Port Role: Root)
        0... .... = Topology Change Acknowledgment: No
        .1.. .... = Agreement: Yes
        ..1. .... = Forwarding: Yes
        ...1 .... = Learning: Yes
        .... 10.. = Port Role: Root (2)
        .... ..0. = Proposal: No
        .... ...0 = Topology Change: No
    Root Identifier: 24676 / 00:d0:04:57:c0:00
    Root Path Cost: 2
    Bridge Identifier: 32868 / 00:0d:ec:d3:86:3c
    Port identifier: 0x9063
    Message Age: 1
    Max Age: 20
    Hello Time: 2
    Forward Delay: 15
    Version 1 Length: 0
.............output truncated
Frame 111 (57 bytes on wire, 57 bytes captured)
    Arrival Time: Mar  1, 2010 11:16:23.973683000
    [Time delta from previous captured frame: 0.000012000 seconds]   [Time delta
from previous displayed frame: 0.000012000 seconds]
```

```
      [Time since reference or first frame: 1267442183.973683000 seconds]
      Frame Number: 111
      Frame Length: 57 bytes
      Capture Length: 57 bytes
      [Frame is marked: False]
      [Protocols in frame: eth:vlan:llc:stp]
Ethernet II, Src: 00:0d:ec:a3:0d:30 (00:0d:ec:a3:0d:30), Dst: 01:80:c2:00:00:00
(01:80:c2:00:00:00)
    Destination: 01:80:c2:00:00:00 (01:80:c2:00:00:00)
        Address: 01:80:c2:00:00:00 (01:80:c2:00:00:00)
        .... ...1 .... .... .... .... = IG bit: Group address (multicast/broadcast)
        .... ..0. .... .... .... .... = LG bit: Globally unique address (factory
default)
    Source: 00:0d:ec:a3:0d:30 (00:0d:ec:a3:0d:30)
        Address: 00:0d:ec:a3:0d:30 (00:0d:ec:a3:0d:30)
        .... ...0 .... .... .... .... = IG bit: Individual address (ungment: No
        .0.. .... = Agreement: No
        ..1. .... = Forwarding: Yes
        ...1 .... = Learning: Yes
        .... 11.. = Port Role: Designated (3)
        .... ..0. = Proposal: No
        .... ...0 = Topology Change: No
    Root Identifier: 32769 / 00:0d:ec:a3:0d:3c
    Root Path Cost: 0
    Bridge Identifier: 32769 / 00:0d:ec:a3:0d:3c
    Port identifier: 0x9063
    Message Age: 0
    Max Age: 20
    Hello Time: 2
    Forward Delay: 15
    Version 1 Length: 0


100 packets captured
CMHLAB-N5K1# dir bootflash:
        47      Dec 17 13:53:06 2009  ..tmp-kickstart
        37      Dec 17 13:53:07 2009  ..tmp-system
   22315520     Dec 17 13:53:06 2009  .tmp-kickstart
  136327913     Dec 17 13:53:07 2009  .tmp-system
       575      Jan 06 21:35:12 2009  N5K1SS.lic
      49152     Dec     Protocol Version Identifier: Rapid Spanning Tree (2)
    BPDU Type: Rapid/Multiple Spanning Tree (0x02)
    BPDU flags: 0x78 (Agreement, Forwarding, Learning, Port Role: Root)
        0... .... = Topology Change Acknowledgment: No
        .1.. .... = Agreement: Yes
        ..1. .... = Forwarding: Yes
```

```
            ...1 .... = Learning: Yes
            .... 10.. = Port Role: Root (2)
            .... ..0. = Proposal: No
            .... ...0 = Topology Change: No
        Root Identifier: 24676 / 00:d0:04:57:c0:00
        Root Path Cost: 2
        Bridge Identifier: 32868 / 00:0d:ec:d3:86:3c
        Port identifier: 0x9063
        Message Age: 1
        Max Age: 20
        Hello Time: 2
        Forward Delay: 15
        Version 1 Length: 0
..............output truncated
Frame 111 (57 bytes on wire, 57 bytes captured)
    Arrival Time: Mar  1, 2010 11:16:23.973683000
    [Time delta from previous captured frame: 0.000012000 seconds]    [Time delta
from previous displayed frame: 0.000012000 seconds]
    [Time since reference or first frame: 1267442183.973683000 seconds]
    Frame Number: 111
    Frame Length: 57 bytes
    Capture Length: 57 bytes
    [Frame is marked: False]
    [Protocols in frame: eth:vlan:llc:stp]
Ethernet II, Src: 00:0d:ec:a3:0d:30 (00:0d:ec:a3:0d:30), Dst: 01:80:c2:00:00:00
(01:80:c2:00:00:00)
    Destination: 01:80:c2:00:00:00 (01:80:c2:00:00:00)
        Address: 01:80:c2:00:00:00 (01:80:c2:00:00:00)
        .... ...1 .... .... .... .... = IG bit: Group address (multicast/broadcast)
        .... ..0. .... .... .... .... = LG bit: Globally unique address (factory
default)
    Source: 00:0d:ec:a3:0d:30 (00:0d:ec:a3:0d:30)
        Address: 00:0d:ec:a3:0d:30 (00:0d:ec:a3:0d:30)
        .... ...0 .... .... .... .... = IG bit: Individual address (unicast)
        .... ..0. .... .... .... .... = LG bit: Globally unique address (factory
default)
    Type: 802.1Q Virtual LAN (0x8100)
802.1Q Virtual LAN
17 13:53:06 2009  lost+found/
      3066     Feb 23 19:54:03 2010  mts.log
   21680640    Nov 16 18:31:06 2009  n5000-uk9-kickstart.4.1.3.N2.1.bin
   22315520    Dec 17 13:34:13 2009  n5000-uk9-kickstart.4.1.3.N2.1a.bin
  136255825    Nov 16 18:32:57 2009  n5000-uk9.4.1.3.N2.1.bin
  136327913    Dec 17 13:33:43 2009  n5000-uk9.4.1.3.N2.1a.bin
     12463     Feb 23 14:22:59 2010  pre-demo.txt
```

```
      8331      Mar 01 11:16:23 2010   stp.pcap
      4096      Jul 31 15:07:28 2009   vdc_2/
      4096      Jul 31 15:07:28 2009   vdc_3/
      4096      Jul 31 15:07:28 2009   vdc_4/
Usage for bootflash://sup-local
  537387008 bytes used
  343097344 bytes free
  880484352 bytes total
CMHLAB-N5K1#
```

In Example 7-22, 100 packets were captured and placed in a file named *stp.pcap* on the switch's bootflash. This file could then be copied off of the switch for analysis.

The embedded analyzer defaults to capturing 100 frames, but this can be changed by using the **limit-captured-frames** command, as demonstrated in Example 7-23.

Example 7-23   *Limiting the Number of Captured Frames*

```
CMHLAB-N5K1# ethanalyzer local interface inbound-hi display-filter "stp" limit-
captured-frames 20 write bootflash:stp1.pcap
Capturing on eth4
Frame 2 (68 bytes on wire, 68 bytes captured)
    Arrival Time: Mar  1, 2010 11:21:39.881854000
    [Time delta from previous captured frame: 0.075555000 seconds]
    [Time delta from previous displayed frame: 1267442499.881854000 seconds]
    [Time since reference or first frame: 1267442499.881854000 seconds]
    Frame Number: 2
    Frame Length: 68 bytes
    Capture Length: 68 bytes
    [Frame is marked: False]
    [Protocols in frame: eth:vlan:llc:stp]
Ethernet II, Src: 00:0d:ec:d3:86:30 (00:0d:ec:d3:86:30), Dst: 01:00:0c:cc:cc:cd
(01:00:0c:cc:cc:cd)
    Destination: 01:00:0c:cc:cc:cd (01:00:0c:cc:cc:cd)
        Address: 01:00:0c:cc:cc:cd (01:00:0c:cc:cc:cd)
        .... ...1 .... .... .... .... = IG bit: Group address (multicast/broadcast)
        .... ..0. .... .... .... .... = LG bit: Globally unique address (factory
default)
    Source: 00:0d:ec:d3:86:30 (00:0d:ec:d3:86:30)
        Address: 00:0d:ec:d3:86:30 (00:0d:ec:d3:86:30)
        .... ...0 .... .... .... .... = IG bit: Individual address (unicast)
        .... ..0. .... .... .... .... = LG bit: Globally unique address (factory
default)
    Type: 802.1Q Virtual LAN (0x8100)
802.1Q Virtual LAN
    111. .... .... .... = Priority: 7
```

```
       ...0 .... .... .... = CFI: 0
       .... 0010 0000 0001 = ID: 513
     Length: 50
Logical-Link Control
     DSAP: SNAP (0xaa)
     IG Bit: Individual
     SSAP: SNAP (0xaa)
     CR Bit: Command
     Control field: U, func=UI (0x03)
          000. 00.. = Command: Unnumbered Information (0x00)
          .... ..11 = Frame type: Unnumbered frame (0x03)
     Organization Code: Cisco (0x00000c)
     PID: PVSTP+ (0x010b)
Spanning Tree Protocol
     Protocol Identifier: Spanning Tree Protocol (0x0000)
     BPDU Type: Rapid/Multiple Spanning Tree (0x02)
     BPDU flags: 0x78 (Agreement, Forwarding, Learning, Port Role: Root)
          0... .... = Topology Change Acknowledgment: No
          .1.. .... = Agreement: Yes
          ..1. .... = Forwarding: Yes
          ...1 .... = Learning: Yes
          .... 10.. = Port Role: Root (2)
          .... ..0. = Proposal: No
          .... ...0 = Topology Change: No
     Root Identifier: 24676 / 00:d0:04:57:c0:00
     Root Path Cost: 2
     Bridge Identifier: 32868 / 00:0d:ec:d3:86:3c
     Port identifier: 0x9063
     Message Age: 1
     Max Age: 20
     Hello Time: 2
     Forward Delay: 15
     Version 1 Length: 0


..............output truncated


Frame 21 (68 bytes on wire, 68 bytes captured)
     Arrival Time: Mar  1, 2010 11:21:39.977388000
     [Time delta from previous captured frame: 0.000005000 seconds]
     [Time delta from previous displayed frame: 0.000005000 seconds]
     [Time since reference or first frame: 1267442499.977388000 seconds]
     Frame Number: 21
     Frame Length: 68 bytes
     Capture Length: 68 bytes
```

```
     [Frame is marked: False]
     [Protocols in frame: eth:vlan:llc:stp]
Ethernet II, Src: 00:0d:ec:a3:0d:0c (00:0d:ec:a3:0d:0c), Dst: 01:00:0c:cc:cc:cd
(01:00:0c:cc:cc:cd)
     Destination: 01:00:0c:cc:cc:cd (01:00:0c:cc:cc:cd)
         Address: 01:00:0c:cc:cc:cd (01:00:0c:cc:cc:cd)
             .... ...1 .... .... .... .... = IG bit: Group address (multicast/broadcast)
             .... ..0. .... .... .... .... = LG bit: Globally unique address (factory
default)
     Source: 00:0d:ec:a3:0d:0c (00:0d:ec:a3:0d:0c)
         Address: 00:0d:ec:a3:0d:0c (00:0d:ec:a3:0d:0c)
             .... ...0 .... .... .... .... = IG bit: Individual address (unicast)
             .... ..0. .... .... .... .... = LG bit: Globally unique address (factory
default)
     Type: 802.1Q Virtual LAN (0x8100)
802.1Q Virtual LAN
     111. .... .... .... = Priority: 7
     ...0 .... .... .... = CFI: 0
     .... 0000 0001 0011 = ID: 19
     Length: 50
Logical-Link Control
     DSAP: SNAP (0xaa)
     IG Bit: Individual
     SSAP: SNAP (0xaa)
     CR Bit: Command
     Control field: U, func=UI (0x03)
         000. 00.. = Command: Unnumbered Information (0x00)
         .... ..11 = Frame type: Unnumbered frame (0x03)
     Organization Code: Cisco (0x00000c)
     PID: PVSTP+ (0x010b)
Spanning Tree Protocol
     Protocol Identifier: Spanning Tree Protocol (0x0000)
     Protocol Version Identifier: Rapid Spanning Tree (2)
     BPDU Type: Rapid/Multiple Spanning Tree (0x02)
     BPDU flags: 0x3c (Forwarding, Learning, Port Role: Designated)
         0... .... = Topology Change Acknowledgment: No
         .0.. .... = Agreement: No

         ..1. .... = Forwarding: Yes
         ...1 .... = Learning: Yes
         .... 11.. = Port Role: Designated (3)
         .... ..0. = Proposal: No
         .... ...0 = Topology Change: No
     Root Identifier: 32778 / 00:0d:ec:a3:0d:3c
     Root Path Cost: 0
```

```
        Bridge Identifier: 32778 / 00:0d:ec:a3:0d:3c
        Port identifier: 0x8085
        Message Age: 0
        Max Age: 20
        Hello Time: 2
        Forward Delay: 15
        Version 1 Length: 0


20 packets captured
CMHLAB-N5K1# dir
            47    Dec 17 13:53:06 2009  ..tmp-kickstart
            37    Dec 17 13:53:07 2009  ..tmp-system
       22315520   Dec 17 13:53:06 2009  .tmp-kickstart
      136327913   Dec 17 13:53:07 2009  .tmp-system
           575    Jan 06 21:35:12 2009  N5K1SS.lic
         49152    Dec 17 13:53:06 2009  lost+found/
          3066    Feb 23 19:54:03 2010  mts.log
       22315520   Dec 17 13:34:13 2009  n5000-uk9-kickstart.4.1.3.N2.1a.bin
      136255825   Nov 16 18:32:57 2009  n5000-uk9.4.1.3.N2.1.bin
      136327913   Dec 17 13:33:43 2009  n5000-uk9.4.1.3.N2.1a.bin
         12463    Feb 23 14:22:59 2010  pre-demo.txt
          8331    Mar 01 11:16:23 2010  stp.pcap
          1696    Mar 01 11:21:39 2010  stp1.pcap
          4096    Jul 31 15:07:28 2009  vdc_2/
          4096    Jul 31 15:07:28 2009  vdc_3/
          4096    Jul 31 15:07:28 2009  vdc_4/


Usage for bootflash://
  537391104 bytes used
  343093248 bytes free
  880484352 bytes total
CMHLAB-N5K1#
```

In the output in Example 7-23, you see that 20 frames were captured rather than the default of 100, and they were saved to a file named *stp1.pcap* on the switch's bootflash.

Smart Call Home

Smart Call Home is an embedded feature for NX-OS platforms with a distinct hardware component, currently the Nexus 7000 and the Nexus 5000/2000 combination. As the Nexus 1000V does not have a distinct hardware component because it leverages the server hardware running VMware vSphere, it does not use Smart Call Home. Smart Call Home provides an automated notification system for policies the network administrator defines. For example, Smart Call Home can automate the process of opening a case with the Cisco Technical Assistance Center (TAC) for a hardware failure and attach the appropriate supporting CLI output. This helps customers simplify their support needs and maintain the integrity of their environment through automation.

Smart Call Home is email-based and supports multiple message formats including Short Text, Long Text, and Extensible Markup Language (XML). This enables the network administrator to configure profiles that are the best use case in their environment. Short-text format is good for pagers and printed reports whereas full text is formatted for ease of reading. The XML format is a machine-readable format and is the format used when NX-OS communicates with Cisco TAC.

Smart Call Home uses multiple configuration elements to provide a customizable utility that can meet many different configuration scenarios. Smart Call Home has destination profiles that define who and with what message format is the recipient of a Smart Call Home message. The destination profile also determines the alert group that is used to trigger specific Smart Call Home messages.

NX-OS provides preconfigured alert groups that can be modified to add or remove specific commands to collect. Table 7-4 displays the predefined alert groups and their executed commands.

Table 7-4   *Nexus 7000 Smart Call Home Alert Groups and Executed Commands*

Alert Group	Description	Executed Commands
Cisco-TAC	All critical alerts from the other alert groups destined for Smart Call Home.	Execute commands based on the alert group that originates the alert.
Configuration	Periodic events related to configuration.	show module show running-configuration vdc-all all show startup-configuration vdc-all show vdc current show vdc membership show version
Diagnostic	Events generated by diagnostics.	show diagnostic result module all detail show diagnostic result module number detail show hardware show logging last 200 show module show sprom all show tech-support gold show tech-support platform show tech-support sysmgr show vdc current show vdc membership show version

Table 7-4 *Nexus 7000 Smart Call Home Alert Groups and Executed Commands*

Alert Group	Description	Executed Commands
EEM	Events generated by EEM.	show diagnostic result module all detail show diagnostic result module number detail show module show tech-support gold show tech-support platform show tech-support sysmgr show vdc current show vdc membership
Environmental	Events related to power, fan, and environment-sensing elements such as temperature alarms.	show environment show logging last 200 show module show vdc current show vdc membership show version
Inventory	Inventory status that is provided whenever a unit is cold booted, or when FRUs are inserted or removed. This alert is considered a noncritical event, and the information is used for status and entitlement.	show inventory show license usage show module show system uptime show sprom all show vdc current show vdc membership show version
License	Events related to licensing and license violations.	show license usage vdc all show logging last 200 show vdc current show vdc membership
Linemodule hardware	Events related to standard or intelligent switching modules.	show diagnostic result module all detail show diagnostic result module number detail show hardware show logging last 200 show module show sprom all show tech-support ethpm show tech-support gold show tech-support platform show tech-support sysmgr show vdc current show vdc membership show version

Table 7-4   *Nexus 7000 Smart Call Home Alert Groups and Executed Commands*

Alert Group	Description	Executed Commands
Supervisor hardware	Events related to supervisor modules.	show diagnostic result module all detail show hardware show logging last 200 show module show sprom all show tech-support ethpm show tech-support gold show tech-support platform show tech-support sysmgr show vdc current show vdc membership show version
Syslog port group	Events generated by the syslog PORT facility.	show license usage show logging last 200 show vdc current show vdc membership
System	Events generated by a failure of a software system that is critical to unit operation.	show diagnostic result module all detail show hardware show logging last 200 show module show sprom all show tech-support ethpm show tech-support gold show tech-support platform show tech-support sysmgr show vdc current show vdc membership
Test	User-generated test message.	show module show vdc current show vdc membership show version

Note   You can add more **show** commands only to full text and XML destination profiles. Short text profiles allow only 128 bytes of text.

Smart Call Home provides the ability to filter messages based on urgency. This allows the network administrator to have flexibility in defining which messages are critical by defining the urgency level in the destination profile.

Note Smart Call Home does not change the syslog message level.

Table 7-5 shows the default Smart Call Home Severity and Syslog Level.

Smart Call Home configuration can be distributed among NX-OS switches that participate in a Cisco Fabric Services (CFS) domain. When CFS is leveraged for this function, all Smart Call Home parameters except SNMP sysContact and the device priority are distributed. Chapter 8, "Unified Fabric," provides additional information on CFS.

Table 7-5 *Nexus 7000 and 5000 Smart Call Home Severity and Syslog Level Mapping*

Call Home Level	Keyword	Syslog Level	Description
9	Catastrophic	N/A	Networkwide catastrophic failure.
8	Disaster	N/A	Significant network impact.
7	Fatal	Emergency (0)	System is unusable.
6	Critical	Alert (1)	Critical conditions that indicate that immediate attention is needed.
5	Major	Critical (2)	Major conditions.
4	Minor	Error (3)	Minor conditions.
3	Warning	Warning (4)	Warning conditions.
2	Notification	Notice (5)	Basic notification and informational messages. Possibly independently insignificant.
1	Normal	Information (6)	Normal event signifying return to normal state.
0	Debugging	Debug (7)	Debugging messages.

Smart Call Home Configuration

Smart Call Home configuration begins with defining a system contact, contract number, and other key attributes such as site address, phone number, and email address. Example 7-24 shows this initial step.

Example 7-24 *Defining Key Attributes for Smart Call Home*

```
Jealousy# confi t
Enter configuration commands, one per line.  End with CNTL/Z.
Jealousy(config)# snmp-server contact Cisco
Jealousy(config)# callhome
Jealousy(config-callhome)# email-contact smartcallhome@cisco.com
Jealousy(config-callhome)# phone-contact +1-800-123-4567
Jealousy(config-callhome)# streetaddress 123 Main Street Data Center
Jealousy(config-callhome)# contract-id 1
Jealousy(config-callhome)# exit
Jealousy(config)# exit
Jealousy# show callhome
callhome disabled
Callhome Information:
contact person name(sysContact):Cisco
contact person's email:smartcallhome@cisco.com
contact person's phone number:+1-800-123-4567
street addr:123 Main Street Data Center
site id:
customer id:
contract id:1
switch priority:7
duplicate message throttling : enabled
periodic inventory : enabled
periodic inventory time-period : 7 days
periodic inventory timeofday : 08:00 (HH:MM)
Distribution : Disabled
```

The next step in Smart Call Home configuration is to define a destination profile. The desitnation profile is where key elements such as message format, message urgency level, destination email address, or URL for alerts and the message transport are defined. Example 7-25 illustrates a destination profile for a Network Operations Center (NOC) team that will receive full-text messages via email for all major conditions.

Example 7-25 *Creation of a Smart Call Home Destination Profile for a NOC*

```
Jealousy# confi t
```

```
Enter configuration commands, one per line.  End with CNTL/Z.
Jealousy(config)# callhome
Jealousy(config-callhome)# destination-profile NOC-email
Jealousy(config-callhome)# destination-profile NOC-email email-addr
noc@whereiwork.com
Jealousy(config-callhome)# destination-profile NOC-email format full-txt
Jealousy(config-callhome)# destination-profile NOC-email message-level 5
Jealousy(config-callhome)# destination-profile NOC-e-mail transport-method e-mail
Jealousy(config-callhome)# destination-profile NOC-e-mail alert-group All
```

The new destination profile can be verified by using the command shown in Example 7-26.

Example 7-26   *Displaying a Smart Call Home Destination Profile*

```
Jealousy# show callhome destination-profile profile NOC-e-mail
NOC-e-mail destination profile information
maximum message size:2500000
message format:full-txt
message-level:5
transport-method:email
email addresses configured:
noc@whereiwork.com

url addresses configured:

alert groups configured:
all
```

Smart Call Home enables network administrators to customize the output collected by adding commands to be executed through an Alert group. Example 7-27 illustrates this by adding the CLI command **show cdp neighbors** to the Linecard-Hardware Alert group.

Example 7-27   *Modification of an Existing Alert Group to Collect Additional Output*

```
Jealousy# confi t
Enter configuration commands, one per line.  End with CNTL/Z.
Jealousy(config)# callhome
Jealousy(config-callhome)# alert-group Linecard-Hardware user-def-cmd show cdp
neighbor
Jealousy(config-callhome)# end

Jealousy# show callhome user-def-cmds
User configured commands for alert groups :
alert-group linecard-hardware user-def-cmd show cdp neighbor
```

If the email transport option is selected, Smart Call Home requires additional information about the email server it is to use to send its messages through. In Example 7-28, an email server is added to the configuration.

Example 7-28 *Adding an Email Server for Smart Call Home to Use*

```
Jealousy# confi t
Enter configuration commands, one per line.  End with CNTL/Z.
Jealousy(config)# callhome
Jealousy(config-callhome)# transport email smtp-server 10.100.10.1 port 25 use-vrf
management
Jealousy(config-callhome)# transport email from Jealousy-Nexus@whereiwork.com
Jealousy(config-callhome)# transport email reply-to noc@whereiwork.com
Jealousy(config-callhome)# end

Jealousy# show callhome transport-email
from email addr:Jealousy-Nexus@whereiwork.com
reply to email addr:noc@whereiwork.com
smtp server:10.100.10.1
smtp server port:25
```

Smart Call Home supports Cisco Fabric Services (CFS) configuration distribution across CFS enabled platforms in a CFS domain. Example 7-29 illustrates how to configure Smart Call Home to use CFS.

Example 7-29 *Configuring Smart Call Home to Use CFS*

```
Jealousy# confi t
Enter configuration commands, one per line.  End with CNTL/Z.
Jealousy(config)# callhome
Jealousy(config-callhome)# distribute
Jealousy(config-callhome)# commit
Jealousy(config-callhome)# end

Jealousy# show cfs application
----------------------------------------------
Application    Enabled    Scope
----------------------------------------------
ntp            No         Physical-fc-ip
stp            Yes        Physical-eth
l2fm           Yes        Physical-eth
role           No         Physical-fc-ip
radius         No         Physical-fc-ip
callhome       Yes        Physical-fc-ip
```

```
Total number of entries = 6

Jealousy#
```

Configuration Checkpoint and Rollback

NX-OS on the Nexus 7000 provides the capability for a network administrator to capture the configuration of the switch in a snapshot or checkpoint. The checkpoint can then be re-applied to the switch via rollback to facilitate the restoration of the original configuration captured in the checkpoint. Checkpoint enables the network administrator to implement changes in the devices configuration and back those changes out if required in a fast and reliable manner.

When checkpoints are created by a network administrator, they are stored on the switch rather than an external server or device. Checkpoints can also be reviewed prior to application on the switch, and their execution is configurable in three modes:

■   **Atomic:** Implements a rollback only if no errors occur

■   **Best-Effort:** Implements a rollback and skips any errors

■   **Stop-at-First-Failure:** Implements a rollback that stops if an error occurs

Note   Atomic is the default rollback mode.

NX-OS can generate checkpoints automatically when specific events happen. The intent for the automatic checkpoints is to minimize network downtime due to disabling key features or when a license expires. Specific triggers for these automated checkpoints include

■   Disabling a feature with the **no** feature command

■   Removing an instance of a Layer 3 protocol, such as EIGRP or PIM

■   License expiration of a feature

The system-generated checkpoint names begin with **system-** and includes the feature name. Example 7-30 shows the system-generated checkpoint.

Example 7-30   *System-Generated Checkpoints*

```
Jealousy(config)# feature eigrp
Jealousy(config)# router eigrp 1
Jealousy(config-router)# autonomous-system 100
Jealousy(config-router)# exit
Jealousy(config)# no feature eigrp
Jealousy(config)# show check all
```

```
Name: system-fm-__inst_1__eigrp
```

Checkpoint Creation and Rollback

The creation of a checkpoint is done on per-VDC basis, and the switch can store up to ten user-defined checkpoints.

> **Note** System checkpoints do not reduce the number of user-defined checkpoints.

Checkpoints can be given a name and description and can be redirected to a file. Example 7-31 shows the creation of a checkpoint named **one**.

Example 7-31 *Creation of a Checkpoint*

```
Jealousy # checkpoint one
.....................Done
Jealousy #
Jealousy # show checkpoint summary
User Checkpoint Summary
1) one:
Created by admin
Created at Wed, 07:54:07 16 Dec 2009
Size is 16,350 bytes
Description: None
```

> **Note** Checkpoints are not preserved after execution of **write erase** and **reload**. The **clear checkpoint database** also removes all checkpoints.

NX-OS provides context-sensitive help for checkpoint filenames and displays them when you use the **?** on the **show checkpoint** command. Example 7-32 demonstrates this behavior and shows all user- and system-created checkpoints.

Example 7-32 *Checkpoint Context-Sensitive Help*

```
Jealousy# show checkpoint ?
  <CR>
  >                     Redirect it to a file
  >>                    Redirect it to a file in append mode
  all (no abbrev)       Show default config
  five                  Checkpoint name
  four                  Checkpoint name
  one                   Checkpoint name
```

```
summary (no abbrev)           Show configuration rollback checkpoints summary
system (no abbrev)            Show only system configuration rollback checkpoints
system-fm-__inst_1__eigrp    Checkpoint name
three                        Checkpoint name
two                          Checkpoint name
user (no abbrev)              Show only user configuration rollback checkpoints
|                             Pipe command output to filter
```

When checkpoints are established, the need to perform a rollback might arise. Before a rollback is performed, it might be prudent to review the differences in the checkpoint to the running configuration. Example 7-33 shows the creation of a checkpoint named **six**. In the time since the checkpoint was made, EIGRP has been added to the running configuration. NX-OS displays the differences in the configuration.

Example 7-33   *Comparing a Checkpoint to the Running Configuration*

```
Jealousy# show diff rollback-patch checkpoint six running-config
Collecting Running-Config
Generating Rollback Patch
..
!!
!
feature eigrp
!
router eigrp 1
 autonomous-system 100
```

After a review of the differences, rolling the system back to the checkpoint named **six** is illustrated in Example 7-34.

Example 7-34   *Rollback of the Configuration from a Checkpoint*

```
Jealousy# rollback running-config checkpoint six
Note: Applying config parallelly may fail Rollback verification
Collecting Running-Config
Generating Rollback Patch
Executing Rollback Patch
Generating Running-config for verification
Generating Patch for verification
Jealousy# show run eigrp
                     ^
% Invalid command at '^' marker.
```

NetFlow

NX-OS on the Nexus 7000 and Nexus 1000V provides a powerful tool for collecting network statistics, NetFlow. Network administrators use NetFlow to provide statistics for network monitoring, planning, and accounting. An ecosystem of NetFlow analysis tools and packages exist that enable network administrators to parse, report, and audit the NetFlow records to suit their needs.

NX-OS defines a flow as a unidirectional stream of packets that arrive on a source interface or VLAN and has the same values for the keys that are an identified value for a field or fields within a packet. The network administrator creates a flow though a flow record that defines the keys that will be unique to the flow.

NetFlow needs to be exported for analysis, and NX-OS uses the concept of an exporter to do this task. NetFlow exports the flow data using UDP and supports both Version 5 and Version 9 formats.

Note   Cisco recommends that you use the Version 9 export format for the following reasons:

■   Variable field specification format

■   Support for IPv6, Layer 2, and MPLS fields

■   More efficient network utilization

For information about the Version 9 export format, see RFC 3954.

The Version 5 export format will have these limitations:

■   Fixed field specifications

■   A 16-bit representation of the 32-bit interface index used in Cisco NX-OS

■   No support for IPv6, Layer 2, or MPLS fields

NetFlow on NX-OS can operate in one of two modes:

■   **Full mode:** NX-OS analyzes all packets on the interface.

■   **Sampled mode:** NX-OS uses a user-defined sampling algorithm and rate to analyze packets on interfaces with NetFlow configured.

NX-OS uses the concept of a monitor that in turn references a flow record and flow exporter. The monitor is applied to an interface and is the mechanism that enables NetFlow on the interface.

Configuring NetFlow on Nexus 7000

The first step to configure NetFlow is to enable it in global configuration mode using the **feature** command. With the modular nature of NX-OS, using the **feature** command loads the NetFlow modular code into memory for execution. Without the feature enabled, it would not be resident in memory. Example 7-35 demonstrates enabling NetFlow.

Example 7-35   *Enabling NetFlow*

```
Jealousy# confi t
Enter configuration commands, one per line.  End with CNTL/Z.
Jealousy(config)# feature NetFlow
Jealousy(config)# end
Jealousy# show feature | include NetFlow
NetFlow                 1          enabled
```

The next step is to define a flow record that determines the keys that will be used to define the flow. Example 7-36 shows the creation of a flow that matches on source and destination interfaces and collects both byte and packet counters.

Example 7-36   *Creating a Flow Record*

```
Jealousy# confi t
Enter configuration commands, one per line.  End with CNTL/Z.
Jealousy(config)# flow record inbound
Jealousy(config-flow-record)# match ipv4 source address
Jealousy(config-flow-record)# match ipv4 destination address
Jealousy(config-flow-record)# collect counter packets
Jealousy(config-flow-record)# collect counter bytes
Jealousy(config-flow-record)# end

Jealousy# show flow record
Flow record inbound:
    No. of users: 0
    Template ID: 0
    Fields:
        match ipv4 source address
        match ipv4 destination address
        match interface input
        match interface output
        match flow direction
        collect counter bytes
        collect counter packets
```

Now that a flow record is defined, the next step is to configure a flow exporter. The flow exporter is the destination for NetFlow data for further analysis. Example 7-37 demonstrates the process for defining a flow exporter.

Example 7-37 *Defining a Flow Exporter*

```
Jealousy# confi t
Enter configuration commands, one per line.  End with CNTL/Z.
Jealousy(config)# flow exporter NetFlowcollector
Jealousy(config-flow-exporter)# destination 10.100.100.235
Jealousy(config-flow-exporter)# source loopback 0
Jealousy(config-flow-exporter)# version 9
Jealousy(config-flow-exporter-version-9)# exit
Jealousy(config-flow-exporter)# end

Jealousy# show flow exporter
Flow exporter NetFlowcollector:
    Destination: 10.100.100.235
    VRF: default (1)
    Source Interface loopback0 (192.168.1.1)
    Export Version 9
    Exporter Statistics
        Number of Flow Records Exported 0
        Number of Templates Exported 0
        Number of Export Packets Sent 0
        Number of Export Bytes Sent 0
        Number of Destination Unreachable Events 0
        Number of No Buffer Events 0
        Number of Packets Dropped (No Route to Host) 0
        Number of Packets Dropped (other) 0
        Number of Packets Dropped (LC to RP Error) 0
        Number of Packets Dropped (Output Drops) 0
        Time statistics were last cleared: Never
```

With both a flow and an exporter defined, the last step is to define a flow monitor, which then is applied to interfaces to begin matching and exporting flows. Example 7-38 defines a flow monitor and applies it to interface Ethernet 1/9.

Example 7-38 *Definition and Application of a Flow Monitor*

```
Jealousy# config t
Enter configuration commands, one per line.  End with CNTL/Z.
Jealousy(config)# flow monitor NetFlowmonitor
Jealousy(config-flow-monitor)# exporter NetFlowcollector
Jealousy(config-flow-monitor)# record inbound
```

```
Jealousy(config-flow-monitor)# exit
Jealousy(config)# int e1/9
Jealousy(config-if)# ip flow monitor NetFlowmonitor in

Jealousy# show flow interface e1/9
Interface Ethernet1/9:
    Monitor: NetFlowmonitor
    Direction: Input

Jealousy# show flow monitor
Flow Monitor NetFlowmonitor:
    Use count: 1
    Flow Record: inbound
    Flow Exporter: NetFlowcollector
```

The Nexus 7000 supports the collection of NetFlow at Layer 2 in addition to the rich set of attributes that can be collected at Layer 3. With the NetFlow modular configuration, enabling Layer 2 NetFlow is a matter of defining a flow record to match on Layer 2 attributes. Example 7-39 defines a Layer 2 NetFlow flow record.

Note   Layer 2 NetFlow cannot be applied to Layer 3 interfaces such as routed ports and VLAN interfaces.

Layer 2 NetFlow cannot be applied in the egress direction; it is an ingress-only feature.

Example 7-39   *Defining a Flow Record for Layer 2 NetFlow*

```
Jealousy# confi t
Enter configuration commands, one per line.  End with CNTL/Z.
Jealousy(config)# flow record l2NetFlow
Jealousy(config-flow-record)# match datalink mac destination-address
Jealousy(config-flow-record)# match datalink mac source-address
Jealousy(config-flow-record)# collect counter bytes
Jealousy(config-flow-record)# collect counter packets
Jealousy(config-flow-record)# end

Jealousy# show flow record l2NetFlow
Flow record l2NetFlow:
    No. of users: 0
    Template ID: 0
    Fields:
        match interface input
        match interface output
```

```
        match datalink mac source-address
        match datalink mac destination-address
        match flow direction
        collect counter bytes
        collect counter packets
Jealousy#
```

NX-OS enables the network administrator to be granular with the amount of NetFlow data collected with one of the mechanisms to facilitate this granularity being sampled NetFlow. Example 7-40 shows the configuration of a sampler and subsequent application to an interface monitor.

Example 7-40   *Defining a NetFlow Sampler*

```
Jealousy# config t
Enter configuration commands, one per line.  End with CNTL/Z.
Jealousy(config)# sampler netflowsampler
Jealousy(config-flow-sampler)# desc Netflow Sampler 1 out of 100
Jealousy(config-flow-sampler)# mode 1 out-of 100
Jealousy(config-flow-sampler)# exit
Jealousy(config)# interface e1/9
Jealousy(config-if)# ip flow monitor netflowmonitor input sampler netflowsampler
Jealousy(config-if)# end

Jealousy# show sampler
Sampler: netflowsampler
    Description: Netflow Sampler 1 out of 100
    ID: 65537
    mode 1 out-of 100
```

Configuring NetFlow on Nexus 1000V

The first step to enable NetFlow on the Nexus 1000V is to define a flow record that determines the keys that will be used to define the flow. Example 7-41 shows the creation of a flow that matches on source and destination interfaces and collects both byte and packet counters.

Example 7-41   *Creating a Flow Record*

```
CMHLAB-DC2-VSM1# confi t
CMHLAB-DC2-VSM1(config)# flow record inbound
CMHLAB-DC2-VSM1(config-flow-record)# match ipv4 source address
CMHLAB-DC2-VSM1(config-flow-record)# match ipv4 destination address
CMHLAB-DC2-VSM1(config-flow-record)# match transport source-port
```

```
CMHLAB-DC2-VSM1(config-flow-record)# match transport destination-port
CMHLAB-DC2-VSM1(config-flow-record)# collect counter bytes
CMHLAB-DC2-VSM1(config-flow-record)# collect counter packets
CMHLAB-DC2-VSM1(config-flow-record)# end


CMHLAB-DC2-VSM1# show flow record inbound
Flow record inbound:
    No. of users: 0
    Template ID: 0
    Fields:
        match ipv4 source address
        match ipv4 destination address
        match transport source-port
        match transport destination-port
        match interface input
        match interface output
        match flow direction
        collect counter bytes
        collect counter packets           collect counter bytes
        collect counter packets
```

Now that a flow record is defined, the next step is to configure a flow exporter. The flow exporter is the destination for NetFlow data for further analysis. Example 7-42 demonstrates the process for defining a flow exporter.

Example 7-42 *Defining a Flow Exporter*

```
CMHLAB-DC2-VSM1# config t
CMHLAB-DC2-VSM1(config)# flow exporter NetFlowcollector
CMHLAB-DC2-VSM1(config-flow-exporter)# destination 10.100.100.235
CMHLAB-DC2-VSM1(config-flow-exporter)# source mgmt0
CMHLAB-DC2-VSM1(config-flow-exporter)# version 9
CMHLAB-DC2-VSM1(config-flow-exporter-version-9)# end


CMHLAB-DC2-VSM1# show flow exporter NetFlowcollector
Flow exporter NetFlowcollector:
    Destination: 10.100.100.235
    VRF: default (1)
    Source Interface mgmt0 (10.2.9.10)
    Export Version 9
        Data template timeout 0 seconds
    Exporter Statistics
        Number of Flow Records Exported 0
        Number of Templates Exported 0
```

```
      Number of Export Packets Sent 0
      Number of Export Bytes Sent 0
      Number of No Buffer Events 0
      Number of Packets Dropped (other) 0
      Number of Packets Dropped (LC to RP Error) 0
      Number of Packets Dropped (Output Drops) 0
      Time statistics were last cleared: Never
```

With both a flow and an exporter defined, the last step is to define a flow monitor, which then is applied to interfaces to begin matching and exporting flows. Example 7-43 defines a flow monitor and applies it to port profile DC2-N1K-VLAN100.

Example 7-43   *Definition and Application of a Flow Monitor*

```
CMHLAB-DC2-VSM1# confi t
CMHLAB-DC2-VSM1(config)# flow monitor netflowmonitor
CMHLAB-DC2-VSM1(config-flow-monitor)# record inbound
CMHLAB-DC2-VSM1(config-flow-monitor)# exporter NetFlowcollector
CMHLAB-DC2-VSM1(config-flow-monitor)# exit
CMHLAB-DC2-VSM1(config)# port-profile DC2-N1K-VLAN100
CMHLAB-DC2-VSM1(config-port-prof)# ip flow monitor netflowmonitor in
CMHLAB-DC2-VSM1(config-port-prof)# end

CMHLAB-DC2-VSM1# show flow monitor
Flow Monitor netflowmonitor:
    Use count: 3
    Flow Record: inbound
    Flow Exporter: NetFlowcollector
    Inactive timeout: 15
    Active timeout: 1800
    Cache Size: 4096
CMHLAB-DC2-VSM1#
```

Summary

NX-OS has a rich set of serviceability features embedded into the operating system to simplify the day-to-day operations and maintenance tasks of the network administrator. Ubiquitous capabilities such as SPAN cross all three Nexus platforms, and for the Nexus 1000V, gain additional functionality with the addition of ERSPAN.

Smart Call Home provides opportunities for organizations to streamline their processes and enable automation of TAC case creation for different issues that might arise in the network. Layering configuration checkpoints and rollback on the Nexus 7000 equates to a platform that is scalable and takes operational considerations into account.

Finally, leveraging features such as NetFlow on the Nexus 7000 and Nexus 1000V provides insight to traffic on the network and empowers network administrators to project growth, defend the network, and provide accounting information.

Chapter 8

Unified Fabric

This chapter covers the following topics related to Unified Fabric:

- Unified Fabric Overview

- Enabling Technologies

- Nexus 5000 Unified Fabric Configuration

- N-Port Virtualization (NPV)

- FCoE Configuration

The Nexus family of switches represents a revolutionary approach to I/O within the data center that is referred to as Unified Fabric.

Unified Fabric Overview

One of the biggest trends in data centers today is consolidation, which can mean many different things. In some cases, consolidation refers to a physical consolidation of data centers themselves where dozens or even hundreds of data centers are geographically dispersed and consolidated into a smaller number of large data centers. Consolidation can also exist within a data center where a large number of underutilized physical servers are consolidated, usually by leveraging some type of virtualization technology, into a smaller number of physical servers. Although virtualization offers many benefits, including consolidation of processors, memory, and storage, little is done to consolidate the amount of adapters, cables, and ports within the data center. In most virtualization implementations, there is actually a requirement for more adapters, cables, and ports to achieve the dense I/O requirements associated with virtualization. Data centers today contain multiple network fabrics that require discreet connectivity components to each fabric.

I/O consolidation is a trend within data centers that refers to the capability to aggregate connectivity to multiple fabrics into a single or redundant pair of adapters, cables, and port. Although new technologies have emerged to enable this consolidation to occur, the concept itself is not new. Fibre Channel, iSCSI, Infiniband, and others were all introduced in an attempt to consolidate I/O. Although the merits or consolidation capabilities of each of these technologies might be open to debate, for one reason or another, all failed to reach mainstream adoption as the single fabric for all I/O requirements.

As a consolidation technology, Unified Fabric offers several benefits to customers, including

- **Lower capital expenditures:** Through the reduction of adapters, cables, and ports required within the infrastructure.

- **Lower operational expenses:** Through the reduction of adapters, cables, and ports drawing power within the data center.

- **Reduced deployment cycles:** Unified Fabric provides a "wire once" model, in which all LAN, SAN, IPC, and management traffic is available to every server without requiring additional connectivity components.

- **Higher availability:** Quite simply, fewer adapters and ports means fewer components that could fail.

Enabling Technologies

Ethernet represents an ideal candidate for I/O consolidation. Ethernet is a well-understood and widely deployed medium that has taken on many consolidation efforts already. Ethernet has been used to consolidate other transport technologies such as FDDI, Token Ring, ATM, and Frame Relay networking technologies. It is agnostic from an upper layer perspective in that IP, IPX, AppleTalk, and others have used Ethernet as transport. More recently, Ethernet and IP have been used to consolidate voice and data networks. From a financial aspect, there is a tremendous investment in Ethernet that also must be taken into account.

For all the positive characteristics of Ethernet, there are several drawbacks of looking to Ethernet as an I/O consolidation technology. Ethernet has traditionally not been a lossless transport and relied on other protocols to guarantee delivery. Additionally, a large portion of Ethernet networks range in speed from 100 Mbps to 1 Gbps and are not equipped to deal with the higher bandwidth applications such as storage.

New hardware and technology standards are emerging that will enable Ethernet to overcome these limitations and become the leading candidate for consolidation.

10-Gigabit Ethernet

10-Gigabit Ethernet (10G) represents the next major speed transition for Ethernet technology. Like earlier transitions, 10G started as a technology reserved for backbone applications in the core of the network. New advances in optic and cabling technologies have made the price points for 10G attractive as a server access technology as well. The desire for 10G as a server access technology is driven by advances in compute technology in the way of multisocket/multicore, larger memory capacity, and virtualization technology. In some cases, 10G is a requirement simply for the amount of network throughput required for a device. In other cases, however, the economics associated with multiple 1G ports versus a single 10G port might drive the consolidation alone. In addition, 10G becoming the de facto standard for LAN-on-motherboard implementations is driving this adoption.

In addition to enabling higher transmission speeds, current 10G offerings provide a suite of extensions to traditional Ethernet. These extensions are standardized within IEEE 802.1 Data Center Bridging. Data Center Bridging is an umbrella referring to a collection of specific standards within IEEE 802.1, which are as follows:

- **Priority-based flow control (PFC; IEEE 802.1Qbb):** One of the basic challenges associated with I/O consolidation is that different protocols place different requirements on the underlying transport. IP traffic is designed to operate in large WAN environments that are global in scale, and as such applies mechanisms at higher layers to account for packet loss, for example, Transmission Control Protocol (TCP). Due to the capabilities of the upper layer protocols, underlying transports can experience packet loss and in some case even *require* some loss to operate in the most efficient manner. Storage-area networks (SAN), on the other hand, are typically smaller in scale than WAN environments. These protocols typically provide no guaranteed delivery mechanisms within the protocol and instead rely solely on the underlying transport to be completely lossless. Ethernet networks traditionally do not provide this lossless behavior for a number of reasons including collisions, link errors, or most commonly congestion. Congestion can be avoided with the implementation of PAUSE frames. When a receiving node begins to experience congestion, it transmits a PAUSE frame to the transmitting station, notifying it to stop sending frames for a period of time. Although this link level PAUSE creates a lossless link, it does so at the expense of performance for protocols equipped to deal with it in a more elegant manner. PFC solves this problem by enabling a PAUSE frame to be sent only for a given Class of Service (CoS) value. This per-priority pause enables LAN and SAN traffic to coexist on a single link between two devices.

- **Enhanced transmission selection (ETS; IEEE 802.1Qaz):** The move to multiple 1-Gbps connections is done primarily for two reasons. One reason is that the aggregate throughput for a given connection exceeds 1 Gbps; this is straightforward but is not always the only reason that multiple 1-Gbps links are used. The second case for multiple 1-Gbps links is to provide a separation of traffic, guaranteeing that one class of traffic will not interfere with the functionality of other classes. ETS provides a way to allocate bandwidth for each traffic class across a shared link. Each class of traffic can be guaranteed some portion of the link, and if a particular class doesn't use all the allocated bandwidth, that bandwidth can be shared with other classes.

- **Congestion notification (IEEE 802.1Qau):** Although PFC provides a mechanism for Ethernet to behave in a lossless manner, it is implemented on a hop-by-hop basis and provides no way for multihop implementations. 802.1Qau is currently proposed as a mechanism to provide end-to-end congestion management. Through the use of backward congestion notification (BCN) and quantized congestion notification (QCN),

Ethernet networks can provide dynamic rate limiting similar to what TCP provides only at Layer 2.

- **Data Center Bridging Capability Exchange Protocol extensions to LLDP (IEEE 802.1AB):** To negotiate the extensions to Ethernet on a specific connection and to ensure backward compatibility with legacy Ethernet networks, a negotiation protocol is required. Data Center Bridging Capability Exchange (DCBX) represents an extension to the industry standard Link Layer Discovery Protocol (LLDP). Using DCBX, two network devices can negotiate the support for PFC, ETS, and Congestion Management.

Fibre Channel over Ethernet

Fibre Channel over Ethernet (FCoE) represents the latest in standards-based I/O consolidation technologies. FCoE was approved within the FC-BB-5 working group of INCITS (formerly ANSI) T11. The beauty of FCoE is in its simplicity. As the name implies, FCOE is a mechanism that takes Fibre Channel (FC) frames and encapsulates them into Ethernet. This simplicity enables for the existing skillsets and tools to be leveraged while reaping the benefits of a Unified I/O for LAN and SAN traffic.

FCoE provides two protocols to achieve Unified I/O:

- **FCoE:** The data plane protocol that encapsulates FC frames into an Ethernet header.

- **FCoE Initialization Protocol (FIP):** A control plane protocol that manages the login/logout process to the FC fabric.

FCoE standards also defines several new port types:

- **Virtual N_Port (VN_Port):** An N_Port that operates over an Ethernet link. N_Ports, also referred to as Node Ports, are the ports on hosts or storage arrays used to connect to the FC fabric.

- **Virtual F_Port (VF_Port):** An F_port that operates over an Ethernet link. F_Ports are switch or director ports that connect to a node.

- **Virtual E_Port (VE_Port):** An E_Port that operates over an Ethernet link. E_Ports or Expansion ports are used to connect fibre channel switches together; when two E_Ports are connected the link, it is said to be an interswitch link or ISL.

Nexus 5000 Unified Fabric Configuration

The Nexus 5000 product line represents the industry's first product that enables Unified I/O through the use of FCoE. The remainder of this chapter discusses the FCoE implementation on the Nexus 5000.

FCoE can be deployed in many different scenarios; however, the maturity of the technology, product availability, and economics are dictating the first implementations of FCoE. As a result of the large number of adapters, cables, and ports that exist at the server interconnect or access layer, this has been the target of organizations wanting to take immediate advantage of the benefits of Unified I/O. This topology takes advantage of the Nexus 5000 as an access layer FCoE switch, connecting to hosts equipped with a Converged Network Adapter (CNA). CNAs present the host with standard 10G ports, as well as native FC ports. The first generation of CNAs focus on maintaining compatibility with existing chipsets and drivers. As such, from the server administrators' standpoint, FCoE is completely transparent to operational practices.

Figure 8-1 shows how a CNA appears in Device Manager of a Microsoft Windows Server.

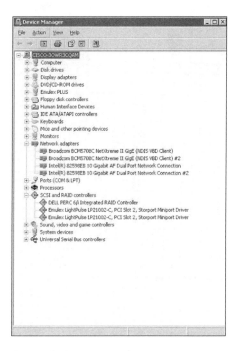

Figure 8-1   *CNA in Device Manager*

Figure 8-2 shows a common FCoE topology.

This topology reduces the requirements on the existing infrastructure, while still taking advantage of the consolidation of adapters, cables, and ports to each server connected to the Nexus 5000.

With the Nexus 5000 switch, FCoE functionality is a licensed feature. After the license is installed, FCoE configuration can be completed.

Note   Enabling FCoE functionality on a Nexus 5000 requires a reboot of the system. Planning for this feature should take this into account.

Example 8-1 shows how to verify the installed licenses.

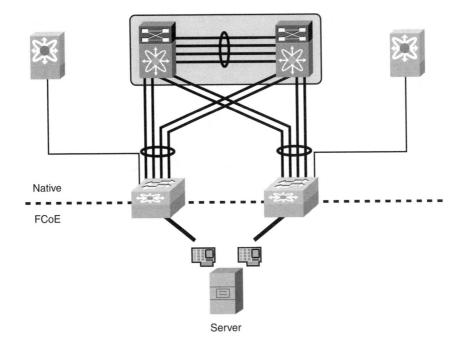

Figure 8-2 *FCoE Network Topology*

Example 8-1 *Verifying FCoE License*

```
Nexus5000(config)# sho license usage
Feature                   Ins  Lic   Status Expiry Date Comments
                               Count
FM_SERVER_PKG             No    -    Unused              -
ENTERPRISE_PKG            Yes   -    Unused Never        -
FC_FEATURES_PKG           Yes   -    Unused Never        -
Nexus5000(config)# -----------------------------------------------------------
Nexus5000(config)#
```

Example 8-2 shows how to enable the FCoE feature.

Example 8-2 *Enabling FcoE*

```
Nexus5000(config)# feature fcoe
Nexus5000(config)# 2009 Nov  3 20:46:23 Nexus5000 %PLATFORM-3-FC_LICENSE_DESIRED:
FCoE/FC feature will be enabled after the configuration is saved followed by a
reboot
Nexus5000(config)# exit
Nexus5000# copy running-config startup-config
[#######################################] 100%
```

```
Packaging and storing to flash: /
Nexus5000#
Nexus5000# reload
WARNING: This command will reboot the system
Do you want to continue? (y/n) [n] y

Broadcast message from root (pts/0) (Tue Nov  3 20:49:15 2009):

The system is going down for reboot NOW!
Connection closed by foreign host.
```

N-Port Virtualization (NPV)

The fibre channel module of the Nexus 5000 series switch can operate in two modes:

- Fabric mode

- NPV (N-Port Virtualization) mode

When in fabric mode, the switch module operates as any switch in a fibre channel network does.

Fabric mode switches have the following characteristics:

- Unique domain ID per virtual storage area network (VSAN)

- Participation in all domain services (zoning, fabric security, Fibre Channel Identification [FCID] allocation, and so on)

- Support for interoperability modes

When the fibre channel module is configured in NPV mode, it does not operate as a typical fibre channel switch and leverages a service, N-Port ID Virtualization (NPIV), on the upstream or core fibre channel switch for domain services. The switch operates in a similar fashion as an NPIV-enabled host on the fabric. The advantage NPV provides the network administrator is the control of domain IDs and points of management on a fibre channel network as it scales.

Note   The fibre channel specification supports 239 domain IDs per VSAN; however, the reality is that many SAN vendors recommend and support a much lower number. Consult your storage vendor (Original Storage Manufacturer [OSM]) for specific scalability numbers.

Additional benefits of NPV include the capability to manage the fibre channel switch as a discrete entity for tasks such as software management and debugging the fibre channel network. NPV also enables network administrators to connect FCoE hosts to non-FCoE-enabled SANs and simplifies third-party interoperability concerns because the NPV enabled fibre channel module does not participate in domain operations or perform local switching. This enables multivendor topologies to be implemented without the restrictions interoperability mode requires.

The fibre channel module in the Nexus 5000 creates a new port type to the fibre channel network when in NPV mode—the NP-port. The NP-port proxies fabric login (FLOGI) requests from end stations and converts them to Fabric Discoveries (FDISC) dynamically and transparently to the end device. The result is that end systems see the NPV-enabled switch as a Fabric Port (F-port), and the upstream/core switch sees the NPV-enabled switch as an F-port as well. Figure 8-3 illustrates the port roles used in a NPV-enabled network.

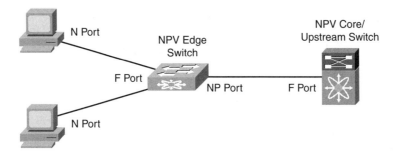

Figure 8-3   *Port Roles in an NPV-Enabled Network*

N-Port Identification Virtualization

A key component to enable the proper operation of NPV is the need for N-Port Identification Virtualization (NPIV) on the core/upstream fibre channel switch. NPIV is an industry-standard technology defined by the T11 committee as part of the Fibre Channel Link Services (FC-LS) specification and enables multiple N Port IDs or FCIDs to share a single physical N Port. Prior to NPIV, it was not possible to have a system that used multiple logins per physical port—it was a one login to one port mapping. With the increasing adoption of technologies such as virtualization, the need to allow multiple logins was created. NPIV operates by using Fabric Discovery (FDISC) requests to obtain additional FCIDs.

Enabling NPV mode can cause the current configuration to be erased and the device rebooted. It is therefore recommended that NPV be enabled prior to completing any additional configuration, as demonstrated in Example 8-3.

Example 8-3   *Enabling NPV Mode*

```
Verify that boot variables are set and the changes are saved. Changing to npv mode
erases the current configuration and reboots the switch in npv mode. Do you w
ant to continue? (y/n):y
Unexporting directories for NFS kernel daemon...done.
Stopping NFS kernel daemon: rpc.mountd rpc.nfsddone.
```

```
Unexporting directories for NFS kernel daemon...
done.
Stopping portmap daemon: portmap.
Stopping kernel log daemon: klogd.
Sending all processes the TERM signal... done.
Sending all processes the KILL signal... done.
Unmounting remote filesystems... done.
Deactivating swap...done.
Unmounting local filesystems...done.
mount: you must specify the filesystem type
Starting reboot command: reboot
Rebooting...
Restarting system.
```

FCoE Configuration

The remainder of this chapter provides a step-by-step configuration of a simple FCoE configuration, depicted in the topology shown in Figure 8-4.

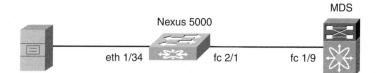

Figure 8-4 *Network Topology for FCoE Configuration*

The first step in the configuration is to configure the connectivity between the Nexus 5000 and the existing SAN environment. The following examples show this configuration on a Cisco MDS SAN director.

Example 8-4 shows how to configure the ISL between the MDS and the Nexus 5000.

Example 8-4 *Enabling MDS Port*

```
MDS-FCOE# conf t
Enter configuration commands, one per line. End with CNTL/Z.
MDS-FCOE(config)# int fc1/9
MDS-FCOE(config-if)# no shutdown
```

Example 8-5 shows how to configure the fibre channel uplink to the SAN core.

Example 8-5 *Configuring FC Uplink*

```
Nexus5000# conf t
Nexus5000(config)# int fc2/1
Nexus5000(config-if)# no shut
Nexus5000(config-if)# exit
Nexus5000(config)#
Nexus5000(config)# sho run int fc2/1
version 4.0(1a)N2(1a)

interface fc2/1
  no shutdown
```

To verify the MDS and Nexus 5000 are configured correctly, the FC uplink port can be verified, as shown in Example 8-6.

Zoning is a typical task within FC SANs to restrict the storage targets that a particular host has access to. Zonesets can be thought of as access lists that grant a particular initiators access to a target. FCoE is transparent to the zoning process. The active zoneset from the SAN fabric should be automatically downloaded to the Nexus 5000. To verify the zoneset, you issue the **show zoneset active** command on the Nexus 5000, as demonstrated in Example 8-7.

Example 8-6 *Verifying FC Uplink*

```
Nexus5000(config)# sho interface fc2/1
fc2/1 is trunking
    Hardware is Fibre Channel, SFP is short wave laser w/o OFC (SN)
    Port WWN is 20:41:00:0d:ec:a3:fd:00
    Peer port WWN is 20:09:00:0d:ec:34:37:80
    Admin port mode is auto, trunk mode is on
    snmp link state traps are enabled
    Port mode is TE
    Port vsan is 1
    Speed is 2 Gbps
    Transmit B2B Credit is 255
    Receive B2B Credit is 16
    Receive data field Size is 2112
    Beacon is turned off
    Trunk vsans (admin allowed and active) (1)
    Trunk vsans (up)                       (1)
    Trunk vsans (isolated)                 ()
    Trunk vsans (initializing)             ()
    5 minutes input rate 784 bits/sec, 98 bytes/sec, 1 frames/sec
    5 minutes output rate 736 bits/sec, 92 bytes/sec, 1 frames/sec
      492492 frames input, 38215024 bytes
```

```
     0 discards, 0 errors
     0 CRC,  0 unknown class
     0 too long, 0 too short
492223 frames output, 28507204 bytes
     0 discards, 0 errors
2 input OLS, 4 LRR, 1 NOS, 0 loop inits
6 output OLS, 4 LRR, 2 NOS, 0 loop inits
16 receive B2B credit remaining
255 transmit B2B credit remaining
```

Example 8-7   *Verifying Active Zoneset*

```
Nexus5000# sho zoneset active
zoneset name ZS_FCoE vsan 1
  zone name z_FCoE vsan 1
  * fcid 0x970002 [pwwn 10:00:00:00:c9:76:f7:e5]
  * fcid 0x6a00ef [pwwn 50:06:01:61:41:e0:d5:ad]
```

Each VSAN is represented as an FCoE VLAN and is required for FCoE functionality.

Example 8-8 configures VLAN 100 as an FCoE VLAN for VSAN 1.

Example 8-8   *Creating an FCoE VLAN*

```
Nexus5000# conf t
Nexus5000(config)# vlan 100
Nexus5000(config-vlan)# name FCoE
Nexus5000(config-vlan)# fcoe vsan 1
Nexus5000(config-vlan)# exit
```

Note   The FCoE VLAN should not be a VLAN, which is the native for any trunk links.

Finally, you define the Virtual Fibre Channel (vfc) port and bind it to a physical interface.

Example 8-9 shows how to create a vfc interface and bind it to a physical interface.

Example 8-9   *Creating a Virtual Fibre Channel Interface*

```
Nexus5000# conf t
Nexus5000(config)# interface vfc34
Nexus5000(config-if)# no shutdown
Nexus5000(config-if)# bind interface ethernet1/34
Nexus5000(config-if)# exit
Nexus5000(config)# exit
```

To carry data traffic and the FCoE traffic, the physical interface must be defined as an 802.1Q trunk carrying the necessary VLANs. Example 8-10 defines the physical interface as a 802.1Q trunk and enables the data and FCoE VLANs.

Example 8-10 *Creating an 802.1Q Trunk*

```
Nexus5000# conf t
Nexus5000(config)# interface ethernet 1/34
Nexus5000(config-if)# switchport mode trunk
Nexus5000(config-if)# switchport trunk native vlan 89
Nexus5000(config-if)# spanning-tree port type edge trunk
Nexus5000(config-if)# switchport trunk allowed vlan 89,100
Nexus5000(config-if)# exit
```

Finally, you can verify that the VFC interface is operational with the **show interface vfc34 brief** command that provides a brief overview of the status of a VFC interface, as demonstrated in Example 8-11.

Example 8-11 *Verifying VFC Interfaces*

```
Nexus5000# show int vfc34 brief

Interface  Vsan   Admin  Admin  Status     SFP    Oper   Oper   Port
                  Mode   Trunk                    Mode   Speed  Channel
                         Mode                            (Gbps)
vfc34      1      F      --     up         --     F      auto --
```

Example 8-12 shows a more detailed status of the VFC interface.

Example 8-12 *VFC Interface Information*

```
Nexus5000# show interface vfc34
vfc34 is up
    Bound interface is Ethernet1/34
    Hardware is GigabitEthernet
    Port WWN is 20:21:00:0d:ec:a3:fd:3f
    Admin port mode is F
    snmp link state traps are enabled
    Port mode is F, FCID is 0x970002
    Port vsan is 1
    Beacon is turned unknown
    5 minutes input rate 0 bits/sec, 0 bytes/sec, 0 frames/sec
    5 minutes output rate 0 bits/sec, 0 bytes/sec, 0 frames/sec
      212797 frames input, 18750280 bytes
        0 discards, 0 errors
```

```
    213056 frames output, 57436752 bytes
      0 discards, 0 errors
```

Summary

Unified Fabric offers several benefits to customers, including

■ **Lower capital expenditures:** Through the reduction of adapters, cables, and ports required within the infrastructure.

■ **Lower operational expenses:** Through the reduction of adapters, cables, and ports drawing power within the data center.

■ **Reduced deployment cycles:** Unified Fabric provides a "wire once" model, where all LAN, SAN, IPC, and management traffic is available to every server without requiring additional connectivity components.

■ **Higher availability:** Few adapters and fewer ports means fewer components that could fail.

By taking advantage of enhancements to traditional Ethernet technologies, and the emergence of technologies such as FCoE, customers can realize these benefits with minimal disruption to operational models. This chapter showed the basic Nexus 5000 configurations necessary to provide a Unified access method for LAN data traffic and SAN storage traffic.

Chapter 9

Nexus 1000V

This chapter covers the following topics:

■ Hypervisor and vSphere Introduction

■ Nexus 1000V System Overview

■ Nexus 1000V Switching

■ Nexus 1000V Installation

■ Nexus 1000V Port Profiles

Hypervisor and vSphere Introduction

A hypervisor, also called a virtual machine manager, is a program that allows multiple operating systems to share a single hardware host. Each operating system appears to have the host's processor, memory, and other resources. The hypervisor controls the host processor, memory, and other resources and allocates what is needed to each operating system. Each operating system is called a *guest operating system* or *virtual machine* running on top of the hypervisor.

The Cisco Nexus 1000V Series Switch is a software-based Cisco NX-OS switch with intelligent features designed specifically for integration with VMware vSphere 4 environments. As more organizations move toward cloud services, VMware vSphere manages collections of CPU(s), storage, and networking as a seamless and dynamic operating environment. The Nexus 1000V operates inside the VMware ESX hypervisor. The Cisco Nexus 1000V Series supports Cisco VN-Link server virtualization technology to provide:

- Policy-based virtual machine (VM) connectivity

- Mobile VM security

- Network policy

- Non-disruptive operational model for your server virtualization, and networking teams

With the Nexus 1000V, virtual servers have the same network configuration, security policy, diagnostic tools, and operational models as physical servers. The Cisco Nexus 1000V Series is certified by VMware to be compatible with VMware vSphere, vCenter, ESX, and ESXi. VMware vCenter provides a single point of management for VMware virtual envonments providing access control, performance monitoring, and configuration. The main difference between ESX and ESXi is that ESXi does not contain the service console. The VSM can be deployed in high-availability mode; each VSM in an active-standby pair; the active and standby should run on separate VMware ESX hosts. This requirement helps ensure high availability if one of the VMware ESX servers fails. A hardware appliance will be available as an alternative optive option in the future.

Nexus 1000V System Overview

The Cisco Nexus 1000V Series Switch has two major components:

- **Virtual Ethernet Module (VEM):** Executes inside the hypervisor

- **External Virtual Supervisor Module (VSM):** Manages the VEMs.

Figure 9-1 shows the Cisco Nexus 1000V Architecture

The Cisco Nexus 1000V Virtual Ethernet Module (VEM) executes as part of the VMware ESX or ESXi kernel. The VEM uses the VMware vNetwork Distributed Switch (vDS) application programming interface (API). The API is used to provide advanced networking capability to virtual machines; allowing for integration with VMware VMotion and Distributed Resource Scheduler (DRS). The VEM takes configuration information from the VSM and performs Layer 2 switching and advanced networking functions:

- Port channels

- Quality of service (QoS)

- Security, including Private VLAN, access control lists, and port security

- Monitoring, including NetFlow, Switch Port Analyzer (SPAN), and Encapsulated Remote SPAN (ERSPAN)

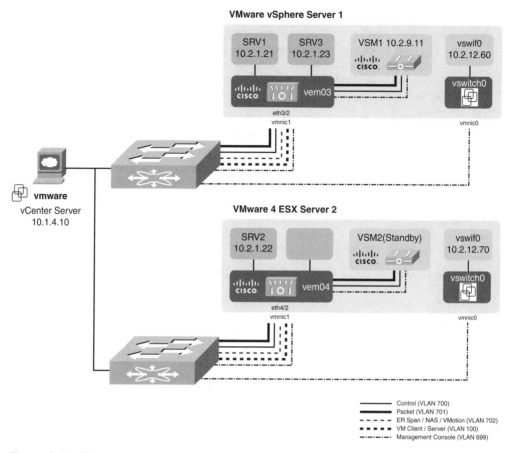

Figure 9-1 *Cisco Nexus 1000V Series Architecture*

Note For more details on VMWare DRA and HA, please visit the following links:

http://www.vmware.com/products/drs/

http://www.vmware.com/products/vmotion/

The Cisco Nexus 1000V Series VSM controls multiple VEMs as one logical modular switch. Instead of physical line card modules, the VSM supports multiple VEMs running in software inside of the physical servers. Configuration is performed through the VSM and is automatically propagated to the VEMs. Instead of configuring soft switches inside the hypervisor on a host-by-host basis, administrators can define configurations for immediate use on all VEMs being managed by the VSM from a single interface.

There are two distinct VLAN interfaces used for communication between the VSM and VEM. These two VLANs need L2 Adjacency between the VEM and VSM; these two VLANs are the Control and Packet VLANs. The Control VLAN is used for:

■   Extended Management communication between the VEM and VSM similar to control communication of chassis-based solutions Nexus 7000, Catalyst 6500.

■   Carrying low-level messages to ensure proper configuration of the VEM.

■   Maintaining a 2-second heartbeat with the VSM to the VEM (timeout 6 seconds).

■   Maintaining synchronization between primary and secondary VSMs.

The Packet VLAN is used for carrying network packets from the VEM to the VSM, such as Cisco Discovery Protocol (CDP) and Interior Gateway Management Protocol (IGMP).

By using the capabilities of Cisco NX-OS, the Cisco Nexus 1000V Series provides the following benefits:

■   **Flexibility and scalability:** Port profiles provide configuration of ports by category enabling the solution to scale to a large number of ports.

■   **High availability:** Synchronized, redundant VSMs enable rapid, stateful failover and ensure an always available virtual machine network.

■   **Manageability:** The Cisco Nexus 1000V Series can be accessed through the XML Management interface, Cisco command-line interface (CLI), Simple Network Management Protocol (SNMP), and CiscoWorks LAN Management Solution (LMS).

Note   With the release of the Nexus 1000V software release 4.0(4)SV1(2), Layer 3 Control between the VSM and the VSM is supported. With Layer 3 Control, the spanning of the Control and Packets VLANs is no longer required; this is covered in more detail in the Layer 3 Control section.

The VSM is also integrated with VMware vCenter Server so that the virtualization administrator can take advantage of the network configuration in the Cisco Nexus 1000V. The Cisco Nexus 1000V includes the port profile feature to address the dynamic nature of server virtualization. Port profiles allow you to define VM network policies for different types or classes of VMs from the Cisco Nexus 1000V VSM. The port profiles are applied to individual VM virtual network interface cards (NICs) through VMware's vCenter GUI for transparent provisioning of network resources. Port profiles are a scalable mechanism to configure networks with large numbers of VMs.

Network and security policies defined in the port profile follow the VM throughout its lifecycle whether it is being migrated from one server to another, suspended, hibernated, or restarted. In addition to migrating the policy, the Cisco Nexus 1000V VSM also moves the VM's network state, such as the port counters and flow statistics. VMs participating in traffic monitoring activities, such as Cisco NetFlow or Encapsulated Remote Switched Port Analyzer (ERSPAN), can continue these activities uninterrupted by VMotion/migration operations. When a specific port profile is updated, the Cisco Nexus 1000V automatically provides live updates to all of the virtual ports using that same port profile. With the capability to migrate network and security policies through VMotion, regulatory compliance is much easier to enforce with the Cisco Nexus 1000V, because the security policy is defined in the same way as physical servers and constantly enforced by the switch.

Nexus 1000V Switching Overview

The VEM differentiates between the following interface types: VEM Virtual Ports and VEM Physical Ports.

The Nexus 1000V supports the following scalability numbers:

- 2 VSMs (High Availability)
- 64 VEMs
- 512 Active VLANs
- 2048 Ports (Eth + vEth)
- 256 Port channels

Each VEM supports:

- 216 Ports (vEths)
- 32 Physical NICs
- 8 Port channels

VEM virtual ports are classified into the three port types:

■ **Virtual NIC:** There are three types of virtual NIC in VMware:

  ■ **virtual NIC (vnic):** Part of the VM, and represents the physical port of the host which is plugged into the switch.

  ■ **virtual kernel NIC (vmknic):** Used by the hypervisor for management, VMotion, iSCSI, NFS, and other network access needed by the kernel. This interface would carry the IP address of the hypervisor itself, and is also bound to a virtual Ethernet port.

  ■ **vswif:** The VMWare Service Console network interface, the Service Console network interface. The first Service Console / vswif interface is always referenced as "vwsif0". The vswif interface is used as the VMware management port; these interface types map to a veth port within Nexus 1000V.

■ **Virtual Ethernet (vEth) port:** Represent a port on the Cisco Nexus 1000V Distributed Virtual Switch. These vEth ports are what the virtual "cable" plugs into, and are moved to the host that the VM is running on; Virtual Ethernet ports are assigned to port groups.

■ **Local Virtual Ethernet (lvEth) port:** Dynamically selected for vEth ports needed on the host.

Note Local vEths do not move, and are addressable by the module/port number.

VEM physical ports are classified into the three port types:

■ VMware NIC

■ Uplink port

■ Ethernet port

Each physical NIC in VMware is represented by an interface called a VMNIC. The VMNIC number is allocated during VMware installation, or when a new physical NIC is installed, and remains the same for the life of the host. Each uplink port on the host represents a physical interface. It acts like an lvEth port; however, because physical ports do not move between hosts, the mapping is 1:1 between an uplink port and a VMNIC. Each physical port added to Cisco Nexus 1000V appears as a physical Ethernet port, just as it would on a hardware-based switch.

Note For more information on interface relationship mapping, refer to the follwing URL: http://tinyurl.com/ydgmens

The Nexus 1000V does not run Spanning Tree Protocol (STP), the Nexus 1000V adheres to the following rules to obtain loop prevention without STP:

■ STP BDPUs are dropped

■ No switching from physical NIC to NIC

■ Layer 2 local MAC address packets dropped on ingress

Figure 9-2 shows how the VEM achieves loop prevention without running STP.

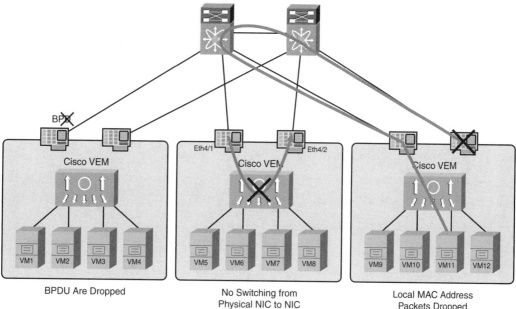

Figure 9-2   *VEM Loop Prevention*

Each VEM learns independently and maintains a separate MAC table. The virtual machine MAC addresses are statically mapped including vEthernet interfaces, vmknics, and vswifs; devices external to the VEM are learned dynamically.

Note   While the interfaces are up, there is no aging.

Nexus 1000V VSM Installation

The Nexus 1000V VSM installation will be shown using the Open Virtualization Appliance / Open Virtualization Format (OVA/OVF) method. There are two modes of installation:

- Manual Installation
- Nexus 1000V Installer

Both methods of installation will be demonstrated throughout this section.

Note To use an ISO image to create a 1000V Virtual Machine (VM), use the following attributes when creating the VM:

- VMType: Other 64-bit Linux
- 1 processor
- 2 GB RAM
- 3 NICs
- Minimum 3GB SCSI hard disk
- LSILogic adapter
- Reserve 2 GB RAM for the VM
- Configure VM network adapters and attach ISO to VM and power on.

The Nexus 1000V virtual appliance has two different modes of installation with the 4.0(4)SV1(2) software release. The next section covers the manual installation of the VSM virtual appliance. The section, "Nexus 1000V GUI Installation," covers the GUI installation. Refer back to the topology in Figure 9-1 for the configuration that follows.

Nexus 1000V Manual Installation

To ensure proper Nexus 1000V manual installation, perform the following steps outlined below:

Step 1. Launch VMware vCenter, select **File > Deploy OVF Template** as shown in Figure 9-3.

Step 2. This brings up the deploy OVF template window. Select the Browse button and enter the location of the Cisco Nexus 1000V OVA Image downloaded, as shown in Figure 9-4.

Step 3. The OVF Template detail dialog window appears, click **Next**. Figure 9-5 shows the VSM deploy OVF template deployment details.

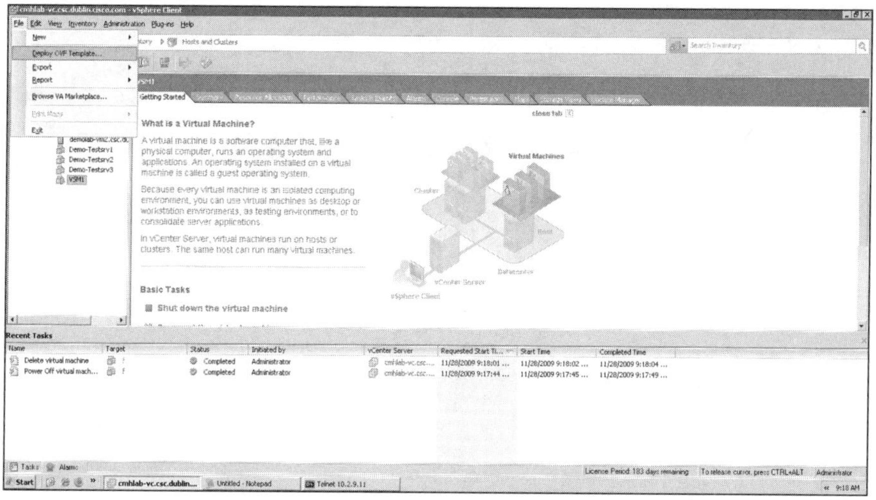

Figure 9-3 *Virtual Center to Deploy an OVF Template*

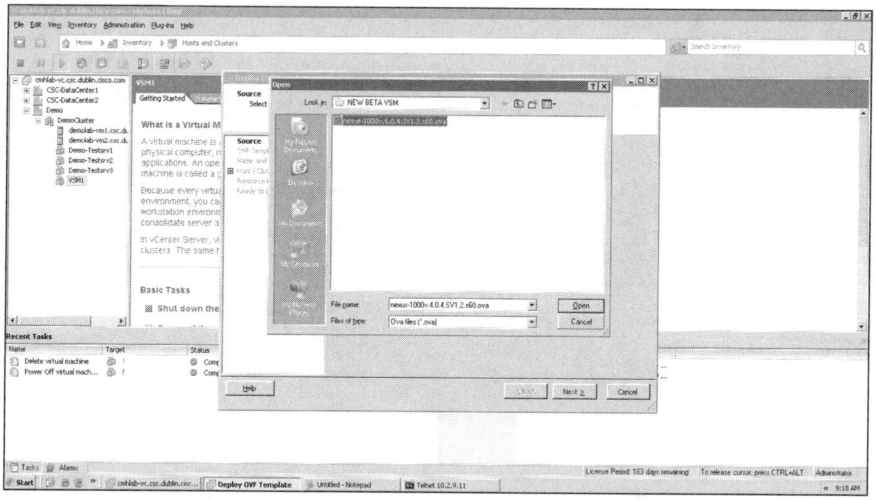

Figure 9-4 *Selecting the VSM OVA Image to Deploy*

Step 4.   Accept the End User License Agreement.

Figure 9-6 shows the end user license agreement. Click **Accept** to continue.

Step 5.   Provide a Name and Location for the VSM. The name in this example is VSM1 in the Demo Data Center.

Figure 9-7 shows where to provide a name for the VSM as well as a virtual center data center container.

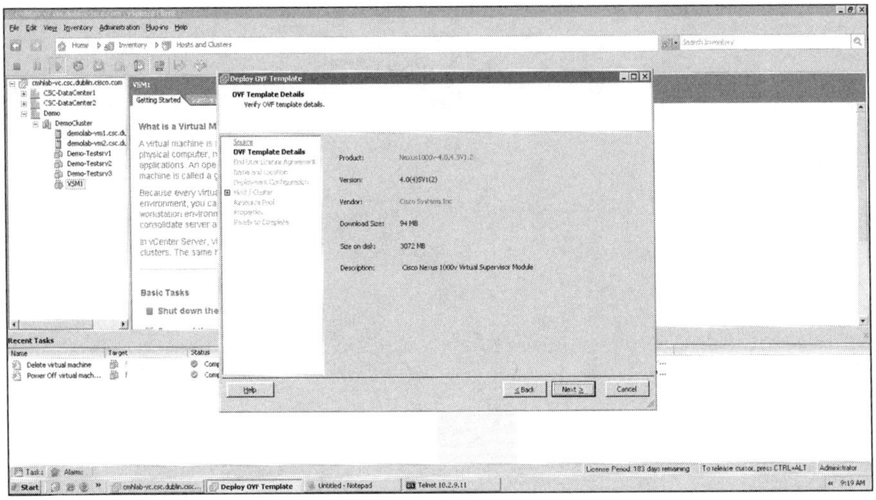

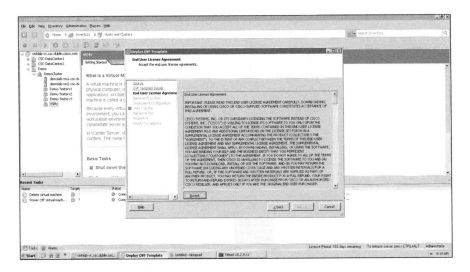

Figure 9-5   *VSM Deploy OVF Template Deployment Details*

Figure 9-6   *End User License Agreement, Accept License Agreement to Continue*

Step 6.   Select **Manually Configure Nexus 1000V** for the deployment option.

Figure 9-8 shows where to select **Manually Configure Nexus 1000V** for the deployment option.

Step 7.   Select the ESX host or cluster to deploy the template, "DemoCluster" is selected in this example, which is a DRS cluster containing two ESX hosts.

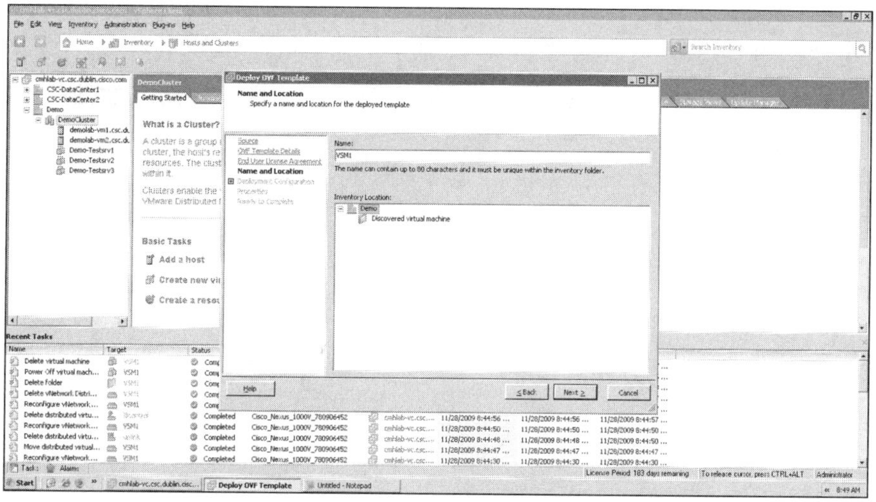

Figure 9-7 *Naming the VSM, Virtual Center Data Center Container*

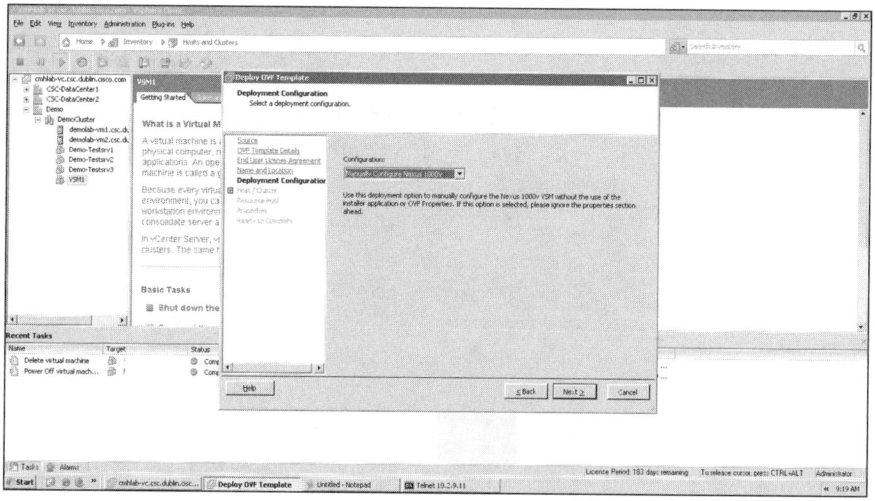

Figure 9-8 *Selecting Manually Configure Nexus 1000V for the Deployment Option*

Figure 9-9 shows selecting an ESX host in the data center container to deploy the VSM template

Step 8.   Select the datastore in which to store the virtual machine file, as shown in Figure 9-10.

Step 9.   Map the Control, Packet, and Management Networks, as shown in Figure 9-11.

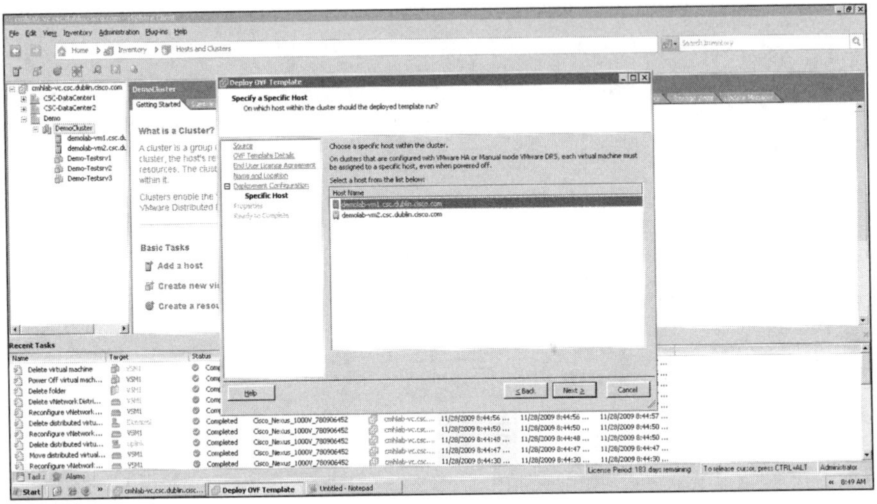

Figure 9-9   *Selecting an ESX Host in the Data Center Container to Deploy the VSM Template*

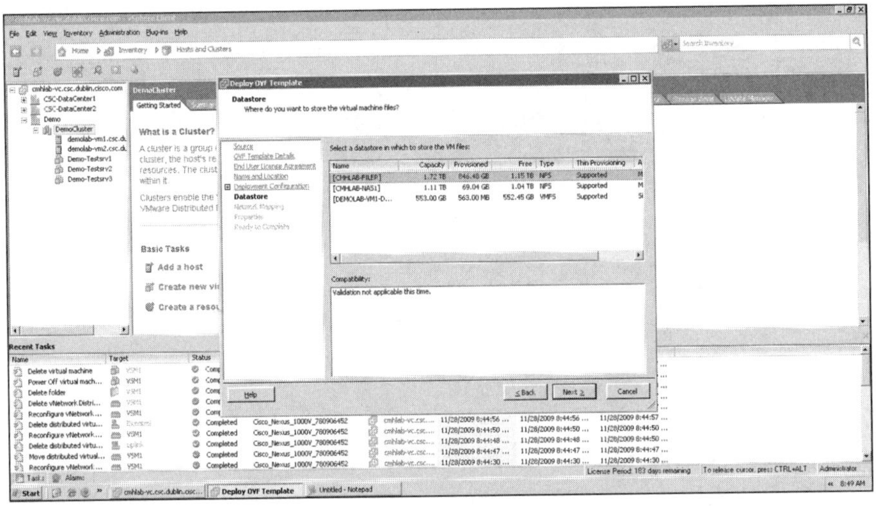

Figure 9-10   *Selecting the Datastore to Store the VM Files*

Step 10.   Enter the VSM specific attributes within the Properties dialog window, such as:

- Do not enter anything in the Nexus 1000V VSM Admin password.

- Enter the Management IP address of the Nexus 1000V VSM.

- Enter the management IP subnet mask.

- Enter the management IP default gateway.

Figure 9-12 shows how to allow the creation of the IP management properties for the VSM MGMT0 interface.

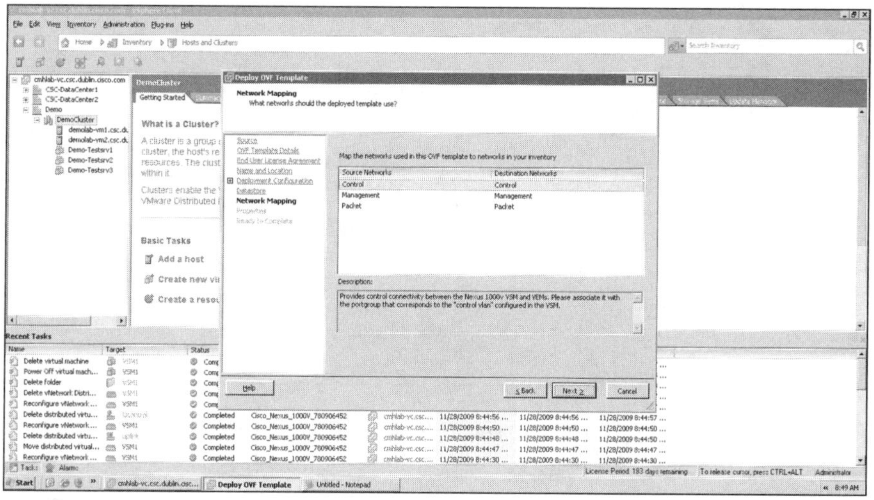

Figure 9-11   *Selecting the Network Mappings for the Control, System, and Management Interfaces*

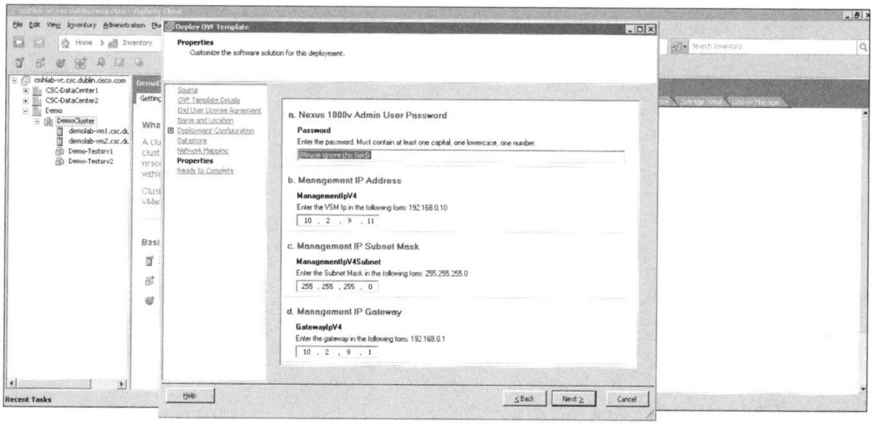

Figure 9-12   *Allowing the Creation of the IP Management Properties for the VSM MGMT0 Interface*

Step 11.   Verify deployment settings for the VSM, as shown in Figure 9-13; click **Finish** to accept or **Back** to modify settings.

The deployment progress window appears as shown in Figure 9-14.

VSM1 is now deployed in the host and clusters navigation window within the Demo data center where specified during installation, as shown in Figure 9-15.

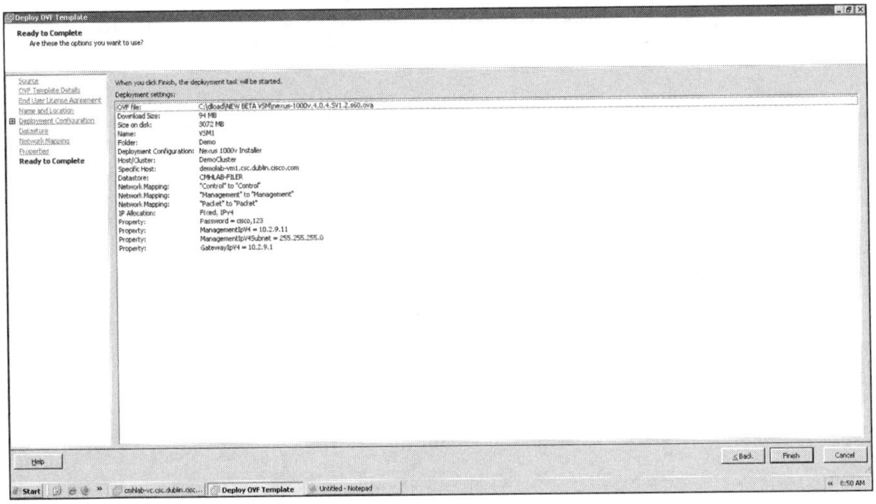

Figure 9-13 *Verifying the Deployment Settings for the VSM*

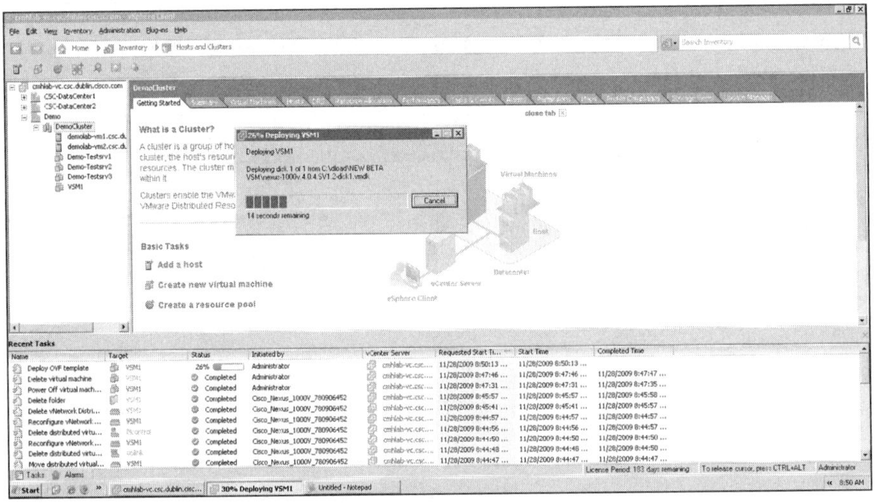

Figure 9-14 *VSM Deployment Progress*

Step 12. Power on the VSM1 Nexus 1000V VSM virtual machine, as shown in Figure 9-16.

Step 13. Open a Virtual Machine Console Windows to the VSM1 Nexus 1000V VSM virtual machine just powered on, as shown in Figure 9-17.

Step 14. The setup script will run. Enter the admin password, domain ID, and VSM role as shown in Figure 9-18. You will also have the option to select the high-availability mode for the VSM; recommend the role of the primary for the initial VSM installation.

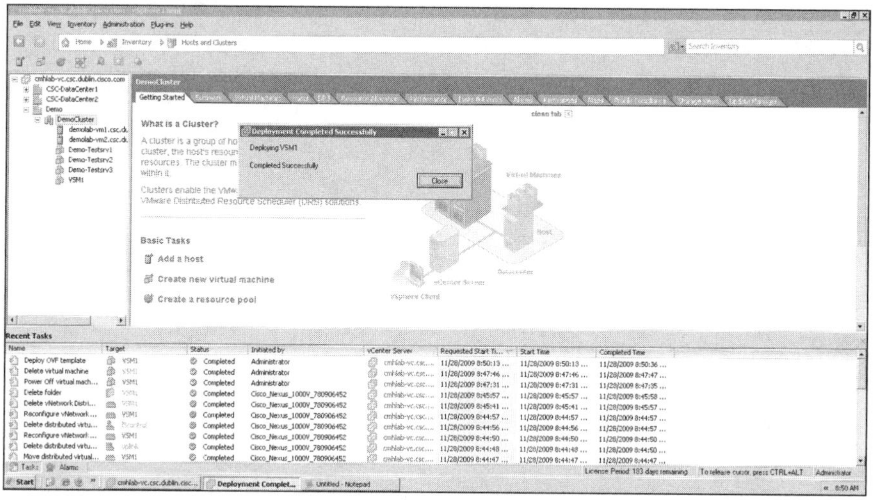

Figure 9-15 *VSM Deployment Completed Successfully*

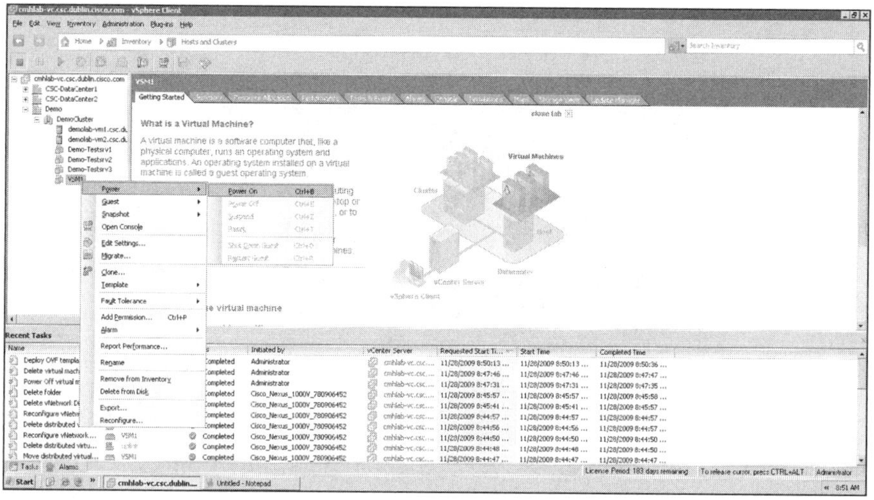

Figure 9-16 *Powering on VSM1 That Was Just Deployed*

Note You can initiate the setup script again by running the EXEC **setup** command.

Registering the Nexus 1000V Plug-in to VMware Virtual Center Management Application

The VSM maintains a communication link to VMware vCenter Server. The communication link is used to maintain definitions and propagate port profiles to VMware virtual center. The Cisco Nexus 1000V uses a VMware vCenter Server plug-in to properly

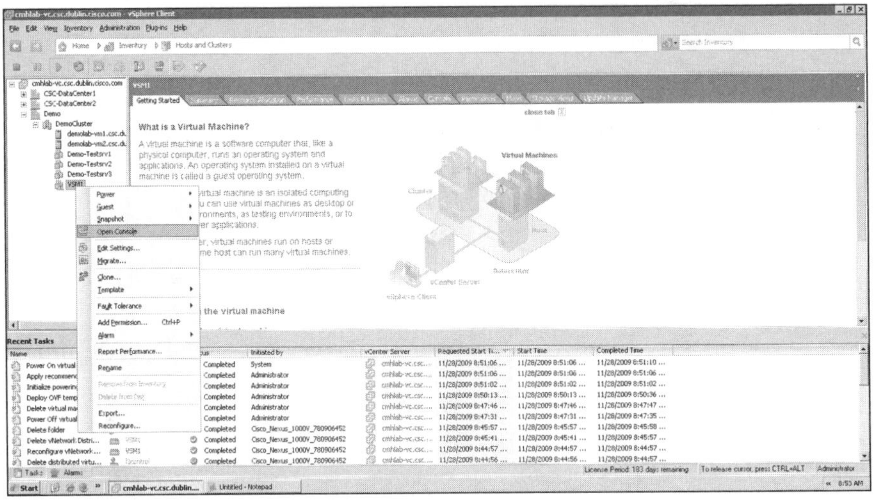

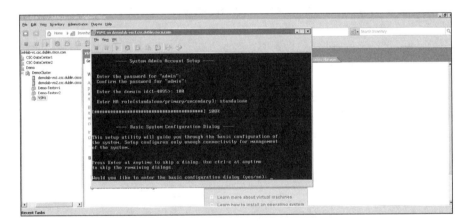

Figure 9-17   *Opening a Console Window to "VSM1"*

Figure 9-18   *Setup Script Runs: Enter the Admin Password, Domain ID, VSM Role*

display a representation of the Cisco Nexus 1000V. The Cisco Nexus 1000V plug-in is an XML file that is downloaded from the VSM's management IP address using a web browser; the XML plug-in must be installed before the VSM can communicate to VMware vCenter Server. A common question is, what if the connection between the VSM and VMware virtual center goes down? If the connection between the VSM and VMware vCenter Server is disrupted, changes made on the VSM will not be propagated to VMware Virtual Center; the VEM(s) will still continue to forward traffic on the dataplane. The VSM ensures that any configuration changes that have been made during this period of disruption; the changes will be propagated when the communication link is restored.

Step 1.   Obtain the IP address / DNS information of the Virtual Center Server. The
following example shows how to verify IP Address / DNS host information on
the VMWare vCenter server:

```
C:\Documents and Settings\Administrator>ipconfig
Windows IP Configuration


Ethernet adapter vCenter Server:

    Connection-specific DNS Suffix  . :
    IP Address. . . . . . . . . . . : 10.1.4.10
    Subnet Mask . . . . . . . . . . : 255.255.255.0
    Default Gateway . . . . . . . . : 10.1.4.1
```

Step 2.   Verify IP connectivity between the VMware virtual center management
station and the Cisco 1000V, as demonstrated in the following example:

```
VSM1# ping 10.1.4.10
PING 10.1.4.10 (10.1.4.10): 56 data bytes
64 bytes from 10.1.4.10: icmp_seq=0 ttl=124 time=1.201 ms
64 bytes from 10.1.4.10: icmp_seq=1 ttl=124 time=1.196 ms
64 bytes from 10.1.4.10: icmp_seq=2 ttl=124 time=0.914 ms
64 bytes from 10.1.4.10: icmp_seq=3 ttl=124 time=0.917 ms
64 bytes from 10.1.4.10: icmp_seq=4 ttl=124 time=0.958 ms


--- 10.1.4.10 ping statistics ---
5 packets transmitted, 5 packets received, 0.00% packet loss
round-trip min/avg/max = 0.914/1.037/1.201 ms
VSM1#
```

Step 3.   From the virtual center desktop, launch your web browser and point to the management interface of the Nexus 1000V VSM, as demonstrated in Figure 9-19.

Step 4.   Under the section, Cisco Nexus 1000V Extension, right mouse click and save
the file named *cisco_nexus_1000v_extension.xml* and save it to your desktop, as demonstrated in Figure 9-20.

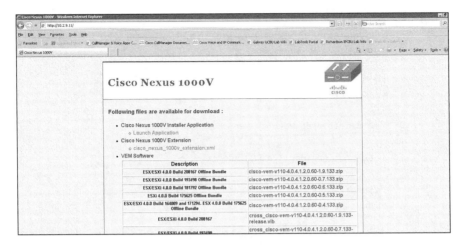

Figure 9-19   *Launching the Web Browser on the vCenter Server and Pointing to the mgmt0 Interface of the VSM*

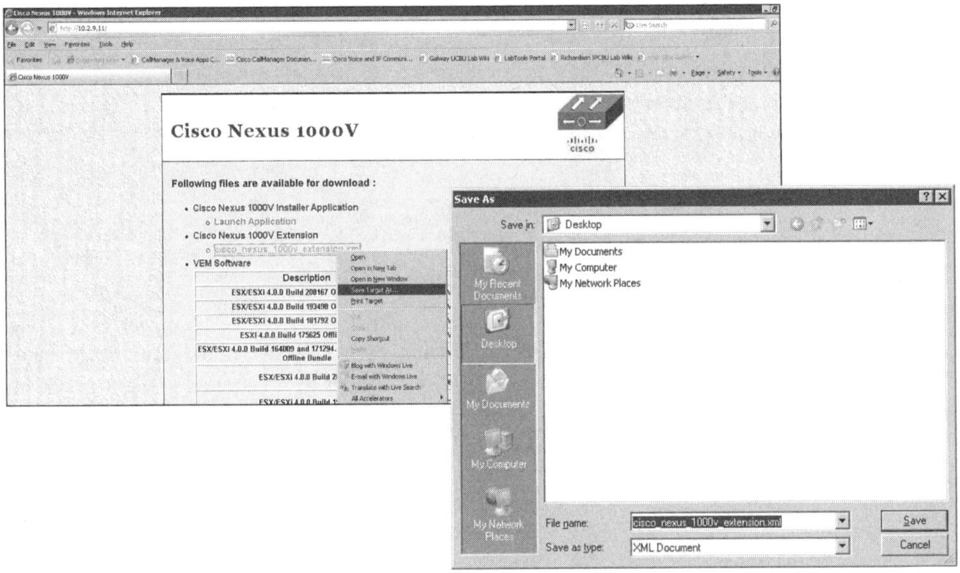

Figure 9-20   *Saving the cisco_nexus_1000v_extension.xml File from the VSM*

Step 5.   Go back to VMware Virtual Center management application and select **Plug-ins > Manage Plug-ins**, as shown in Figure 9-21.

Step 6.   Right-click under **Available Plug-ins** and select **New Plug-in**, as demonstrated in Figure 9-22.

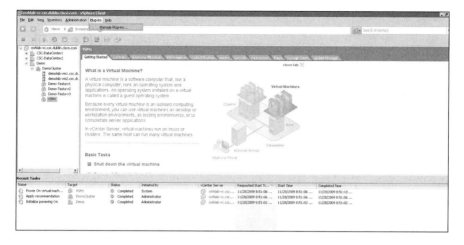

Figure 9-21 *Selecting the Plug-ins Menu Option from vCenter*

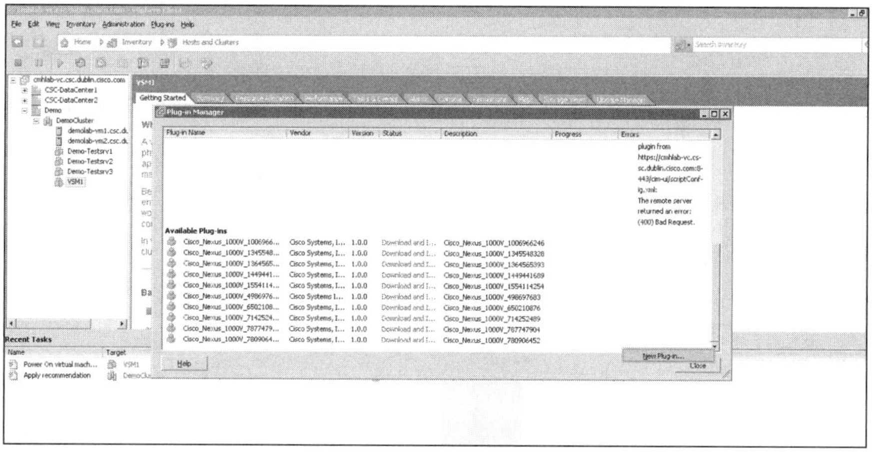

Figure 9-22 *Creating a New Managed Plug-in from vCenter*

Step 7. The Register Plug-in window appears. As shown in Figure 9-23, select the browse button and find the file downloaded in step 4, *cisco_nexus_1000v_extension.xml*.

Step 8. The Register Plug-in window appears. click on the **Register Plug-in** button, as shown in Figure 9-24.

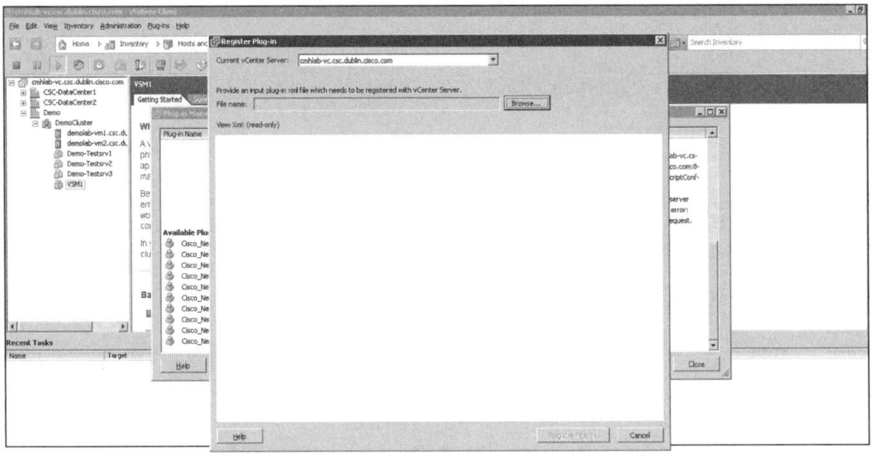

Figure 9-23 *Browsing for the cisco_nexus_1000v_extension.xml File That Was Downloaded to the Desktop in Step 4*

Figure 9-24 *Registering the Plug-in*

Step 9. The Security Warning dialog box appears, as there is a new SSL cert being installed. Click the **Ignore** button. Figure 9-25 shows the certificate security warning dialog box.

Step 10. You should receive a successful Register Plug-in window, as shown in Figure 9-26. Click **OK** to close this window.

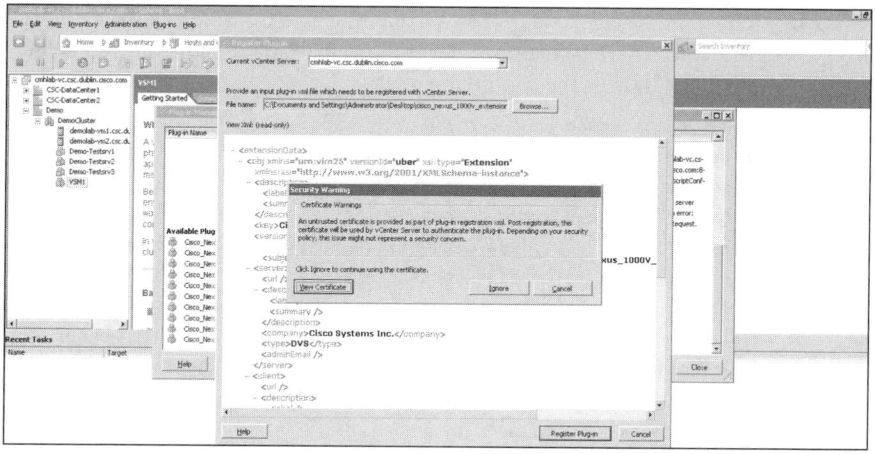

Figure 9-25 *Certificate Security Warning Dialog Box*

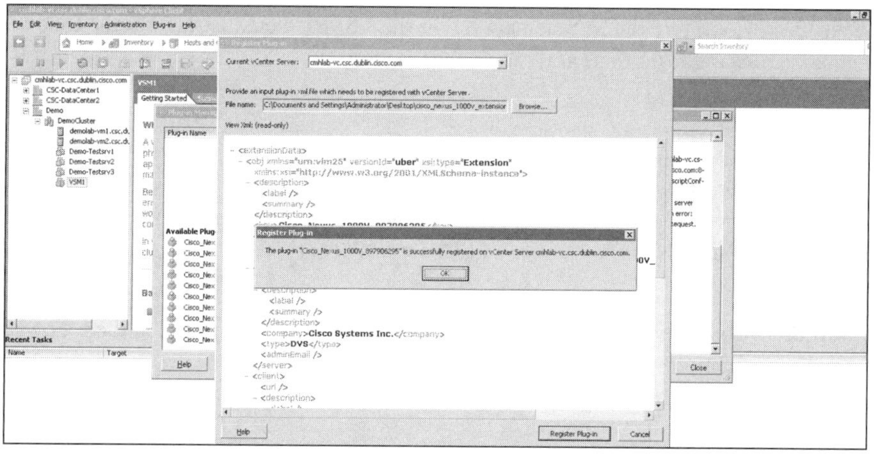

Figure 9-26 *Successful Register Plug-in Dialog Window*

Configuring the SVS Domain and Networking Characteristics

A domain ID is a parameter of the Cisco Nexus 1000V Series that is used to identify a VSM and VEM. The domain ID of the Cisco Nexus 1000V is defined when the VSM is first installed and becomes part of the opaque data that is transmitted to VMware vCenter Server. Each command sent by the VSM to any associated VEMs is tagged with this domain ID. When a VSM and VEM share the same domain ID, the VEM will accept and respond to requests and commands from the VSM. If the VEM receives a command or configuration request that is not tagged with the proper domain ID, that request is ignored. Similarly, if the VSM receives a packet from a VEM that is tagged with the wrong domain ID, it will be ignored.

Step 1.   Open the Nexus 1000V VSM Virtual Machine Console window or Telnet to the VSM MGMT0 Interface. The following example shows how to Telnet to the IP address of the mgmt0 interface:

```
VSM1 login: admin
Password:
Cisco Nexus Operating System (NX-OS) Software
TAC support: http://www.cisco.com/tac
Copyright (c) 2002-2009, Cisco Systems, Inc. All rights reserved.
The copyrights to certain works contained in this software are
owned by other third parties and used and distributed under
license. Certain components of this software are licensed under
the GNU General Public License (GPL) version 2.0 or the GNU
Lesser General Public License (LGPL) Version 2.1. A copy of each
such license is available at
http://www.opensource.org/licenses/gpl-2.0.php and
http://www.opensource.org/licenses/lgpl-2.1.php
VSM1#
```

Step 2.   Configure the SVS domain ID on the VSM as demonstrated in the following example (in this case, the domain ID is 100):

```
VSM1# conf t
VSM1(config)# svs-domain
VSM1(config-svs-domain)#  domain id 100
VSM1(config)# exit
VSM1# copy running-config startup-config
[#####################################] 100%
VSM1#
```

Step 3.   Configure the Control and Packet vLANS as demonstrated in the following example:

```
VSM1# conf t
VSM1(config)# svs-domain
VSM1(config-svs-domain)#  control vlan 700
VSM1(config-svs-domain)#  packet vlan 701
VSM1(config-svs-domain)#  svs mode L2
VSM1(config-svs-domain)# exit
VSM1(config)# exit
VSM1# copy running-config startup-config
[#####################################] 100%
VSM1#
```

Connecting the Nexus 1000V VSM to the vCenter Server

After the plug-in is installed, the network administrator can define the SVS connection. The SVS connection defines the link between the VSM and VMware vCenter Server. The connection contains the following parameters:

- VMware vCenter Server IP address

- Communication protocol (always VMware VIM over HTTPS)

- Name of the VMware data center in which the VMware ESX hosts reside

The Nexus 1000V Plug-in must be registered before you connect it to the vCenter server.

Step 1.   Open the Nexus 1000V VSM Virtual Machine Console window or Telnet to the VSM mgmt0 interface, as demonstrated in the following example:

```
VSM1 login: admin
Password:
Cisco Nexus Operating System (NX-OS) Software
TAC support: http://www.cisco.com/tac
Copyright (c) 2002-2009, Cisco Systems, Inc. All rights reserved.
The copyrights to certain works contained in this software are
owned by other third parties and used and distributed under
license. Certain components of this software are licensed under
the GNU General Public License (GPL) version 2.0 or the GNU
Lesser General Public License (LGPL) Version 2.1. A copy of each
such license is available at
http://www.opensource.org/licenses/gpl-2.0.php and
http://www.opensource.org/licenses/lgpl-2.1.php
VSM1#
```

Step 2.   Configure the connection on the Nexus 1000V VSM. The following example shows how to Telnet to the IP address of mgmt0 interface:

```
VSM1# conf t
VSM1(config)# svs connection vcenter
VSM1(config-svs-conn)# protocol vmware-vim
VSM1(config-svs-conn)# vmware dvs datacenter-name Demo
VSM1(config-svs-conn)# remote ip address 10.1.4.10
VSM1(config-svs-conn)# connect
VSM1(config-svs-conn)# exit
VSM1(config)# exit
VSM1# copy running-config startup-config
[#####################################] 100%
VSM1#
```

Step 3.   After issuing the **connect** command, verify output on the vCenter server as demonstrated in the following example:

```
VSM1# show svs connections vcenter
connection vcenter:
  ip address: 10.1.4.10
  remote port: 80
  protocol: VMware-vim https
  certificate: default
```

```
            datacenter name: Demo
            DVS uuid: 14 8a 06 50 08 62 41 c2-b8 7d 46 56 1a 62 93 b4
            config status: Enabled
            operational status: Connected
            sync status: Complete
            version: VMware vCenter Server 4.0.0 build-162856
        VSM1#
```

Step 4.   Create VLANs on the VSM as demonstrated in the following example:

```
        VSM1# conf t
        VSM1-VSM(config)# vlan 700
        VSM1-VSM(config-vlan)# name Control
        VSM1-VSM(config-vlan)# exit
        VSM1-VSM(config)# vlan 701
        VSM1-VSM(config-vlan)# name Packet
        VSM1-VSM(config-vlan)# exit
        VSM1-VSM(config)# vlan 699
        VSM1-VSM(config-vlan)# name Management
        VSM1-VSM(config-vlan)# exit
        VSM1-VSM(config)# vlan 702
        VSM1-VSM(config-vlan)# name ERSPAN-NAS-vMotion
        VSM1-VSM(config-vlan)# exit
        VSM1-VSM(config)# vlan 100
        VSM1-VSM(config-vlan)# name ClientServer
        VSM1-VSM(config-vlan)# exit
        VSM1-VSM(config)# exit
        VSM1# copy running-config startup-config
        [#####################################] 100%
        VSM1#
```

Step 5.   Verify the VLAN configuration as demonstrated in the following example:

```
        VSM1# show vlan

        VLAN Name                             Status    Ports
        ---- -------------------------------- --------- ------------------------

        1    default                          active
        100  ClientServer                     active
        699  Management                       active
        700  Control                          active
        701  Packet                           active
        702  ERSPAN-NAS-vMotion               active


        VLAN Type
```

```
---- -----
1    enet
100  enet
699  enet
700  enet
701  enet
702  enet


Remote SPAN VLANs
---------------------------------------------------------------------------


Primary  Secondary  Type              Ports
-------  ---------  ----------------  --------------------------------

VSM1#
```

Nexus 1000V GUI Installation

Nexus 1000V software release 4.0(4)SV1(2) adds a GUI to reduce the installation and configuration time. The GUI installer provides initial configuration for the following operations:

■   Creating the SVS connection between the VSM and vCenter

■   Creating VMware port groups for Control, Packet, and Management

■   Creating the Control, Packet, and Management VLANs

■   Enabling SSH and configuring the SSH connection

■   Enabling the option to Telnet on the VSM

■   Creating a Cisco Nexus 1000V plug-in and registering it on the vCenter server

During the Nexus 1000V OVF/OVA deployment, select **Nexus 1000V Installer**; all other steps are the same as described in the Manual installation process.

Note   The GUI installer requires a minimum of JRE 1.5, here is the link used to download JRE 6u17:

http://java.sun.com/javase/downloads/index.jsp#jre

Figure 9-27 shows how to download the Java Network Launching Protocol (jnlp) file from the VSM and start the installer.

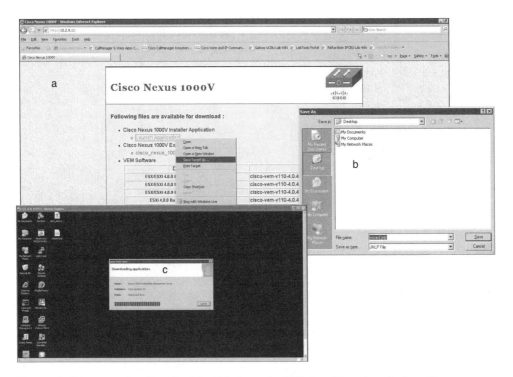

Figure 9-27   *Downloading the jnlp File from the VSM and Starting the Installer*

After the application download completes, the Nexus 1000V Installer window appears to enter the VSM IP address, username, and password, as shown in Figure 9-28.

Figure 9-29 shows how to enter the vCenter IP address, vCenter user ID, and password.

Figure 9-30 shows how to select the VSM's host to install the VSM.

Figure 9-31 shows how to select VSM's VM and port-group configuration.

Figure 9-32 shows how to enter the VSM configuration options.

Figure 9-33 shows the verification of the configuration summary to be deployed.

Figure 9-34 shows the 1000V Install installation status.

Figure 9-35 show the VSM installation completion as well as the svs-connection to vCenter "connected" status.

The Nexus 1000V GUI installation significantly reduces the installation time. The GUI does not cover all features such as High Availability and Layer 3 Control configuration; future releases will incorporate these enhancements.

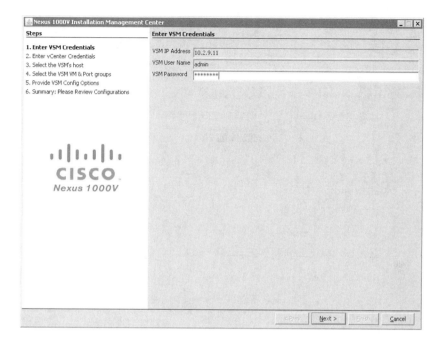

Figure 9-28 *Nexus 1000V Installer Window to Enter the VSM IP Address, Username, and Password*

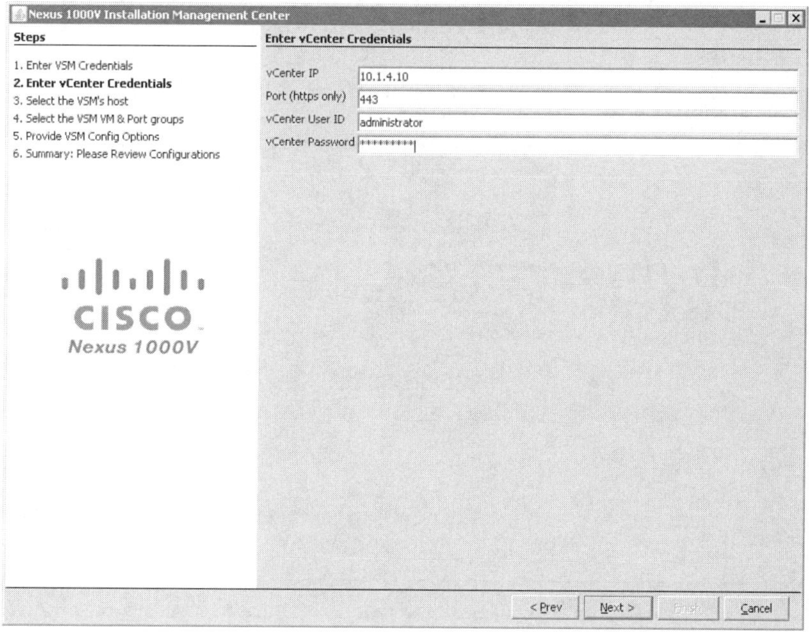

Figure 9-29 *Entering the vCenter IP Address, vCenter User ID, and Password*

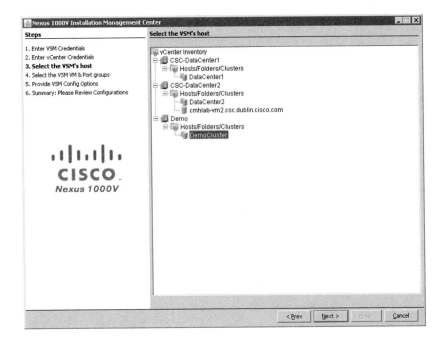

Figure 9-30   *Selecting the VSM's Host to Install the VSM*

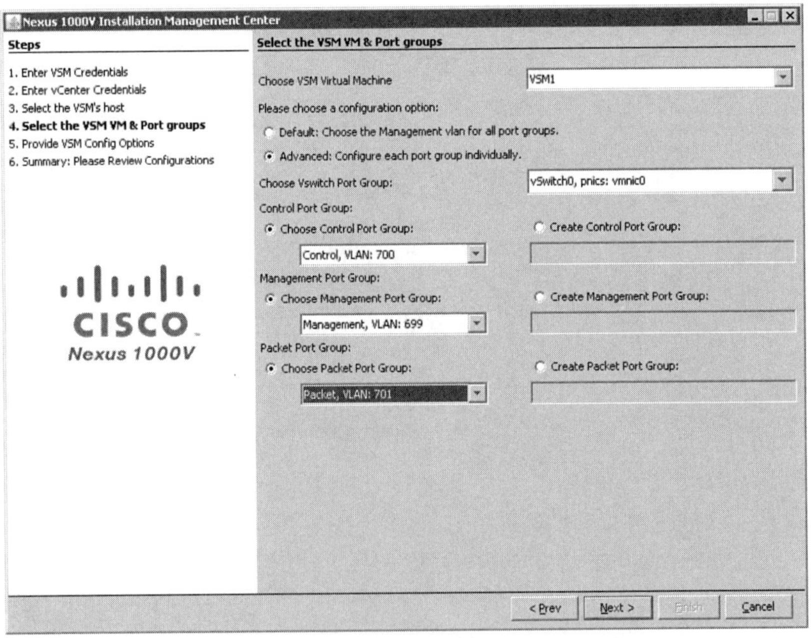

Figure 9-31   *Selecting VSM's VM and Port-Group Configuration*

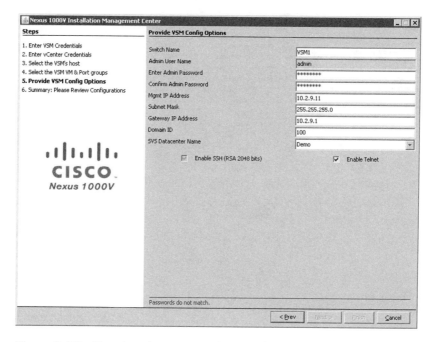

Figure 9-32   *Entering the VSM Configuration Options*

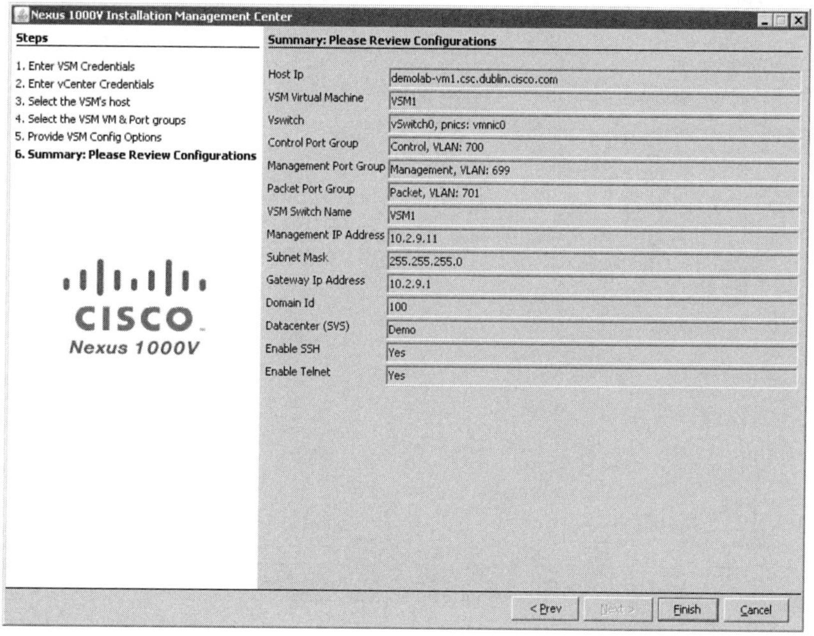

Figure 9-33   *Verifying the Configuration Summary to Be Deployed*

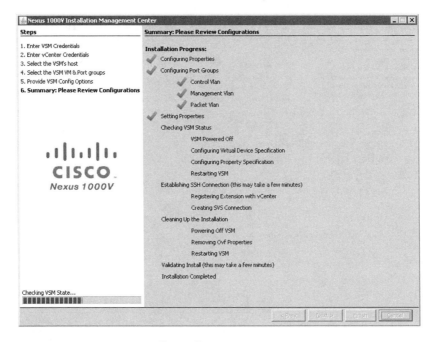

Figure 9-34   *1000V Install Installation Status*

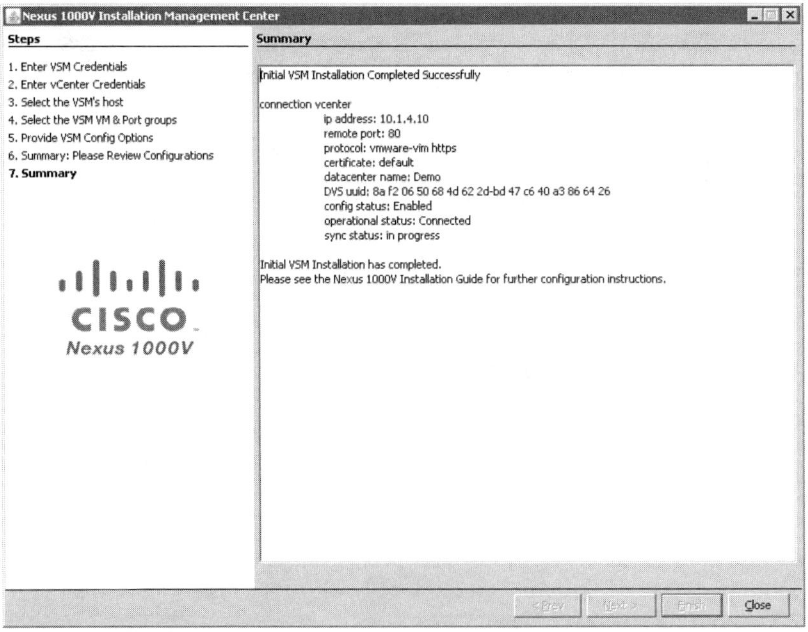

Figure 9-35   *VSM Installation Completion as Well as the svs-connection to vCenter "connected" Status*

Creating the Uplink Profile

With VMWare vSphere 4.0, VMWare introduced the vNetwork Distributed Switch (DVS) Feature, the Cisco VEM plugs directly into the VMWare DVS. The DVS functionality spans many ESX/ESXi hosts. The DVS reduces network maintenance, increases network capacity, and allows virtual machines to maintain consistent network configuration. Before you can add a host to the DVS on vCenter Server, you must first create an uplink port-profile; this will allow for a Virtual Ethernet Module (VEM) to be added to the VSM. Example 9-1 shows the Layer 2 communication mode between the VSM and the VEM(s) via the Control and Packet VLANs.

Note   You can find a feature comparison of the Virtual Networking features of the VMware vNetwork Distributed Switch and Cisco Nexus 1000V Switches at the following URL: https://www.myciscocommunity.com/docs/DOC-8666.

Example 9-1   *Verifying Control and Packet System VLANs, Which Are Used for VEM to VSM Communication*

```
VSM1# show vlan

VLAN Name                            Status    Ports
---- -------------------------------- --------- -------------------------------

1    default                         active
100  ClientServer                    active
699  Management                      active
700  Control                         active
701  Packet                          active
702  ERSPAN-NAS-vMotion              active
```

Example 9-2 shows how to create the uplink profile on the Nexus 1000V VSM, the port-profile will be named "uplink" in this example.

Example 9-2   *Creating the Uplink Profile on the Nexus 1000V VSM*

```
VSM1# conf t
VSM1(config)#
VSM1(config)# port-profile uplink
VSM1(config-port-prof)# capability uplink
VSM1(config-port-prof)# switchport mode trunk
VSM1(config-port-prof)# switchport trunk allowed vlan 100, 699, 700, 701, 702
VSM1(config-port-prof)# no shutdown
VSM1(config-port-prof)# system vlan 700, 701
VSM1(config-port-prof)# VMware port-group
VSM1(config-port-prof)# state enabled
```

The output in Example 9-3 verifies the port-profile "uplink" configuration.

Example 9-3 *Verifying Port-Profile "Uplink" Configuration*

```
VSM1(config-port-prof)# show port-profile name uplink
port-profile uplink
  description:
  type: ethernet
  status: enabled
  capability l3control: no
  pinning control-vlan: -
  pinning packet-vlan: -
  system vlans: 700-701
  port-group: uplink
  max ports: -
  inherit:
  config attributes:
    switchport mode trunk
    switchport trunk allowed vlan 100,699-702
    no shutdown
  evaluated config attributes:
    switchport mode trunk
    switchport trunk allowed vlan 100,699-702
    no shutdown
  assigned interfaces:
VSM1(config-port-prof)# exit
VSM1(config)# exit
VSM1# copy running-config startup-config
[#######################################] 100%
VSM1#
```

Note In the previous example, if the optional **VMware port-group uplink** *name* command was used in the port-profile configuration, the *name* parameter would specify the name that is displayed in the vCenter Server. If the command is not used, the port-profile name will be used.

Figure 9-36 verifies that the port-profile **uplink** is in vCenter by selecting **Networking** from the navigation window.

Adding the VEM to a ESX vSphere 4 Host

The VEM provides the Cisco Nexus 1000V Series with network connectivity and forwarding capabilities and each VEM acts as an independent switch from a forwarding perspective. The VEM is tightly integrated with VMware ESX and is installed on each

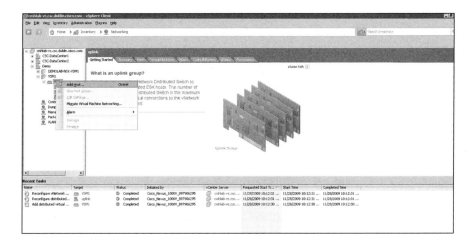

Figure 9-36 *port-profile Uplink Is in vCenter*

VMware ESX host as a kernel component. Each instance of the Cisco Nexus 1000V
Series is composed of two VSMs and one or more VEMs. The maximum number of
VEMs supported by a pair of VSMs is 64.

Note   VMware update manager was installed prior to this configure, the manual VEM
installation will not be shown.

Step 1.   Right mouse click on the vNetwork Distributed Switch named **VSM1** and
select **Add Host**. Figure 9-37 shows how to start the process of adding a
VEM to the ESX host in Virtual Center.

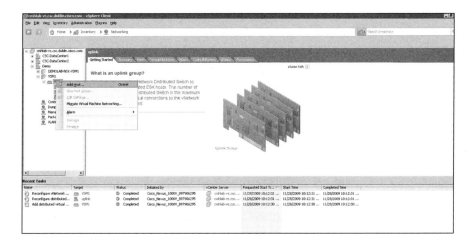

Figure 9-37 *Starting the Process of Adding a VEM to the ESX Host in Virtual
Center*

Step 2.   Select the ESX host and the physical network adapters; make sure you have **uplink** profile selected in the DVUplink port group column, as shown in Figure 9-38.

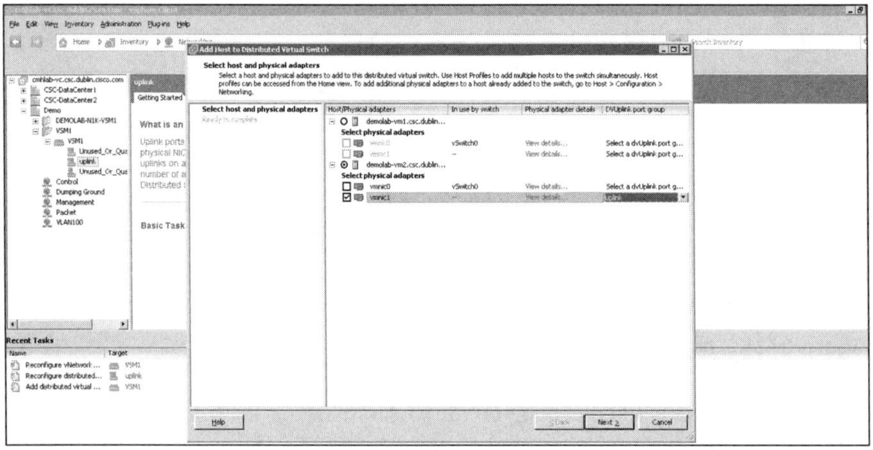

Figure 9-38   *Selecting the ESX Host and the Physical Network Adapters*

Step 3.   Verify the settings for the new VEM to be installed and click the **Finish** button as demonstrated in Figure 9-39.

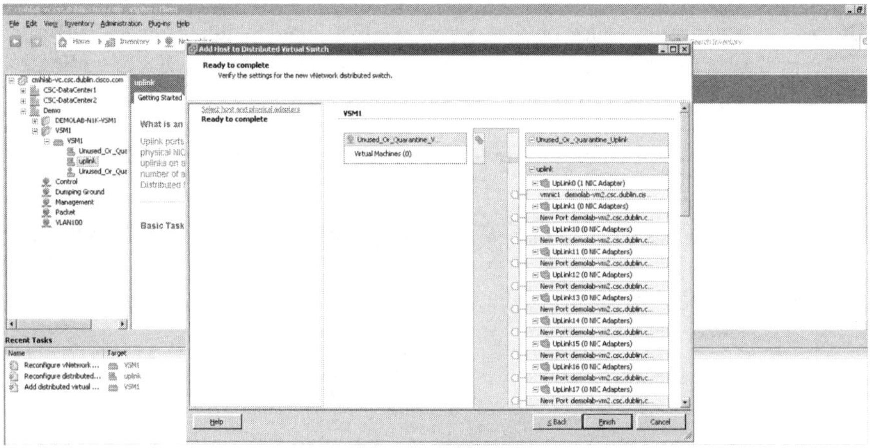

Figure 9-39   *Verifying the Settings for the New VEM to Be Installed*

Step 4.   Verify that the ESX host was added to the Hosts tab of VSM1 as shown in Figure 9-40.

Step 5.   Verify the VEM was added to the VSM, **VSM1**. The following example shows the VEM being powered up on VSM1:

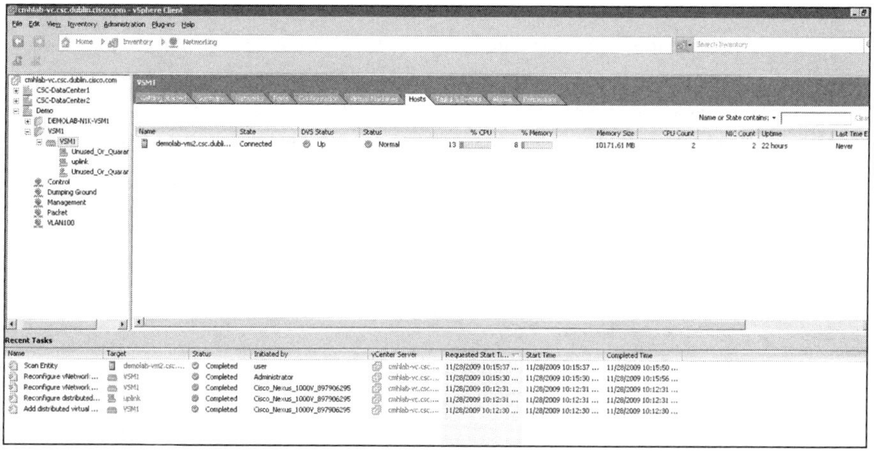

Figure 9-40 *Verifying That the ESX Host Was Added to the "Hosts" Tab of VSM1*

```
VSM1# 2009 Nov 28 15:14:54 VSM1 %PLATFORM-2-MOD_PWRUP: Module 3 powered
up (Serial number)


VSM1# show module
Mod  Ports  Module-Type                         Model              Status
---  -----  --------------------------------    -----------------  -------
-----
1    0      Virtual Supervisor Module           Nexus1000V         active
*
3    248    Virtual Ethernet Module             NA                 ok


Mod  Sw               Hw
---  --------------   ------
1    4.0(4)SV1(2)     0.0
3    4.0(4)SV1(2)     0.4


Mod  MAC-Address(es)                          Serial-Num
---  --------------------------------------   ----------
1    00-19-07-6c-5a-a8 to 00-19-07-6c-62-a8   NA
3    02-00-0c-00-03-00 to 02-00-0c-00-03-80   NA


Mod  Server-IP        Server-UUID                          Server-Name
---  --------------   ------------------------------------ ------------
--------
1    10.2.9.11        NA                                   NA
3    10.2.12.70       34313937-3536-5553-4537-30324e305331 demolab-vm2


* this terminal session
```

```
VSM1#
The following output shows the full running-config on VSM1:
VSM1# show running-config
version 4.0(4)SV1(2)
username admin password 5 $1$zOAxtvcu$EvFPLY4rt.21MlKR0PBfd0  role
network-admin
telnet server enable
ssh key rsa 2048
ip domain-lookup
ip host VSM1 10.2.9.11
kernel core target 0.0.0.0
kernel core limit 1
system default switchport
vem 3
  host VMware id 34313937-3536-5553-4537-30324e305331
vem 4
  host VMware id 8fd290ce-4ed2-3ea5-a3df-f35c3e85ab27
snmp-server user admin network-admin auth md5
0xa0ec81a6f2a7638882d8ec88574043ec
  priv 0xa0ec81a6f2a7638882d8ec88574043ec localizedkey
snmp-server enable traps license
vrf context management
  ip route 0.0.0.0/0 10.2.9.1
hostname VSM1
vlan 1
vlan 100
  name ClientServer
vlan 699
  name Mgmt
vlan 700
  name Control
vlan 701
  name Packet
vlan 702
  name NASvMotion
vdc VSM1 id 1
  limit-resource vlan minimum 16 maximum 513
  limit-resource monitor-session minimum 0 maximum 64
  limit-resource vrf minimum 16 maximum 8192
  limit-resource port-channel minimum 0 maximum 256
  limit-resource u4route-mem minimum 32 maximum 80
  limit-resource u6route-mem minimum 16 maximum 48
port-profile type ethernet Unused_Or_Quarantine_Uplink
  description Port-group created for Nexus1000V internal usage. Do not
use.
  VMware port-group
```

```
    shutdown
    state enabled
port-profile type vethernet Unused_Or_Quarantine_Veth
    description Port-group created for Nexus1000V internal usage. Do not
use.
    VMware port-group
    shutdown
    state enabled
port-profile type ethernet uplink
    VMware port-group
    switchport mode trunk
    switchport trunk allowed vlan 100,699-702
    no shutdown
    system vlan 700-701
    state enabled

interface Ethernet3/2
    inherit port-profile uplink

interface Ethernet4/2
    inherit port-profile uplink

interface mgmt0
    ip address 10.2.9.11/24

interface control0
boot kickstart bootflash:/nexus-1000v-kickstart-mz.4.0.4.SV1.2.bin sup-
1
boot system bootflash:/nexus-1000v-mz.4.0.4.SV1.2.bin sup-1
boot kickstart bootflash:/nexus-1000v-kickstart-mz.4.0.4.SV1.2.bin sup-
2
boot system bootflash:/nexus-1000v-mz.4.0.4.SV1.2.bin sup-2
svs-domain
    domain id 100
    control vlan 700
    packet vlan 701
    svs mode L2
svs connection vcenter
    protocol VMware-vim
    remote ip address 10.1.4.10 port 80
    VMware dvs uuid "8a f2 06 50 68 4d 62 2d-bd 47 c6 40 a3 86 64 26"
datacenter-n
ame Demo
    connect

VSM1# show module
Mod  Ports  Module-Type                          Model            Status
```

```
---  -----  ------------------------------------  ------------------  -------
-----
1    0      Virtual Supervisor Module             Nexus1000V          active
*
3    248    Virtual Ethernet Module               NA                  ok
4    248    Virtual Ethernet Module               NA                  ok


Mod  Sw               Hw
---  ---------------  ------
1    4.0(4)SV1(2)     0.0
3    4.0(4)SV1(2)     0.4
4    4.0(4)SV1(2)     0.4


Mod  MAC-Address(es)                           Serial-Num
---  ---------------------------------------   ----------
1    00-19-07-6c-5a-a8 to 00-19-07-6c-62-a8    NA
3    02-00-0c-00-03-00 to 02-00-0c-00-03-80    NA
4    02-00-0c-00-04-00 to 02-00-0c-00-04-80    NA


Mod  Server-IP        Server-UUID                              Server-Name
---  ---------------  ------------------------------------     ------------
1    10.2.9.11        NA                                       NA
3    10.2.12.70       34313937-3536-5553-4537-30324e305331     demolab-
vm2.csc.dubl
in.cisco.com
4    10.2.12.60       8fd290ce-4ed2-3ea5-a3df-f35c3e85ab27     demolab-
vm1.csc.dubl
in.cisco.com


* this terminal session
VSM1#
```

Example 9-4 shows how to install the Nexus 1000V license. A Cisco Nexus 1000V license is required for each server CPU in your system.

Example 9-4 *Installing the Nexus 1000V License*

```
VSM1# copy tftp://10.1.4.10/N1KVFEAT20091108140613428.lic bootflash:
Enter vrf (If no input, current vrf 'default' is considered): management
Trying to connect to tftp server......
Connection to Server Established.
|
TFTP get operation was successful
VSM1# conf t
VSM1-VSM(config)# exit
```

```
VSM1# install license bootflash:N1KVFEAT20091108140613428.lic
Installing license .....done
VSM1# show license
N1KVFEAT20091108140613428.lic:
SERVER this_host ANY
VENDOR cisco
INCREMENT NEXUS1000V_LAN_SERVICES_PKG cisco 1.0 permanent 2 \
        HOSTID=VDH=4459104771250635013 \
        NOTICE="<LicFileID>20091108140613428</LicFileID><LicLineID>1</LicLineID> \
        <PAK>FXPAK2485D0</PAK>" SIGN=BD161668DEB2

VSM1# dir bootflash:
        146     Nov 08 20:11:21 2009   .ovfconfigured
        253     Nov 08 22:09:38 2009   N1KVFEAT20091108140613428.lic
      77824     Nov 08 20:10:58 2009   accounting.log
      16384     Aug 18 22:34:51 2009   lost+found/
    1335170     Aug 18 22:35:40 2009   nexus-1000v-dplug-mzg.4.0.4.SV1.2.bin
   21732352     Aug 18 22:35:42 2009   nexus-1000v-kickstart-mzg.4.0.4.SV1.2.bin
   73375005     Aug 18 22:35:53 2009   nexus-1000v-mzg.4.0.4.SV1.2.bin

Usage for bootflash://sup-local
  211210240 bytes used
 1383665664 bytes free
 1594875904 bytes total
VSM1#
```

Note There is a 60-day evaluation license part of the OVF VSM installation, this can be verified with the following command:

```
VSM1# show mod vem internal license-info
License Sync Initiator      : VEM 3
License Sync Stages         : Complete
Num of Def Licenses in Use : 0
Num of Sync participants    : 2
License Host-ID             : 3730446821259416248
Eval time remaining         : 47 days
Installed lic count         : 0
-------------------VEM License Info ---------------------
Vem     Current License Operation      License Status  License Flags
---     -------------------------      --------------  ------------
  3                       None            licensed  None
  4                       None            licensed  None
```

```
----------------VEM Socket License Info ------------------
Vem     Sync     License Usage     Sockets License Version
---     ----     -------------     ------- ---------------
 3      Yes            2              2           1.0
 4      Yes            1              1           1.0
```

Enabling the Telnet Server Process

Example 9-5 shows how to enable Telnet server, which is disabled by default.

Example 9-5   *Enabling Telnet Server*

```
switch# conf t
switch(config)# telnet server enable
switch(config)# exit
switch# show telnet server
telnet service enabled
switch#
```

Changing the VSM Hostname

Example 9-6 shows how to change the Nexus 1000V VSM hostname.

Example 9-6   *Changing the Nexus 1000V VSM Hostname*

```
Change Nexus 1000V Hostname
switch# conf t
switch(config)# hostname Nexus1000V-VSM1
Nexus1000V-VSM1(config)# exit
Nexus1000V-VSM1#
```

Layer 3 Control

The Nexus 1000V software release 4.0(4)SV1(2) adds the capability for Layer 3 Control between the VEM(s) and VSM; Layer 3 Control no longers the Control and Packet VLANs. Layer 3 Control capability offers the following capabilities and requirements:

■   The transport mode for the VSM domain can be configured for Layer 3.

■   The VEM VM kernel NIC must connect to this Layer 3 control port profile when adding the host to the Cisco Nexus 1000V DVS.

- Only one VM kernel NIC can be assigned to this Layer 3 Control port profile per host.

- The VLAN assigned to this Layer 3 Control port profile must be a system VLAN.

- The port profile must be an access port profile; it cannot be a trunk port profile.

- Different hosts can use different VLANs for Layer 3 Control.

Figure 9-41 shows the Cisco Nexus 1000V Series Architecture for L3 Control

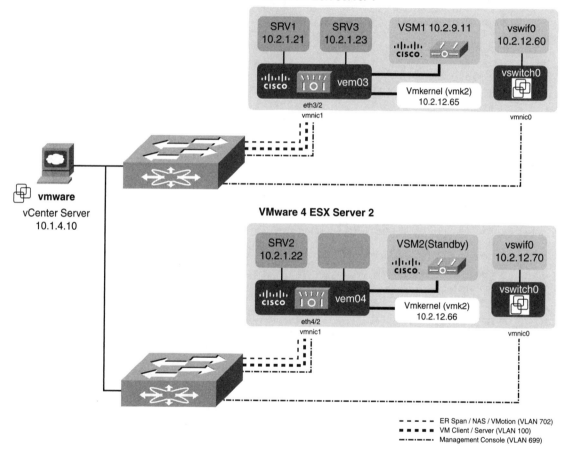

Figure 9-41   *Cisco Nexus 1000V Series Architecture for L3 Control*

Example 9-7 shows how to create a port-profile for Layer 3 Control mode.

Example 9-7   *Create a Port-Profile for L3 Control Mode*

```
VSM1(config)# port-profile type vethernet l3control
VSM1(config-port-prof)#    capability l3control
```

```
VSM1(config-port-prof)#   VMware port-group
VSM1(config-port-prof)#   switchport mode access
VSM1(config-port-prof)#   switchport access vlan 702
VSM1(config-port-prof)#   no shutdown
VSM1(config-port-prof)#   system vlan 702
VSM1(config-port-prof)#   state enabled
```

Example 9-8 shows how to verify the Layer 3 Control port-profile.

Example 9-8 *Verifying the Layer 3 Control Port-Profile*

```
VSM1(config-port-prof)# show port-profile name l3control
port-profile l3control
  description:
  type: vethernet
  status: enabled
  capability l3control: yes
  pinning control-vlan: -
  pinning packet-vlan: -
  system vlans: 702
  port-group: l3control
  max ports: 32
  inherit:
  config attributes:
    switchport mode access
    switchport access vlan 702
    no shutdown
  evaluated config attributes:
    switchport mode access
    switchport access vlan 702
    no shutdown
  assigned interfaces:
VSM1(config-port-prof)#
```

Example 9-9 shows how to enable SVS Layer 3 mode feature level.

Example 9-9 *Enabling SVS L3 Mode Feature Level*

```
VSM1(config)# system update vem feature level 1
old feature level: 4.0(4)SV1(1) new feature level: 4.0(4)SV1(2)
VSM1(config)#
```

Example 9-10 shows how to nullify the Control and Packet VLANs, which will show both Control and Packet VLANs as 1; this is OK.

Example 9-10   *Nullifying the Control and Packet VLANs*

```
VSM1(config-svs-domain)# no packet vlan
VSM1(config-svs-domain)# no control vlan
```

Example 9-11 shows how to change SVS mode from Layer 2 to Layer 3 and specify the Layer 3 Management interface of mgmt0. The Control0 interface could be used as well.

Example 9-11   *Changing SVS Mode from Layer 2 to Layer 3 and Specifying the Layer 3 Management Interface of mgmt0*

```
VSM1(config-svs-domain)# svs mode l3 interface mgmt0
```

Example 9-12 shows how to change the system VLAN on the uplink profile.

Example 9-12   *Changing the System VLAN on the Uplink Profile*

```
VSM1# conf t
VSM1(config)# port-profile uplink
VSM1(config-port-prof)# system vlan 702
```

Example 9-13 shows how to verify the L3 Control configuration.

Example 9-13   *Verifying the Layer 3 Control Configuration*

```
VSM1# show svs domain
SVS domain config:
  Domain id:    100
  Control vlan: 1
  Packet vlan:  1
  L2/L3 Control mode: L3
  L3 control interface: mgmt0
  Status: Config push to VC successful.
VSM1#
```

Figure 9-42 shows (sequentially in windows a through h) how to add a vmkernel interface to vNetwork Distributed Switch. The vmkernel interface will have an IP address on it for the Layer 3 Control.

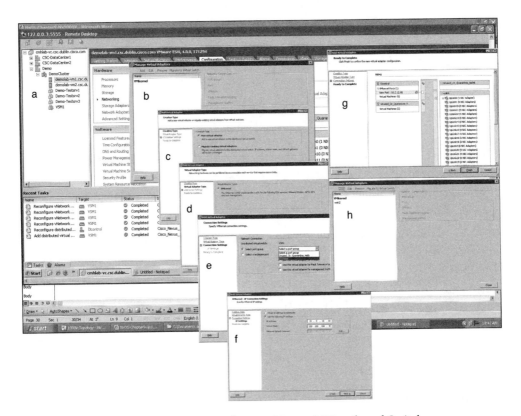

Figure 9-42 *Adding a vmkernel Interface to vNetwork Distributed Switch*

Example 9-14 shows the running configuration for the Layer 3 Control configuration.

Example 9-14 *Running-Configuration for the Layer 3 Control Configuration*

```
VSM1# show running-config
version 4.0(4)SV1(2)
username admin password 5 $1$zOAxtvcu$EvFPLY4rt.21MlKR0PBfd0   role network-admin
telnet server enable
ssh key rsa 2048
ip domain-lookup
ip host VSM1 10.2.9.11
kernel core target 0.0.0.0
kernel core limit 1
system default switchport
vem 3
  host VMware id 34313937-3536-5553-4537-30324e305331
vem 4
  host VMware id 8fd290ce-4ed2-3ea5-a3df-f35c3e85ab27
snmp-server user admin network-admin auth md5 0xa0ec81a6f2a7638882d8ec88574043ec
```

```
  priv 0xa0ec81a6f2a7638882d8ec88574043ec localizedkey
snmp-server enable traps license
vrf context management
  ip route 0.0.0.0/0 10.2.9.1
hostname VSM1
vlan 1
vlan 100
  name ClientServer
vlan 699
  name Mgmt
vlan 700
  name Control
vlan 701
  name Packet
vlan 702
  name NASvMotion
vdc VSM1 id 1
  limit-resource vlan minimum 16 maximum 513
  limit-resource monitor-session minimum 0 maximum 64
  limit-resource vrf minimum 16 maximum 8192
  limit-resource port-channel minimum 0 maximum 256
  limit-resource u4route-mem minimum 32 maximum 80
  limit-resource u6route-mem minimum 16 maximum 48
port-profile type ethernet Unused_Or_Quarantine_Uplink
  description Port-group created for Nexus1000V internal usage. Do not use.
  VMware port-group
  shutdown
  state enabled
port-profile type vethernet Unused_Or_Quarantine_Veth
  description Port-group created for Nexus1000V internal usage. Do not use.
  VMware port-group
  shutdown
  state enabled
port-profile type vethernet l3control
  capability l3control
  VMware port-group
  switchport mode access
  switchport access vlan 702
  no shutdown
  system vlan 702
  state enabled
port-profile type ethernet uplink
  VMware port-group
  switchport mode trunk
```

```
  switchport trunk allowed vlan 100,699-702
  no shutdown
  system vlan 702
  state enabled

interface Ethernet3/2
  inherit port-profile uplink

interface Ethernet4/2
  inherit port-profile uplink

interface mgmt0
  ip address 10.2.9.11/24

interface Vethernet1
  inherit port-profile l3control
  description VMware VMkernel, vmk2
  VMware dvport 100

interface Vethernet2
  inherit port-profile l3control
  description VMware VMkernel, vmk2
  VMware dvport 101

interface control0
boot kickstart bootflash:/nexus-1000v-kickstart-mz.4.0.4.SV1.2.bin sup-1
boot system bootflash:/nexus-1000v-mz.4.0.4.SV1.2.bin sup-1
boot kickstart bootflash:/nexus-1000v-kickstart-mz.4.0.4.SV1.2.bin sup-2
boot system bootflash:/nexus-1000v-mz.4.0.4.SV1.2.bin sup-2
svs-domain
  domain id 100
  control vlan 1
  packet vlan 1
  svs mode L3 interface mgmt0
svs connection vcenter
  protocol VMware-vim
  remote ip address 10.1.4.10 port 80
  VMware dvs uuid "8a f2 06 50 68 4d 62 2d-bd 47 c6 40 a3 86 64 26" datacenter-n
ame Demo
  connect
VSM1#
```

The mgmt0 interface will be used for the Layer 3 Control traffic, interface control0 can be used as well. Port-profile named "l3control" was created and defined the system vLAN of 702 as well as capability of l3control.

VSM High Availability: Adding a Secondary VSM

If redundant VSM(s) are required, the VSM(s) can be deployed in a High Availability configuration. The VSM High Availability deployment configuration is the same as the dual supervisors in a physical chassis. The two VSMs are deployed in an active-standby configuration, the first VSM will function as the primary role and the second VSM will function as the secondary role. If the primary VSM fails, the secondary VSM will take over.

Note   When deploying VSM redundancy (HA), it is not possible to use Layer 3 between the two VSM(s); a Layer 2 adjacency is required between them.

Step 1.   Verify the current VSM role as demonstrated in the following output:

```
VSM1# show system redundancy status


Redundancy role
---------------
      administrative:   standalone
         operational:   standalone


Redundancy mode
---------------
      administrative:   HA
         operational:   None


This supervisor (sup-1)
-----------------------
    Redundancy state:   Active
    Supervisor state:   Active
      Internal state:   Active with no standby


Other supervisor (sup-2)
-----------------------
    Redundancy state:   Not present
VSM1# show module
Mod  Ports  Module-Type                              Model                Status
---  -----  ---------------------------------------- ------------------   --------
1    0      Virtual Supervisor Module                Nexus1000V           active
*
```

```
3    248     Virtual Ethernet Module          NA              ok
4    248     Virtual Ethernet Module          NA              ok


Mod  Sw               Hw
---  ---------------  ------
1    4.0(4)SV1(2)     0.0
3    4.0(4)SV1(2)     0.4
4    4.0(4)SV1(2)     0.4


Mod  MAC-Address(es)                          Serial-Num
---  ---------------------------------------  ----------
1    00-19-07-6c-5a-a8 to 00-19-07-6c-62-a8   NA
3    02-00-0c-00-03-00 to 02-00-0c-00-03-80   NA
4    02-00-0c-00-04-00 to 02-00-0c-00-04-80   NA


Mod  Server-IP        Server-UUID                            Server-Name
---  ---------------  -------------------------------------  -----------
1    10.2.9.11        NA                                     NA
3    10.2.12.70       34313937-3536-5553-4537-30324e305331   demolab-
vm2.csc.dubl
in.cisco.com
4    10.2.12.60       8fd290ce-4ed2-3ea5-a3df-f35c3e85ab27   demolab-
vm1.csc.dubl
in.cisco.com


* this terminal session
VSM1# show system redundancy ha status
VDC No    This supervisor                    Other supervisor

------    ---------------                    ---------------


vdc 1     Active with no standby             N/A

VSM1#
```

Step 2. Change the role of the VSM from standalone to primary as demonstrated in the following example:

```
VSM1# conf t
VSM1-VSM(config)# system redundancy role primary
VSM1-VSM(config)# exit
VSM1# show system redundancy status
Redundancy role
---------------
```

```
        administrative:   primary
          operational:    primary


Redundancy mode
. . . . . . . . . . . . . . .

        administrative:   HA
          operational:    None


This supervisor (sup-1)
. . . . . . . . . . . . . . . . . . . . . .

      Redundancy state:   Active
      Supervisor state:   Active
        Internal state:   Active with no standby


Other supervisor (sup-2)
. . . . . . . . . . . . . . . . . . . . . .

      Redundancy state:   Not present
VSM1#
```

Step 3. Install the secondary VSM as outlined here: To install the secondary VSM, change the **Deployment Configuration** options. Change the selection from **Nexus 1000V installer** to **Manually Configure Nexus 1000V**, as shown in Figure 9-43.

Step 4. On the Deploy OVF Template properties page, do not fill in any of the fields; just select **Next** as shown in Figure 9-44.

Step 5. Power on the new VSM just deployed and open the console within vCenter (recommended practice dictates picking a different ESX within the cluster or data center). The system setup script will appear in the console window and you should perform the following steps:

a. Enter the admin password.

b. Enter the same domain ID as the initial domain ID on the first VSM, in this case it is 100. The domain ID needs to be the same that was configured on the primary VSM.

c. Enter the VSM role as secondary.

d. Verify the VSM role as secondary as the VSM will want to reboot, the secondary VSM will reboot.

Figure 9-45 shows powering on the newly installed VSM from the OVF process and opening a console window to the VSM.

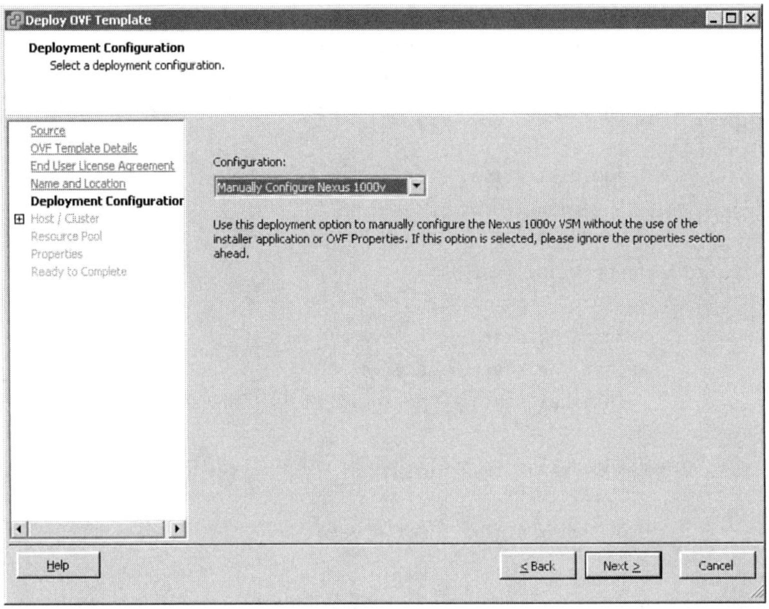

Figure 9-43 *Deployment Configuration: Changing the Selection from Nexus 1000V Installer to Manually Configure Nexus 1000V*

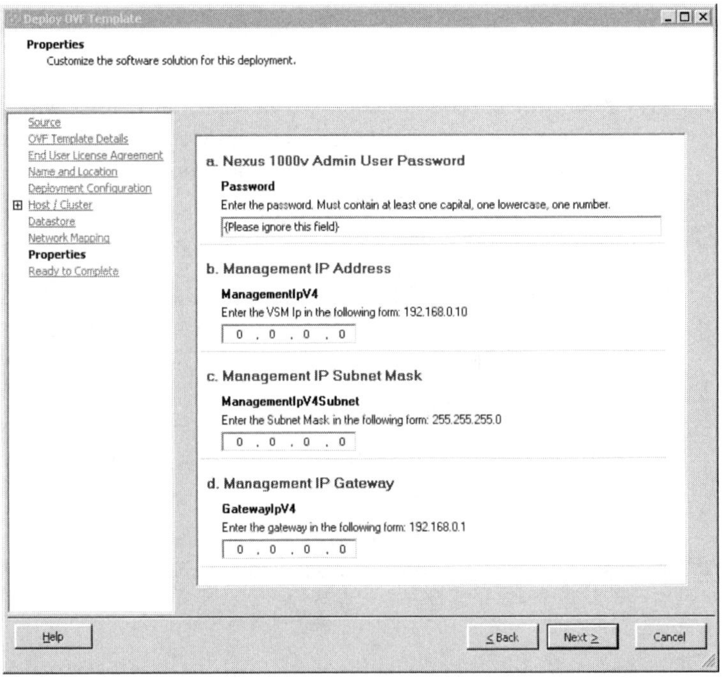

Figure 9-44 *Do Not Fill in Any Fields in the Deploy OVF Template Properties Page*

Figure 9-45 *Powering on the Newly Installed VSM from the OVF Process and Opening a Console Window to the VSM*

Example 9-15 shows how to verify VSM HA after the secondary VSM reboots.

Example 9-15 *Verifying VSM HA After the Secondary VSM Reboots*

```
VSM1# show system redundancy status
Redundancy role
---------------

     administrative:   primary
        operational:   primary


Redundancy mode
---------------

     administrative:   HA
        operational:   None


This supervisor (sup-1)
-----------------------
```

```
        Redundancy state:    Active
       Supervisor state:    Active
         Internal state:    Active with HA standby


Other supervisor (sup-2)
-----------------------

      Redundancy state:    Standby
      Supervisor state:    HA standby
        Internal state:    HA synchronization in progress


VSM1# show system redundancy status
Redundancy role
--------------

         administrative:    primary
            operational:    primary


Redundancy mode
--------------

         administrative:    HA
            operational:    None


This supervisor (sup-1)
-----------------------

      Redundancy state:    Active
      Supervisor state:    Active
        Internal state:    Active with HA standby


Other supervisor (sup-2)
-----------------------

      Redundancy state:    Standby
      Supervisor state:    HA standby
        Internal state:    HA synchronization in progress
VSM1#
```

Example 9-16 shows how to verify VSM roles after synchronization is complete.

Example 9-16   *Verifying VSM Roles After Synchronization Is Complete*

```
VSM1# show system redundancy status
Redundancy role
----------------

         administrative:    primary
            operational:    primary
```

```
Redundancy mode
---------------

        administrative:   HA
            operational:   HA

This supervisor (sup-1)
-----------------------

    Redundancy state:   Active
    Supervisor state:   Active
      Internal state:   Active with HA standby

Other supervisor (sup-2)
------------------------

    Redundancy state:   Standby
    Supervisor state:   HA standby
      Internal state:   HA standby


VSM1# show system redundancy ha status
VDC No    This supervisor                     Other supervisor


-------    ---------------                     ---------------


vdc 1     Active with HA standby              HA standby


VSM1#
```

Figure 9-46 verifies the secondary VSM is in standby mode from the standby VSM.

Example 9-17 shows how to verify VSM roles after synchronization is complete from the primary VSM. This will also verify that both the VSM are present in the system.

Example 9-17 *Verify VSM Roles After Synchronization Is Complete from the Primary VSM*

```
VSM1# show module
Mod   Ports  Module-Type                        Model               Status
---   -----  ---------------------------------  ------------------  -----------
1     0      Virtual Supervisor Module          Nexus1000V          active *
2     0      Virtual Supervisor Module          Nexus1000V          ha-standby
3     248    Virtual Ethernet Module            NA                  ok
4     248    Virtual Ethernet Module            NA                  ok

Mod   Sw                     Hw
```

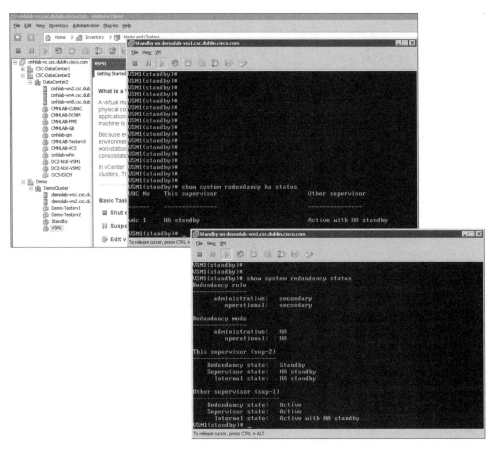

Figure 9-46   *Verifying the Secondary VSM Is in Standby Mode from the Standby VSM*

```
---   ---------------   ------
1     4.0(4)SV1(2)      0.0
2     4.0(4)SV1(2)      0.0
3     4.0(4)SV1(2)      0.4
4     4.0(4)SV1(2)      0.4


Mod   MAC-Address(es)                           Serial-Num
---   ---------------------------------------   ----------
1     00-19-07-6c-5a-a8 to 00-19-07-6c-62-a8    NA
2     00-19-07-6c-5a-a8 to 00-19-07-6c-62-a8    NA
3     02-00-0c-00-03-00 to 02-00-0c-00-03-80    NA
4     02-00-0c-00-04-00 to 02-00-0c-00-04-80    NA


Mod   Server-IP         Server-UUID                           Server-Name
---   --------------    -----------------------------------   --------------------
```

```
1     10.2.9.11      NA                                   NA
2     10.2.9.11      NA                                   NA
3     10.2.12.70     34313937-3536-5553-4537-30324e305331 demolab-vm2.csc.dubl
in.cisco.com
4     10.2.12.60     8fd290ce-4ed2-3ea5-a3df-f35c3e85ab27 demolab-vm1.csc.dubl
in.cisco.com


* this terminal session
VSM1#
```

Note A manual switchover can be forced with the **system switchover** command; this will force primary on the standby VSM.

Nexus 1000V Port Profiles

Port profiles are used to configure interfaces on the Virtual Ether Module (VEM). A port profile can be assigned to multiple interfaces this allows for standardized interface configurations across multiple VEM(s). When changes are applied to a port profile, the changes can be propagated automatically to the configuration of any interface assigned to it.

In the VMware vCenter Server, a port profile is represented as a port group. The VEthernet or Ethernet interfaces are assigned in vCenter Server to a port profile for:

■ Defining port configuration by policy.

■ Applying a single policy across a large number of ports.

■ Supporting both VEthernet and Ethernet ports.

Port profiles that are configured as uplinks can be assigned by the server administrator to physical ports (a vmnic or a physical NIC [pnic]). Port profiles that are not configured as uplinks can be assigned to a VM virtual port.

Note Manual interface configuration overrides the port-profile configuration; it is recommended to use this method for temporary changes or configuration changes.

Port profiles have two states, Enabled and Disabled. When a port-profile state is disabled, the port-profile has the following behavior:

■ Its configuration is not applied to assigned ports.

■ If exporting policies to a VMware port group, the port group is not created on the vCenter Server.

When a port-profile state is enabled, the port-profile has the following behavior:

■ Its configuration is applied to assigned ports.

■ If inheriting policies from a VMware port group, the port group is created on the vCenter Server.

Note   The default state of a port-profile is disabled.

A port profile can have the following characteristics defined:

■ ACL

■ capability (uplink, l3control)

■ Channel-group

■ Description

■ Inherit

■ Default, resets characteristics to default settings

■ Interface state (shutdown / no shutdown)

■ Name

■ Netflow

■ Port-security

■ Private-VLAN

■ QoS policy

■ State (enabled / disabled)

■ Switchport mode (access port or trunk port)

■ System VLAN

■ VLAN configuration

■ VMware max-ports

■ VMware port-group name

Port Profile Inheritance allows one port profile to inherit the policies from another port profile. The characteristics of the parent profile become the default settings for the child. The inheriting port profile ignores any non-applicable configuration.

Table 9-1 lists the the port profile characteristics that can and cannot be inherited:

Table 9-1 *Port Profile Characteristic Inheritance Properties*

Port Profile Characteristics That Can Be Inherited	Port Profile Characteristics That Cannot Be Inherited
ACL	Capability
Channel-group	Description
Default	State
Inherit	System vlan list
Interface state	VMware max-port
Name	VMware port-group name
Netflow	
Port-security	
QoS	
Private vlan	
Switchport mode	
VLAN configuration	

A system port profile is designed to establish vCenter Server connectivity. The system port-profile carries the following VLANs:

- System VLANs or VNICs used when bringing up the ports before communication is established between the VSM and VEM.

- The uplink that carries the control VLAN.

- Management uplink(s) used for VMware vCenter Server connectivity or SSH or Telnet connections. There can be more than one management port or VLAN—for example, one dedicated for vCenter Server connectivity, one for SSH, one for SNMP, a switch interface, and so forth.

- VMware kernel NIC for accessing VMFS storage over iSCSI or NFS.

The system port-profile system VLANs have the following characteristics:

- System VLANs cannot be deleted when the profile is in use.

- Non-system VLANs in a system port profile can be freely added or deleted, even when the profile is in use; that is, one or more DVS ports are carrying that profile.

- System VLANs can always be added to a system port profile or a non-system port profile, even when the profile is in use.

- The native VLAN on a system port profile may be a system VLAN or a non-system VLAN.

Example 9-18 shows how to create the port-profile on the VSM.

Example 9-18   *Creating the Port-Profile on the VSM*

```
VSM1(config)# port-profile HR-APPS
SVS domain config:
VSM1(config-port-prof)# vmware port-group
VSM1(config-port-prof)# switchport mode access
VSM1(config-port-prof)# switchport access vlan 701
VSM1(config-port-prof)# service-policy type qos output qos-stat
VSM1(config-port-prof)# no shutdown
VSM1(config-port-prof)# system vlan 701
VSM1(config-port-prof)# state enabled
VSM1(config-port-prof)# exit


VSM1(config)# port-profile Web
VSM1(config-port-prof)# vmware port-group
VSM1(config-port-prof)# switchport mode access
VSM1(config-port-prof)# switchport access vlan 78
VSM1(config-port-prof)# ip flow monitor IPv4Monitor input
VSM1(config-port-prof)# service-policy type qos output qos-stat
VSM1(config-port-prof)# no shutdown
VSM1(config-port-prof)# state enabled
VSM1(config-port-prof)# exit


VSM1(config)# port-profile NAS
VSM1(config-port-prof)# vmware port-group
VSM1(config-port-prof)# switchport mode access
VSM1(config-port-prof)# switchport access vlan 702
VSM1(config-port-prof)# ip flow monitor IPv4Monitor input
VSM1(config-port-prof)# service-policy type qos output mark-control-packet-vlans
VSM1(config-port-prof)# no shutdown
VSM1(config-port-prof)# system vlan 702
VSM1(config-port-prof)# state enabled
VSM1(config-port-prof)# exit


VSM1(config)# port-profile ERSPAN
VSM1(config-port-prof)# capability l3control
VSM1(config-port-prof)# vmware port-group
VSM1(config-port-prof)# switchport mode access
VSM1(config-port-prof)# switchport access vlan 702
VSM1(config-port-prof)# no shutdown
```

```
VSM1(config-port-prof)# system vlan 702
VSM1(config-port-prof)# state enabled
VSM1(config-port-prof)# exit
```

Example 9-19 shows how to verify the port-profiles on the VSM.

Example 9-19   *Verifying the Port-Profiles on the VSM*

```
VSM1# show port-profile usage


---------------------------------------------------------------------------
Port Profile              Port        Adapter        Owner
---------------------------------------------------------------------------
HR-APPS                   Veth3       Net Adapter 1  Demo-Testsrv2
Web                       Veth2       Net Adapter 1  Demo-Testsrv1
l3control                 Veth1       vmk2           Module 4
uplink                    Eth4/2      vmnic1         demolab-vm1.csc.dublin.ci
VSM1#
VSM1# show running-config interface vethernet 3
version 4.0(4)SV1(2)

interface Vethernet3
  inherit port-profile HR-APPS
  description Demo-Testsrv2, Network Adapter 1
  vmware dvport 160

VSM1# show running-config interface vethernet 2
version 4.0(4)SV1(2)

interface Vethernet2
  inherit port-profile Web
  description Demo-Testsrv1, Network Adapter 1
  vmware dvport 192

VSM1# show running-config interface vethernet 1
version 4.0(4)SV1(2)

interface Vethernet1
  inherit port-profile l3control
  description VMware VMkernel, vmk2
  vmware dvport 100

VSM1# show int vethernet 3
Vethernet3 is up
```

```
      Port description is Demo-Testsrv2, Network Adapter 1
      Hardware is Virtual, address is 0050.5686.3f96
      Owner is VM "Demo-Testsrv2", adapter is Network Adapter 1
      Active on module 4
      VMware DVS port 160
      Port-Profile is HR-APPS
      Port mode is access
      5 minute input rate 168 bits/second, 0 packets/second
      5 minute output rate 0 bits/second, 0 packets/second
      Rx
      45 Input Packets 0 Unicast Packets
      3 Multicast Packets 42 Broadcast Packets
      5932 Bytes
      Tx
      1 Output Packets 0 Unicast Packets
      1 Multicast Packets 0 Broadcast Packets 1 Flood Packets
      60 Bytes
      0 Input Packet Drops 0 Output Packet Drops


VSM1# show port-profile usage


--------------------------------------------------------------------------
Port Profile             Port        Adapter       Owner
--------------------------------------------------------------------------
HR-APPS                  Veth3       Net Adapter 1 Demo-Testsrv2
Web                      Veth2       Net Adapter 1 Demo-Testsrv1
l3control                Veth1       vmk2          Module 4
uplink                   Eth4/2      vmnic1        demolab-vm1.csc.dublin.ci
VSM1# show port-profile name web
ERROR: port-profile web does not exist
VSM1# show port-profile name Web
port-profile Web
  description:
  type: vethernet
  status: enabled
  capability l3control: no
  pinning control-vlan: -
  pinning packet-vlan: -
  system vlans: none
  port-group: Web
  max ports: 32
```

```
    inherit:
    config attributes:
      switchport mode access
      switchport access vlan 78
      ip flow monitor IPv4Monitor input
      service-policy type qos output qos-stat
      no shutdown
    evaluated config attributes:
      switchport mode access
      switchport access vlan 78
      ip flow monitor IPv4Monitor input
      service-policy type qos output qos-stat
      no shutdown
    assigned interfaces:
      Vethernet2
VSM1# show int brie


--------------------------------------------------------------------------
Port     VRF          Status IP Address              Speed    MTU
--------------------------------------------------------------------------
mgmt0     --            up      10.2.9.11            1000     1500


--------------------------------------------------------------------------
Ethernet     VLAN  Type Mode   Status Reason          Speed    Port
Interface                                                        Ch #
--------------------------------------------------------------------------
Eth4/2       1     eth  trunk  up     none           1000(D) --


--------------------------------------------------------------------------
Interface   VLAN  Type Mode   Status Reason          MTU
--------------------------------------------------------------------------
Veth1       702   virt access up     none           1500
Veth2       78    virt access down   inactive       1500
Veth3       701   virt access up     none           1500


--------------------------------------------------------------------------
Port     VRF          Status IP Address              Speed    MTU
--------------------------------------------------------------------------
ctrl0     --            up      --                   1000     1500
VSM1#
```

Figure 9-47 shows the port-profiles that were created on the VSM pushed to Virtual Center port-groups.

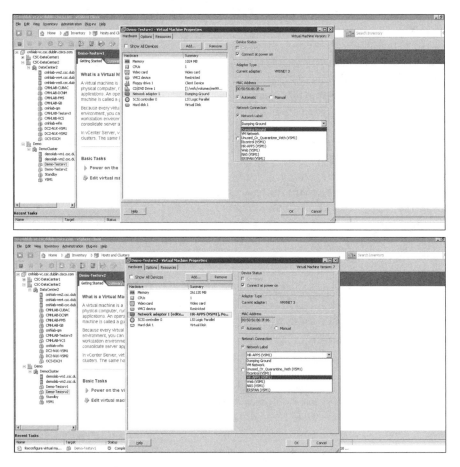

Figure 9-47   *Verifying the Port-Profiles That Were Created on the VSM Pushed to Virtual Center Port-Groups*

Example 9-20 shows port-profile mobility; virtual machine "Demo-Testsrv2" was vMotioned to another ESX host. Interface Vethernet 3 is now installed on another VEM; the interface counters were not changed.

Example 9-20   *Port-profile Mobility, Virtual Machine "Demo-Testsrv2" Was vMotioned to Another ESX Host*

```
VSM1# show int vethernet 3
Vethernet3 is up
    Port description is Demo-Testsrv2, Network Adapter 1
    Hardware is Virtual, address is 0050.5686.3f96
    Owner is VM " Demo-Testsrv2", adapter is Network Adapter 1
    Active on module 5
    VMware DVS port 160
```

```
    Port-Profile is HR-APPS
    Port mode is access
    Rx
    116110 Input Packets 102386 Unicast Packets
    15 Multicast Packets 13709 Broadcast Packets
    21252722 Bytes
    Tx
    1162978 Output Packets 125195 Unicast Packets
    72181 Multicast Packets 965602 Broadcast Packets 0 Flood Packets
    169423238 Bytes
    98 Input Packet Drops 0 Output Packet Drops

VSM1# show int vethernet 3
Vethernet3 is up
    Port description is Demo-Testsrv2, Network Adapter 1
    Hardware is Virtual, address is 0050.5686.3f96
    Owner is VM " Demo-Testsrv2", adapter is Network Adapter 1
    Active on module 4
    VMware DVS port 160
    Port-Profile is HR-APPS
    Port mode is access
    Rx
    116113 Input Packets 102386 Unicast Packets
    18 Multicast Packets 13709 Broadcast Packets
    21252902 Bytes
    Tx
    1163004 Output Packets 125196 Unicast Packets
    72185 Multicast Packets 965623 Broadcast Packets 6 Flood Packets
    169425525 Bytes
    100 Input Packet Drops 0 Output Packet Drops
```

Example 9-21 shows a sample QoS policy that was part of the port-profiles configured.

Example 9-21 *Sample QoS Policy That Was Part of the Port-Profiles Configured*

```
Sample QoS Configure for the QoS
ip access-list match-control-vlans
  statistics per-entry
  10 permit ip 10.1.12.0/24 any
  20 permit ip any 10.1.12.0/24
class-map type qos match-any EF
  match dscp 46
class-map type qos match-any CS3
  match dscp 24
```

```
class-map type qos match-any cs0
  match dscp 0
class-map type qos match-any cs1
  match dscp 8
class-map type qos match-any cs2
  match dscp 16
class-map type qos match-any cs3
  match dscp 24
class-map type qos match-any cs4
  match dscp 32
class-map type qos match-any cs5
  match dscp 40
class-map type qos match-any cs6
  match dscp 48
class-map type qos match-any cs7
  match dscp 56
class-map type qos match-any AF31
  match dscp 26
class-map type qos match-any af11
  match dscp 10
class-map type qos match-any af12
  match dscp 12
class-map type qos match-any af13
  match dscp 14
class-map type qos match-any af21
  match dscp 18
class-map type qos match-any af22
  match dscp 20
class-map type qos match-any af23
  match dscp 22
class-map type qos match-any af31
  match dscp 26
class-map type qos match-any af32
  match dscp 28
class-map type qos match-any af33
  match dscp 30
class-map type qos match-any af41
  match dscp 34
class-map type qos match-any af42
  match dscp 36
class-map type qos match-any af43
  match dscp 38
class-map type qos match-any match-control-vlans
    match access-group name match-control-vlans
```

```
policy-map type qos qos-stat
  class cs7
  class cs6
  class cs5
  class cs4
  class cs3
  class cs2
  class cs1
  class af43
  class af42
  class af41
  class af33
  class af32
  class af31
  class af23
  class af22
  class af21
  class af13
  class af12
  class af11
  class EF
  class cs0
policy-map type qos mark-control-packet-vlans
  class match-control-vlans
    set cos 6
```

As you can see in Example 9-21, port-profiles offer a tremendous amount of flexibility, control, and details on a per virtual machine basis. Example 9-21 demonstrates a very detailed QoS policy that can be customized to meet different requirements and applications.

Summary

The Nexus 1000V offers tight integration between server and network environments; this integration helps to ensure consistent, policy-based network capabilities to all servers in your data center. The chapter covered several benefits such as policy-based virtual machine connectivity, mobile VM security, network policy, and operation models. Having real-time coordinated configuration of network and security services will allow for enterprises to increase the scale of the VM deployments and have the tools to maintain, monitor, and troubleshoot these dynamic environments.

Index

Numerics

10-Gigabit Ethernets, 362-363

A

AAA (Authentication, Authorization, and Accounting), 202

access

groups, 233

switch configuration, 57

access control lists. *See* ACLs

accounting, 202

ACLs (access control lists), 2

interfaces, applying, 233

IP configuration, 232-234

MAC configuration, 234-236

sequence numbers, modifying, 236

VLAN configuration, 236-237

actions

process restarts, 297

security, 240-242

active zoneset verification, 371

adding

email servers, 349

ports to VLANs, 52

static IP source entries, 252

static secure MAC addresses, 239

SVIs, 101

VEMs, 406-414

VLANs, 50

addresses

BGP, 140

IP management, 54

MAC, 38

DHCP snooping, 245

enabling sticky learning, 238

maximum number of, 241

OSPF summary, 122

Advanced Encryption Standard. *See* AES

advantages of Cisco NX-OS, 1

advertisements, networks, 117, 148-150

AES (Advanced Encryption Standard), 2, 224

B

C

F

G

O

P